CISCO CATALYST LAN
SWITCHING

McGRAW-HILL CISCO TECHNICAL EXPERT SERIES

Cisco Catalyst LAN Switching

Louis R. Rossi,
Louis D. Rossi,
and
Thomas L. Rossi

McGraw-Hill
New York   San Francisco   Washington, D.C.
Auckland   Bogotá   Caracas   Lisbon   London
Madrid   Mexico City   Milan   Montreal   New Delhi
San Juan   Singapore   Sydney   Tokyo   Toronto

McGraw-Hill

A Division of The McGraw-Hill Companies

1 2 3 4 5 6 7 8 9 0   DOC/DOC   9 0 4 3 2 1 0 9

0-07-134982-0

The sponsoring editor for this book was Steven Elliot, the editing supervisor was Ruth W. Mannino, and the production supervisor was Claire Stanley. It was set in New Century Schoolbook by Victoria Khavkina of McGraw-Hill's desktop composition unit in cooperation with Spring Point Publishing Services.

Printed and bound by R. R. Donnelley & Sons Company

This book is printed on recycled, acid-free paper containing a minimum of 50% recycled, de-inked fiber.

CONTENTS

v

Contents

Contents

PREFACE

This book covers switching from the basics to advanced features, such as multilayer switching, as they pertain to Cisco's Catalyst products. Because of the rapidly changing Catalyst product line, I was unable to include all the latest products. However, I am sure that this is one of the most up-to-date reference materials available.

The audience for this book is anyone working with the Catalyst products. The recommended level of the reader is intermediate; an understanding of TCP/IP addressing, client server architectures, and routing is strongly recommended. This book is intended to be a reference guide to understanding and configuring the Catalyst switch from Cisco Systems. It also covers all material that may be found on Cisco's CLSC written exam, which is required for the Cisco Certified Networking Professional (CCNP) certification.

This book was written using the Catalyst IOS 4.5(1). There have been numerous changes in the Catalyst IOS since its inception. You should always be aware of the version you are currently running when reading this book. I have tried to mention several of these differences, but I am sure there are some that I have not yet encountered.

The first four chapters of this book give a general overview of bridging and switching concepts, including transparent and source-route bridging. These chapters are designed to be a quick overview. For a more detailed explanation, see Radia Perlman, *Interconnections: Routers and Bridges*.

Chapters 5 and 6 provide as complete a product overview as possible. These chapters will always be a work in progress because of the many new products that Cisco introduces each week. I apologize for not including the Catalyst 8500 Series in these descriptions. However, the Catalyst 8500 Series is really a Switch-Router that runs the Cisco IOS and not the Catalyst IOS. For further information on Cisco IOS, I would recommend reading some of the other books in McGraw-Hill's Cisco Technical Expert Series.

Chapters 7, 8, 9, and 10 cover the many different configuration options that are available for the Catalyst IOS. Although I used the Catalyst 5000 Series in writing this book, the Catalyst 4000 and 6000 series run the Catalyst IOS as well. And many of the commands and procedures discussed in these chapters will be the same when working with the 4000 and 6000.

In these chapters I have included some Tech Tips and Bonehead Alerts. The Tech Tips are recommendations that I have developed over the past two years. Bonehead Alerts are errors that I have made while working with these products. In this case the Bonehead would be myself. They say we are to learn from our mistakes, I hope you will learn from mine!

No, this is not me!

There are review exercises at the end of each chapter of this book. I will be posting the answers to these on the www.CCprep.com website. Here you can also make comments about these answers.

—Louis R. Rossi

ACKNOWLEDGMENTS

First and foremost, I would like to thank the hundreds of Catalyst switch students who have been in my classes for the past two years. I have learned as much from you as, hopefully, you have learned from me. This book would not be possible without your constant input. Thank you.

I would especially like to thank my wife Kim, who has worked very hard on this book. Although I have written the material, she has taken on the task of printing out the many manuscript copies for the editing process. I would like to also thank my father, his wife Annette, and my brother for their continuing work on CCprep.com while I was working on this book. And I would like to thank my mother, Della Caldwell, and her husband, Bill, for putting up with me these last several months while I have been working on this book—thanks for the barbecue when I needed it.

Many thanks to the GeoTrain Corporation for taking a chance on a small company like CCprep.com and myself.

Many other people have helped me, either directly or indirectly. My thanks go (listed in no particular order) to:

My family: Adam Legault, Damon Legault, Catherine Walter, Debi Kamla, Todd Kamla, Elden Kamla, Karmen Kamla, Wynn Legault, Mark Walter, Robert Walter, Lucy Walter, Ralph and Jane Box.

My friends: Stuart Higgins, John Gorman at Tech Force, Karl Schuman at Tech Force, Barry Gursky at Geotrain, Steven Sowell, Robert Hasty, Todd Hasty, Gary Andrews, Dr. Derek Eisnor, Chris Patron, David Patron, and Rudy Kohele.

The McGraw-Hill crew: Steven Elliot, Ruth Mannino, Victoria Khavkina, and the others who worked on this book.

And others: Elaine Crutchfield, Martha Hasty, Dr. Robert C. Atkins, and The Florida State University.

ABOUT THE REVIEWERS

As the leading publisher of technical books for more than 100 years, McGraw-Hill prides itself on bringing you the most authoritative and up-to-date information available. To ensure that our books meet the highest standards of accuracy, we have asked a number of top professionals and technical experts to review the accuracy of the material you are about to read.

We take great pleasure in thanking the following technical reviewers for their insights:

Mark Freivald MCP, CCNP is a Network Operator at Inacom's Enterprise Management Center. His primary responsibility is in network management. Mark is currently working toward the CCIE certification.

Chad Marsh, CCNP, CCDA, is the Communications/WAN technician for the Tacoma School District #10, in Tacoma, WA. He supports and maintains an integrated voice/data wide area network of 60+ locations, and has been in the communications field for 10 years. He is currently working toward CCIE certification, and is scheduled to take the lab exam in October.

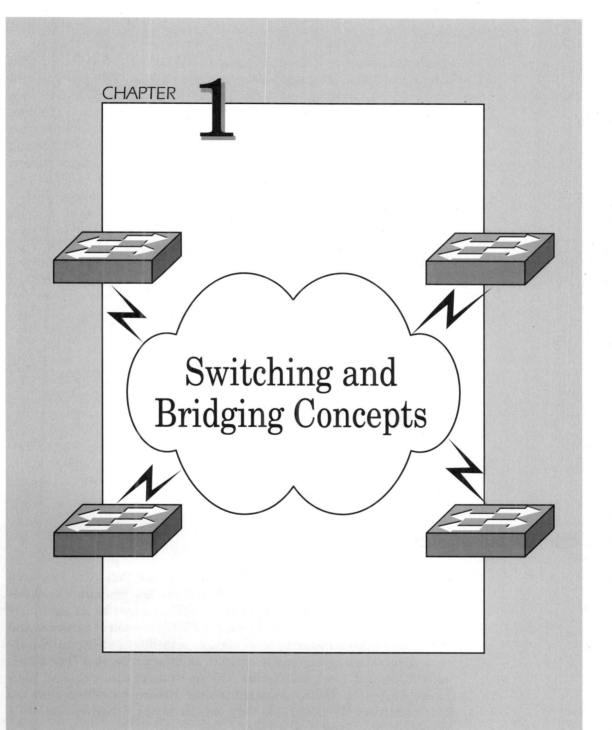

Switching and Bridging Concepts

In today's marketplace, the demand for bandwidth has far exceeded what anyone could have imagined 5 years ago. We have seen Ethernet become the dominant local-area networking (LAN) medium. With the development of Fast Ethernet and Gigabit Ethernet, we are assured that Ethernet will continue to be the medium of choice for the local-area infrastructure. Even with the increased bandwidth of Fast Ethernet and Gigabit Ethernet, there is still the need for physical and logical segmentation. This segmentation requires the use of switches and routers. This book examines Cisco's switching product line—its features and capabilities.

Cisco has exhibited dominance in the networking field with its impressive line of routing products. However, the need for increased bandwidth has increased the demand for products that give physical segmentation as well as logical segmentation. Cisco, having identified this growing marketplace, has developed the Catalyst line of switching products. Catalyst products support all the major media, i.e., Ethernet, Fast Ethernet, Gigabit Ethernet, FDDI, Token Ring, and ATM. Cisco also has incorporated many proprietary features to help limit or eliminate the number of bottlenecks in a network infrastructure.

The Cisco Catalyst product line consists of products that were manufactured originally by such companies as Crescendo and Kalpana. Kalpana is the company often credited with invention of the Ethernet switch. Cisco has adeptly acquired these companies to create its own line of switching products.

To better understand the need for segmentation, one must learn how to segment. This chapter details the different methods of segmentation and when to use each.

Ethernet

Ethernet was developed in the mid-1970s by the Palo Alto Research Center (PARC), a division of Xerox Corporation. The medium was developed so that Xerox could interconnect many machines to its extremely large printers. Xerox originally created a 2-Mb/s version of Ethernet and later codeveloped a faster 10-Mb/s version with Intel and Digital Equipment Corporation, commonly referred to as *Ethernet version II* or *Ethernet DIX* (Digital, Intel, and Xerox). The Institute of Electrical and Electronics Engineers (IEEE) standardized the Ethernet medium with the 802 Committee. IEEE 802.3 is very similar to the Ethernet version II created by Intel, Digital, and Xerox.

Ethernet is a medium by which computers can communicate with each other, similar to the way in which air is a medium for human communication. Humans talk by causing reverberations in the air that are perceived as sound by our ears. These sounds are strung together to form words, and the words are strung together to form sentences, and so on. Ethernet uses bits that are strung together to form octets or bytes, and these bytes are strung together to form frames. The bits are electrical impulses that traverse a wire, rather than reverberations in the air.

Ethernet is broken into *physical segments,* and each segment consists of a wire and the nodes connected to it, as in Figure 1-1. A hub, although it uses a star topology, will repeat every bit in one port out to all other ports, essentially becoming a multiport repeater and thus emulating the Ethernet wire. All nodes connected to the wire see all traffic on the wire. This is a potential security risk. A network analyzer that is attached to the Ethernet wire will see all traffic traveling on that wire. In many cases, data are not encrypted over the local-area medium, making it easy for engineers to decode the data in the encapsulated frames traveling on the wire.

Traffic is simply electrical charges transmitted across the wire. It is these charges that indicate 1s and 0s (Figure 1-2), and these bits travel

Figure 1–1
Ethernet Physical
Segment

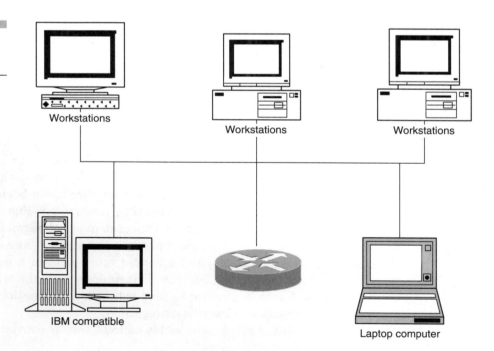

Workstations

Workstations

Workstations

IBM compatible

Laptop computer

Figure 1–2
Ethernet Physical
Segment

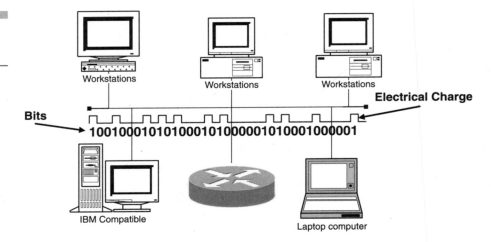

Figure 1–3
An Ethernet Frame

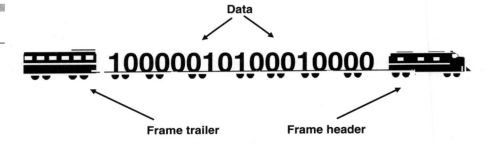

in a stream. You can think of the stream of bits as a train traveling down a track. The train can only travel on the track and has a beginning and an end, the locomotive and the caboose. The train is called an *Ethernet frame,* and it is a collection of bits that traverse the Ethernet wire. The frame that travels on an Ethernet wire has a beginning, called the *frame header,* and an end, called the *frame trailer* (Figure 1-3).

With many stations on an Ethernet physical segment and every station receiving every frame, how does the station "know" if the frame is directed to it? Every frame header must contain a destination *media access control (MAC) address.* This address tells the station whether or not the frame is directed to it or not. When destination MAC addresses do not match, the frame is disregarded.

The MAC address is a 48-bit address that is converted into 12 hexa-

Figure 1–4
MAC Addresses

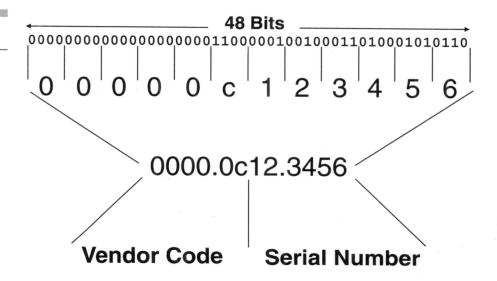

decimal groups of 4 bits separated by dots. This notation is sometimes referred to as *dotted hexadecimal* (Figure 1-4). The MAC address is burned into the ROM of all network interface controllers (NICs). To ensure that MAC addresses are unique, the IEEE administers these addresses. Each address is split into two parts—the *vendor code* and the *serial number*. The vendor code is given to the manufacturer of the NIC card and makes up the first 6 hex digits, or 24 bits, of the MAC address. The serial numbers are administered by the vendor, and they make up the remaining 6 hex digits, or last 24 bits, of the address. If a vendor runs out of serial numbers, it must apply for another vendor code.

Ethernet Frame Formats

Figure 1-5 shows some common frame types used today. Ethernet II is the oldest of the Ethernet frame headers and, as mentioned earlier, is sometimes referred to as *Ethernet DIX,* where DIX stands for Digital, Intel, and Xerox, the original three companies that formed an alliance to manufacturer Ethernet equipment.

The *preamble field* is used for synchronization and is 7 bytes in length. It is followed by a 1-byte field called the *start-of-frame delimiter.* The preamble field consists of the binary value "10" repeated, whereas

Ethernet II or Ethernet DIX

Preamble	Destination MAC	Source MAC	Type	Layer 3 packet (46-1500 bytes)	Frame Check Sum

IEEE 802.3 Ethernet With 802.2 Logical Link Control

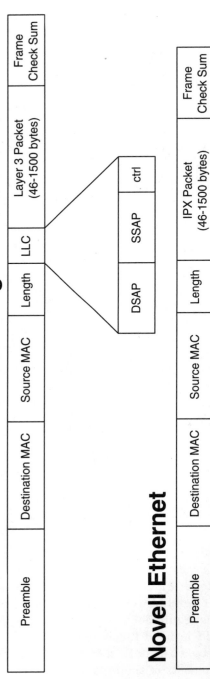

Preamble	Destination MAC	Source MAC	Length	LLC	Layer 3 Packet (46-1500 bytes)	Frame Check Sum

DSAP	SSAP	ctrl

Novell Ethernet

Preamble	Destination MAC	Source MAC	Length	IPX Packet (46-1500 bytes)	Frame Check Sum

IEEE 802.3 Sub-Network Access Protocol (Ethernet SNAP)

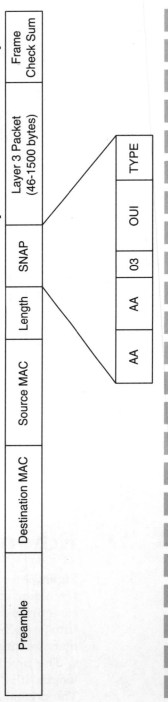

Preamble	Destination MAC	Source MAC	Length	SNAP	Layer 3 Packet (46-1500 bytes)	Frame Check Sum

AA	AA	03	OUI	TYPE

Figure 1-5 Ethernet Frame Types

Figure 1–6
The Preamble and
Start-of-Delimiter
Fields

56 Bits   **8 Bits**

1010101010101010101010101010101010101010101010101010101010101011

Preamble

Start-of-Delimiter

the start-of-frame delimiter consists of "10" repeated up to the final 2 bits, which end in "11" (see Figure 1-6). Most often, the start-of-frame delimiter is considered part of the preamble field. The *destination MAC* and *source MAC* addresses are used to identify where the frame is going and where the frame is coming from. These fields are each 6 bytes in length.

Ethernet II

Each frame header is responsible for identifying the type of Layer 3 packet encapsulated in the frame. Ethernet II uses the *type field,* which is 2 bytes in length. Some popular type codes are listed in Appendix C. Many manufacturers and software developers wanted to use Ethernet for their own Layer 3 protocols, so they needed a unique type code that would not be confused with another protocol. Xerox, credited with the invention of Ethernet, was in control of these codes and therefore had an unfair advantage over its competitors.

IEEE 802.3 with 802.2 Logical Link Control

The IEEE designed its own Ethernet frame type based on the original Ethernet II frame. The IEEE 802.3 Ethernet frame header is very similar to that of Ethernet II except the type field is changed to represent the length and another field, called *logical link control (LLC),* is added. The LLC is responsible for identifying the Layer 3 protocol that the packet is using. The LLC header, or IEEE 802.2 header, consists of a *destination service access point (DSAP), source service access point (SSAP),* and a *control field.* The DSAP and SSAP, when combined, identify the type of Layer 3 protocol in use.

IEEE 802.3 Sub-Network Access Protocol (Ethernet SNAP)

When Ethernet became very popular in the mid-1980s, the IEEE was becoming concerned that it would run out of possible DSAP and SSAP codes. Therefore, it created a new frame format called the *Ethernet Sub-Network Access Protocol* or, affectionately, *Ethernet SNAP*. This frame header replaced the DSAP and SSAP with "AA." When "AA" appears in both the DSAP and SSAP fields, the frame is an Ethernet SNAP frame. The Layer 3 protocol will be represented in a type field that follows the *organizational unique identifier (OUI) field*. The OUI is a 6-hex-digit number that uniquely represents an organization. The IEEE assigns the OUI. Cisco Systems' OUI is 00000c. This number was used in the vendor code portion of the MAC address until Cisco ran out of possible serial numbers.

Novell Ethernet

The Novell Ethernet frame type is used only for IPX traffic. Novell never envisioned a time when IPX would be run alongside other Layer 3 protocols. Therefore, there was no need to have a field that identified the Layer 3 protocol. If you were running Novell, you used IPX. The Novell Ethernet frame format replaces the type field with a length field, the same way the IEEE did. However, there is no LLC field following the length field. The IPX packet immediately follows the length field. Therefore, there is no way to identify the Layer 3 protocol that is being encapsulated. This is the reason only IPX traffic can be encapsulated in the Novell Ethernet frame. Because the Novell Ethernet header looks the same as the IEEE 802.3 header, Novell often refers to this framing as "Ethernet 802.3," but it is not the IEEE 802.3 Ethernet frame because it does not have LLC.

Carrier Sense Multiple Access with Collision Detection (CSMA/CD)

Ethernet uses Carrier Sense Multiple Access with Collision Detection (CSMA/CD). CSMA/CD can be likened to a polite conversation. In a polite conversation, if you have something to say, you listen to see if anyone is already speaking (i.e., Carrier Sense). If someone is talking, you wait patiently until that person finishes talking, and then you begin to speak. What happens if two people begin to talk at the same time? It becomes very difficult to make out what either is saying. In a polite conversation when two people begin speaking at the same time, both parties will hear that they have started speaking at the same time (i.e., Collision Detection), cease to speak, and wait a random amount of time before speaking again. The first person to start talking controls the medium, and the second person will have to wait for the first person to finish before he or she can talk.

Ethernet works in the same way, except with computers. Nodes on an Ethernet segment that want to transmit data will first listen to the wire. This procedure is the Carrier Sense of CSMA/CD. If a node is transmitting, then the listening node will have to wait until the transmitting node is finished. If two stations transmit at the same time, the Ethernet segment is said to have a "collision." The collision can be detected by all stations on the node because the voltage on the wire exceeds the typical value. Immediately after a collision, the two nodes involved in the collision send a jam signal to ensure that everyone has detected the collision and the bandwidth on the wire is 0 Mb/s. No data will traverse the wire during the recovery process. Nodes on the segment that were not part of the collision will not transmit until the collision is over. Once the two nodes finish transmitting the jam signal, they set a random timer and begin counting to zero. The first station to reach zero listens to the wire, hears that no one is transmitting, and begins to transmit. When the second station finishes counting to zero, it listens to the wire and hears that the first station has already begun transmitting and must now wait.

NOTE: *In reality, the random time is generated through an algorithm that can be found on page 55 of the IEEE's 802.3 Standard CSMA/CD document.*

With CSMA/CD, only one node can be transmitting on the wire at a time. If more than one node needs to transmit, one must wait for the other. The very fact that all nodes share the same wire is why Ethernet is commonly referred to as a *shared medium*.

Fast Ethernet

Now that you have a general understanding of Ethernet, it is appropriate to mention Fast Ethernet. In an effort to improve the performance of Ethernet, many organizations tried to create a 100-Mb/s version of Ethernet. Although the IEEE's 802.3u 100-MB standard was not the first on the market, it quickly became the status quo. All Catalyst products support Fast Ethernet.

Fast Ethernet became extremely popular because of the simple fact that it was merely Ethernet yet 10 times faster. The framing used on Fast Ethernet is the same as that used for regular Ethernet. This made it easier for engineers to understand Fast Ethernet as opposed to some of the other new 100-MB technologies, such as ATM. Fast Ethernet also uses CSMA/CD, making it easy for engineers who were familiar with Ethernet to become comfortable with the new medium.

When implementing Fast Ethernet, the same concepts mentioned earlier apply. Therefore, the more nodes you place on a Fast Ethernet segment, the more collisions that will occur, slowing the overall performance of the Fast Ethernet wire.

Gigabit Ethernet

With the implementation of Fast Ethernet came the need for a larger-backbone medium. ATM was moving along nicely with its 155- and 622-Mb/s versions, but they were still very difficult to implement. The IEEE 802.3z Committee then introduced Gigabit Ethernet, which is very similar to Ethernet except that it is 100 times faster. At the time of this writing, the only major difference between Gigabit Ethernet, Fast Ethernet, and Ethernet is that Gigabit Ethernet does not have a copper wiring standard.

Gigabit Ethernet is a 1000-Mb/s medium that is just as simple as Ethernet and Fast Ethernet, giving it a major advantage over its competitors, primarily ATM. ATM was thought to be the medium of the future, replacing Ethernet in its entirety. Indeed, ATM has many advantages, which will be discussed later, but its primary advantage over Ethernet and Fast Ethernet is increased bandwidth. The standardization of Gigabit Ethernet, however, brings a medium that rivals the high bandwidth of ATM but is much easier to implement. Talk of Desktop ATM is a thing of the past, with Fast Ethernet giving us the speed necessary to the desktop without the complexity of ATM.

Gigabit Ethernet will only be considered in the backbone and wiring closet; Gigabit Ethernet to the desktop is not a reality at this time. The limiting factor is the architecture of today's PC. A typical PC bus cannot handle Fast Ethernet, much less Gigabit Ethernet. In the backbone there will be the need to pass traffic now flowing from Fast Ethernet and Switched Ethernet stations as opposed to the Shared Ethernet stations of the past. Gigabit Ethernet will be an easy-to-implement option. Gigabit Ethernet uses the same framing and access methods of Ethernet and Fast Ethernet, making it easier to manage at such a large throughput. The Catalyst product line currently has several models designed primarily for connectivity to these types of backbones.

Full-Duplex Ethernet

When two Ethernet nodes are connected directly to each other using 10baseT cabling, the wiring looks similar to that shown in Figure 1-7. There are two separate pathways for transmitting and receiving. With only two nodes, there is no hub, and therefore, it is possible to have traffic flowing in both directions at the same time without a collision occurring. This is referred to as *full-duplex Ethernet*. To perform full-duplex Ethernet, two nodes must be connected directly together using 10baset, and the NICs must support full duplex.

With full-duplex Ethernet theoretically you could have 10 Mb/s going in both directions. It is for this reason that full-duplex Ethernet is described as a 20-Mb/s medium. It is also supported on Fast Ethernet and Gigabit Ethernet. Therefore, Fast Ethernet with full duplex would be considered 200 Mb/s, and Gigabit Ethernet with full duplex would be considered 2 Gb/s.

Physical Segmentation

Collisions are an unfortunate necessity, and they reduce the total bandwidth of an Ethernet wire. As more and more nodes are connected to a wire, the number of collisions goes up. The maximum number of nodes that can be placed on an Ethernet segment will depend on the type of

Figure 1–7
Crossover Cable between Two Workstations

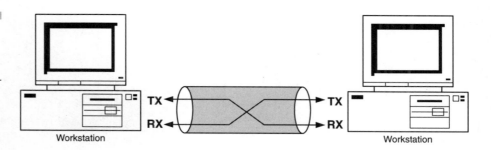

traffic traversing the wire. The obvious solution is to limit the number of nodes on the Ethernet wire. This process is often referred to as *physical segmentation.*

A *physical segment* is defined as all stations connected to the same wire. In other words, all nodes that can have a possible collision with another are said to be on the same physical segment. Another term often used to describe a physical segment is *collision domain.* The two terms refer to the same thing, however. Frequently in this industry terminology is inconsistent, therefore making it difficult for new members of the community to learn certain concepts. It is therefore important to realize that a physical segment and a collision domain are one and the same.

Physical segmentation can occur when certain internetworking devices are used to create more Ethernet wires or physical segments. In Figure 1-8, a *bridge* is used to break the Ethernet wire in Figure 1-1 into

Figure 1–8
Physical
Segmentation

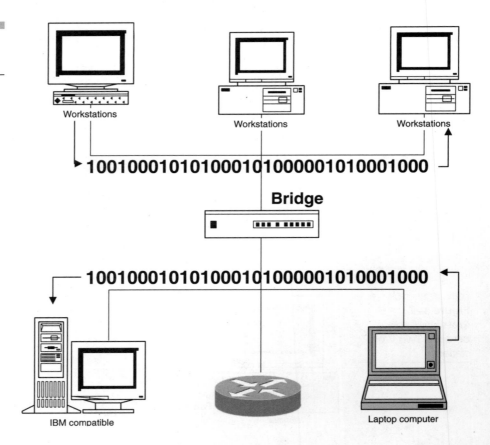

two separate physical wires or two separate physical segments. The bridge accomplishes this by forwarding only traffic that is destined for the other physical segment. Therefore, if all traffic is destined for the local physical segment, then no traffic will pass through the bridge. Communication can occur between hosts simultaneously, as in Figure 1-8. The network now has two 10-Mb/s physical segments, increasing the aggregate bandwidth to 20 Mb/s. We will examine how the bridge knows when to forward traffic in the bridging section.

A router also may be used to create physical segmentation, as shown in Figure 1-9. However, as we will also see later, the router does a bit more.

Figure 1–9
Physical Segmenta-
tion with a Router

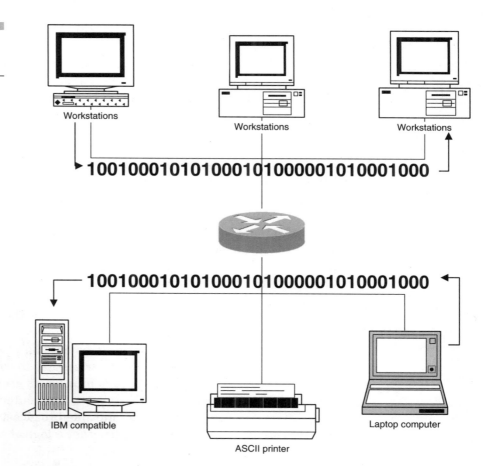

Broadcasts and Logical Segmentation

In the last section we saw the disadvantages of using a shared medium such as Ethernet and the effect of collisions on physical segments. Now we will look at another cause of degradation of network performance—broadcasts.

Broadcasts can be found on all networks, and they can account for a majority of network traffic if they are not maintained and controlled properly. Network operating systems (NOSs) use broadcasts for many different reasons. TCP/IP uses a broadcast to resolve a MAC address from an IP address. It also uses broadcasts to advertise routes with its RIP and IGRP routing protocols. Appletalk uses broadcasts with its distance vector routing protocol, the Routing Table Maintenance Protocol (RTMP). RTMP updates are sent out every 10 seconds on an Appletalk network. Novell uses the Service Advertising Protocol (SAP) to advertise network services on its networks. Each service advertises every 60 seconds. If your network has 1000 Novell servers running a multitude of services, your network will have thousands of broadcasts every minute.

Broadcasts consume bandwidth and therefore limit the bandwidth available to users for actual data. Broadcasts consume not only bandwidth but also processing power on your users' workstations. A broadcast will have the destination address of ffff.ffff.ffff. This address tells all stations that receive the frame to forward the encapsulated packet to the appropriate protocol software. This takes processing power regardless of whether or not the encapsulated packet is of any use to the workstation. If an Appletalk router sends an RTMP update, every workstation receives it and forwards the encapsulated packet to the upper-layer protocols. Of course, only routers will use RTMP updates, leaving all your workstations to discard the packet after it has been deencapsulated. This procedure requires CPU cycles and consumes the processing power of an already slow workstation.

A bridge will forward all broadcasts, whereas a router will not. It is simple to deduce that a router will be necessary to control broadcasts. All nodes that can receive each other's broadcasts are said to be on the same *broadcast domain* or *logical segment*. The router will filter broadcast traffic, allowing one to create multiple broadcast domains or logical segments. It is important to realize that a logical segment defines a

Layer 3 network. An IP subnet, an IPX network, and an Appletalk cable-range will be defined by the broadcast domain or logical segment.

Figure 1-10 shows two logical segments defined by a router interface. These logical segments also define the IP subnets, IPX networks, and Appletalk cable-ranges. All nodes on Broadcast Domain 1 will have IP addresses in the 172.16.0.0 network, whereas the workstations in Broadcast Domain 2 will have IP addresses in the 172.17.0.0 network.

Figure 1–10
Broadcast Domains
and Logical
Addressing

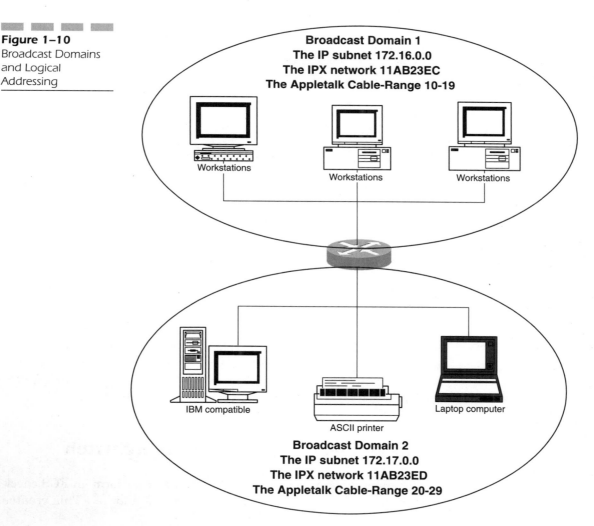

Broadcast Domain 1
The IP subnet 172.16.0.0
The IPX network 11AB23EC
The Appletalk Cable-Range 10-19

Workstations   Workstations   Workstations

IBM compatible   ASCII printer   Laptop computer

Broadcast Domain 2
The IP subnet 172.17.0.0
The IPX network 11AB23ED
The Appletalk Cable-Range 20-29

Multicasts

Multicasts are similar to broadcasts, but rather than being destined for all nodes, they are destined for only a specific type of node. The type of node is defined by the address. For example, a frame with a destination MAC address of 01000CCCCCCC is destined for all Cisco devices. A switch or a bridge will forward these frames in the same way that it would forward a broadcast.

What Is the Difference between a Switch and a Bridge?

In the preceding discussion of segmentation we have looked at segmenting with a router and with a bridge, but we have failed to mention the very device that appears in the title of this book—a switch cover? A switch and a bridge accomplish segmentation in the same way. A switch is essentially a multiport bridge. There are generally only three major differences between a switch and a bridge:

1. A bridge usually has only two ports, whereas a switch generally has many more than two ports.
2. A bridge usually is slower than a switch.
3. A bridge always receives the entire frame and performs a *frame check sum (FCS)* before forwarding, whereas a switch can start to forward a frame before it is completely received.

The second difference can be attributed to the fact that most switches use more modern hardware architecture than older bridges. Many engineers will point to numerous other minor differences, but such differences have no real effect on the issues discussed in this book.

Frame-Forwarding Methods of a Switch

A bridge must receive a frame in its entirety and perform an FCS check before it can forward a frame from one port to another. This creates latency as the bridge is forwarding frames. *Latency* is a fancy term for the length of time it takes a device to receive a frame on a port and forward it to the appropriate destination. This method of frame forwarding is called *store and forward.*

A switch can perform store and forward frame forwarding but sometimes can perform *cut-through frame forwarding.* A cut-through switch will not wait until the entire frame has been received before forwarding. This means that an FCS cannot be performed. Therefore, a frame with errors may be forwarded, raising the bandwidth use on both the source physical segment and the destination physical segment for a frame that will eventually be discarded. If a network is not prone to frame errors, cut-through frame forwarding will increase the performance of the network.

Bridges and Segmentation

Bridges are used to physically segment a network. By placing bridges in a network, the number of nodes on a physical segment can be reduced. When this occurs, there will be fewer collisions and a higher total aggregate throughput for the network. Figure 1-11 shows six hubs daisy-chained together to form a single physical segment. There can be collisions between any of the nodes shown in the figure. The total aggregate throughput of the network is 10 Mb/s. In Figure 1-12, bridges have been inserted to create more physical segments. With the addition of bridges, there is now a total of six physical segments, five more than in Figure 1-11. With each physical segment providing 10 Mb/s of throughput, there is now a total of 60 Mb/s of throughput.

The next question one needs to ask is, How many logical segments are there? If a broadcast were sent by any of the stations in Figure 1-11, who would receive it? Bridges, by default, forward broadcasts; therefore, all stations in Figure 1-12 would receive a broadcast on the network. There is a single collision domain or physical segment in Figure 1-12. The same can be said of Figure 1-11 because only hubs are used in its network. It can be said that bridges will *not* logically segment a network. All nodes in Figure 1-12 are in the same IP subnet, the same IPX network, and the same Appletalk cable-range. Bridges can increase bandwidth and reduce collisions but cannot stop broadcasts or logically segment a network.

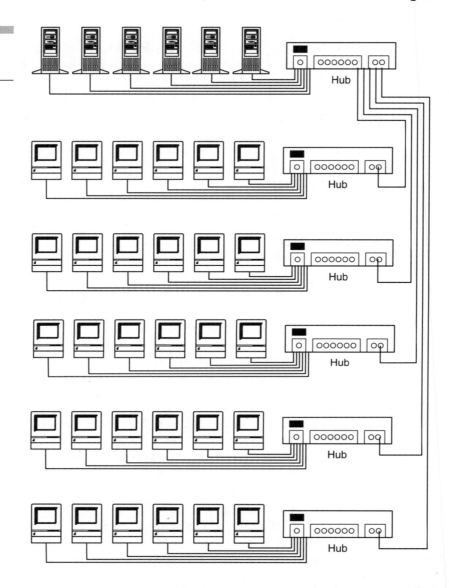

Figure 1-11
A Single Physical
Address

Switches and Segmentation

Because a switch performs segmentation in the same way as a bridge, using switches can further increase throughput. Switches will have more ports and less latency when forwarding frames from one physical

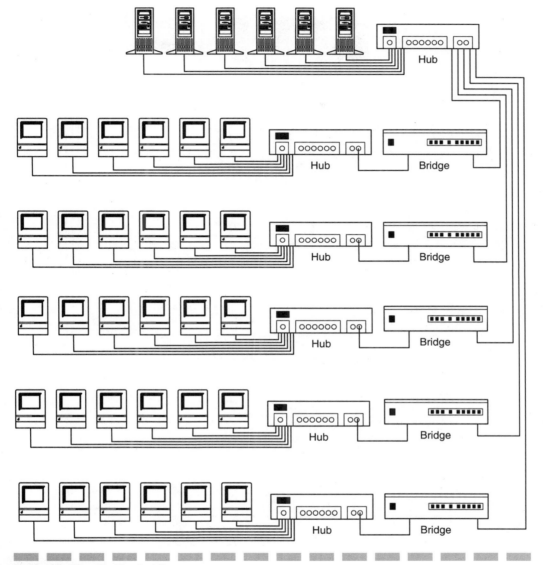

Figure 1–12 *Six Physical Segments*

segment to another. Switches almost always support full duplex, thus doubling the bandwidth, theoretically, on those ports which are connected directly to another node. Full-duplex Ethernet is often said to double the bandwidth, when in actuality this is not the case.

Figure 1–13

*Thirty-six Physical
Segments, One
Logical Segment*

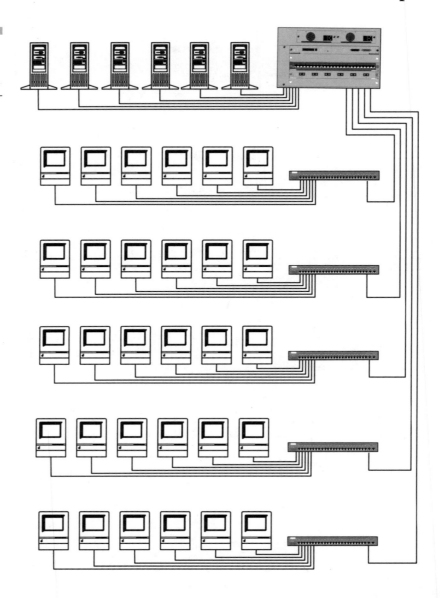

In Figure 1-13, the bridges and hubs have been replaced with switches, yielding numerous physical segments with the ability to use full-duplex Ethernet. Each port on the switch is its own physical segment. This network configuration would be considered switched Ethernet to the desktop. Switches will have no effect on the logical segmentation of this network. Thus broadcast traffic is propagated onto each of the physical segments that has been created by the switches. These broadcasts continue to impede network throughput, as discussed previously. All nodes in Figure 1-13 are in the same IP subnet, the same IPX network, and the same Appletalk cable-range. Switches, like bridges, can increase bandwidth and reduce collisions but cannot stop broadcasts or logically segment a network.

NOTE: *I am often contradicted when I say that a switch does not logically segment a network because of the fact that Virtual Local Area Networks, orVLANs, actually create logical segmentation. However, for VLANs to have any practical application, a router must be employed.*

Routers and Segmentation

A router will physically segment a network in the same way as a switch or a bridge, but it also will create logical segmentation. Routers make forwarding decisions based on the Layer 3 header, the destination IP address, the destination IPX address, or the destination Appletalk address. Broadcasts will not be forwarded by a router. Therefore, a router will create more broadcast domains or logical segments.

In Figure 1-14, the switches have been replaced with a router and some hubs. The router will create five Ethernet physical segments and five Ethernet logical segments. The servers are placed on an FDDI ring, and the ring is used as a collapsed backbone. The term *collapsed backbone* in this case refers to the fact that all workstations will be transmitting to the FDDI ring where the servers reside—hence the traffic collapses into the FDDI ring.

Comparing Segmentation with Routers, Bridges, and Switches

The collapsed FDDI backbone was a common configuration in the "old days," 1992 to 1995. The router provided all the physical and logical segmentation. This created many problems and limitations. When traffic on the hubs became such that the collision rates went above acceptable limits, 3 to 10 percent, users would see considerable performance degradation.

The only solution, at the time, was to use more router interfaces. Routers are not inexpensive, so IS managers were not quick to approve

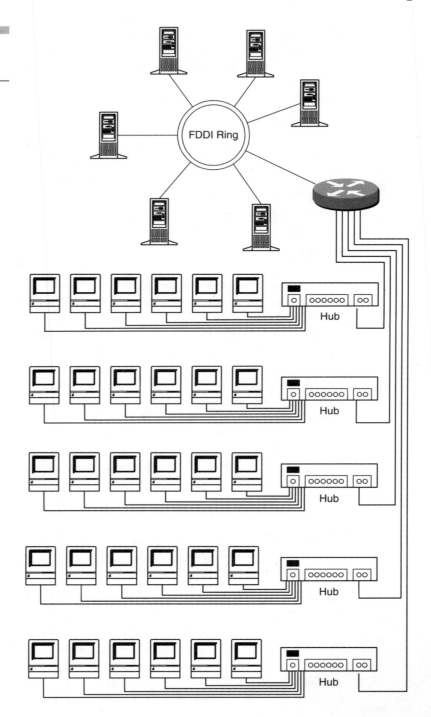

Figure 1–14
Routers and Logical
Segmentation

such expenditures, regardless of the performance degradations. With the invention and mass production of switches, physical segmentation could be accomplished and collisions could be reduced without the purchase of router interfaces.

Another advantage of the switch was the low latency in forwarding frames it provided. Routers have to go through the lengthy process of stripping off frame headers, comparing the Layer 3 destination address with its routing tables, making a forwarding decision, and reencapsulating the packet in a frame. A switch, which is essentially a bridge, could make its forwarding decision based only on the destination MAC address. Figure 1-5 shows that the first field after the preamble is the destination MAC address. A switch or bridge will compare that value to its forwarding tables and then copy the frame to the destination port(s).

What to Buy, Routers or Switches

When switches first hit the market, many engineers were under the impression that routers would be replaced in the marketplace by switches. This was a huge fallacy. Switches could provide all the physical segmentation but offered no means of logical segmentation. Many organizations tried to implement "flat networks," thinking that the switch provided all the segmentation necessary. A *flat network* is a network with little or no logical segmentation. The networks in Figures 1-11 through 1-13 are all flat networks. These figures show only a few workstations in total, but in the real world, flat networks have been attempted with more than 10,000 workstations. The broadcast traffic on these networks is not controlled, and thus every station receives every broadcast. As mentioned earlier, this produces added traffic to all physical segments, even if switched Ethernet to the desktop has been implemented. It also causes unnecessary processing on all devices on the network. A flat network is not an organization's ideal network.

How Many Nodes Should Be Placed on a Physical Segment?

The number of nodes that are placed on a physical segment is determined by a single factor—money. How much can your organization afford to pay? The ideal number of nodes on a physical segment is two.

Some would disagree and suggest that one is the ideal number of nodes. However, if this were the case, the node would have no one with whom to communicate, making it unnecessary to have the node connected to a network. Engineers often do not realize that the port that a node is connected to is considered a node. Communication will occur directly between the port and the node, and it is possible for a collision to occur. Many engineers erroneously believe that with only a single node connected to a switch or a bridge port, collisions cannot occur.

With the understanding that the ideal number of nodes on a physical segment is two, an organization will have to determine the number of switch ports that must be purchased. If the number determined is unacceptable to the powers that be, a combination of hub ports and switch ports will be necessary. The number of ports on the hubs will determine the number of nodes that are eventually placed on the physical segments.

Figure 1-15 shows a configuration with 12 port hubs in combination with a Cisco Catalyst switch. It should be observed that each hub has 11 workstations connected to it, with the twelfth port being used to connect to the switch. This configuration creates four physical segments. Each segment is defined by a port on the Catalyst switch. The total aggregate bandwidth is 40 Mb/s, excluding the physical segment to the Cisco router. Clearly, this organization felt it unnecessary to use all switches. This is usually attributed to a limited budget. However, the price of switches has come down to the point where an organization would have to be painfully frugal not to install all switches, as in Figure 1-16.

In the configuration in Figure 1-16, the organization has implemented *switched Ethernet* to the desktop. The total number of physical segments has been increased dramatically to 48, excluding the physical segment to the router. This implementation will not be significantly more expensive, but it will increase total aggregate bandwidth to 480 Mb/s as opposed to the 40 Mb/s in Figure 1-15. If full-duplex Ethernet were to be implemented, total aggregate bandwidth would be 960 Mb/s.

How Many Nodes Should Be Placed on a Logical Segment?

It is very easy to determine the optimal number of nodes on a physical segment because one only has to consider collisions. However, with logical segmentation, the only factor is broadcasts. The number of broadcasts that is acceptable to an organization determines the size of a logical seg-

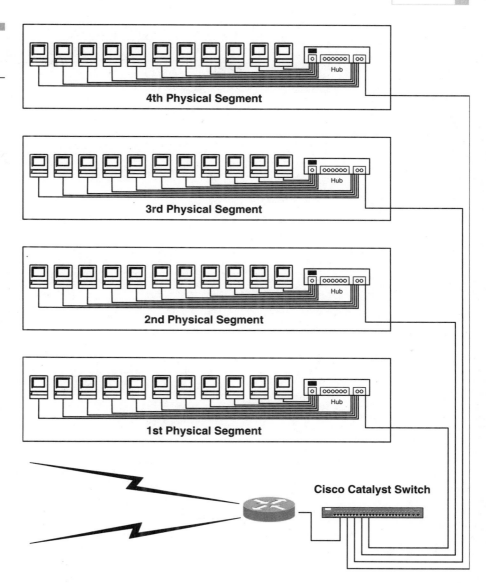

Figure 1–15
Segmentation Using
Switches and Hubs

ment. This is not an easy value to ascertain. In general, I have found that 100 to 1000 broadcast packets per second (BPPS) is the typical range of acceptable broadcasts. This value will vary based on several factors:

1. *The processing power and applications running on a workstation.* Low processing power or more applications running will require a lower BPPS level.

Figure 1–16
Switched Ethernet to
the Desktop

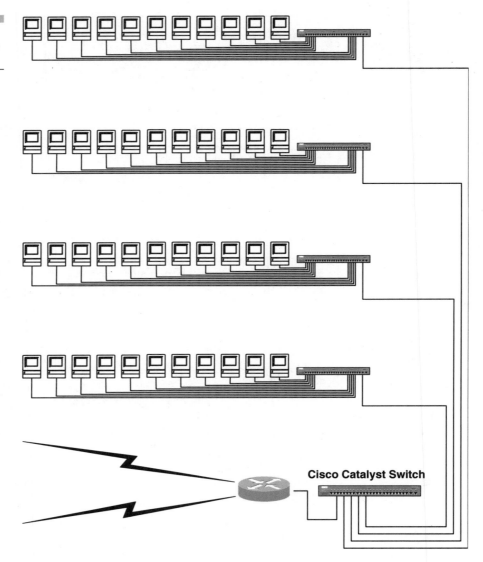

Cisco Catalyst Switch

2. *The bandwidth of the medium in use.* The higher the bandwidth of
the medium, the lower will be the percentage of bandwidth used for
broadcast traffic. Therefore, a high BPPS level will be acceptable.

3. *Application and NOS in use.* There is a small chance that certain applications will be affected by excessive broadcasts, as well as some NOSs.

Once an acceptable BPPS level has been established, it is necessary to determine the number of broadcasts generated by an organization's particular environment. For example, through testing, an organization has determined that based on its current applications and NOS, 500 BPPS will be generated on a logical segment with 500 nodes. If 500 BPPS is an acceptable level, the number of nodes allowed on a logical segmentation will be 500.

To determine the number of broadcasts that will be generated by a particular environment many factors must be considered:

1. *The NOS.*   NOSs such as Windows NT, Appletalk, and Novell Netware will generate many broadcasts, whereas certain UNIX environments will generate far fewer.

2. *The applications running on the network.*   Certain network applications will use broadcasts to operate. One must be aware of these applications and the number of broadcasts that the application may generate based on a function of the number of nodes. For instance, an application that runs on a logical segment of 100 users generates 50 BPPS but generates 500 BPPS when there are 200 users.

3. *The Layer 3 protocol in use.*   This is usually determined by the NOS, but there are certain processes that occur at Layer 3, such as routing protocols and the Address Resolution Protocol (ARP), that generate broadcasts.

All these factors must be taken into consideration when determining the number of nodes on a logical segment. Unfortunately, these values may be impossible to predict without first implementing the system. A protocol analyzer can be set up to monitor only broadcast traffic, and then the BPPS level can be determined more accurately.

Another factor to consider when determining the number of nodes on a logical segment is IP subnetting. About 95 percent of the world's networks use IP. IP subnets will be determined by the size of a logical segment. It is a clean solution to have the number of nodes on a logical segment equal the number of nodes on an IP subnet. When determining the number of nodes, try to choose one of the following values:

Class of Address	Subnet Mask	Number of Nodes
Class A, B, and C	255.255.255.252	2
	255.255.255.248	6
	255.255.255.240	14
	255.255.255.224	30
	255.255.255.192	62
Class A and B	255.255.255.128	126
	255.255.255.0	254
	255.255.254.0	510
	255.255.252.0	1022
	255.255.248.0	2046
	255.255.240.0	4094
	255.255.224.0	8190
	255.255.192.0	16382
Class A	255.255.128.0	32764

Of course, the extreme top and bottom of this table are rarely used. It is unrealistic to build a network with 2 or 32,764 nodes on a single logical segment. This does not mean that it has not been tried, but those who have tried have failed miserably and have created an administrative nightmare.

NOTE: *The two-node subnet mask is actually quite common on point-to-point serial links, but a router typically is used, not a bridge or a switch.*

As can be seen in the preceding discussion, choosing the correct number of nodes for a logical segment often can be difficult and time-consuming. Another approach commonly used today is to simply guess (not very scientific but often effective). I would recommend placing 254 nodes on a logical segment. This is typically a safe number regardless of application or NOS. It is also one of the most common subnet masks.

There will be times when broadcasts are not the most important factor in choosing the size of a logical segment. Sometimes the wide-area network (WAN) may define a network's logical segmentation. In Figure 1-17,

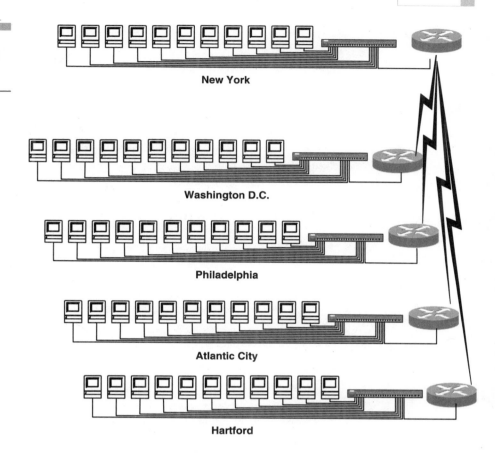

Figure 1–17
Wide-Area Network
of a Small
Organization

New York

Washington D.C.

Philadelphia

Atlantic City

Hartford

each site of an organization's network has so few users that logical segmentation is not required at each site. Although there are only 11 workstations at each site, the routers required for the WAN connection will define the logical segmentation.

SUMMARY

This chapter has described the Ethernet medium and the problems associated with using it in local-area networks (LAN). To resolve these problems, LANs using Ethernet must be segmented. There are two types of segmentation, logical and physical. A router must be used to perform logical segmentation, whereas a bridge or switch must be used to perform physical segmentation.

A bridge makes its forwarding decision based on the destination MAC address, whereas a router makes its forwarding decision based on the destination Layer 3 address. This creates more latency in the router, so forwarding with a bridge or switch is faster.

The number of nodes placed on a physical segment is optimally 2, whereas the number of nodes on a logical segment depends on many different factors such as the application, NOS, and Layer 3 protocol.

EXERCISES

1. If an engineer were to place a protocol analyzer on an Ethernet physical segment, what traffic would the analyzer see?

2. How does an Ethernet station know when it sees a frame on the Ethernet physical segment that the frame is directed to it?

3. What are the differences between the Ethernet II frame type and the Standard IEEE 802.3 frame type?

4. Why is IPX the only Layer 3 protocol supported by the Novell Ethernet frame type?

5. If two stations on a physical segment were to have a collision, describe the steps that are taken to recover from the collision.

6. Define the term *shared medium* and indicate how it compares with a switched network.

7. What are the major differences between Ethernet, Fast Ethernet, and Gigabit Ethernet from a practical standpoint?

8. What is *full-duplex Ethernet,* and what are its requirements?

9. How many physical and logical segments are shown in Figure 1-18?

10. At what layer of the OSI model does a switch operate, and how does this compare with a bridge?

11. What are the advantages of physical segmentation?

12. What are the advantages of logical segmentation?

13. Describe the possible forwarding methods of a switch and the advantages and disadvantages to each?

14. Why is it necessary to use routers in larger networks, excluding the fact that they are necessary for WAN connections?

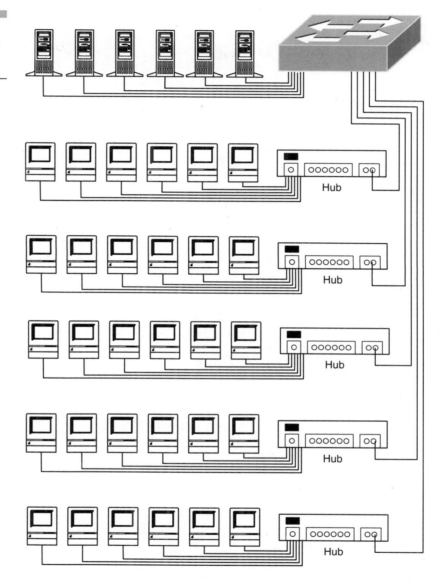

Figure 1–18
Physical Segments(?)
and Logical
Segments(?)

Hub

Hub

Hub

Hub

Hub

15. When would an organization choose to have more than two nodes on a physical segment? What would be a commonly used term to describe the use of only two nodes on a physical segment?

16. What is the maximum number of nodes that can be placed on a logical segment, and why?

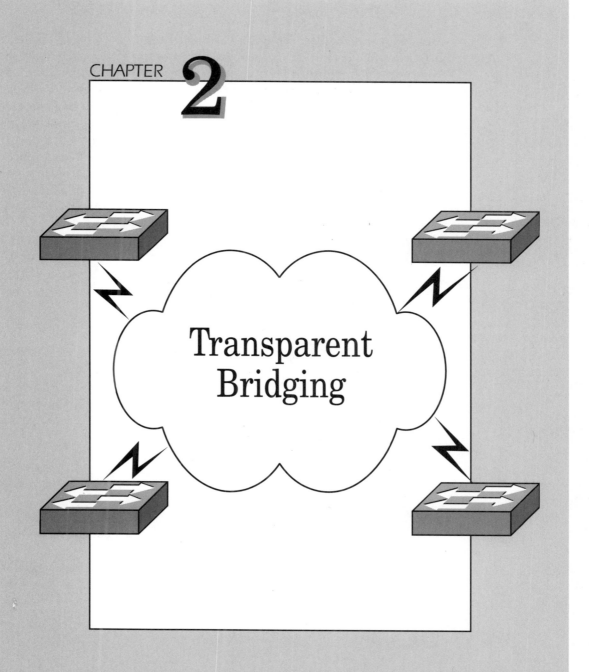

Transparent
Bridging

Chapter 1 talked about what kind of segmentation a switch, a bridge, or a router provides but did not discuss how a bridge or a switch makes its forwarding decision. This chapter addresses the functions of a bridge/switch in an Ethernet environment. In fact, bridges and switches provide frame forwarding in the same manner, so I will use the term *bridge* throughout most of this chapter. These concepts, however, also apply to switches.

Because a bridge makes its forwarding decision based solely on the destination MAC address, no address hierarchy can be created as in routing. Every node will have to be "learned" and stored in a table that will be placed in RAM or cache memory. This chapter describes this process, as well as the problems and solutions that come with it.

With Ethernet, the process of making the forwarding decisions is called *transparent bridging,* whereas in Token Ring environments the process is a little different and is called *source route bridging.* This is discussed in Chapter 3.

The Three Functions of a Transparent Bridge

A transparent bridge is used primarily in Ethernet environments and is designed to be transparent to the end nodes—hence the name. A transparent bridge has three major functions:

1. Learning

2. Forwarding and filtering

3. Avoiding loops

A transparent bridge performs all three functions concurrently while it is operational. It should be noted that some published material lists a total of four functions, in that forwarding and filtering are split into individual functions. Cisco, however, considers them to be the same function, and hence so will I.

Learning

A bridge must make forwarding decisions based on the destination MAC address. Therefore, it must "learn" the locations of MAC addresses so that it can make accurate forwarding decisions. All stations on an Ethernet physical segment see all frames transmitted on that segment. When a bridge is connected to a physical segment, it examines all the frames it sees. It reads the source MAC address field of the frame and makes an assumption. It assumes that if it sees a frame coming from a node on a particular port, then the workstation must reside on that port. It will place this information in what is called a *bridge table*. The bridge will perform the frame check sum (FCS) before placing the entry in the bridge table, thereby eliminating erroneous entries. On a Catalyst switch, this table is called the *content addressable memory (CAM)*. A bridge table and a CAM table are basically the same, with some small differences that will be discussed later.

Figure 2-1 shows four workstations: A, B, C, and D. There is also a bridge with two ports connected to two physical segments. When workstation A transmits to workstation B, the frame traverses Ethernet Segment 1 and is received by both the bridge and workstation B.

When the bridge receives the frame, it will learn that workstation A is on its port 1, since this is the port on which the frame was received. The bridge puts an entry into its bridge table recording the MAC address of workstation A as being on port 1, as in Figure 2-2.

Conversely, when workstation B responds to workstation A, the bridge sees a frame with workstation B's MAC address as the source, as shown in Figure 2-3.

Figure 2-1
Workstation A transmits to workstation B on Ethernet Segment 1

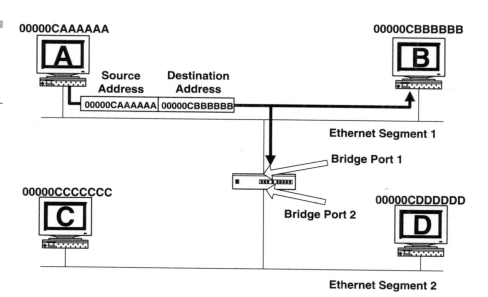

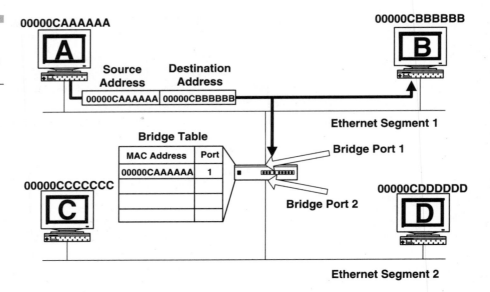

Figure 2-2
The Bridge Learns
That Workstation A Is
Attached to Its Port 1

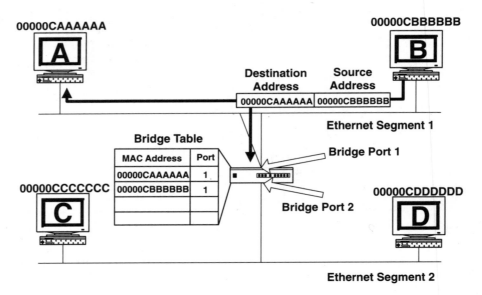

Figure 2-3
The Bridge Learns
That Workstation B Is
Attached to Its Port 1

Bridges learn continuously. Entries remain in the bridge table until no traffic is seen coming from that MAC address for 5 minutes. This time interval is configurable on almost all switches and bridges and is referred to as the *aging time*. Entries also may be entered manually into the bridge table, and these entries will not time-out.

Eventually, all MAC addresses will be known by the bridge, assuming that all workstations are in use.

Forwarding and Filtering

The second major function of a bridge is to forward and filter. Using the bridge table, a bridge makes a decision as whether to forward or not forward (i.e., filter) a frame. This decision is based on the destination MAC address in the frame header.

If workstation A were to transmit to workstation C and workstation C had an entry in the bridge table, the bridge would forward the frame onto Ethernet Segment 2 (Figure 2-4).

If workstation A were to transmit to workstation B, forwarding of frames would be unnecessary because workstation B is on the same physical segment. Therefore, the bridge would filter, or not forward (Figure 2-5).

What happens if workstation A sends a frame to workstation C and the bridge does not have workstation C in its bridge table? Bridges forward frames directed to unknown destination MAC addresses to all ports. The bridge behaves as a hub in this scenario to ensure that it is not preventing traffic from flowing (Figures 2-6 and 2-7).

Figure 2-4
Forwarding

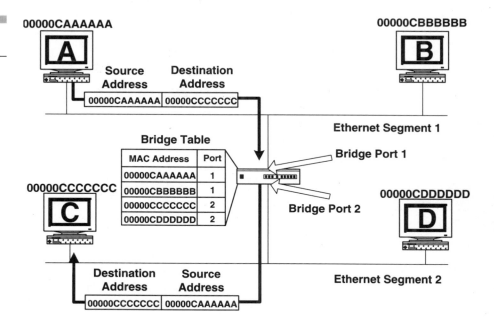

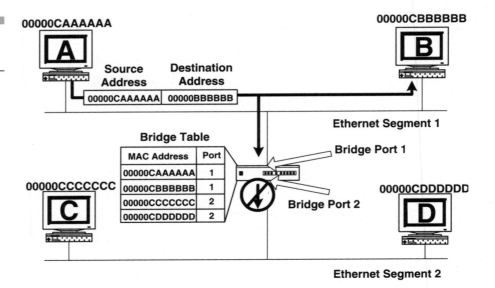

Figure 2-5
Filtering, or Not
Forwarding

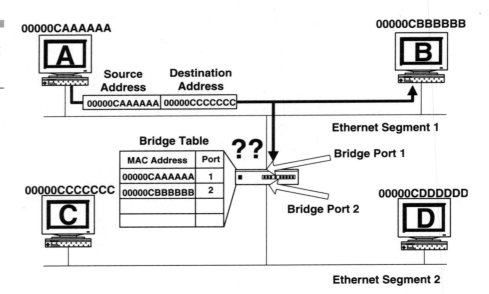

Figure 2-6
The Destination MAC
Address Is Not in the
Bridge Table

If the bridge did not forward frames with unknown destination MAC addresses, workstation A would not have connectivity with workstation C until workstation C transmitted a frame. This would be unacceptable.

Bridges also forward broadcasts and multicasts out all ports, much the same as frames with unknown destination ports.

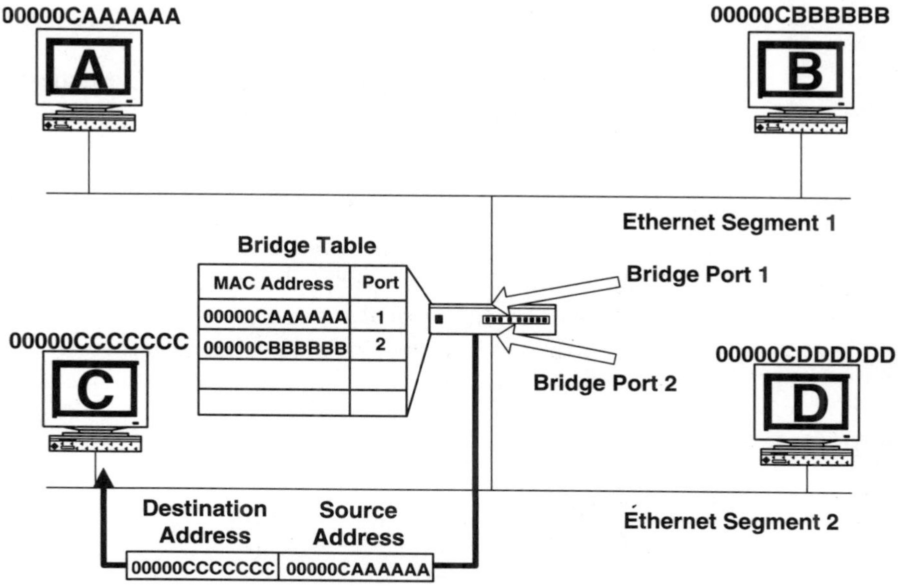

Figure 2-7
The Bridge Forwards
the Frame Out All
Ports

Figure 2-7
The Bridge Forwards
the Frame Out All
Ports

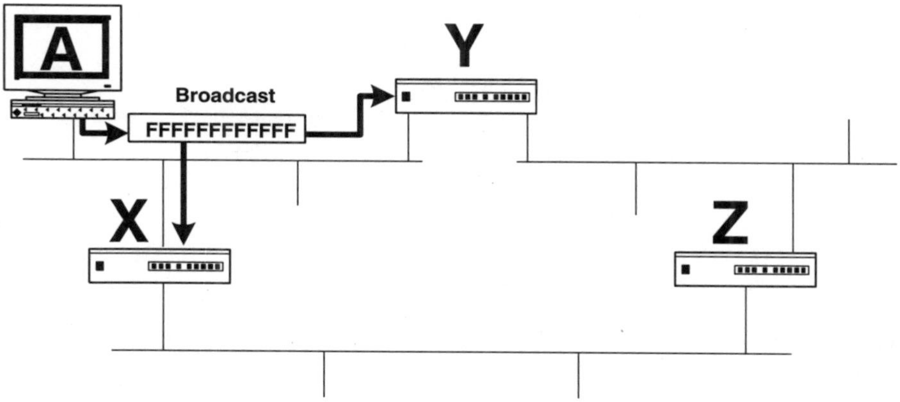

Figure 2-8
Bridge Loops

Avoiding Loops

The final function of a transparent bridge is to avoid loops. This is by far the most difficult of the three functions to comprehend. Figure 2-8 shows multiple bridges used for redundancy. A broadcast is sent from a workstation in the upper right-hand corner of the figure.

Bridges X and Y, which are connected to the first segment, see the broadcast and then forward it out all other ports, which in this case is only one (Figure 2-9).

The broadcast is propagated onto the second and third Ethernet segments, both of which have a connection to bridge Z, and bridge Z will forward the broadcasts to the third and second Ethernet segments (Figure 2-10).

This little problem is called a *bridge loop,* and there is nothing little about it. This single broadcast will kill the three physical segments shown in Figures 2-8 through 2-10. In the real world, there may be hundreds of these physical segments. Such a situation could lead to hours of downtime while an engineer tries to locate the loop. Once the loop is located, the simple solution would be to remove the offending connection.

Figure 2-9
Bridge Loops

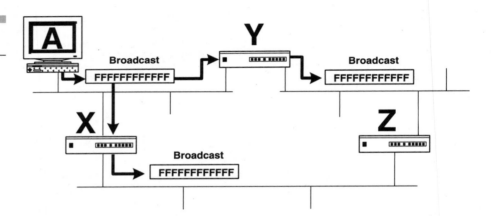

Figure 2-10
Bridge Loops

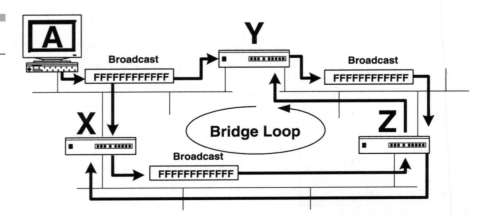

The third major function of a bridge is to locate and eliminate the redundant connections. To do this, a bridge must be aware of other bridges. The assumption that the source MAC address is located on the port on which a frame is received does not work when there is more than one bridge. The protocol used by bridges to exchange information with one another is called the *Spanning Tree Protocol (STP)*.

There are several different versions of the STP, and they are not compatible with one another. It is important to verify that all bridges and switches use the same version of STP because different versions of the STP can cause bridge loops, which kill Ethernet physical segments. The two most commonly used STPs are DEC and IEEE. There are several other versions that have not been very popular. Therefore, it is important to verify that you are not using one of these rarely used STPs because it could create a potential problem in the future. Most switches do not support anything other than DEC and IEEE. The Cisco Catalyst switch uses the IEEE version of STP on its Ethernet ports and the IBM version of STP on its Token Ring ports.

Spanning Tree Protocol

A bridge must transmit small packets out all ports to let other bridges know that it exists and can be a potential cause of bridge loops. These small packets are called *bridge protocol data units (BPDUs)*. A Catalyst switch sends a BPDU out all its active ports every 10 seconds. These BPDUs are received, and the bridge uses a mathematical formula called the *spanning tree algorithm (STA)*. The STA lets a bridge know when there is a loop and determines which of the redundant ports needs to be shut down. The process of shutting down a port is called *blocking*. A port that is blocking is still an active port; i.e., it is still receiving and reading BPDUs. It will wait until a failure or topology change eliminates the loop. When this occurs, the port will start to forward frames because the loop is no longer present (Figure 2-11).

The purpose of the BPDUs and the STA is to create a "loopless" environment. A tree is free of loops naturally. All trees have a root at the bottom of a trunk, the trunk breaks into branches, and the branches divide into smaller branches, and so on. A branch, however, never grows into another branch—thus a "loopless" environment.

The STA can be very complex, but if one understands several small concepts, one can understand which ports will go into the blocking state.

Figure 2-11
All Bridges Will Send
BPDUs

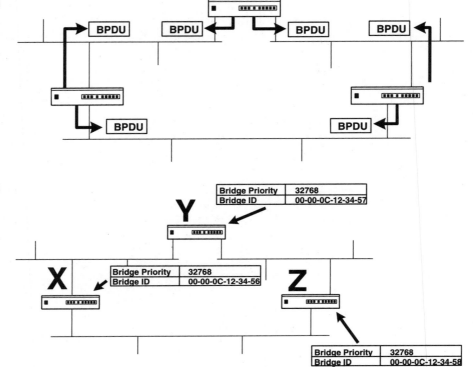

Figure 2-12
All Bridges Will Send
BPDUs

The Root Bridge

All trees have a root, so a spanning tree also has a root. This will be a special bridge appropriately called the *root bridge*. All bridges are assigned a numerical value called *bridge priority,* and the bridge with the lowest priority is the root bridge. By default, a Catalyst switch has a bridge priority of 32768. Therefore, if you only use Catalyst switches, all your bridges have the lowest bridge priority, or the highest if you are a "glass is half full" kind of engineer. A tiebreaker must be used, and unlike the NFL playoffs, a coin toss will not be a good last resort considering that most switches do not have a dime to their name. On a Catalyst switch, the lowest MAC address in the pool assigned to the supervisor engine is used. This MAC address is commonly referred to as the *bridge ID*. The bridge ID is the tiebreaker; i.e., the bridge with the lowest bridge ID will be the root bridge. Using the MAC address as the bridge ID ensures that one and only one bridge will have the lowest value because MAC addresses are globally unique. In Figure 2-12, all the bridges used have the same bridge priority, so the tiebreaker will be the bridge ID. Bridge X has the lowest bridge ID and thus will be the root bridge.

Which Ports Should Be Blocked?

Using BPDUs, the bridges must locate the loops and shut down or block those ports which are causing a loop. There will always be two or more ports involved in a loop, so which one should go into the blocking state? A decision must be made. *Port* cost is an arbitrary parameter that is assigned to ports in a bridged environment, usually by default and based on medium rate. A Catalyst switch has default values based on the medium of the port. The default cost can usually be derived by dividing 1000 by the speed of the media in megabytes per second. For example, Ethernet's default port cost will be 1000/10 MB/s, or 100. A bridge always looks for the port that will lead to the root bridge in the cheapest fashion. This could be likened to traveling into New York City from JFK Airport. You could take a cab or a limousine service. Sometimes the limousine service is cheaper, and sometimes the cab is cheaper. The obvious choice is the cheapest method, unless you are independently wealthy and like to spend money frivolously.

Everything is viewed in relation to the root bridge. As far as the bridge is concerned, no more than one port is needed that can lead to the root bridge. Thus the port that is "closest" to the root bridge or "cheapest" is called the *root port* (not a very exciting name).

Looking at our three-bridge scenario (Figure 2-13), we can see that the ports that are connected directly to the root bridge will be the root ports because they are the "cheapest" of the two ports on bridges Y and Z.

Figure 2-13
Designated Ports

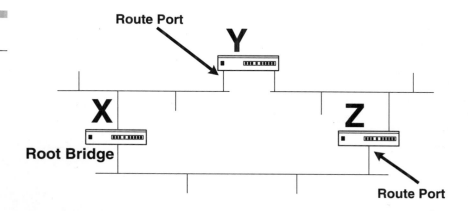

Route Port

Y

X

Root Bridge

Z

Route Port

There is a loop in this situation, and one of the two ports on either bridge Y or bridge Z must go into the blocking state to break the loop. In order to determine which one it will be, one must understand the concept of a designated port (or bridge). A *designated* port is the bridge port that is closest to the root bridge on a physical segment. Looking at the third physical segment in Figure 2-13, it is apparent that there are two bridge ports to chose from. Now I know what you are thinking—that both these bridge ports are equally close to the root bridge. The tiebreaker, however, will be a parameter called the *port ID,* which is usually the MAC address of the port. Thus there will be a designated port (bridge) on all physical segments, and the designated port will be the bridge advertising, via BPDUs, the lowest cost to the root. In the event of a tie, the port ID with the lowest MAC address will be the designated port because the MAC address is globally unique, thus preventing a tie.

If the cost of all ports in Figure 2-14 is the same, then the port with the higher MAC address will be the port to enter the blocking state. In this case, bridge Y has a port ID of 00-00-0C-00-00-0A, which is higher than bridge Z's port ID. Therefore, bridge Y's port will enter the blocking state (Figure 2-15).

The designated port (or bridge) is determined by physical segment. The two physical segments that are connected directly to the root bridge will use the two ports of the root bridge as the designated port. The root bridge will always be the designated port on all physical segments to which it is directly connected.

A bridge will calculate which port is the root port and determine if any of its ports are the designated port of a physical segment. It will block all other ports. In Figure 2-16, all the root ports and designated bridges are identified, leaving a single port to be blocked. Please note

Figure 2-14
Port Ids

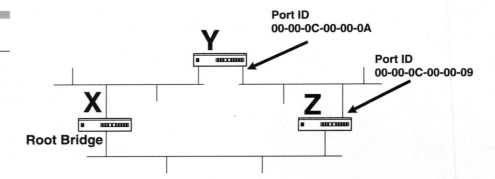

Port ID
00-00-0C-00-00-0A

Port ID
00-00-0C-00-00-09

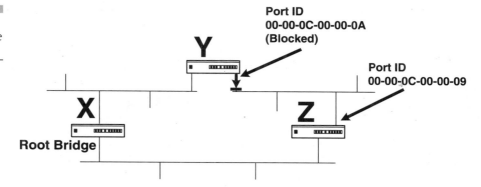

Figure 2-15
Workstation Y's Bridge
Will Be Blocked

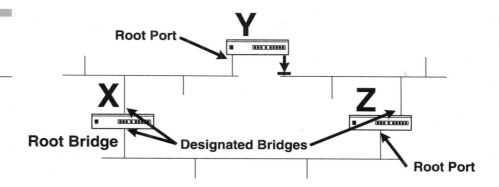

Figure 2-16
Root Ports and
Designated Bridge
Ports

that the root bridge will be the designated bridge on all its ports and therefore will never block any of its ports.

To further illustrate these concepts, let's look at a much more complex environment, much like we would expect in the real world. Figure 2-17 shows a network diagram with the workstations left out. A lot of redundancy has been built into this configuration because this organization is very paranoid that something may go wrong.

All the port IDs have been listed as well as the bridge IDs. The bridge priority and port cost are left the same to illustrate situations in the real world. A lot of times these parameters will be left at default. It is important to look at each physical segment individually and then to divide and conquer. To determine which ports will be forwarding and which will be blocking, I would suggest taking the following steps:

1. *Determine the root bridge.* The bridge with the lowest bridge priority will be the root bridge. If there is a tie, the bridge ID will be used as the tiebreaker.

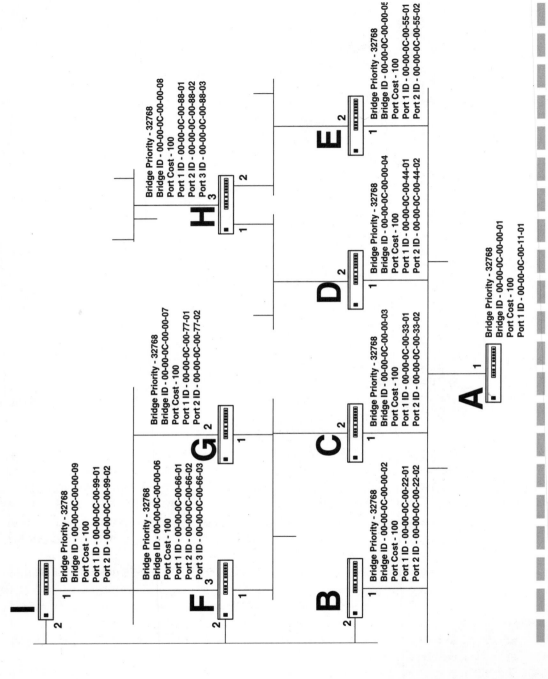

Figure 2-17 Complex Spanning Tree

2. *Determine the designated bridges.* The bridge port advertising the lowest cost to the root will be the designated root. In the event of a tie, the port ID will be the tiebreaker.

3. *Determine the root ports.* On all bridges, determine which port has the lowest cost to the root bridge. This port will be the root port.

4. *Determine which ports will be blocking.* After the first three steps, one needs simply set all ports to blocking except the ports that are the designated bridge or root ports.

5. *Determine which ports will be forwarding.* All root ports and designated bridges will forward.

Let's examine these steps in greater detail.

Step 1: Determine the Root Bridge. All bridges have the same priority, so the bridge ID will be used. Bridge A has the lowest bridge ID, so it will be the root bridge (Figure 2-18).

Step 2: Determine the Designated Bridges of All Physical Segments. The first physical segment is the physical segment connected to the root bridge and is the simplest of the segments on which to determine the designated bridge. The root bridge obviously will have the lowest cost to the root bridge (Figure 2-19).

The second physical segment has three bridges, and Figure 2-20 shows that bridge B is closest to the root bridge. Because all the port costs are the same, the bridge that has to traverse the least number of bridges to the root will be the designated bridge. This is very similar to the distance vector routing protocol RIP. However, if the port costs were different, a comparison could be made to link state routing. Because bridge B is the least number of hops from the root, it will be the designated bridge for physical segment 2.

The third physical segment will use bridge C as the designated bridge because it has the least number of hops to the root bridge (Figure 2-21).

The fourth physical segment is a little more difficult. Both bridges F and G are one hop from the root bridge. Thus the port ID is used as the tiebreaker. Bridge F's port 3 ID is smaller than bridge G's port 2 ID, so bridge F's port 3 will be the designated bridge of the fourth physical segment (Figure 2-22). Then it is easy to see that bridges D and E are the designated bridges of the fifth and sixth physical segments, respectively (Figures 2-23 and 2-24).

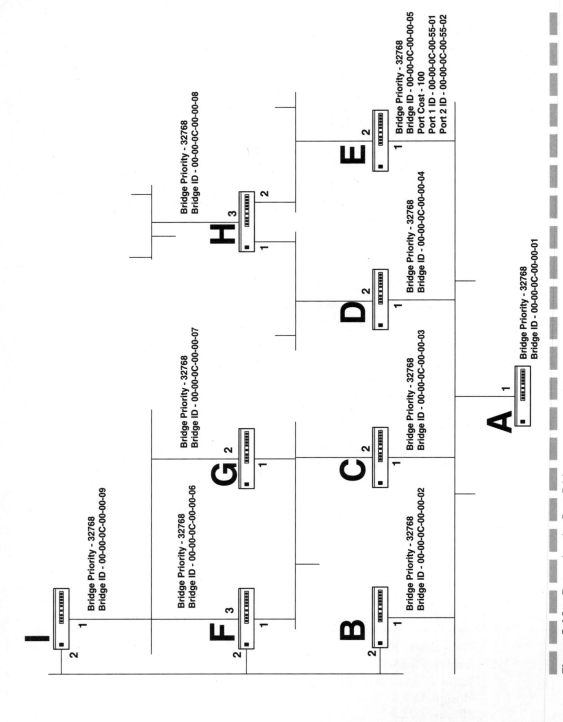

Figure 2-18 Determine the Root Bridge

48

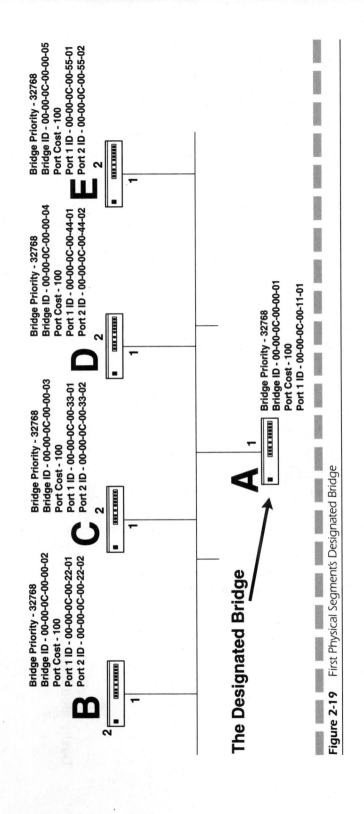

The Designated Bridge

Figure 2-19   First Physical Segment's Designated Bridge

49

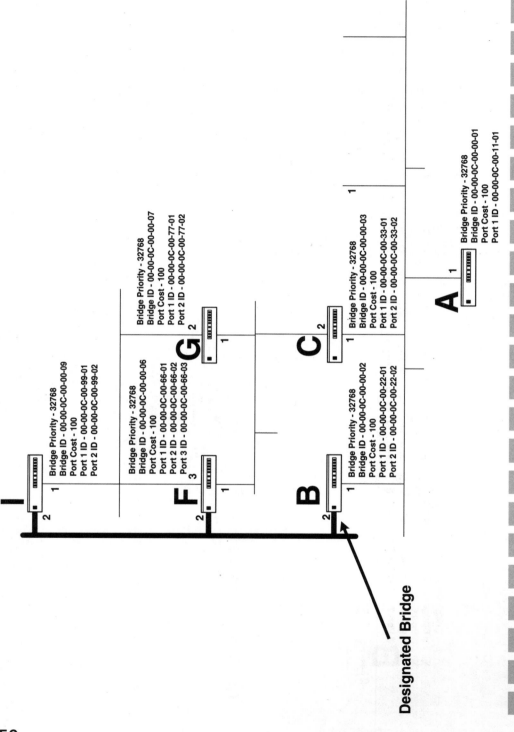

Bridge Priority - 32768
Bridge ID - 00-00-0C-00-00-09
Port Cost - 100
Port 1 ID - 00-00-0C-00-99-01
Port 2 ID - 00-00-0C-00-99-02

Bridge Priority - 32768
Bridge ID - 00-00-0C-00-00-06
Port Cost - 100
Port 1 ID - 00-00-0C-00-66-01
Port 2 ID - 00-00-0C-00-66-02
Port 3 ID - 00-00-0C-00-66-03

Bridge Priority - 32768
Bridge ID - 00-00-0C-00-00-07
Port Cost - 100
Port 1 ID - 00-00-0C-00-77-01
Port 2 ID - 00-00-0C-00-77-02

Bridge Priority - 32768
Bridge ID - 00-00-0C-00-00-02
Port Cost - 100
Port 1 ID - 00-00-0C-00-22-01
Port 2 ID - 00-00-0C-00-22-02

Bridge Priority - 32768
Bridge ID - 00-00-0C-00-00-03
Port Cost - 100
Port 1 ID - 00-00-0C-00-33-01
Port 2 ID - 00-00-0C-00-33-02

Bridge Priority - 32768
Bridge ID - 00-00-0C-00-00-01
Port Cost - 100
Port 1 ID - 00-00-0C-00-11-01

Designated Bridge

Figure 2-20   Second Physical Segment's Designated Bridge

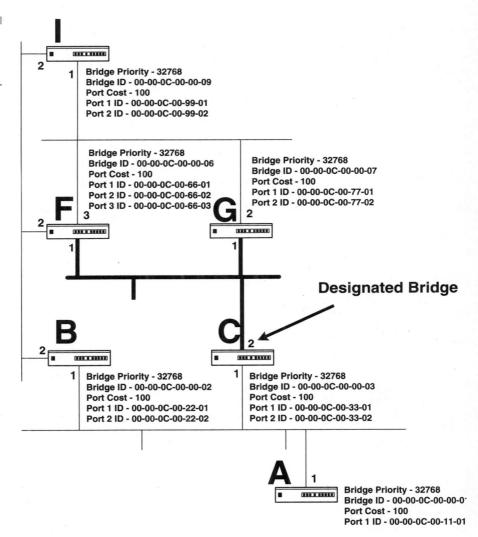

Figure 2-21
Third Physical
Segment's Designated
Bridge

Bridge Priority - 32768
Bridge ID - 00-00-0C-00-00-09
Port Cost - 100
Port 1 ID - 00-00-0C-00-99-01
Port 2 ID - 00-00-0C-00-99-02

Bridge Priority - 32768
Bridge ID - 00-00-0C-00-00-06
Port Cost - 100
Port 1 ID - 00-00-0C-00-66-01
Port 2 ID - 00-00-0C-00-66-02
Port 3 ID - 00-00-0C-00-66-03

Bridge Priority - 32768
Bridge ID - 00-00-0C-00-00-07
Port Cost - 100
Port 1 ID - 00-00-0C-00-77-01
Port 2 ID - 00-00-0C-00-77-02

Designated Bridge

Bridge Priority - 32768
Bridge ID - 00-00-0C-00-00-02
Port Cost - 100
Port 1 ID - 00-00-0C-00-22-01
Port 2 ID - 00-00-0C-00-22-02

Bridge Priority - 32768
Bridge ID - 00-00-0C-00-00-03
Port Cost - 100
Port 1 ID - 00-00-0C-00-33-01
Port 2 ID - 00-00-0C-00-33-02

Bridge Priority - 32768
Bridge ID - 00-00-0C-00-00-0'
Port Cost - 100
Port 1 ID - 00-00-0C-00-11-01

Bridge H is the only bridge on the seventh physical segment, so it must be the designated bridge (Figure 2-25).

Step 3: Determine the Root Ports. The port closest to the root bridge is the root port. This port will be easy to determine for bridges B, C, D, and E. However, when examining bridge F, we see that there are two possible paths to the root bridge, each with an equal cost. The tiebreaker once again will be the port ID. Bridge B's port 2 ID is smaller

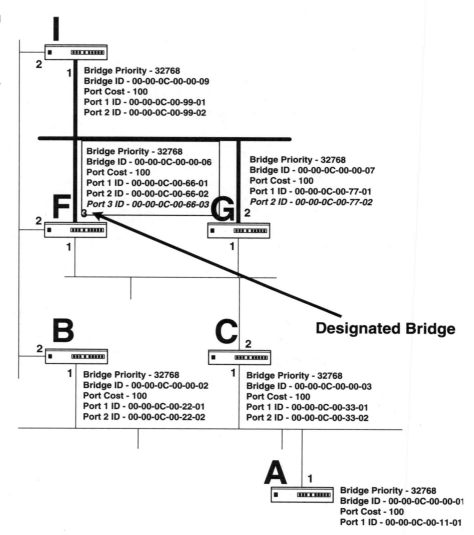

than bridge C's port 3 ID and will cause bridge F to select its port 2 as the root port. A similar scenario occurs with bridge H, whereby port 1 of bridge H will be elected the root port because bridge D's port 2 ID is lower than bridge E's port 2 ID (Figure 2-26).

Step 4: Determine Which Ports Will Be Blocking. Once the designated bridge ports and root ports have been identified, all other ports will be placed in the blocking state (Figure 2-27).

Figure 2-23
Fifth Physical
Segment's Designated
Bridge

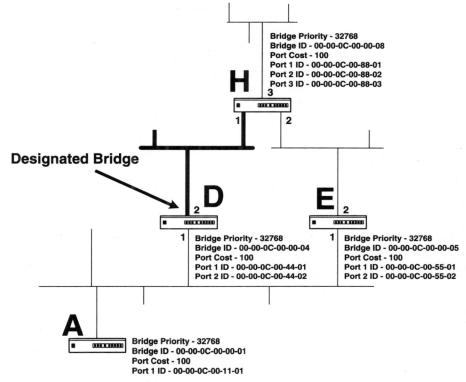

Step 5: Determine Which Ports Will Be Forwarding. After we remove the blocked ports, we can see the spanning tree (Figure 2-28). Bridge A is the root and forwards on all its ports, creating a sort of bush, not really a tree. When one thinks of a tree, there is only one trunk, but with a spanning tree, it is more of an oleander or rhododendron. Whatever it is, it works.

Spanning Tree Port States

When a bridge or switch has a port become active (i.e., the link light turns on), it will go through several states before it actually begins forwarding or blocking. A port will first enter the listening state, listening for BPDUs. It will read these BPDUs to determine its root port and the designated bridge on that port. If it has been determined that a port needs to be placed in the blocking mode, it will enter that state when lis-

Figure 2-24
Sixth Physical
Segment's Designated
Bridge

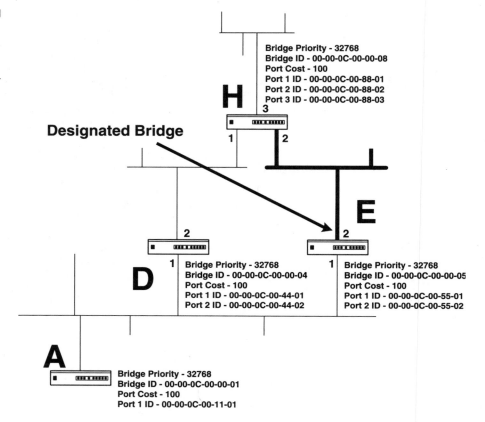

Figure 2-24
Sixth Physical
Segment's Designated
Bridge

tening mode is complete. If it is determined that the port should be in the forwarding mode, the port will enter an intermediate state called *learning,* so called because the port will be examining source MAC addresses and placing entries in the bridge table. Once learning mode is complete, forwarding begins (Figure 2-29). If there is a change in the link state or spanning tree topology, the spanning tree states will be cycled. This may cause short periods of downtime on the network. To avoid these downtime periods, I recommend not making substantial changes to a bridged environment during mission-critical times of the day.

While a bridge or switch port is in the listening and learning modes, it is not forwarding. This can be a source of great problems when using switched Ethernet to the desktop. When workstations are plugged directly into a switch port, the link state will change whenever the machine is power cycled. When a user comes into the office in the morn-

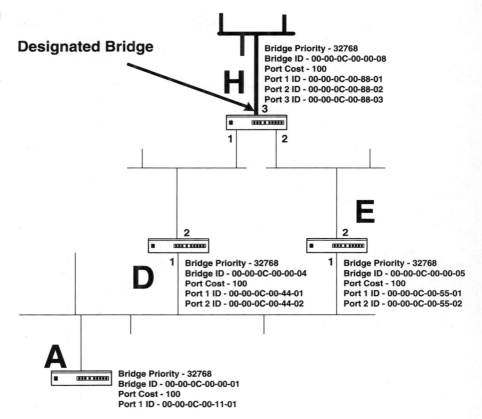

Figure 2-25
Seventh Physical Segment's Designated Bridge

ing and turns on his or her workstation, the switch port must go through the spanning tree states. These states can take a minute or more depending on the switch settings. The NOS client software that is running on the workstation may have problems with this delay in connectivity. Once the machine loads the client software, e.g., Novell DOS or Windows Requester or Windows NT, the workstation will look for a server. If no server is found, the workstation often will not have connectivity to the resources it needs, rendering the user unable to work (assuming that he or she actually does work in the first place). This can be fixed simply by rebooting the workstation, but such a solution usually is not acceptable to the user. A configurable parameter called *forward delay* will set the amount of time a port will be in the listening and learning modes. Listening mode and learning mode each will be half the forward delay time. However, this is not a parameter that I would recommend changing

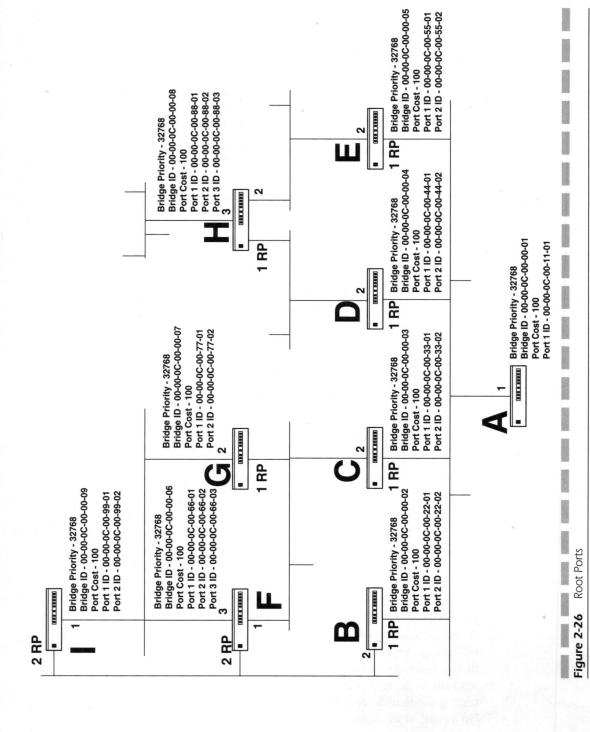

Figure 2-26 Root Ports

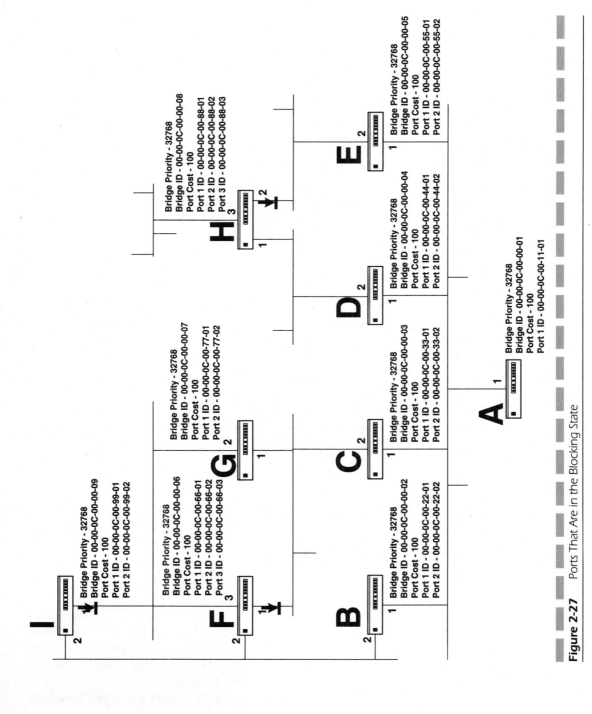

Figure 2-27   Ports That Are in the Blocking State

57

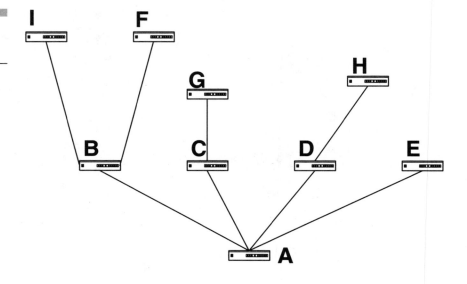

Figure 2-28
The Spanning Tree
(Loopless)

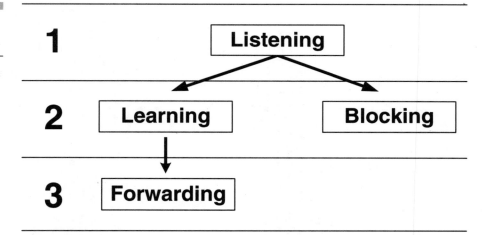

Figure 2-29
Spanning Tree States
of a Port

because these times are for the entire switch or bridge, and a change thus will affect the entire switch. This would include ports that may need to spend the whole minute to accurately calculate whether or not they belong in the forwarding state or blocking state.

On a Catalyst switch, a port can be configured to enter the forwarding state immediately to ensure connectivity to servers. This will not affect other ports on the switch. This also will not turn off the Spanning Tree Protocol. I have often heard engineers refer to this as turning off spanning tree, but you are not really turning it off. You are simply allowing the switch to forward while it goes through the learning and listening modes. We will revisit the subject when we get to configurations.

The spanning tree disabled state occurs when a port is administratively shut down. In this state, a port will not listen for BPDUs, forward frames, or learn MAC addresses. A disabled port must be reenabled manually. It will then go through the normal cycling of states described earlier.

SUMMARY

When using switches with Ethernet, Fast Ethernet, or Gigabit Ethernet, transparent bridging will be used. There are two popular Spanning Tree Protocols (STPs) that can be used to identify and stop loops, DEC and IEEE. Catalyst switches only use the IEEE version. Therefore, it is important to verify that all switches and bridges in a Catalyst environment use the IEEE version of STP.

A transparent bridge has three major functions:

1. Learning

2. Forwarding and filtering

3. Avoiding loops (Spanning Tree Protocol)

A bridge or switch will learn the location of end stations by examining the source MAC addresses of all frames on its ports. It will then make forwarding and filtering decisions based on what it has learned. To avoid loops, a bridge will transmit BPDUs out all its ports and listen for BPDUs from other bridges. Using the spanning tree algorithm (STA), it will determine which ports need to enter the blocking state to stop loops.

It is important to understand the different spanning tree states that a port will go through when it first becomes active. The forward delay parameter changes the amount of time a port spends in the learning and listening states.

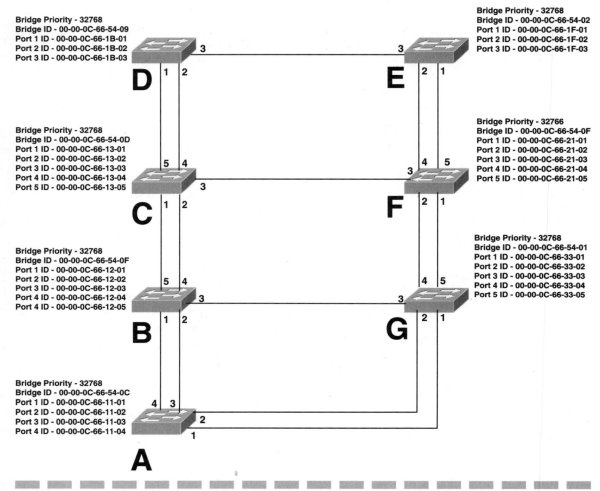

Figure 2-30   Catalyst Switched Infrastructure

EXERCISES

1. Which field in the frame header does a bridge or switch use when learning? Which field in the frame header does a bridge or switch use when making a forwarding decision?

2. What is the purpose of the bridge table or CAM table of a bridge or switch?

3. When does a bridge not learn on a port? Why?

4. List three possible scenarios where a bridge or switch behaves as a hub?

5. Describe the problems associated with using different versions of the Spanning Tree Protocol and what can be done to avoid the situation.

6. What is the purpose of the Spanning Tree Protocol?

7. What parameter(s) are used in determining the root bridge? What happens if these parameters are all the same?

8. What is the difference between the root bridge and the root port?

Use Figure 2-30 to answer Exercises 9 through 12.

9. Which of the switches is the root bridge, and why?

10. Identify all the ports that are designated bridges. How did you determine the designated bridges?

11. Identify all the root ports. How did you determine the root ports?

12. Identify which ports will enter the blocking state after listening mode. Why do these ports enter the blocking state?

13. Explain the problems with spanning tree states and switched Ethernet to the desktop.

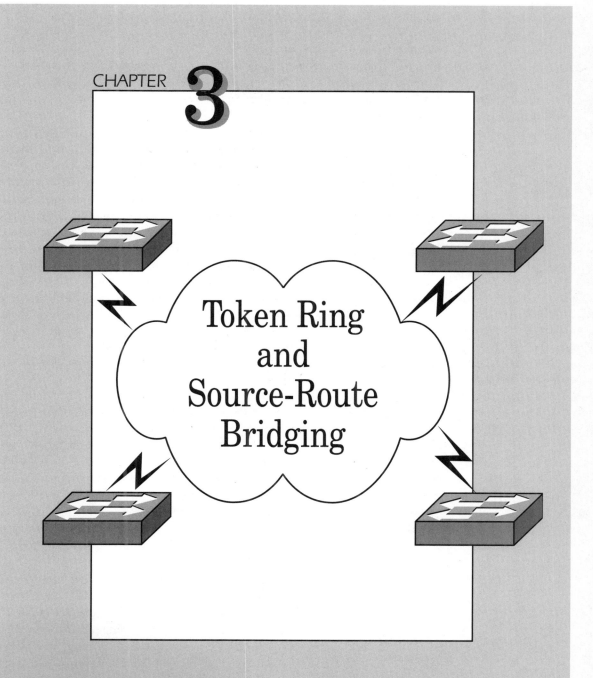

CHAPTER 3

Token Ring
and
Source-Route
Bridging

Although the medium for most networks is one of the three available forms of Ethernet, Token Ring remains an ever-present nuisance. Its unusual method of transmission and nonconventional representation of MAC addresses have caused many engineers a great deal of pain and heartache.

The Institute of Electrical and Electronics Engineers (IEEE) has adopted the original Token Ring specifications with small modifications, and this document is referred to as IEEE 802.5. It was released in 1985. Used primarily in environments where IBM is the dominant vendor, Token Ring will be around for awhile. IBM's omnipotent presence in the computer industry in the early 1980s has led many organizations to this peculiar medium. Financial institutions, insurance organizations, government agencies, and government contractors are the major organizations where Token Ring is still present. Many organizations are in the process of moving away from Token Ring, but there are still a few that cannot remove it because of legacy applications and the inability to fund a transition to Ethernet.

Token Ring Architecture

In the middle to late 1970s, as local-area networks (LANs) were becoming popular, IBM felt the need to develop a LAN medium of its own. Ethernet would not have been a good fit with IBM's practices in those days. IBM was a very strict organization in the 1960s and 1970s. Its male employees were required to wear blue suits with white shirts, not off-white or light pink. Surely a company this strict could not endorse a medium that let a workstation transmit whenever it wanted, provided no other workstation was transmitting. I do not know the real story of why IBM developed Token Ring, but this theory has always helped me remember the Token Ring architecture.

Rather than placing stations on a wire or segment, Token Ring builds a ring of stations. Most of the time, a *multiaccess unit* (*MAU*), a Token Ring hub but with a fancier name, is used to create the ring. Figure 3-1 shows an organization whose workstations are all plugged into an MAU to create a Token Ring. The logical representation is a ring, but physically it looks like a star topology. Normal Category 5 cabling will work with Token Ring. The Cisco Catalyst Token Ring switching products all use RJ-45 connectors.

With Ethernet, a *nondeterministic* method of passing data was used.

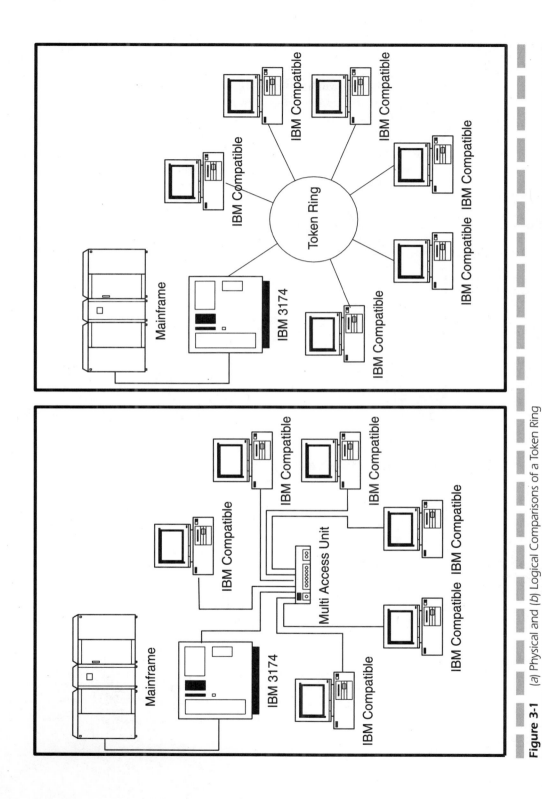

Figure 3-1 (a) Physical and (b) Logical Comparisons of a Token Ring

In other words, a workstation could transmit whenever it wanted as long as another workstation was not already using the wire. Token Ring uses a *deterministic* method. In Token Ring, a token is passed around the ring. When a workstation has the token, it may transmit a frame. The frame passes around to all workstations, which would include the destination (Figure 3-2). The destination station copies the frame and sets a bit in

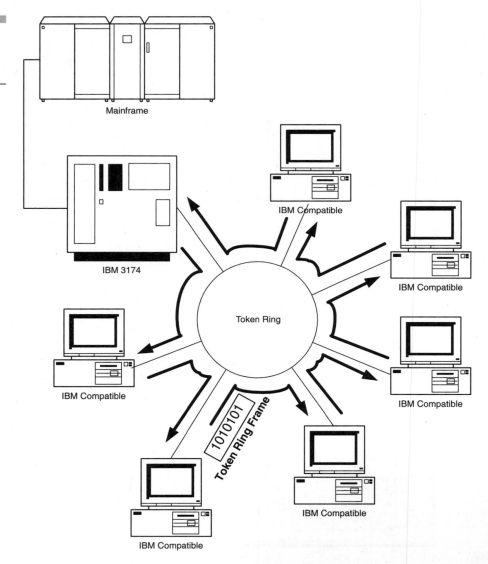

Figure 3-2

Physical and Logical Comparisons of a Token Ring

the Token Ring frame header to indicate that it has received the data. The frame then continues around the ring to the source workstation. This workstation knows that the frame has been read by the destination, so it regenerates the token and passes it to the next workstation in the ring. Token Ring is still a shared medium because stations have to wait for the token. But because of its deterministic nature, Token Ring uses its bandwidth much more efficiently. In Token Ring a workstation is always assured of its turn to transmit because of the token, whereas in Ethernet a workstation is never guaranteed of having access to the medium. However, the more workstations on a Token Ring, the longer a workstation will have to wait for the token to come around to it.

A special workstation, called the *active monitor*, handles maintenance of the ring. The active monitor ensures that the token is being passed around the ring. If the workstation with the token were to fail, the active monitor would regenerate the token and transmit it to the next workstation in the ring.

Token Ring has two speeds at which it can transmit data, 16 Mb/s and 4 Mb/s. The 4-Mb/s version is rarely used today and is not supported on many products. In addition, Token Ring's ability to run at different speeds can cause problems. Most Token Ring network interface cards (NICs) support both speeds, but before autosensing, they defaulted to 4 Mb/s. Workstations with Token Ring NICs that had not been configured would try to insert into a ring at 4 Mb/s. Unfortunately, the ring almost certainly would be 16 Mb/s. When this occurred, the entire ring would lose connectivity for a short period of time, causing workstations to lock and other various problems. Thus it is extremely important to verify the speed of a workstation before allowing it to insert itself into the ring.

Token Ring Segmentation

Like Ethernet, Token Ring is a shared medium. If too many workstations are placed on a ring, performance is reduced and timeouts at the transport layer may occur. The obvious solution is to create more rings. As with Ethernet, there are two types of ring segmentation, physical and logical. Physical segmentation will create more rings without affecting the Layer 3 protocols. Physical segmentation results in multiple tokens, which in turn allow for simultaneous conversations. Broadcasts still will be propagated onto all rings, leaving the IP, IPX, or Appletalk addressing undisturbed.

Figures 3-3 and 3-4 show a large Token Ring that is broken into three smaller rings with more tokens. This configuration allows for a greater aggregate throughput. In Figure 3-3, the total aggregate throughput would be 16 Mb/s, assuming a ring speed of 16 Mb/s. In Figure 3-4, the

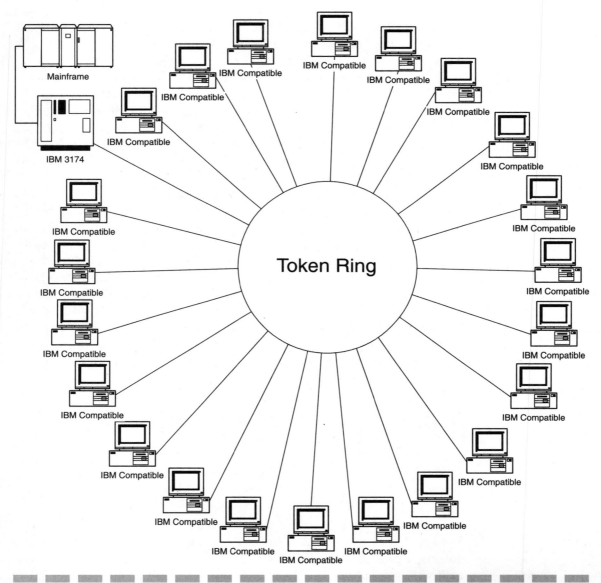

Figure 3-3 Single Ring

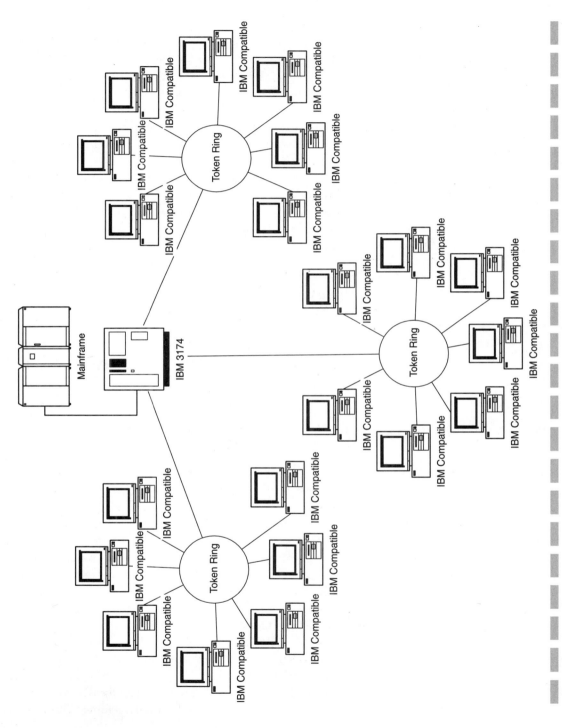

Figure 3-4 Three Physical Rings

single ring is broken into three separate rings, creating three tokens and allowing a total aggregate bandwidth of 48 Mb/s. The IBM 3174 is connected to all three rings for connectivity. All three rings are still a part of the same IP subnet, IPX network, and Appletalk cable-range. The broadcast domain is not affected by the physical segmentation.

Token Ring physical segmentation can be performed with a bridge, a switch, or a router with Token Ring interfaces. As discussed in Chapter 1, all three devices segment in the same way, only now it is Token Ring segmentation, whereas before we were discussing Ethernet segmentation. The main difference between Ethernet and Token Ring bridging is the fact that an Ethernet bridge uses transparent bridging and a Token Ring bridge uses source-route bridging most of the time. It is possible for a Token Ring bridge or switch to transparently bridge, but this will be discussed later.

Token Ring logical segmentation must be performed by a router, as with Ethernet. Setting up switched Token Ring to the desktop is a reality with Catalyst Token Ring switches, but this still does not solve the problems associated with broadcasts that were discussed in Chapter 1. Just as in Ethernet, too many nodes on a logical ring or flat network will create excess broadcast traffic and seriously degrade the throughput of a network.

Source-Route Bridging

Source-route bridging is the bridging method used by Token Ring bridges and switches most of the time. It is very similar to Layer 3 routing in that every physical ring receives a number to identify that ring, similar to a network number with Layer 3 protocols. Each bridge in the source-route environment receives a bridge number. Figure 3-5 shows six physical Token Rings interconnected with six source-route bridges. End nodes have been omitted to make the illustration easier to read. Each ring has been given a ring number, and each bridge has been given a bridge number.

Built into the Token Ring frame header is a field called the *routing information field* (*RIF*). The RIF contains the route a frame must take through the source-route bridged environment to reach its destination. The source workstation builds the RIF into every single data packet it transmits. The source workstation is the device that actually routes the frame through the source-route bridged environment—hence the name.

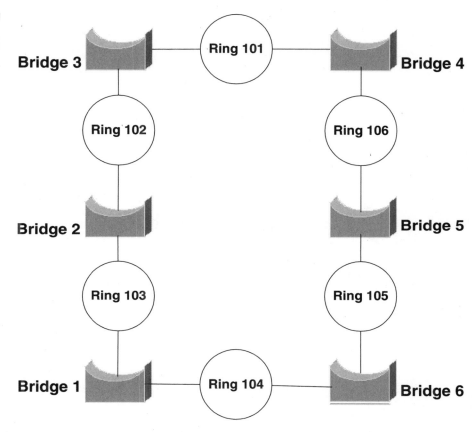

Figure 3-5
Source-Route Bridged
Environment

This requires end nodes to have software to enable them to build an RIF. A source-route bridge reads the RIF and determines whether or not to forward the frame to the adjoining ring. In this sense, a source-route bridge is not nearly as intelligent as a transparent bridge. A transparent bridge learns where all nodes reside relative to its ports, whereas a source-route bridge does as it is told and does not learn end-node addresses.

The RIF contains two parts. The *route control (RC) field* is the first part and consists of 16 bits. The second part of the RIF is a series of 16-bit fields called *route designators (RDs)*. The number of RDs will vary based on the number of bridges and rings the frame must traverse to reach its destination. The first 12 bits of the RD is a ring number, and the last 4 bits is a bridge number (Figure 3-6). The RDs are the actual fields that are read by the bridges so as to route the frame properly.

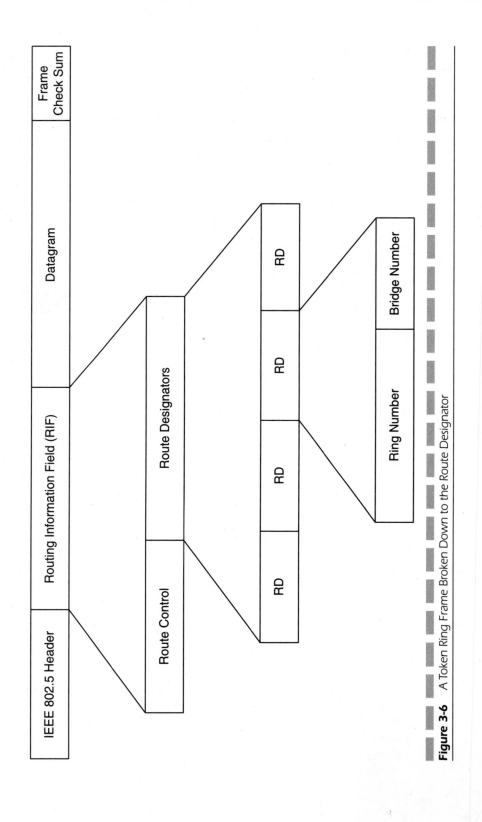

Figure 3-6 A Token Ring Frame Broken Down to the Route Designator

There can be a maximum of 14 RDs in an RIF, restricting the size of a source-route bridged environment to 13 bridge hops.

If a workstation wants to communicate with the server in the network in Figure 3-7, its RIF would have to contain an RD for every bridge hop plus one. The last RD would have the destination ring number and a bridge number of zero, indicating that the frame need not be forwarded further. Figure 3-7 uses decimals to represent the ring and bridge numbers; however, when a packet analysis tool is used, the fields are represented in hexadecimal.

Figure 3-7
Sample RIF

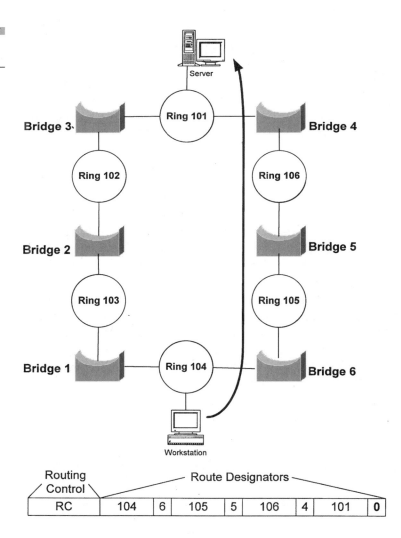

Routing Control	Route Designators						
RC	104	6	105	5	106	4	101	0

Route Discovery

In the preceding section the workstation built an RIF detailing the exact path that all frames would take through the bridged environment to reach the server. The obvious question that must be going through your mind is, How did the workstation know how to get to the server? In source-route bridging, the source must discover the route to the destination. To do this, a source node uses special packets called *explorer packets*. These packets go in search of the destination. There are several types of explorer packets, and the following paragraphs discuss two of them.

All-Routes Explorer Packets

The *all-routes explorer (ARE) packet* is a packet that will be forwarded by all bridges. This can create excess traffic when there are multiple paths. The explorer packets will have RDs added by each of the bridges as each packet is forwarded. In Figure 3-8, the workstation sends ARE packets to discover the path to the server. As the ARE packets are forwarded by the bridges, each bridge adds an RD recording the path the ARE is taking through the bridged environment. When the ARE packets reach the destination node, the destination node responds to each one it receives. The direction bit inside the RC field informs the bridges of which direction the frame is traveling. When the destination node responds to the ARE packet, it reverses the direction bit and swaps the source and destination addresses of the ARE packet. The workstation will cache the route from the first ARE reply it receives, and all others will be discarded.

As mentioned, the ARE packets will create excess traffic when there are multiple paths. When the packets reach the destination ring, they will continue to be forwarded until the maximum number of RDs is entered or the bridge realizes that it has already entered an RD. In Figure 3-9, the ARE packets will continue beyond ring 101 in both directions until both ARE packets cycle back to ring 104. In this case there are two ARE packets traveling across the network, the first moving counterclockwise around the bridges and the second moving clockwise. The first ARE packet travels in the following order: bridge 1, bridge 2, bridge 3, bridge 4, bridge 5, and bridge 6. The ring numbers have been omitted. When the first ARE packet comes full circle back to bridge 1, bridge 1 sees that it has already entered an RD and will not forward the packet further. The second ARE packet will travel in the reverse order, and will not be forwarded by bridge 6.

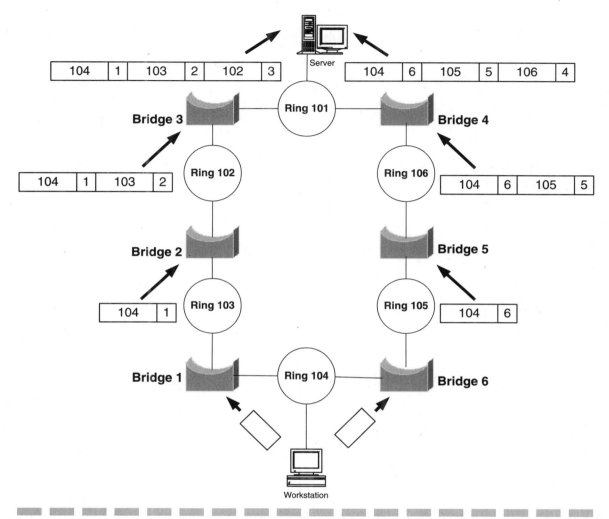

Figure 3-8   RDs Are Added as the Explorer Packets Are Forwarded

Spanning Tree Explorer Packets

An ARE packet can lead to multiple explorer packets reaching a destination, creating excess traffic. To eliminate multiple explorer packets, *spanning tree explorer* (*STE*) or *single-route explorer* (*SRE*) packets may be used. Source-route bridges run a spanning tree algorithm and will forward STE packets only out those ports designated "forwarding." This

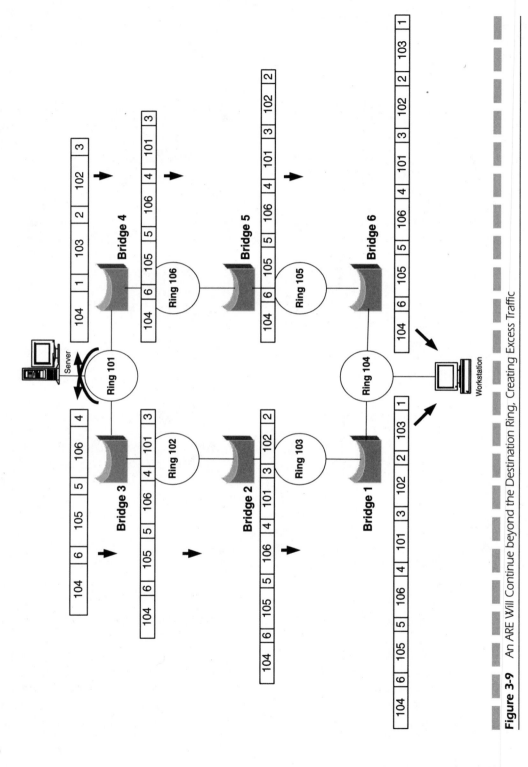

Figure 3-9 An ARE Will Continue beyond the Destination Ring, Creating Excess Traffic

ensures that the explorer packets will discover only a single route to the destination.

This also eliminates multiple responses to an explorer packet. In Figure 3-8, the server responded to each explorer packet it received. In that case there were two responses. If STE packets had been used, the server would have received only one explorer packet, and thus only one response would have been generated. It is important to remember that in a large network environment these responses could reach numbers in the thousands per second range. STE packets therefore can reduce the bandwidth consumed by explorer packets.

The spanning tree algorithm used by source-route bridges in most cases is the IBM version, not the standard IEEE or older DEC version. Cisco Catalyst switches use the IBM version only.

Source-Route Transparent Bridging

In some environments, end nodes may not have the necessary software to build an RIF. In such cases, a source-route bridge can be configured to do both forms of bridging, source-route and transparent. These bridges are commonly referred to as *source-route transparent (SRT) bridges*. An SRT bridge will look to a special bit in the Token Ring frame header called the *routing information indicator (RII)*. The RII is actually the first bit of the destination MAC address. The RII, when set, indicates that there is an RIF in the frame. Therefore, the frame will be source-route bridged. And conversely, when the RII is not set, the SRT bridge will transparently bridge the frame.

Source-Route Translational Bridging

When both Token Ring and Ethernet are implemented in the same environment, a router typically is used. However, when a router is used, the Ethernet and Token Ring stations are on different logical segments. If this is not desirable, a *source-route translational bridge (SRT/LB)* may be used. An SRT/LB is a very busy bridge. It must perform source-route bridging on the Token Ring ports and transparent bridging on the Ethernet ports. It also must have the ability translate the Ethernet frames into Token Ring frames, and vice versa, when its bridging functions deem it necessary. SRT/LB is not supported on a Catalyst switch without the use of an external router or route-switch module.

SUMMARY

Token Ring, although different and often difficult to work with, is still used with many legacy applications in today's marketplace. Token Ring is a deterministic medium developed by IBM. A small group of bits called a token is passed around a ring of nodes. The node with the token may transmit; when finished, it passes the token to the next node on the ring.

A source-route bridge does bridging in a Token Ring environment. It requires the end nodes to be configured with software that can discover the route to a destination and then build a routing information field (RIF) into the frame header. Source-route bridges read the RIF in a frame header to properly route the frame.

In environments where end nodes do not have source-route bridging software loaded, a source-route transparent (SRT) bridge may be used. In this case, an SRT will look to the routing information indicator (RII) to determine if there is an RIF present. If no RIF is present, the SRT bridge will transparently bridge the frame; if there is an RIF present, the SRT bridge will source-route bridge the frame.

In environments where both Ethernet and Token Ring are in use, a source-route translational bridge (SRT/LB) may be used to bridge between the different media. An SRT/LB has the ability to translate Ethernet frames into Token Ring frames and perform both source-route bridging and transparent bridging.

EXERCISES

1. List the primary differences between Token Ring and Ethernet.

2. Describe the advantages and disadvantages of using Token Ring. Describe the advantages and disadvantages of using Ethernet.

3. Why is Token Ring able to handle large a large volume of traffic, unlike Ethernet? Why is Ethernet unable to cope with high utilization of its bandwidth?

Figure 3-10
Questions 9–11.

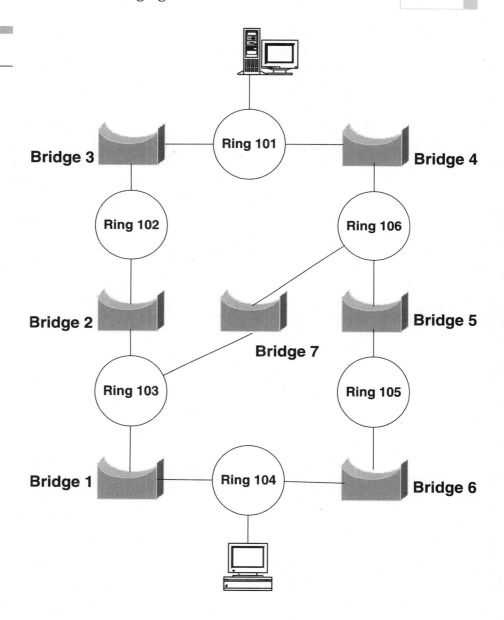

4. Why is it important to check the speed of a Token Ring NIC before being connected to an MAU?

5. When using source-route bridges to physically segment one's network, what is the effect on broadcasts and why? What would be the effect if a transparent bridge were used instead?

6. Which device must be used to logically segment a Token Ring network and why?

7. What are the similarities between a Layer 3 protocol and source-route bridging?

8. Why is source-route bridging called source-route bridging? Describe its operation.

9. In Figure 3-10, if the workstation were to use an all-routes explorer (ARE) packet, how many explorer packets would the server receive? What would the RIFs of those packets look like? How many explorer packets would the server respond to?

10. In Figure 3-10, how many explorer packets would be received by the server if STE packets were used? Why?

11. In Figure 3-10, which version of bridging is necessary for the workstation to communicate with the server? If the Token Ring segment did not need connectivity with the Ethernet segment and vice versa, what kind of bridge would be used?

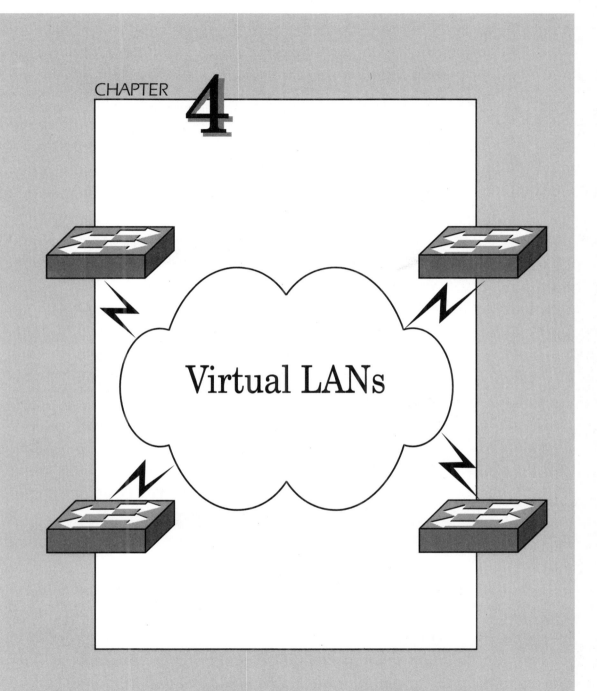

Virtual LANs

With a growing number of users on a network comes the challenges of management, so it is not surprising that virtual local-area networks (VLANs) have become a popular feature of switches. VLANs ease the administrative duties of the network engineer. A VLAN gives an administrator the ability to remove the physical restrictions of the past and control a user's Layer 3 network address regardless of his or her physical location.

Other advantages of VLANs include enhanced security features, easier-to-control broadcasts, and the ability to distribute traffic. Cisco Catalyst switches have the ability to perform numerous functions to enhance and ease the implementation of VLANs.

The use of *trunking* allows a VLAN to span multiple switches that can be separated by small or large areas. Cisco also has implemented the trunking feature in many of its routing products, resulting in many helpful and interesting network designs.

VLAN Defined

A VLAN can be defined in two words—*broadcast domain*. VLANs are broadcast domains, and as we learned in Chapter 1, a broadcast domain is a Layer 3 network. A switch defines a VLAN, and the switch's ports will have membership in one of the defined VLANs. For example, in Figure 4-1, a switch has ports defined in two VLANs, Accounting and Management.

Figure 4-1
Two VLANs on
a Catalyst 1900

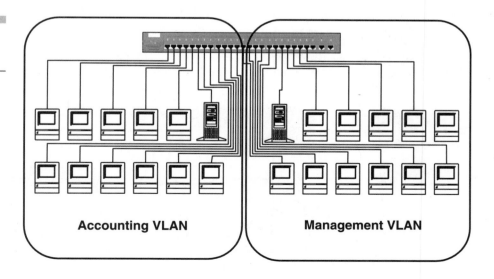

Accounting VLAN   **Management VLAN**

Ports 1 through 12 have been assigned to the Accounting VLAN, and ports 13 through 24 have been assigned to the Management VLAN. The switch will not allow broadcasts to flow between VLANs, thus logically segmenting the network (Figure 4-2).

If workstation A were to send a broadcast, all stations on the Accounting VLAN would receive it. However, the switch would not forward the broadcast to any of the Management VLAN ports. In fact, a switch would not forward a frame from one VLAN to another unless it was a multilayer switch, which will be discussed later. Some of you may still be thinking about Chapter 1 when I said, "A router is the only device that can logically segment." Technically, this is incorrect. A switch *can* logically segment, but in the real world it is ludicrous to use a switch without a router as a device to logically segment because traffic will never be allowed to pass between VLANs. This is a very unlikely scenario and is pointless to discuss.

The workstations in the Accounting VLAN will be in a completely different broadcast domain from the Management VLAN's users and therefore will be in an entirely different IP subnet, IPX network, and Appletalk cable-range. In Figure 4-3, the Accounting VLAN is assigned the IP subnet 172.16.10.0/24, the IPX Network 10, and the Appletalk cable-range 10-10. The Management VLAN is assigned the IP subnet 172.16.20.0/24, the IPX network 20, and the Appletalk cable-range 20-20. Traffic from one VLAN will have no effect on the other, regardless of their physical locations on the floor.

Figure 4-2
Broadcasts Are Kept within All Ports in the VLAN

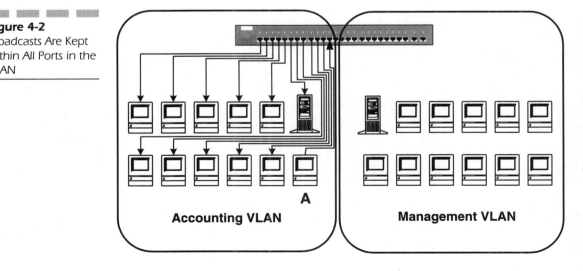

Accounting VLAN   **Management VLAN**

A

Figure 4-3
IP Subnets, IPX
Network, and
Appletalk Cable-Range
Assignments for
Each VLAN

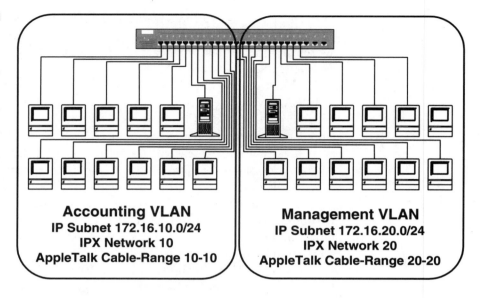

Accounting VLAN
IP Subnet 172.16.10.0/24
IPX Network 10
AppleTalk Cable-Range 10-10

Management VLAN
IP Subnet 172.16.20.0/24
IPX Network 20
AppleTalk Cable-Range 20-20

Cisco's implementation of VLANs is port-centric. The port to which a node is connected will define the VLAN in which it resides. How a port gets assigned to a VLAN can vary with Cisco Catalyst switches. There are two methods of assigning ports to VLANs, static and dynamic.

Static VLANs

The *static* VLAN procedure is to administratively assign a port to a VLAN. An engineer determines which ports he or she would like on a particular VLAN and statically maps that VLAN to a port. For example, in Figure 4-1, the Accounting VLAN is defined to be any node connected to ports 1 through 12. An engineer would enter the appropriate commands, either from the command line interface (CLI) of the switch, an SNMP management station, or Cisco's software management tool CiscoWorks for Switched Internetworks (CWSI) to assign ports 1 through 12 to the Accounting VLAN. This method can be very time-consuming because the engineer has to manually enter the commands necessary to map the ports to their appropriate VLANs. However, it is the most common method of assigning a port to a VLAN.

Dynamic VLANs

A *dynamic* VLAN exists when a port decides what VLAN it belongs in for itself. No, this is not The Terminator or The Forbin Project becoming nonfiction; rather, it is a simple mapping that occurs based on a database created by an engineer. When a port that is assigned to be a dynamic VLAN port becomes active, the switch caches the source MAC address of the first frame (Figure 4-4).

It then makes a request to an external server called a *VLAN management policy server* (*VMPS*) that contains a text file with MAC addresses to VLAN mappings. The switch will download this file and examine it for the source MAC address it has cached for the port in question. If the MAC address is found in the table, the port will be assigned to the listed VLAN. If the MAC address is not in the table, the switch will use the default VLAN, if defined. In the event that the MAC address is not listed in the table and there is no default VLAN, the port will not become active. This can be a very good method of security.

Dynamic VLANs on the surface appear to be very advantageous, but building of the database can be a very painstaking and tortuous task. If a network has thousands of workstations, there will be a lot of typing. Assuming that one could survive the process, there are still other issues with dynamic VLANs. Keeping the database current can become an ongoing time-consuming process. Dynamic VLANs will be discussed further in Chapter 6.

Trunking

An individual switch defines VLANs. How can one extend VLANs beyond a single switch? For example, Figure 4-5 shows nodes on the first and second floors that are part of the Accounting Department and the Management Department. This organization would like its Layer 3 addressing scheme to mirror its organization, not its physical configuration. How can the nodes on both floors participate in the same VLAN?

The physical connection between the two switches could be assigned to the Accounting VLAN, but this would limit traffic between the floors to the Accounting VLAN. A second connection could be made between the switches and placed in the Management VLAN, but this could be costly, especially when there are more than two VLANs. Trunking will

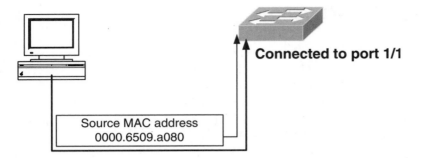

Connected to port 1/1

Source MAC address
0000.6509.a080

The source MAC address of the first frame is cached

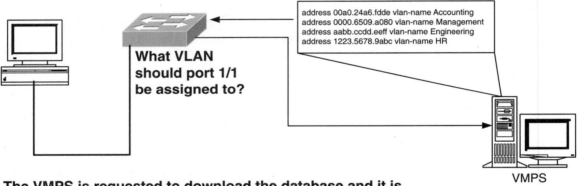

**What VLAN
should port 1/1
be assigned to?**

address 00a0.24a6.fdde vlan-name Accounting
address 0000.6509.a080 vlan-name Management
address aabb.ccdd.eeff vlan-name Engineering
address 1223.5678.9abc vlan-name HR

VMPS

**The VMPS is requested to download the database and it is
examined for the source MAC address**

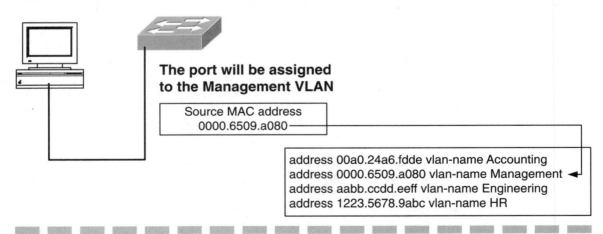

**The port will be assigned
to the Management VLAN**

Source MAC address
0000.6509.a080

address 00a0.24a6.fdde vlan-name Accounting
address 0000.6509.a080 vlan-name Management
address aabb.ccdd.eeff vlan-name Engineering
address 1223.5678.9abc vlan-name HR

Figure 4-4 The Source MAC Address Is Mapped to the Management VLAN

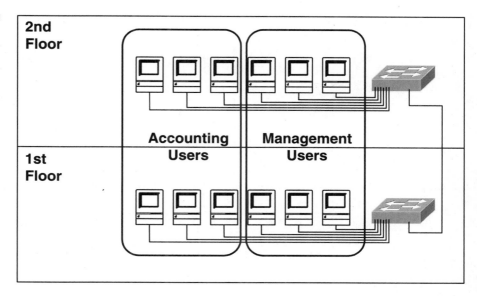

Figure 4-5
Accounting and Management Users

allow multiple VLAN traffic to flow across a single physical connection. If the connection between the two switches in Figure 4-5 were made a trunk connection, both VLANs could communicate across the same physical link. This is accomplished by using a *tag*. Each frame that is transmitted across a trunk line is tagged with the VLAN ID. A Catalyst switch will identify each VLAN with a unique number. If the Accounting VLAN were assigned the VLAN number 100, then all frames that traverse the trunk line for the Accounting VLAN would be tagged with the VLAN number 100 (Figure 4-6).

When the second-floor switch receives the frame over the trunk, it reads the tag and learns that the frame is destined for the Accounting VLAN. In addition, broadcasts will be propagated across trunk lines. This is very important because a VLAN is a broadcast domain. With broadcasts being propagated across the trunk in the appropriate VLAN, the broadcast domain can be extended across multiple switches. The switches keep broadcasts in the appropriate VLANs by reading the tag on the frames that come across the trunks.

Figure 4-7 shows a network made up of six floors with users in the Accounting Department dispersed on all six floors. With trunking, all the accounting users can be placed in the same broadcast domain or VLAN.

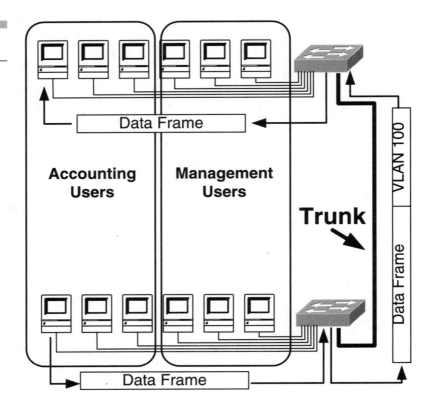

Figure 4-6
Trunk Tagging

All accounting nodes will be connected to a port in VLAN 100, regardless of the floor on which they reside. This will allow all the accounting users to be in the same IP subnet, IPX network, and Appletalk cable-range. It also should be noted that in Figure 4-7, through the use of VLANs, the servers have all been strategically located together yet can remain in the broadcast domains of their respective users.

All VLAN traffic will travel across the trunk if necessary, ensuring that other VLANs will have connectivity across the entire network, as in Figure 4-8.

The workstations in this organization have been assigned their logical addresses according to the departments within the organization, regardless of their physical locations. Before trunking was an option, engineers were unable to easily separate the logical addressing scheme from an organization's physical configuration.

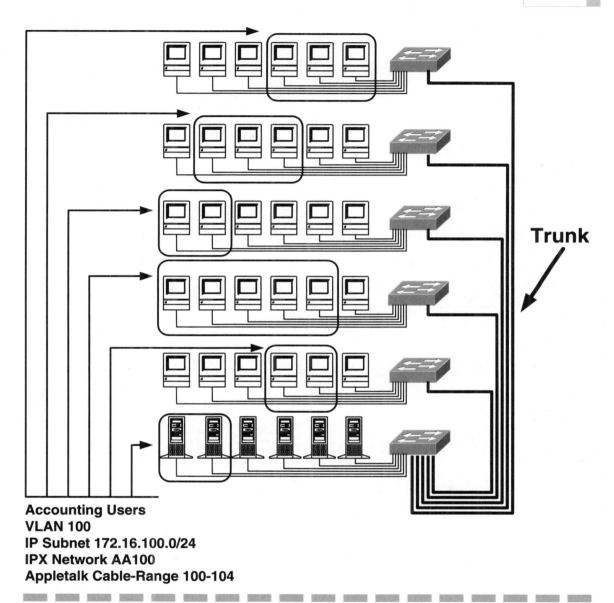

Accounting Users
VLAN 100
IP Subnet 172.16.100.0/24
IPX Network AA100
Appletalk Cable-Range 100-104

Figure 4-7 The Accounting VLAN

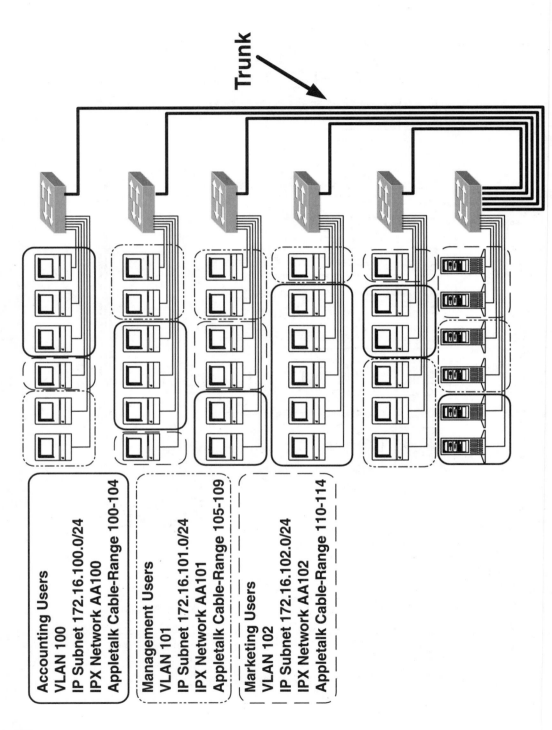

Accounting Users
VLAN 100
IP Subnet 172.16.100.0/24
IPX Network AA100
Appletalk Cable-Range 100-104

Management Users
VLAN 101
IP Subnet 172.16.101.0/24
IPX Network AA101
Appletalk Cable-Range 105-109

Marketing Users
VLAN 102
IP Subnet 172.16.102.0/24
IPX Network AA102
Appletalk Cable-Range 110-114

Trunk

Figure 4-8 The Three VLANs' Layer 3 Addressing Scheme

Trunking over Fast Ethernet and Gigabit Ethernet

A trunk line can be almost any medium supported by a Catalyst switch. Trunking with Fast Ethernet and Gigabit Ethernet can use one of two types of tags:

1. Inter-Switch Link
2. IEEE 802.1Q

The Inter-Switch Link (ISL) tag is a Cisco proprietary tag used over most Fast Ethernet trunks. The IEEE 802.1Q tag is a standard tag that is supported by some of the Cisco Catalyst switch line cards but not all. Trunking is performed by application-specific integrated circuits (ASICs) on the line module, so the line module must contain the necessary ASICs. Trunking is hardware-based; upgrading Catalyst software will not enable it. The IEEE 802.1Q tag is used when not all the switches are Cisco Catalyst switches.

Inter-Switch Link (ISL)

The ISL tag is used on Fast Ethernet and Gigabit Ethernet trunk lines when an environment consists of primarily Cisco Catalyst switches. Figure 4-9 breaks down the fields of the ISL tag.

The most important field in this header is the VLAN field. It is this field that identifies the VLAN to which the encapsulated frame belongs. It is important to remember that non-Cisco devices will not be able to read the ISL tag.

IEEE 802.1Q

The Institute of Electrical and Electronics Engineers (IEEE), as of late 1998, is still working on the final draft the IEEE 802.1Q standard. However, the tag format has been completed. Unlike ISL, 802.1Q has different formats based on the medium that is used. ISL is for Fast Ethernet and Gigabit Ethernet only, whereas 802.1Q can be used on all the different media, including FDDI and Token Ring.

The Ethernet form of the tag is described in Figure 4-10.

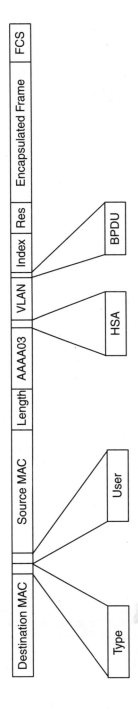

| Destination MAC | | Source MAC | Length | AAAA03 | VLAN | Index | Res | Encapsulated Frame | FCS |

Type   User   HSA   BPDU

Field	Description	# of bits
Destination Address	A multicast address that is destined for trunk ports.	40
Type	Identifies the encapsulated frame [Ethernet-0000, Token Ring-0001, FDDI-0010, ATM-0011].	4
User	A possible addition to the Type field. In Ethernet it can be used to define priorities.	4
Source Address	The Source MAC address of the transmitting switch.	48
Length	Identifies the length of the frame excluding the Destination Address, Type, User, Source Address, Length, and FCS fields.	16
AAAA03	This is the standard IEEE 802.2 Logical Link Control header.	24
HSA	Identifies the Vendor code or OUI of the source station.	24
VLAN	A 15-bit field used to identify the VLAN of the encapsulated frame; currently only the lower 10 bits are used. This will provide for a maximum of 1024 possible VLAN numbers.	15
BPDU	Identifies whether or not the encapsulated frame is a BPDU; if set, could also identify that encapsulated frame as a Cisco Discovery Packet.	1
Index	Used for diagnostic purposes.	16
Reserved	Used for additional information.	16
Total Bits		208 bits or 26 bytes

Figure 4-9   The Inter-Link Switch Tag

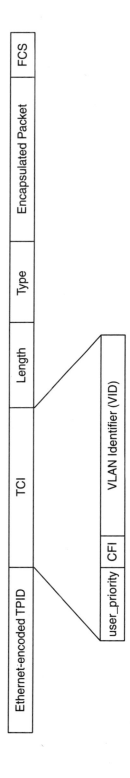

Field	Description	# of Bits
The Ethernet-encoded Tag Protocol Identifier (TPID)	Used to identify this frame as a tagged frame. Currently there is one possible value for this field, 0x8100.	16
The Tag Control Information (TCI)	The name given the three fields listed below.	16
user_priority	Identifies the priority of the encapsulated frame according to ISO/IEC 15802-3. The possible values range from 0-7.	3
The Canonical Format Identifier (CFI)	Identifies whether or not the frame is in a canonical format.	1
The VLAN Identifier (VID)	Uniquely identifies the VLAN where the encapsulated frame belongs. This field will provide for a maximum of 4094 VLANs.	12
Frame Check Sequence	There will be a recomputation of the FCS every time a frame is untagged.	

Figure 4-10 The IEEE 802.1Q Ethernet-Encoded Tag Header

The IEEE 802.1Q tag header will vary on the basis of the medium that is in use. According to the draft IEEE 802.1Q standard, the tag is actually inserted after the source and destination MAC addresses. The tag is smaller than Cisco's ISL and thus will have slightly lower overhead. Cisco commonly refers to this method of trunk encapsulation as "dot1q." The IEEE 802.1Q tag format requires Catalyst IOS 4.1.

Trunking and FDDI

With trunking over FDDI, Cisco uses a different form of the tag. Here Cisco uses the IEEE 802.10 LAN/MAN Standard for Interoperable LAN/MAN Security (SILS) frame header as the tag when sending frames across an FDDI ring configured as a trunk. The 802.10 standard was developed for security in late 1992 but was rarely used. Cisco uses the *security association identifier* (*SAID*) field of the 802.10 header as its VLAN identifier (Figure 4-11).

The 802.10 standard called for a clear header and a protected header. The *protected header* is an encrypted portion of the header. The source MAC address is placed in both the protected header and the clear header. The destination node can then check the protected header MAC address against the clear header MAC address. If they are different, the frame is discarded under the assumption the data has been tampered with. When Cisco implements 802.10, only the LSAP and SAID fields are necessary, minimizing overhead.

ATM and Trunking

Trunking can be accomplished across ATM using a standard ATM procedure called *LAN emulation* (*LANE*). This is different from the tagging methods discussed for Fast Ethernet and FDDI. LANE is much lengthier to understand and implement and will be discussed in Chapter 10.

VLANs and the Spanning Tree Protocol

When implementing a large network with multiple VLANs, the randomness of the Spanning Tree Protocol (STP) may create undesirable topolo-

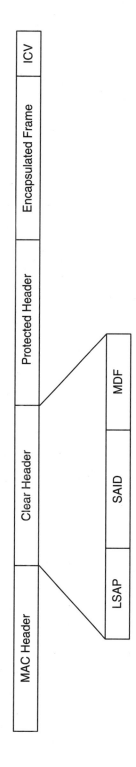

MAC Header	Clear Header	Protected Header	Encapsulated Frame	ICV

LSAP	SAID	MDF

Field	Description	# of Bits
LSAP	The standard 802.2 LLC Service Access Point, indicating an 802.10 VLAN frame.	24
Security Association Identifier (SAID)	Uniquely identifies the VLAN of the encapsulated frame.	32
Management-Defined Field	This field contains management-defined information.	
Integrity Check Value	A security algorithm is used to verify the integrity of the frame, similar to a Frame Check Sequence.	

Figure 4-11 *Cisco's Use of the IEEE 802.10 Header for FDDI Trunking*

Figure 4-12
Undesirable Span-
ning Tree
Configuration

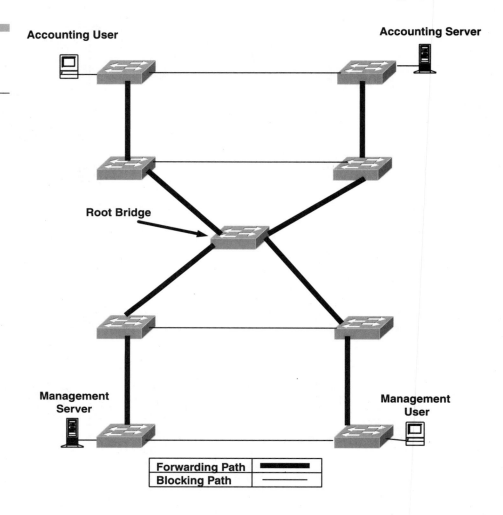

gies. Figure 4-12 shows two VLANs spread over a network. The spanning tree path, indicated by the bold line, creates an undesirable environment.

The accounting user must go through the root bridge to reach the
accounting server, and the same will apply to the management user.
One solution would be to make the accounting server's switch the root
bridge. This would ensure a more direct path for accounting users (Figure 4-13).

However, management users will still have an indirect path. Cisco
implements a version of the STP per VLAN, which allows for different

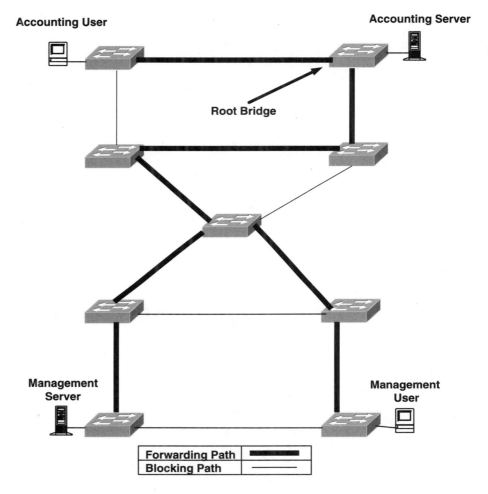

Figure 4-13
Accounting Users
with a Direct Path,
and Management
Users with an Indirect
Path

forwarding paths based on the VLAN. With a separate instance of the STP per VLAN, the accounting VLAN can have as its root bridge the accounting server's switch, whereas the management VLAN can have the management server's switch as its root bridge. Figure 4-14 shows the forwarding path with the management server's switch as the root bridge.

The VLAN to which traffic belongs will determine which forwarding path the traffic follows. Accounting VLAN traffic follows the forwarding path in Figure 4-13, whereas Management VLAN traffic follows the path in Figure 4-14. It is important to note that both forwarding paths act simultaneously, as in Figure 4-15.

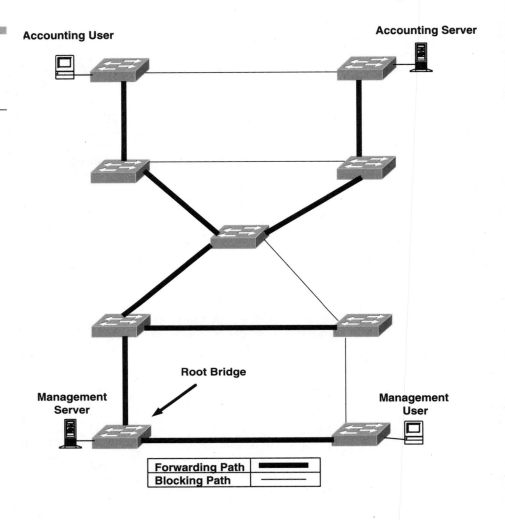

Figure 4-14
The Management
Server's Switch Is the
Root Bridge for the
Management VLAN

Traffic in the Management VLAN may take a different path from traffic in the Accounting VLAN.

Routers and VLANs

Earlier I mentioned that inter-VLAN communication would not be possible without a router. A router is the gateway between broadcast domains or VLANs. An interface for each VLAN may be connected to the switch, as shown in Figure 4-16.

Figure 4-15
Accounting and
VLAN Forwarding
Paths

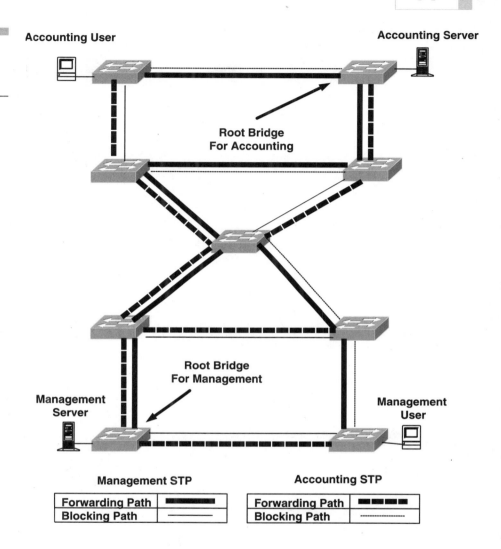

Accounting User

Accounting Server

Root Bridge
For Accounting

Root Bridge
For Management

Management
Server

Management
User

Management STP	
Forwarding Path	▬▬▬▬
Blocking Path	——

Accounting STP	
Forwarding Path	▬ ▬ ▬ ▬
Blocking Path	---------

In this case, the workstations will send any internetwork traffic through the router. The router's interfaces are completely unaware that they are connected to the same switch. They simply see two broadcast domains or IP subnets, IPX networks, and Appletalk cable-ranges. The configuration of the router shown in Figure 4-17 will be exactly the same as the configuration for the router in Figure 4-16.

The router only sees the logical environment.

▬▬ ▬▬ ▬▬ ▬▬
Figure 4-16
A Separate Interface
per VLAN

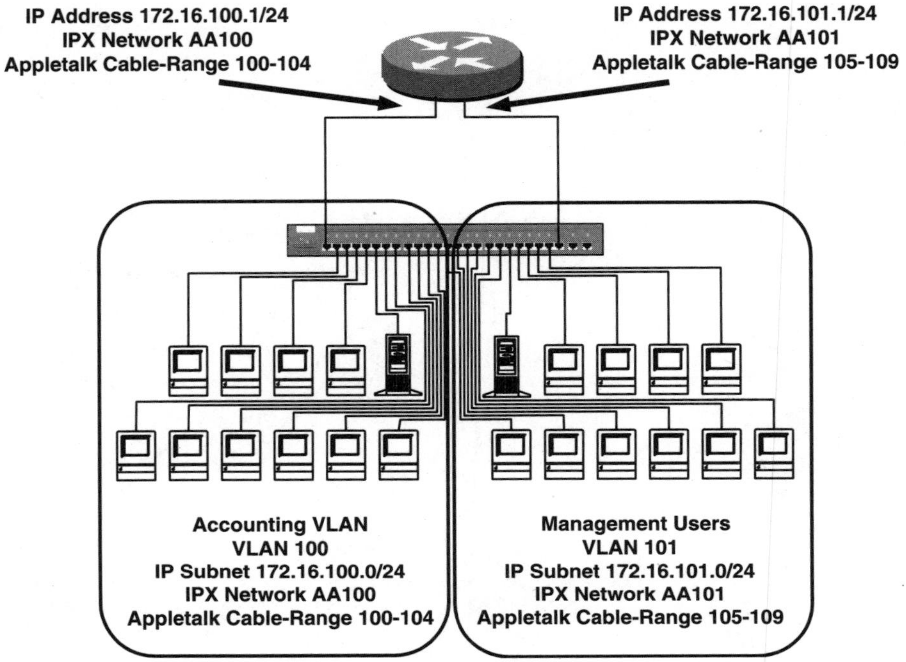

IP Address 172.16.100.1/24
IPX Network AA100
Appletalk Cable-Range 100-104

IP Address 172.16.101.1/24
IPX Network AA101
Appletalk Cable-Range 105-109

Accounting VLAN
VLAN 100
IP Subnet 172.16.100.0/24
IPX Network AA100
Appletalk Cable-Range 100-104

Management Users
VLAN 101
IP Subnet 172.16.101.0/24
IPX Network AA101
Appletalk Cable-Range 105-109

▬▬ ▬▬ ▬▬ ▬▬
Figure 4-17
Logical Configuration
of Figure 4-16

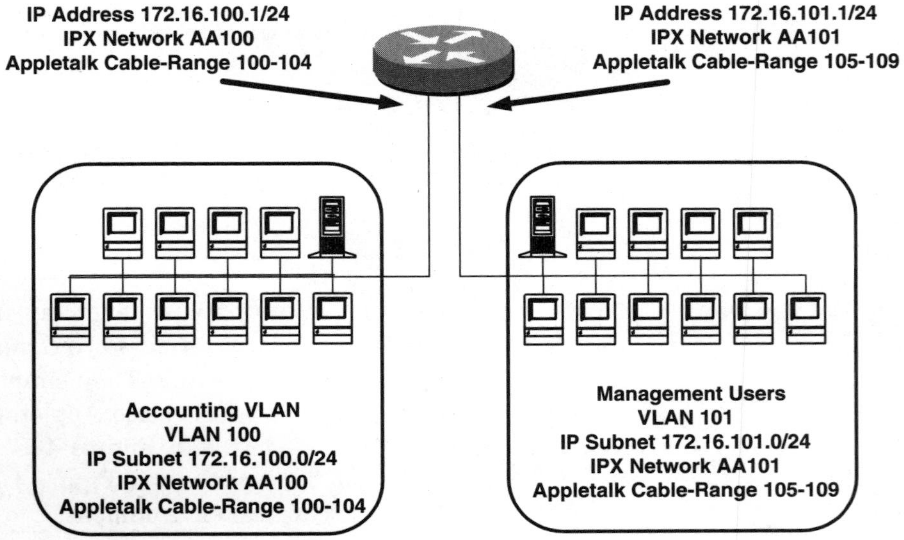

IP Address 172.16.100.1/24
IPX Network AA100
Appletalk Cable-Range 100-104

IP Address 172.16.101.1/24
IPX Network AA101
Appletalk Cable-Range 105-109

Accounting VLAN
VLAN 100
IP Subnet 172.16.100.0/24
IPX Network AA100
Appletalk Cable-Range 100-104

Management Users
VLAN 101
IP Subnet 172.16.101.0/24
IPX Network AA101
Appletalk Cable-Range 105-109

Trunking to Routers (Router on a Stick)

In Figure 4-16, a router interface was required for every VLAN it needed to route. If there were 100 VLANs, the router would need 100 interfaces. Obviously, this is a little expensive. A Cisco router can be configured to trunk so that it may route for multiple VLANs with one interface. The medium that is in use will determine vendor compatibility. Cisco routers are the only routers that support ISL. Cisco Routers also support IEEE 802.1Q, the IEEE 802.10 FDDI trunking method, and ATM LANE.

Figure 4-18 shows a router configured to trunk so that it can route for the Accounting and Management VLANs on the same interface.

This configuration is commonly referred to as "router on a stick" and sometimes is affectionately known as "one-armed routing." The advantage of this type of a configuration is the ability to use a single interface to route for multiple VLANs. The disadvantage is the possibility that the interface may not support enough bandwidth to handle the inter-

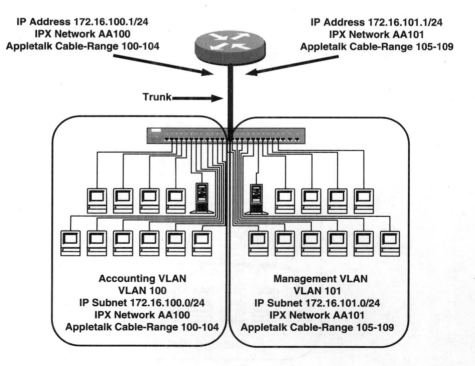

Figure 4-18
Trunking to a Router

IP Address 172.16.100.1/24
IPX Network AA100
Appletalk Cable-Range 100-104

IP Address 172.16.101.1/24
IPX Network AA101
Appletalk Cable-Range 105-109

Trunk

Accounting VLAN
VLAN 100
IP Subnet 172.16.100.0/24
IPX Network AA100
Appletalk Cable-Range 100-104

Management VLAN
VLAN 101
IP Subnet 172.16.101.0/24
IPX Network AA101
Appletalk Cable-Range 105-109

VLAN traffic sufficiently. The router will be configured using Ethernet subinterfaces, which will be discussed in detail in Chapter 8.

Trunking to Servers

Ideally, servers with global services such as e-mail need to be members of every VLAN to which they provide services. If a global server is in a single VLAN, all other VLANs must have their traffic routed to the VLAN where the global server resides. This situation will create latency.

In Figure 4-19, if the mail server resides on the Management VLAN, accounting users would always have to go across the trunk line to the router, which would then route the traffic back out the trunk line with a Management VLAN tag. This creates more work for the router and adds traffic to a trunk line that very well may be oversubscribed to begin with.

Cisco has licensed its Inter-Switch Link (ISL) technology to network interface card (NIC) vendors such as Intel and Sun to manufacture

Figure 4-19
Path Traffic Will Take to the Mail Server from the Management VLAN

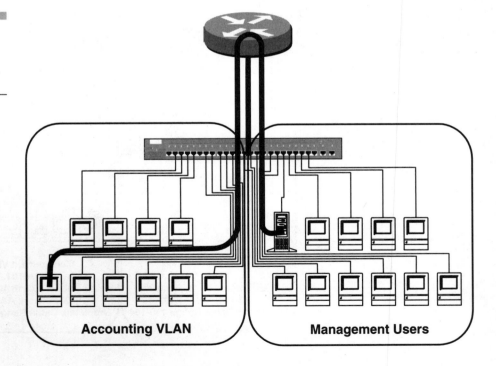

Accounting VLAN   **Management Users**

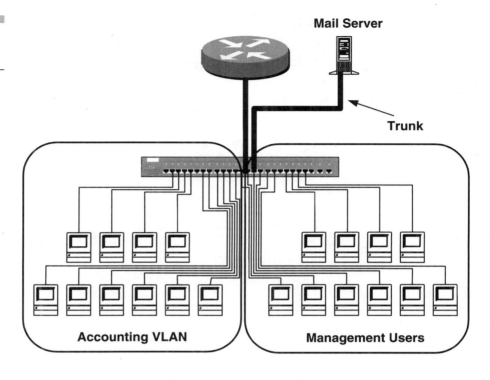

Figure 4-20
Mail Server
Configured to Trunk

NICs that support ISL. This will give servers the ability to read the tags on frames, allowing the servers to connect to more than one VLAN on a single connection. In Figure 4-20, an ISL-capable NIC is installed in the server, and trunking is enabled on the switch port. The server may now directly communicate with both accounting and management users.

The drivers for an ISL-capable NIC will allow for the creation of a Layer 3 address for each VLAN to which it connects. If a server were to be connected to 100 VLANs, it would need to have 100 Layer 3 addresses. It is important to plan accordingly when using ISL-capable adapters.

SUMMARY

A VLAN is a broadcast domain defined by ports on a switch. The switch controls broadcasts but will not allow traffic to pass between broadcast domains. To pass traffic between VLANs, a router must be employed. A Cisco Catalyst switch uses a port-centric method of defining VLANs; i.e., the port will define the VLAN. A port will be assigned to a VLAN by one of two methods:

(1) statically (i.e., a port is assigned administratively to a VLAN) or

(2) dynamically (i.e., a port automatically assigns itself to VLAN based on the source MAC address).

The ability to pass multiple VLAN traffic across a connection is called trunking. Trunking is supported over all the major media supported on a Catalyst switch. Trunking is accomplished by tagging frames going out a trunk port with a VLAN ID. The format of the tag will depend on the medium that is in use:

Medium	Tagging Format
Fast Ethernet	ISL or IEEE 802.1Q
Gigabit Ethernet	ISL or IEEE 802.1Q
FDDI	IEEE 802.10
ATM	LAN emulation (LANE)

Cisco implements a version of the Spanning Tree Protocol per VLAN to allow for multiple bridged topologies based on VLAN.

Trunk connections can be established to Cisco routers and ISL-capable servers.

EXERCISES

1. A VLAN is a broadcast domain and is defined by a switch. However, if a switch can create more broadcast domains, i.e., logically segment, why is a router necessary?

2. Describe the advantages of using VLANs?

3. Describe Cisco's implementation of VLANs. What is meant by the term *port-centric*? What is the difference between a static VLAN and a dynamic VLAN?

4. What is a trunk port, and how does it work?

5. List the media over which trunking is supported and the tagging format required for each. (*Hint:* Read the Summary.)

6. Why would an organization choose to use IEEE 802.1Q over Cisco's Inter-Switch Link?

7. What are the advantages of Cisco's unique implementation of the Spanning Tree Protocol (STP)?

8. What is meant by the term "router on a stick"?

9. What are the advantages of using an ISL-capable NIC?

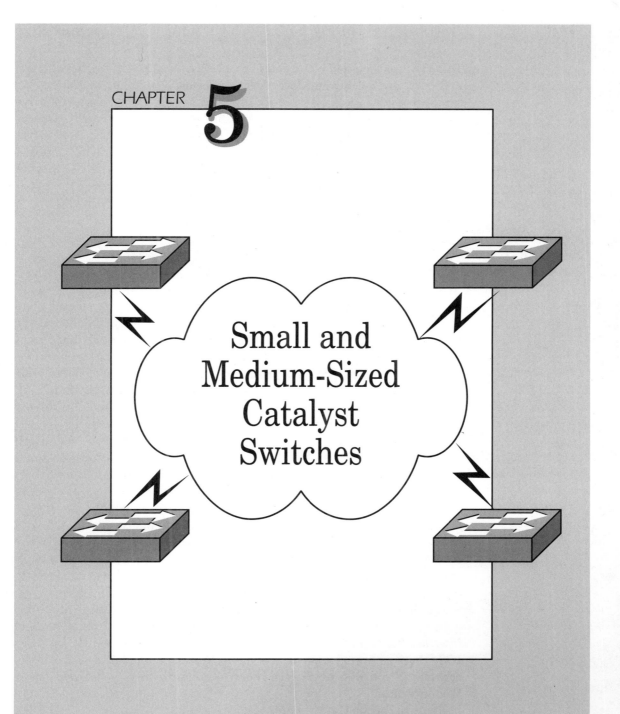

Small and
Medium-Sized
Catalyst
Switches

This chapter focuses on the smaller Catalyst switches, those with model numbers lower than the Catalyst 5000 series. The Catalyst 1900 is the smallest of the Catalyst product line and is one of the least expensive switches in terms of price per port. The Catalyst 2820 is slightly larger and offers more high-speed bandwidth options. The Catalyst 3000 series is a product line spawned from the Kalpana purchase. The Catalyst 4000 series is new to the Catalyst product line and offers small switches with very high port density and Gigabit Ethernet interfaces.

Catalyst 1900

The Catalyst 1900 is the smallest of the Ethernet-capable switches, and currently, there are three models with different versions of software depending on the features. Basically, the Catalyst 1900 incorporates two versions of software—regular and enterprise. The regular version of the operating system for the Catalyst 1900 provides all the basic features of a small switch, such as virtual local-area networks (VLANs) and cut-through switching. The enterprise version of the operating system adds such advanced features as Fast EtherChannel and Inter-Switch Link (ISL) trunking on its Fast Ethernet ports. Enterprise model numbers have an "EN" at the end.

There are three different physical versions of the Catalyst 1900. Each of the versions has a switched AUI (attachment user interface) port and two Fast Ethernet ports. The Catalyst 1912 has twelve 10-Mb/s Ethernet ports, and the Catalyst 1924 has twenty-four 10-Mb/s ports. The Catalyst 1924C has twenty-four 10-Mb/s ports like the 1924 but uses a fiber SC connector on one of the two Fast Ethernet ports. These switches are ideal for small wiring closets and, with the enterprise version of the software, will allow trunking and Fast EtherChannel back to the main wiring closet. The Catalyst 1924C will allow the small wiring closet to be up to 2 km away (Figure 5-1*a* and *b*).

Configuring a Catalyst 1900 switch is very easy. If you are familiar with the Cisco IOS, the Catalyst 1900 series now has a *command line interface (CLI)* that is very similar. If you are not familiar with the Cisco IOS, there is a very easy-to-use menu system that is accessed via the console. If you like neither of those options, there is a browser-based Web interface.

Features of the Catalyst 1900 series include

Standard software upgradable to the enterprise edition

Figure 5-1
Catalyst 1924: (*a*)
front view; (*b*) rear
view

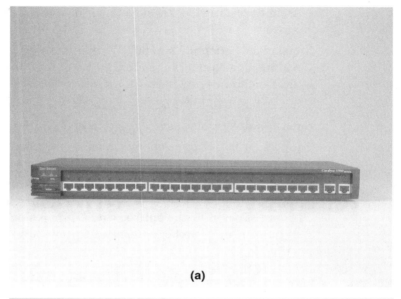

(a)

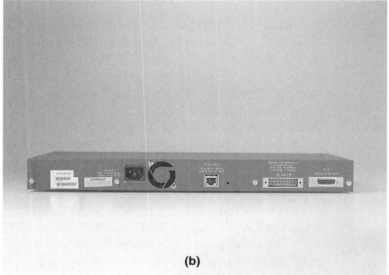

(b)

Full-duplex operation on all Ethernet and Fast Ethernet ports
Congestion-control features, including IEEE 802.3x-based flow control
Web-based network management
Per-port broadcast storm control, preventing faulty end stations

from degrading overall system performance with broadcast storms

Support for optional Cisco 600-W redundant ac power system, providing a backup power source for up to four units for improved fault tolerance and network uptime

Support for 1024 MAC addresses in its bridge table

Simple Network Management Protocol (SNMP) and Telnet support

Support for four groups of embedded remote monitoring (RMON) (history, statistics, alarms, and events)

Support for all nine RMON groups through use of a switch-probe analyzer port that permits traffic monitoring of a single port, a group of ports, or the entire switch from a single network analyzer or RMON probe (enterprise edition only)

Catalyst 2820

The Catalyst 2820 has the same architecture as the Catalyst 1900 except that it is twice the height with two modular bays for high-speed uplink options. The Catalyst 2820 base unit has twenty-four 10-Mb/s RJ-45 ports and one 10-Mb/s AUI port. The two modular bays support a number of modules of varying media types. It is ideal for small wiring closets that require a high-bandwidth connection back to a main wiring closet. For example, a small building, with only 20 users, in a campus needs connectivity to an FDDI or ATM backbone. A router with an FDDI or ATM interface is much too expensive. A Catalyst 5000 would be overkill for such a small office. Thus the Catalyst 2820 allows connectivity to an FDDI or ATM backbone without being too expensive.

Currently, there are two models of the Catalyst 2820 switch. The Catalyst 2822 and Catalyst 2828 are identical in architecture and features with one exception. The Catalyst 2822 can have a maximum of 2048 MAC addresses in its bridge table, whereas the Catalyst 2828 can have a maximum of 8192 MAC addresses in its bridge table. At the time of this writing, Cisco had issued an end-of-life notice on the Catalyst 2822.

The key difference between the Catalyst 2820 and the Catalyst 1900 is the uplink bays. These bays accept FDDI, CDDI, and ATM ports. They also accept 100-Mb/s modules as well. The Fast Ethernet modules for the Catalyst 2820 can be purchased with fiber or copper ports. There is a one-port (switched) fiber Fast Ethernet module and a one-port (switched) copper Fast Ethernet module. There is also a four-port (shared) fiber Fast Ethernet module and an eight-port (shared) Fast Ethernet module. The shared modules are hubs on a module; they are not multiple physical segments. The single-port modules will take up one of the two modules. In my opinion, the Catalyst 2820 is not good as a Fast Ethernet solution. The Catalyst 1900 is cheaper and has the same port density (switched). The only advantage of the Catalyst 2820 is a higher possible port density for Fast Ethernet, but the ports are shared and switched.

The FDDI modules offer both single attached and dual attached options. The ATM modules have their own operating system and are configured in the same way as the Catalyst 5000 ATM line cards. The ATM cards support local-area network emulation (LANE) for trunking capabilities.

All the features listed for the Catalyst 1900 also apply to the Catalyst 2820.

Catalyst 2900XL Series

Cisco introduced the Catalyst 2900XL series of switches after the Catalyst 5000 series, which has caused some confusion. The Catalyst 5000 series has one model called the Catalyst 2900, but this model is in no way related to the 2900XL—the numbers just happen to be the same. The "XL" indicates that the switch is completely different from the Catalyst 5000 series. The Catalyst 2900XL runs true Cisco IOS, unlike the Catalyst 5000 series, which uses its own brand of operating system. The Catalyst 2900XL has a completely different architecture than the Catalyst 5000 series. The Catalyst 2900XL has a 3.2-Gb/s backplane, whereas the Catalyst 5000 has a 1.2-Gb/s backplane. To make things even more confusing, the Catalyst 2900XL looks like the Catalyst 1900 or 2820 (see Figure 5-2), so one should examine the switch carefully before making a determination as to the model. Table 5-1 is a summary of the features of the Catalyst 2900XL models.

The Catalyst 2900XL is much more advanced than the Catalyst 1900 or 2820. For example, all its ports are 10/100 Mb/s, and all are capable of Fast EtherChannel. The Catalyst 2900XL is more expensive than the Catalyst 1900 yet less expensive than the Catalyst 5000. There are several different models of the Catalyst 2900XL, and I separate them into two groups—the modular and the nonmodular. Any Catalyst 2900XL

Figure 5-2
Rear view of Catalyst
2900XL

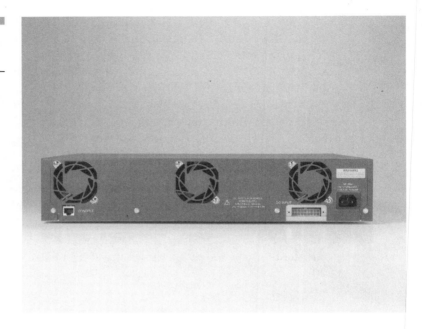

Table 5-1

Catalyst 2900XL
Model Summary

Model	10/100 Mb/s Ports	100baseTX	Expansion Bays
2908XL	8	0	0
2912XL	12	0	0
2912M-XL	12	0	2
2916M-XL	16	0	2
2924XL	24	0	0
2924M-XL	24	0	2
2924C-XL	22	2	0

that has the letter "M" in its model number will have two modular bays that look very similar to the bays in a Catalyst 2820. However, the modules that go in these bays are *not* interchangeable.

Configuring a Catalyst 2900XL is as easy as configuring a Catalyst 1900. The same configuration options available with the Catalyst 1900 and 2820 switches are available with the Catalyst 2900XL except the menu system. The switch can be configured through the Web interface or through the CLI, which is Cisco IOS.

Some of the key features of all the Catalyst 2900XL products are

10baseT/100baseTX ports

A switching fabric of 3.2 Gb/s and a forwarding rate of over 1.19 million packets per second

Full-duplex operation on switched 100baseT ports

4-MB shared memory architecture

Fast EtherChannel technology

Per-port broadcast storm control

Ease of use and ease of deployment

Web-based interface

Default configuration stored in flash memory

Simple Network Management Protocol (SNMP) and Telnet support

Cisco IOS command-line interface (CLI)-based management

Manageable through CiscoWorks Windows network management software on a per-port and per-switch Cisco Discovery Protocol (CDP) embedded RMON software agent with support for four RMON groups (history, statistics, alarms, and events) for enhanced traffic management, monitoring, and analysis

Supports all nine RMON groups through use of a switched-port analyzer (SPAN) port, which permits high-performance traffic monitoring of a single port, a group of ports, or the entire switch from a single network analyzer or RMON probe.

Catalyst 3000 Series

The Catalyst 3000 series uses a completely different architecture than any of the other Catalyst products. Its original design came from the Kalpana line of switches. Its "claim to fame" is its ability to stack. Multiple Catalyst 3000 switches can be stacked together to appear as a single switch. It is very similar to the "Borg" concept on "Star Trek: The Next Generation" or the concept of "Galaxia" in Isaac Asimov's Foundation Series. The stack acts as one switch, each piece becoming part of the whole.

There are three models in the Catalyst 3000 series, and they are all modular. There are two types of modular bays. The regular expansion bay will accept a number of modules (described later), whereas the "flexslot" expansion bay will accept regular expansion modules or a 3011

WAN module. The WAN modules are basically routers on a card that can be placed in the switch. The Catalyst 3000 has sixteen 10-Mb/s Ethernet ports and two expansion bays. The Catalyst 3100 has twenty-four 10-Mb/s Ethernet ports and one flexslot. The Catalyst 3200 has no fixed ports, one flexslot, and six regular expansion slots.

All the Catalyst 3000 series chassis have a modular bay on the back for a Stackport Module. A Stackport Module has one proprietary port and is necessary for the switch to connect into a Catalyst 3000 series stack. The port looks like an SCSI-2 connector and uses a proprietary cable. If only two switches are in the stack, they can be connected together via the Stackport Module. If more than two switches (there can be up to eight) are to be stacked, then a Catalyst Matrix ("What is the Matrix, Keanu?") must be purchased. The Catalyst Matrix is simply a box with SCSI-2 ports so that up to eight switches can all be plugged in. Cisco refers to it as the "switch of switches."

The modules that can be purchased for the regular expansion bays are numerous and sometimes comical. For instance, the Catalyst 100baseVG expansion module is probably not very popular, or how about a 3 port 10base2 module? Also not too popular. There are, however, very useful modules, such as the Dual Fast Ethernet ISL-capable module. This module allows for trunking. There is also an ATM expansion module for ATM backbone connectivity. For a complete listing, please refer to the latest Cisco product catalog.

The 3011 wide-area network (WAN) module that can be placed in the flexslot of the Catalyst 3100 and 3200 is a Cisco IOS router on a card. It is based on the Cisco 2503 router and has two high-speed serial interfaces and an ISDN BRI interface. It will use the same IOS image as that of the Cisco 2500 series of routers, and it must be release 11.1(6) or higher. The 3011 WAN module will be useful for small offices that need serial connectivity without the added expense or space of an external router.

Catalyst 3900 Series

In an effort to break into the Token Ring switching market, Cisco acquired Nashoba Systems, Inc., a manufacturer of Token Ring switches. This acquisition led to the development of the Catalyst 3900 switch. It has 20 fixed Token Ring ports and a double-wide expansion bay that can accept two single-wide expansion cards or one double-wide expansion card (Why do I feel like I am buying a mobile home?). The Catalyst 3900 is also a stackable switch with support for up to eight switches. Unlike the Catalyst 5000 series Token Ring line card, the Catalyst 3900 is capable of source-route bridging (SRB), source-route transparent bridging (SRT), and source-route switching (SRS).

The Catalyst 3900 supports TokenChannel. TokenChannel, like Fast EtherChannel and EtherChannel, bundles ports together. In this case, though, they are Token Ring ports, and up to eight can be bundled together, yielding a throughput of up to 256 Mb/s between switches.

The Catalyst 3900 double-wide expansion slot can accept ISL uplink modules, and this permits trunking Token Ring VLANs to a larger Catalyst 5000 series switch or another Catalyst 3900. There is also a two-port ATM expansion module for connectivity to an ATM backbone.

The Catalyst 3920 was the last Catalyst Token Ring switch to be introduced. It has 24 fixed Token Ring ports and an integrated Stack-port Module. This allows for stacking of up to eight Catalyst 3920s for a total of 192 switched Token Ring ports. All the features for the Catalyst 3900 apply to the Catalyst 3920.

Catalyst 4000 Series

Not to be confused with the Cisco 4000 series router, the Catalyst 4000 is one of Cisco's newest switches. There is currently a 3-slot chassis, the Catalyst 4003, and a 12-port Gigabit Ethernet fixed-port switch, the Catalyst 4912G. The Catalyst 4003 is a 3-slot switch, with the top slot reserved for the supervisor engine, which is the "brains" of the switch, responsible for most of the switching tasks. The remaining two slots can carry a number of different line cards. The Catalyst 4000 series uses the same operating system as the Catalyst 5000 series, but the Catalyst 4000 series will not accept any of the line cards used by the Catalyst 4000 series.

The Catalyst 4000 series is the lowest-modeled switch to support Gigabit Ethernet. Currently, there is a 6- and an 18-port line card for the Catalyst 4003 chassis. The Catalyst 4912G supports up to 12 Gigabit Ethernet interface controllers (GBICs). The GBIC is a small module that is the Gigabit Ethernet port. The purpose of keeping it modular is to allow organizations to implement various gigabit physical media, depending on the distance required. The Catalyst 4912G has a 24-Gb/s switching fabric for a backplane, ensuring that oversubscription of bandwidth on the backplane never occurs. The Catalyst 4003, configured with two 18-port line cards, can have the 24-Gb/s backplane fabric oversubscribed, but at a less than 2:1 ratio.

Features supported on the Catalyst 4000 series include support for Fast EtherChannel and Gigabit EtherChannel on all ports, VLANs, ISL trunking on all Fast Ethernet ports, and IEEE 802.1Q trunking on all ports. The Catalyst 4000 series also supports protocol filtering. The Catalyst 4000 switch can detect the protocol in use by end nodes connected to its ports and determine which broadcasts to forward on those ports. For example, an IP-only node will not receive IPX broadcasts. The Catalyst 4003 has redundant power supplies, but only one of the slots is "hot swappable."

The Gigabit Ethernet interface controllers (GBICs) come in two different versions. The 1000baseSX "shortwave" GBIC module is used for short distances, less than 2 km. The 1000baseLX/LH "long haul" GBIC module is for longer distances, up to 10 km. These modules may be mixed and matched in any combination on both the Catalyst 4912G and the Gigabit Ethernet line cards for the Catalyst 4003 (Figures 5-3 through 5-5).

Not many line cards are available for the Catalyst 4003 chassis, but their port densities are staggering. In addition to the 6- and 8-port Gigabit Ethernet line cards mentioned previously, there is currently a 48-port

Figure 5-3
Catalyst 4003 with Gigabit Ethernet and 10/100 ports

Figure 5-4
Catalyst 4000 series
Gigabit Ethernet
module

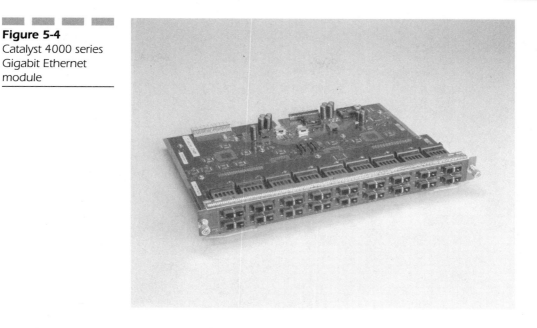

Figure 5-5
Catalyst 4000 series
supervisor engine

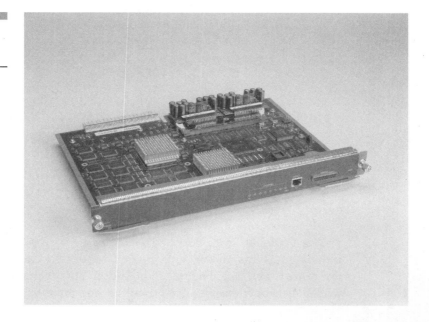

Figure 5-6
Catalyst 4000 series
48-port 10/100
module

Fast Ethernet line card (Figure 5-6), and a 2-port Gigabit Ethernet line card, 32-port 10/100-Mb/s line card (Figure 5-7).

The switch can be configured with up to 96 Fast Ethernet ports or 36 Gigabit Ethernet ports (see Figure 5-8), which is a lot when compared with the Catalyst 5000 series of switches.

SUMMARY

The Catalyst series of switches from Cisco Systems offers everything from an eight-port Ethernet switch to modular, stackable, high-port-density Gigabit Ethernet-capable switches. This chapter examined the small to medium-sized switches.

The Catalyst 1900 and 2820 switches are ideal for small switching implementations and remote wiring closets. The Catalyst 2900XL allows for more Fast Ethernet and included Fast EtherChannel for those wiring closets which required a large connection back to the main wiring

Figure 5-7
Catalyst 4000 series,
2-port Gigabit Ether-
net, 32-port 10/100
line module

Figure 5-8
Catalyst 4003

closet. The Catalyst 3000 series was developed from the older Kalpana switches and offers better legacy connectivity as well as serial connectivity with the 3011 WAN module. The Catalyst 3900 series offers affordable Token Ring switching solutions without requiring the larger Catalyst 5000 switches. And finally, the Catalyst 4000 Series of switches offers capabilities fit for the main wiring closet with a high port density of both Fast Ethernet and Gigabit Ethernet ports.

EXERCISES

1. What is the maximum port density of Fast Ethernet ports for the Catalyst 1900, and what are the possible physical media options?

2. What are the possible ways to configure a Catalyst 1900 or 2820?

3. What is the maximum number of MAC addresses that may be stored in the bridge table of a Catalyst 1900? What are some of the problems with this number?

4. Describe the differences between a Catalyst 1900 and a Catalyst 2820, and explain why you would use one over the other?

5. List the possible media that may be used in the Catalyst 2820 expansion bays?

6. List some of the differences between the Catalyst 2900XL series and the Catalyst 2900 series (only the differences discussed in this chapter).

7. Can the backplane of a Catalyst 2900XL series switch be oversubscribed? Explain.

8. List the three models of Catalyst 3000 series switches and their slots. What is the difference between the "flexslot" and the regular expansion slots?

9. What is the purpose of the Catalyst Matrix?

10. What advantages are there to using the 3011 WAN module? What are the disadvantages?

11. What is the main difference between the Catalyst 3900 series of switches and the rest of the Catalyst product line? What is the difference between the Catalyst 3900 and the Catalyst 3920?

12. Is it possible to build a Catalyst 4003 with 4 Gigabit Ethernet ports and 64 Fast Ethernet ports? What line cards would have to be used to acquire such a configuration?

13. Why is the backplane of the Catalyst 4012G impossible to over-subscribe? Why and when is it possible to oversubscribe the back-plane of the Catalyst 4003?

14. What is the purpose of the GBIC? What are the maximum dis-tances of the two different types of GBICs?

15. Describe the protocol filtering capabilities of the Catalyst 4000 series?

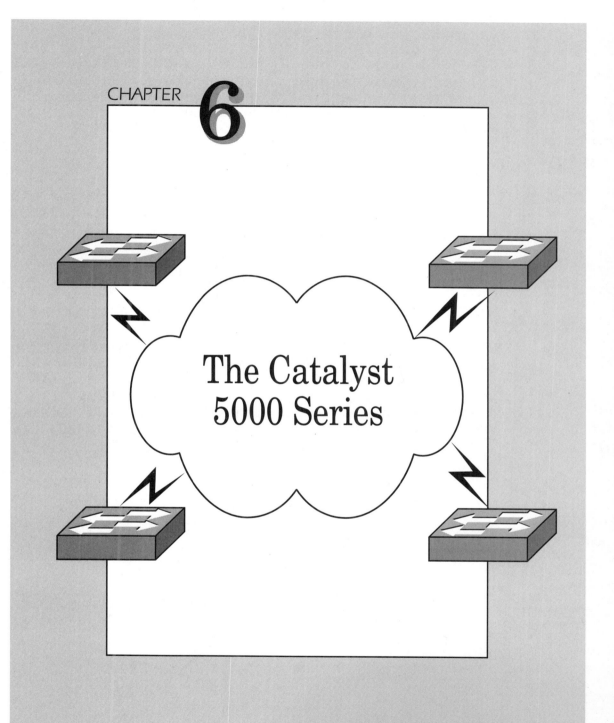

The Catalyst
5000 Series

The Catalyst 5000 series of switches is Cisco's flagship switching product. It currently has support for Gigabit Ethernet, Fast EtherChannel, ATM OC-3, and ATM OC-12. With many different chassis options, it is ideal for almost any switching solution.

Supervisor Engines

The Catalyst 5000 series of switches is a series of chassis that support a number of line cards. The chassis themselves are not capable of frame switching. A separate line card called a *supervisor engine* is the actual "brains" of the switch. The supervisor engine is responsible for almost all the higher-layer functions of the switch. The supervisor engine is responsible for data packet arbitration to the backplane, making frame forwarding decisions, and most Simple Network Management Protocol (SNMP) processes. A supervisor engine is required in all the Catalyst 5000 series chassis types.

Cisco currently has three models of supervisor engines, appropriately named *supervisor engine I, supervisor engine II,* and *supervisor engine III,* with each successive engine delivering more advanced capabilities.

Supervisor engine I was the first implementation and uses a Motorola 68EC040 processor operating at 25 MHz. It has two RJ-45 100-Mb/s-only switched ports, a console port for command line interface (CLI) access, and two medium-independent interfaces (MIIs) that may be used instead of the RJ-45 100-Mb/s-only ports. Its capabilities include *virtual local-area networks (VLANs),* CGMP/IGMP support, port security, and broadcast control. When in use, the backplane capacity of the chassis is 1.2 Gb/s (Figure 6-1).

Supervisor engine II uses the same processor and port configuration as the supervisor engine I, and its capabilities include all those features

Figure 6-1
Supervisor Engine I

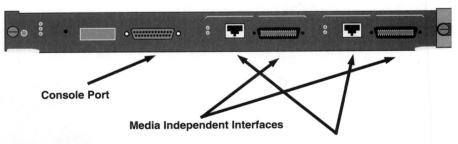

Console Port

Media Independent Interfaces

Fast Ethernet RJ-45 Ports

found in the supervisor engine I with several additions. Supervisor engine II allows for redundant supervisor engines to be placed in some of the Catalyst 5000 series chassis, and this allows for a hot standby. In the event that a supervisor engine II fails, it automatically reboots off the redundant supervisor engine II. This feature is supported in the Catalyst 5500 chassis. Supervisor engine II also supports the use of Fast EtherChannel (Figure 6-2).

Supervisor engine III is the most advanced of the three current products. It uses a RISC based 150-MHz R-4700 processor. The port configuration of supervisor engine III is modular, and there are several different uplink modules from which to choose. The two-port Gigabit Ethernet module has two 1000-Mb/s ports for high-speed uplinks, whereas the two- or four-port 10/100-Mb/s modules allow connectivity with workstations or servers. All the features of both the supervisor engines I and II are supported on supervisor engine III (Figure 6-3). However, supervisor engine III is the only supervisor engine to support the net flow feature card (NFFC) or multilayer switching. It is also the only supervisor engine to support Gigabit EtherChannel. In addition, it also enables the 3.6-Gb/s crossbar matrix on the backplane of all the Catalyst 5500 series chassis (see Table 6-1).

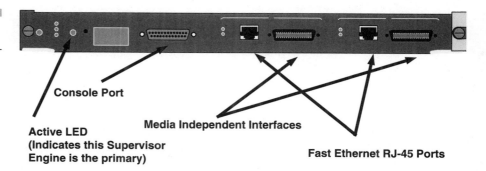

Figure 6-2
Supervisor Engine II

Console Port

Active LED
(Indicates this Supervisor
Engine is the primary)

Media Independent Interfaces

Fast Ethernet RJ-45 Ports

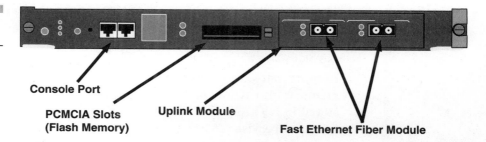

Figure 6-3
Supervisor Engine III

Console Port

PCMCIA Slots
(Flash Memory)

Uplink Module

Fast Ethernet Fiber Module

TABLE 6-1

Supervisor Engine
Feature
Comparison

Feature	Supervisor Engine I	Supervisor Engine II	Supervisor Engine III
Support for VLANs	X	X	X
Number of VLANs supported	1024	1024	1024
SNMP	X	X	X
RMON	X	X	X
Catalyst 5000 chassis	X	X	X
Catalyst 5500 chassis		X	X
Catalyst 5505 chassis		X	X
Catalyst 5509 chassis		X	X
Redundant supervisor engines		X	X
Fast EtherChannel		X	X
Gigabit EtherChannel			X
3.6-Gb/s crossbar fabric			X
Net flow feature card (NFFC)			X

TABLE 6-2

Memory Sizes for
Supervisor Engines

Memory Location	Supervisor Engine I	Supervisor Engine II	Supervisor Engine III
Flash	4 MB	8 MB	8 MB
RAM	20 MB	16 MB	32 MB
NVRAM	256 kB	256 kB	512 kB

Supervisor Engine Memory

Most memory is located in the supervisor engine of Catalyst switches. There are three types of main memory, flash, NVRAM, and RAM. The memory structure in the switch is very similar to that of a router. *Flash memory* is for storage of the operating system, *NVRAM* is used for storing the configuration file of the switch, and *RAM* is used to store the running software of the switch. The operating system loads from flash memory into RAM, and the configuration file is run from RAM but stored in NVRAM. The size of each memory location varies based on the type of supervisor engine (see Table 6-2).

Catalyst 5000 Line Cards

All the Catalyst 5000 chassis will support the line cards available. There are instances where it is unwise to place a particular card in a particular chassis. These situations will be discussed as well as the many different media and numerous connector types (Figure 6-4).

Figure 6-4
Several Ethernet line cards

24 port Ethernet Line Card with Telco Connectors.

48 port Ethernet Line Card with Telco Connectors.

12 port10/100 Ethernet Line Card with RJ-45 Connectors. (This could be a Fast EtherChannel Card)

24 port10/100 Ethernet Line Card with RJ-45 Connectors. (This could be a Fast EtherChannel Card)

6 port Fiber Fast Ethernet Line Card with SC Connectors.

12 port Fiber Fast Ethernet Line Card with SC Connectors.

10-Mb/s Ethernet Line Cards

There are two types of 10-Mb/s Ethernet line cards, the *switched Ethernet line card* and the *group switched Ethernet line card*. The grouped switched Ethernet line card is similar to placing a 10-Mb/s hub on a card and then placing it in a chassis.

At the time of this writing, Cisco offers 10-Mb/s switched Ethernet line cards with port densities of 12, 24, and 48 ports. The 48-port line card uses Telco connectors because of the limited space on a line card. These cards are good solutions for organizations needing to implement switched Ethernet to the desktop.

Cisco also offers 10-Mb/s group switched Ethernet line cards with port densities of 24 and 48 ports. These cards are less expensive and therefore make it easier for an organization to replace its existing shared-medium hubs. The group switched line cards do not provide the physical segmentation of switched cards.

Fast Ethernet Line Cards

Fast Ethernet line cards also come in switched and group switched models. Some cards support Fast EtherChannel and Inter-Switch Link (ISL), while others do not. It is important to check with Cisco to verify the features supported on a Fast Ethernet line card. Table 6-3 provides a summary of cards that are available as of March 1999.

TABLE 6-3

10/100-Mb/s Line Cards Features

Feature	12-Port (WS-X5203)	24-Port (WS-X5224)	24-Port (WS-X5225R)
Half/full-duplex on all ports	Yes	Yes	Yes
Dynamic VLANs	Yes	Yes	Yes
Hot swappable	Yes	Yes	Yes
Broadcast suppression	Yes	Yes	Yes
Auto speed negotiation	Yes	Yes	Yes
ISL trunking	Yes	No	Yes
Fast EtherChannel	Yes	No	Yes
IEEE 802.1 Q	No	No	Yes
Multilayer switching	No	No	Yes

FDDI Line Cards

FDDI is currently supported on the Catalyst 5000 series of switches via an FDDI translational bridge line card. The FDDI line card can use a variety of connectors. Typically, FDDI installations use the media interface connector (MIC) multimode fiber connection, but Cisco also supports single-mode fiber and copper (CDDI) (Figure 6-5).

All the FDDI cards have a maximum of one dual-attached station (DAS) or dual-homed station connection.

All frames will be translationally bridged to the backplane, as in Figure 6-6. This will create unwanted latency when switching from an

Figure 6-5
FDDI/CDDI line cards

Dual Attached or Dual Homed FDDI Line Card

Dual Attached or Dual Homed CDDI Line Card

Figure 6-6
FDDI translational
bridging

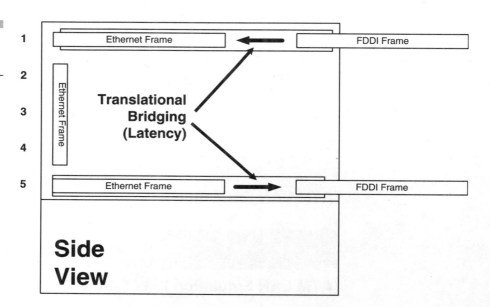

FDDI port to another FDDI port. However, the Catalyst 5000 was not designed to be an FDDI switch, so it should be used only as an end node on an FDDI ring.

ATM LAN Emulation Line Cards

Cisco Catalyst switches currently support several types of LAN Emulation (LANE) cards for connectivity to ATM backbones and wide-area networks (WANs) as is shown in Figure 6-7.

ATM LANE version 1 is a standard specification from the ATM Forum, a group of ATM vendors that agree on specifications. ATM will be discussed further in Chapter 10.

Route-Switch Modules

Cisco currently manufacturers a line card that is a Cisco router on a card. The route-switch module (RSM) frequently is compared with the route-switch processor 2 (RSP2), which was designed for the Cisco 7500 series of routers. The RSM has the ability to route frames from VLAN to VLAN by pulling the frames off the backplane of the switch (Figure 6-8). Currently, the connection to the backplane is limited to 400 Mb/s, not the 1.2 Gb/s that one would expect given the architecture of the Catalyst backplane. The RSM has its own command line interface (CLI) that is

Figure 6-7
ATM LANE line cards

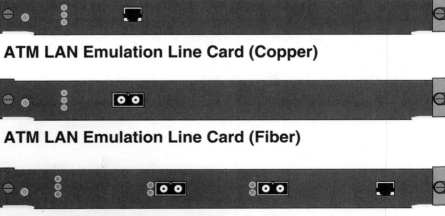

ATM LAN Emulation Line Card (Copper)

ATM LAN Emulation Line Card (Fiber)

ATM LAN Emulation Line Card w/ Dual PHY (Fiber)

Figure 6-8
Route switch module
(RSM)

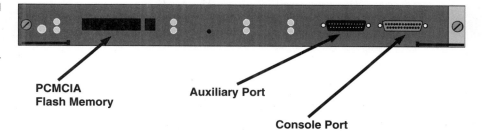

PCMCIA
Flash Memory

Auxiliary Port

Console Port

true Cisco IOS. The RSM has its own NVRAM, flash memory, RAM, and processor. It is an independent card in the switch. The RSM is a Cisco router with only one interface, the connection to the backplane. The RSM is capable of all Cisco IOS routing services including IP, IPX, AppleTalk, VINES IP, DECnet, XNS, SNA, access lists, RSVP, COS, CGMP, and many more. Creating virtual interfaces for each of the VLANs that need to be routed configures the RSM. RSM configurations will be discussed in Chapter 8.

The RSM can have an optional module called a *versatile interface processor* (*VIP*) *module* that supports the many port adapters that Cisco has designed for its 7200 series of routers. There is also a VIP-2 for the 7500 series of routers. The VIP module for the RSM allows a Catalyst switch to have wide-area interfaces such as Fast Serial connected directly into the chassis. The RSM with the VIP option can eliminate the need for an external router.

Gigabit Ethernet Line Cards

The Gigabit Ethernet line cards for the Catalyst 5000 series of switches are the only line cards that have the ability to attach to all three of the 1.2-Gb/s backplanes used by the Catalyst crossbar matrix. Although it is possible to install a Gigabit Ethernet line card in a chassis with only a supervisor engine II, this is generally not a good practice. Doing so will limit the connection to the backplane to 1.2 Gb/s, and thus the card may easily overwhelm the small backplane of the switch. An interesting feature of Gigabit Ethernet line cards is their use of the Gigabit Ethernet interface converter (GBIC). Each of the ports on a Gigabit Ethernet line card requires a GBIC, depending on the type of medium to which the interface is connecting. There are currently two GBICs to choose from, the 1000baseSX or 1000baseLX/LH. These GBICs are hot-swappable.

At present, 3- and 9-port versions of the Gigabit Ethernet line card are available, and all the interfaces use the versatile and convenient GBIC. These line cards are also capable of local switching. They have their own backplanes and can make forwarding decisions locally. This reduces the traffic placed on the backplane of the switch and allows simultaneous switching to occur. Frames can travel between ports of the Gigabit Ethernet line card and on the backplane of the switch. It is important to keep as much traffic on the local card as possible. This will limit the bandwidth consumed on the backplane and ensure that the Gigabit Ethernet ports do not overwhelm the relatively small backplane of the switch.

Catalyst 8510 Line Cards

The Catalyst 5500 chassis can support the switch route processor (SRP) of the Catalyst 8510 for the purpose of allowing Catalyst 8510 line cards to be inserted in slots 9 through 12. However, the Catalyst 8510 backplane that is present in slots 9 through 12 has no physical connection to the frame-switching fabric used by the Catalyst 5000 line cards. The Catalyst 5500/8500 fabric integration module (FIM) internally connects the Catalyst 5500 switch fabric to the Catalyst 8510 switch fabric. This internal connection provides the equivalent of an 800-Mb/s full-duplex pipe composed of a Fast EtherChannel bundle.

The Chassis

Catalyst 2900 Series

The Catalyst 2900 series is the smallest of the 5000 series. It sounds strange, but the Catalyst 2900 is a part of the Catalyst 5000 series. The 2900 series switch has two slots, and the uniqueness of the product lies in the fact that both cards are welded into the chassis. What you buy is what you get, the cards cannot be removed. The supervisor engine is a supervisor engine I, except for the Catalyst 2948G.

The Catalyst 2900 series, because it uses the supervisor engine I, has a 1.2 Gb/s backplane. There are five models in the series: 2901, 2902, 2926, 2926G, and 2948G. The 2901 and 2902 have reached the end of life cycle from Cisco and will no longer be manufactured. However, they are still in use. The Catalyst 2901 has a supervisor engine I in the first slot and a 12 port RJ-45 10/100-Mb/s card in the second slot, thus having a total of twelve 10/100-Mb/s ports and two 100-Mb/s-only ports (Figure 6-9). The Catalyst 2902 also has a supervisor engine I in the top slot but uses a 12-port 100-Mb/s fiber card in the second slot, yielding a total of twelve 100-Mb/s-only fiber ports and two RJ-45 100-Mb/s ports.

The Catalyst 2926 switch has a supervisor engine II in the first slot, but there are two different models to choose from. The Catalyst 2926T has two 100baseTX uplink ports with MII connectors, whereas the Catalyst 2926F has two 100baseFX ports with no MII connectors. Both switches support Fast EtherChannel, allowing for high-speed connections back to the main wiring closet.

The Catalyst 2926GS and 2926GL use a modified supervisor engine III that supports all the features of a supervisor engine III but has no PCMCIA flash card bays for easy storage of the Catalyst operating system. The supervisor engine has no modular uplink ports but instead has a fixed-port configuration depending on the model purchased. The Catalyst 2926GS has two 1000baseSX uplink ports, whereas the Catalyst 2926GL has two 1000baseLX/LH uplink ports. The second slot of the switch has twenty-four 10/100baseTX ports. The Gigabit Ethernet ports allow for very high throughput to the main wiring closet.

The Catalyst 2948G looks out of place in the Catalyst 2900 series but does run a Catalyst operating system, and it supports all the features that are found with supervisor engine III. Like the Catalyst 2926G, it supports two Gigabit Ethernet ports, but instead of twenty-four 10/100-Mb/s ports, it supports forty-eight 10/100-Mb/s ports. It is an ideal switch for closets that require a high density of ports and a high-bandwidth uplink connection to the main wiring closet. Table 6-4 presents a summary of the Catalyst 2900 series.

Catalyst 5002 Series

The Catalyst 5002 chassis is very similar to the Catalyst 2900 series of switches that have two slots. However, the Catalyst 5002 cards are

Figure 6-9
Catalyst 2900 chassis

TABLE 6-4

Catalyst 2900
Series Models and
Features

Feature	2901	2902	2926T	2926F	2926GS	2926GL	2948G
10/100 TX ports	14	2	24	24	24	24	48
10/100 FX ports	0	12	0	2	0	0	0
1000 SX ports	0	0	0	0	2	0	2
1000 LX/LH ports	0	0	0	0	0	2	0
ISL trunking	All ports	All ports	2	2	24	24	0
IEEE 802.1Q trunking	0	0	0	0	24	24	50
Fast EtherChannel	0	0	2	2	24	24	48
Gigabit EtherChannel	0	0	0	0	0	2	2
RAM (MB)	8	8	20	20	32	32	64
Flash (MB)	4	4	4	4	8	8	12
NVRAM (kB)	256	256	256	256	512	512	512
Dynamic VLANs supported	No	No	No	No	Yes	Yes	Yes

Figure 6-10
Catalyst 5002 chassis

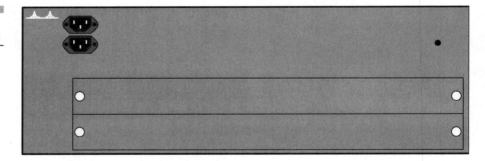

removable. The Catalyst 5002 supports any of the supervisor engines, but to put a supervisor engine III in a Catalyst 5002 would be like placing a $10,000 stereo system in a 1977 El Camino. It will support any of the past or present 5000 series line cards, including ATM LANE (Figure 6-10).

Catalyst 5000

The Catalyst 5000 chassis is a five-slot chassis that can take any of the different Cisco Catalyst 5000 line cards. The top slot must have a supervisor engine installed. Supervisor engine I or II is recommended because

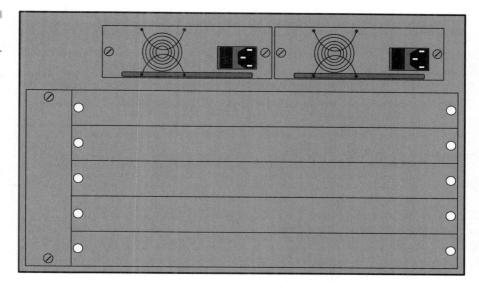

Figure 6-11
Catalyst 5000 chassis

the Catalyst 5000 chassis does not have the 3.6-Gb/s crossbar matrix backplane that supervisor engine III could enable. It has dual hot-swappable power supplies for redundancy. All line cards are hot swappable as well. The Catalyst 5000 chassis supports any of the past or present Catalyst 5000 line cards, including ATM LANE (Figure 6-11).

Catalyst 5505

The Catalyst 5505 chassis is a five-slot chassis that looks almost exactly like the Catalyst 5000 except that it has the number 5505 in place of the number 5000. The major difference between the Catalyst 5505 and 5000 is the backplane. The Catalyst 5505 backplane supports the 3.6-Gb/s crossbar matrix that can be enabled when supervisor engine III is used. Supervisor engine I cannot be used in the Catalyst 5505 chassis. However, the Catalyst 5505 also supports multiple supervisor engines for redundancy (Figure 6-12).

Catalyst 5509

The Catalyst 5509 chassis is a nine-slot chassis that supports all the Cisco Catalyst 5000 line cards, including the Gigabit Ethernet line cards. It also has a 3.6-Gb/s crossbar matrix that can be enabled when supervisor engine III is used. Supervisor engine I cannot be used in the Catalyst 5509

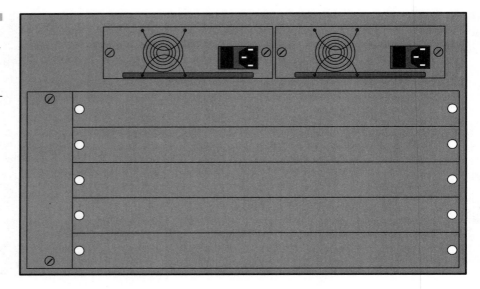

chassis. The Catalyst 5509 is ideal for high-density Gigabit Ethernet installations, and it has the capability to support 38 Gigabit Ethernet ports. This number is by far the largest number of supported ports of any of the Catalyst 5000 series of switches. Redundancy features include multiple supervisor engine support and two hot-swappable power supplies.

Catalyst 5500

The Catalyst 5500 chassis is the largest of the Catalyst 5000 series, with a total of 13 slots. The Catalyst 5500 chassis also supports LightStream 1010 cards in the bottom 5 slots. If one has no need for ATM Light-Stream cards, the chassis also supports the new Catalyst 8500 line cards in the bottom 5 slots only. Like the rest of the Catalyst 5500 series of products, multiple hot-swappable supervisor engines can be used for redundancy and supervisor engine I is not supported.

Although the top slot of the Catalyst 5500 series switches is reserved for the primary supervisor engine, the second slot may be used for a secondary engine if one has been employed. If not, the second slot can be configured with any of the Catalyst 5000 line cards. Slot 13 of the Catalyst 5500 is reserved for a LightStream 1010 ATM switch processor (ASP) or a Catalyst 8500 switch route processor (SRP). If neither is employed, the slot is unusable. All other slots support any of the Catalyst 5000 line cards (Figure 6-13).

Figure 6-13
Catalyst 5500 chassis

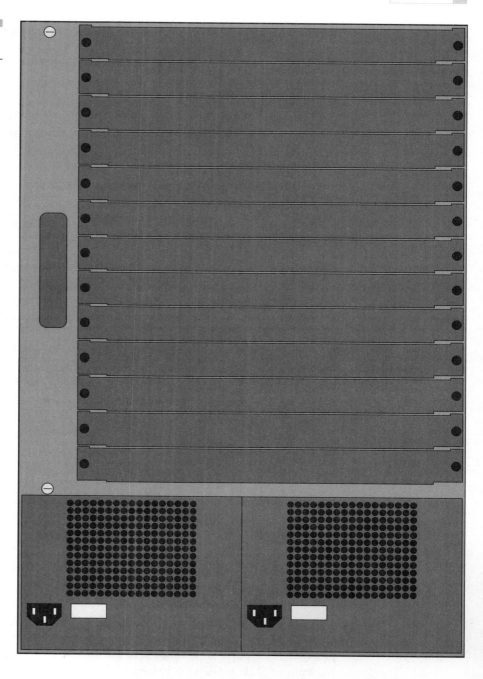

Catalyst 5000 Series Backplane

The backplane of the Catalyst 5000 series switches is somewhat complex. As mentioned earlier, the aggregate backplane bandwidth will vary based on the supervisor engine used. Supervisor engine III enables the 3.6-Gb/s crossbar fabric on any of the 5500 series products. This includes the Catalyst 5505, 5509, and 5500. The 3.6-Gb/s crossbar fabric consists of three 1.2-Gb/s backplanes bridged together and, when properly implemented, can yield an aggregate throughput up to 3.6 Gb/s. A Catalyst 5000 line card connects to only one of the three 1.2-Gb/s backplanes. Therefore, it is helpful to know which slot corresponds to which backplane.

The trick to making use of all three backplanes is to place your clients and servers properly. The clients and servers (that are going to be used by the clients) should be placed on the same backplane. By keeping traffic from being bridged between the backplanes, one can limit the amount of bandwidth used. Doing this, however, can be a problem because Cisco does not document the slot-to-backplane mappings; therefore it is difficult to ascertain the backplane on which a client or server is placed. Figure 6-14 shows the approximate slot-to-backplane mappings for the Catalyst 5500. The bottom five slots of the Catalyst 5500 also have a 5-Gb/s cell-switching backplane. This backplane is used when an ATM switch processor (ASP) is installed. The Catalyst 5000 line card connects to the first backplane (the left-most backplane when looking at the back of the switch) or the side where the line cards are inserted.

At the time of this writing, Cisco has one type of card that makes use of all three backplanes. Gigabit Ethernet line cards connect to all three backplanes. The Catalyst 5500, as shown in Figure 6-14, provides connectivity to all three backplanes in slots 1 through 5. In most cases, however, the first two slots will be used by the redundant supervisor engines, thus leaving only three slots available that connect to all three backplanes. The Gigabit Ethernet line card currently comes in three- and nine-port versions. The unusual number of ports can be attributed to the fact that the ports will be divided evenly into the three backplanes. For example, if the nine-port version were installed in slots 3 through 5 of a Catalyst 5500, ports 1 through 3 would be connected to backplane A, ports 4 through 6 to backplane B, and ports 7 through 9 to backplane C. If a Gigabit Ethernet line card were installed in any slots other than 2 through 5, only the ports connected to the first backplane

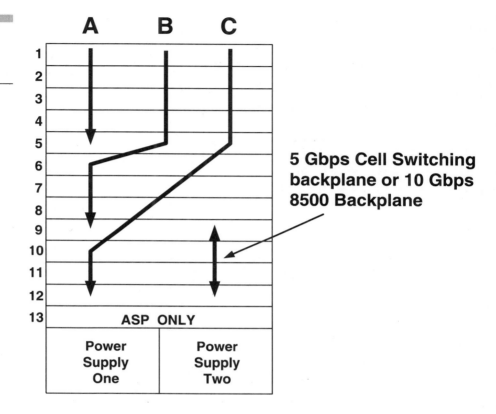

Figure 6-14
Catalyst 5500
backplane
assignments

5 Gbps Cell Switching backplane or 10 Gbps 8500 Backplane

would be available. For example, if a nine-port Gigabit Ethernet line card were installed in slot 10 of a Catalyst 5500, ports 1 through 3 would be connected to backplane C, while ports 4 through 9 would be unusable. If a three-port Gigabit Ethernet line card were installed in slot 10, port 1 would be connected to backplane C and the other ports 2 and 3 would be unusable. It is a waste of money to install Gigabit Ethernet line cards in slots that are not connected to all three backplanes. The maximum number of Gigabit Ethernet line cards that may be installed in a Catalyst 5500 Chassis is three.

The Catalyst 5509 was designed with the Gigabit Ethernet line card in mind. It provides connectivity to all three backplanes on any of its slots (Figure 6-15). A maximum of four Gigabit Ethernet cards can be installed in the Catalyst 5509 chassis. This limitation is set by Cisco.

The Catalyst 5505, like the Catalyst 5509, provides connectivity to all three backplanes in all its slots. Figure 6-16 shows which backplane is assigned to which slot.

Regular line cards installed in slots 2 and 3 will be connected to backplane A; those in slot 4, to backplane B; and those in slot 5, to backplane C. A three-port Gigabit Ethernet line card installed in either slot 2 or 3 would have port 1 connected to backplane A, port 2 to backplane B, and port 3 to backplane C (see Table 6-5). A three-port Gigabit Ethernet line card installed in slot 4 would have port 1 connected to backplane B, port 2 to backplane A, and port 3 to backplane C (see Table 6-6). And a three-port Gigabit Ethernet line card installed in slot 5 would have port 1 connected to backplane C, port 2 to backplane B, and port 3 to backplane A (see Table 6-7).

Figure 6-15
Catalyst 5509
backplane
assignments

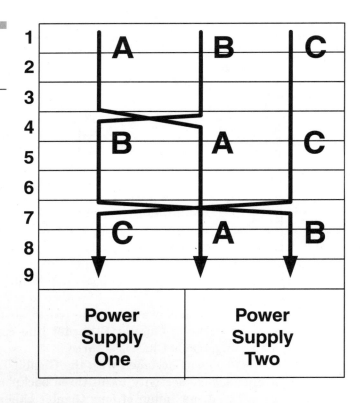

Figure 6-16
Catalyst 5505
backplane
assignments

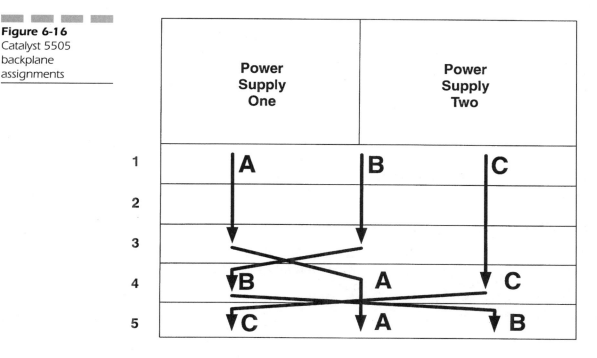

TABLE 6-5

Gigabit Ethernet
Port-to-Backplane
Assignments for
Slots 2 and 3

	Backplane A	Backplane B	Backplane C
3-port Gigabit Ethernet Card	Port 1	Port 2	Port 3
9-port Gigabit Ethernet Card	Ports 1–3	Ports 4–6	Ports 7–9

TABLE 6-6

Gigabit Ethernet
Port-to-Backplane
Assignments for
Slot 4

	Backplane A	Backplane B	Backplane C
3-port Gigabit Ethernet Card	Port 2	Port 1	Port 3
9-port Gigabit Ethernet Card	Ports 4–6	Ports 1–3	Ports 7–9

TABLE 6-7

Gigabit Ethernet
Port-to-Backplane
Assignments for
Slot 5

	Backplane A	Backplane B	Backplane C
3-port Gigabit Ethernet Card	Port 3	Port 2	Port 1
9-port Gigabit Ethernet Card	Ports 4–6	Ports 7–9	Ports 1–3

Processors and Architecture of the Catalyst 5000

Application-Specific Integrated Circuits

The Catalyst 5000 was designed around a distributed processing architecture such that tasks are performed by separate processors built specifically for their application. These processors are called *application-specific integrated circuits (ASICs)*. ASICs are present on all the line cards of a Catalyst switch. Each ASIC performs a different application.

Network Management Processor

The *network management processor (NMP)* resides on the supervisor engine of the switch and is responsible for tasks such as SNMP processing, the command line interface (CLI), and the spanning tree per VLAN calculations. The NMP frequently is mistakenly thought of as the forwarding engine of the switch, the ASIC responsible for the forwarding of frames.

Encoded Address Recognition Logic

The *encoded address recognition logic* ASIC, affectionately called EARL, is responsible for the learning and forwarding/filtering functions of the Catalyst switch. This ASIC resides on the supervisor engine, and its processing speed and responsibilities vary based on the model of the supervisor engine. For example, the EARL+, which is found in supervisor engine II, has the capability to learn and forward/filter Token Ring MAC addresses.

Synergy Advanced Multi-Bus Arbiter

The *synergy advanced multi-bus arbiter (SAMBA)*—this would be Simba's cousin—is an ASIC that is present on all Catalyst line cards. Each line card's SAMBA works in conjunction with all the other SAMBAs to arbitrate access to the switching bus. The supervisor engine's SAMBA is considered the "master," while the SAMBAs on the line cards are the "slaves." Arbitration in the Catalyst switch is a two-tier process, with the master SAMBA arbitrating access to the backplane for its slave SAMBAs and the slave SAMBAs arbitrating access for the individual ports on its line card. There are three possible priority levels that a port may have when accessing the backplane:

1. *Normal.*   This is the normal priority level. When all ports are set to this level, all ports are given equal access to the backplane.
2. *High.*   This level is configurable from the CLI and gives a port a higher priority to the backplane than ports with normal priority.
3. *Critical.*   A port enters this level only when the switch determines that the port's buffer is close to a buffer overflow, in which case it will automatically be placed in the critical priority level. When a port is in the critical priority level, it will have full access to the backplane. Once its buffer is emptied, it will return to its original state.

Master Communications Processor

The master communications processor (MCP)—sounds like the bad guy from TRON—is responsible for communicating management information to the line cards over a separate management bus. The management bus operates at 761 kb/s and carries no frames, only management information. This includes SNMP and RMON statistics coming from the individual line cards.

Line Communications Processor

The *line communications processor (LCP)* is responsible for communicating to the MCP over the management bus. LCPs exist on each of the line cards installed on a Catalyst 5000 series switch.

Synergy Advanced Integrated Network Termination

The *synergy advanced integrated network termination (SAINT)* ASIC is responsible for maintaining an Ethernet or Fast Ethernet port. Each Ethernet or Fast Ethernet port will have its own SAINT ASIC. This ASIC has a 192-kB buffer in which to store incoming and outgoing frames. Of this buffer, 168 kB is for outgoing frames, whereas the remaining 24 kB is used for caching incoming frames. The discrepancy is due to the limited bandwidth when transmitting frames out an Ethernet or Fast Ethernet port. When frames are being transmitted onto the backplane, there is far less a chance of congestion.

The SAINT is also used to perform the Inter-Link Switch (ISL) encapsulation and deencapsulation or IEEE 802.1Q encapsulation and deencapsulation. Trunking is performed in the ASICs, which explains why the capabilities of a port depend on the type of card and not the version of operating system, which is the case with Cisco routers. When frames are transmitted onto the backplane of a switch, they are tagged with a proprietary frame header and another frame check sum (FCS). These fields are for internal use only and will be stripped off before being transmitted out any of the ports. It is also important to note that these fields are not in any way associated with ISL or IEEE 802.1Q trunking headers.

Synergy Advanced Gate-Array Engine

The *synergy advanced gate-array engine (SAGE)* can be used on all non-Ethernet ports. It performs most of the functions of a SAINT but is not be responsible for access to the physical medium. This will involve application-specific processors depending on the medium.

Fast EtherChannel and the Ethernet Bundling Controller

Cisco has developed a proprietary method of combining or bundling Fast Ethernet ports to make them appear as single connection to the Spanning Tree Protocol (STP). This is necessary because of the STP's nasty little habit of eliminating redundancies, which can be a problem if you would like to load share over multiple links between switches. For example, Figure 6-17 shows two switches with four Fast Ethernet connections between them. What is the maximum bandwidth that can be achieved between the two switches?

Only one of the four connections actually will be in the forwarding state, yielding a total throughput of only 200 Mb/s. Thus 600 Mb/s of bandwidth is not being used. Cisco's Fast EtherChannel bundles the four ports together to make them appear as a single port to the STP so that it will not block on any of the ports (Figure 6-18).

The *Ethernet bundling controller (EBC)* performs load sharing across the four ports. There will be one EBC for every four ports. It is for this reason that there are limitations to which ports can be assigned to a channel. The ports must be physically located next to one another and cannot span multiple EBC ASICs. Figure 6-19 shows a possible configuration for multiple Fast EtherChannels on a single 12-port 10/100-Mb/s Fast EtherChannel line card. Figure 6-20 shows two 800-Mb/s Fast

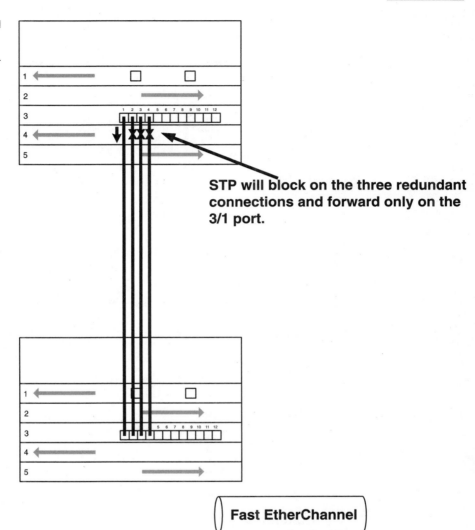

Figure 6-17
Redundancy and STP

STP will block on the three redundant connections and forward only on the 3/1 port.

Fast EtherChannel

EtherChannels that are misconfigured to span multiple EBCs. This is not possible, and any attempt to do so will result in an error.

Load sharing does not occur in the conventional round-robin approach. Instead, load sharing is accomplished by performing an eXclusive OR (XOR) Boolean expression on the last two bits of the source and destination MAC addresses. The purpose of using such an unconventional approach is to ensure that frames arrive in order for a particular flow. This will allow a quality of service (QoS) to be established.

Figure 6-18
Fast EtherChannel

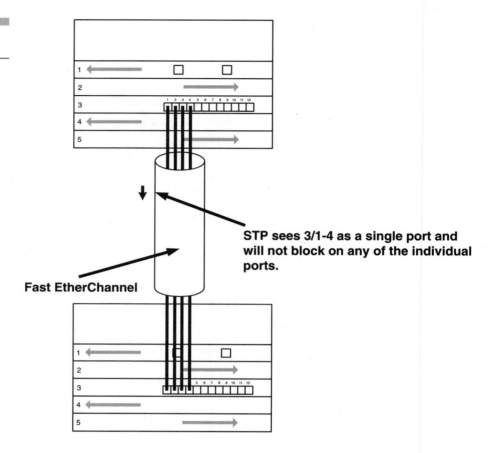

STP sees 3/1-4 as a single port and will not block on any of the individual ports.

Fast EtherChannel

In Figure 6-21, frames coming from host A going to server B are always going to take the same port, in this case the second port in the Fast EtherChannel.

Frames coming from host C destined for server B will always take the same path, but a different path from that of host A to server B traffic (Figure 6-22). This load balancing relies on the randomness of the MAC address involved.

A Fast EtherChannel is very useful for redundancy as well as for creating a larger pipe between switches. In the event that one of the ports should fail, the EBC will drop a four-port Fast EtherChannel to two ports or two-port Fast EtherChannel to the remaining port. Of course,

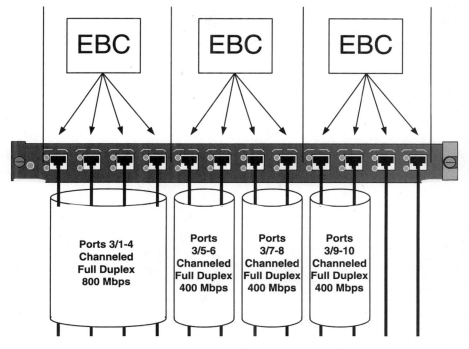

Figure 6-19
Possible Fast
EtherChannel
configuration

EBC   **EBC**   **EBC**

Ports 3/1-4
Channeled
Full Duplex
800 Mbps

Ports
3/5-6
Channeled
Full Duplex
400 Mbps

Ports
3/7-8
Channeled
Full Duplex
400 Mbps

Ports
3/9-10
Channeled
Full Duplex
400 Mbps

Fast EtherChannels cannot span more than one EBC.

this will reduce the bandwidth between the devices but will maintain connectivity (Figure 6-23).

Fast EtherChannel can be configured between switches and routers and between switches and workstations. Cisco has licensed its Fast EtherChannel technology to several vendors, including Intel and Sun Microsystems, for the manufacturing of Fast EtherChannel network interface cards (NICs) (Figures 6-24 and 6-25).

By using Intel's server NICs, an 800-Mb/s path can be created between a server and the switch, eliminating the bottleneck that was encountered frequently in the past between server and switch. However, the bottleneck can easily become the server because currently server buses are limited in their ability to move data when compared with the bandwidth of a four-port Fast EtherChannel. Do not oversubscribe the bus of your server because this could cause numerous network operating system (NOS) errors and even failure.

Figure 6-20
Misconfigured Fast
EtherChannels

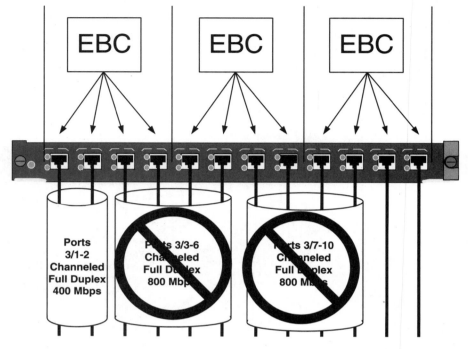

Fast EtherChannels cannot span more than one EBC.

SUMMARY

The Cisco Catalyst 5000 series of switches has numerous chassis and line cards to choose from for applications ranging from a small remote office to a large campus environment. Its line cards support all major media, including Ethernet, Fast Ethernet, Gigabit Ethernet, Token Ring, FDDI, ATM OC-3, and ATM OC-12.

The supervisor engine is responsible for all the higher functions of the switch and comes in three different models. The version of supervisor engine determines the features and capabilities of the switch. Supervisor engine III is the only supervisor engine that will support multilayer switching (MLS) and the 3.6-Gb/s crossbar fabric. There are three main areas of memory on the supervisor engine, flash, RAM, and NVRAM.

The Cisco Catalyst 5000 chassis provide different slot densities as

Figure 6-21
Fast EtherChannel
load balancing

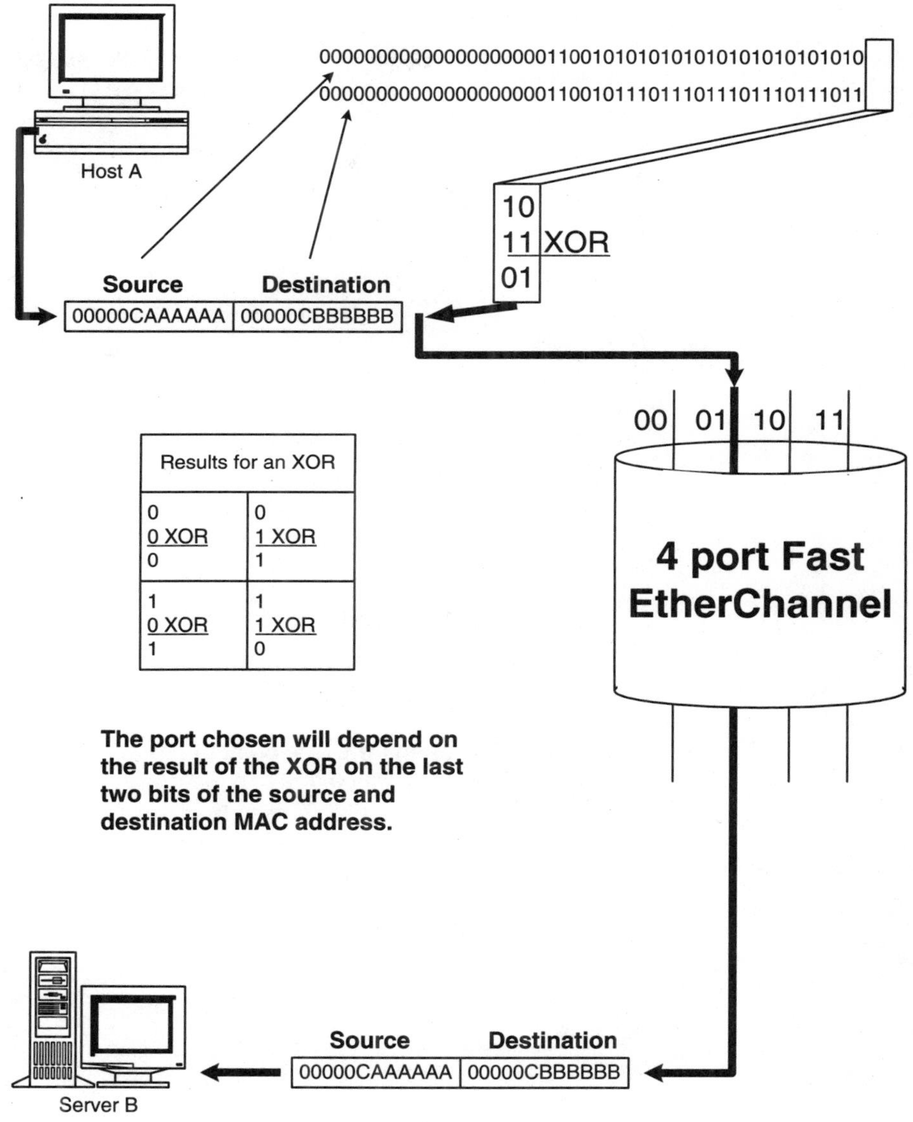

Host A

0000000000000000000000110010101010101010101010101010
0000000000000000000000110010111011101110111011

10
11 XOR
01

Source   **Destination**
00000CAAAAAA   00000CBBBBBB

00 | 01 | 10 | 11

**4 port Fast
EtherChannel**

Results for an XOR	
0 0 XOR 0	0 1 XOR 1
1 0 XOR 1	1 1 XOR 0

**The port chosen will depend on
the result of the XOR on the last
two bits of the source and
destination MAC address.**

Source   **Destination**
00000CAAAAAA   00000CBBBBBB

Server B

well as different backplane capacities. The Catalyst 5500 series of chassis (5505, 5509, 5500) have a 3.6-Gb/s crossbar switching fabric, but the chassis must have a supervisor engine III installed to make use of it.

The Cisco Catalyst 5000 series of switches use a distributed processing architecture with many different application-specific integrated cir-

Figure 6-22
Fast EtherChannel
load balancing for
Host B

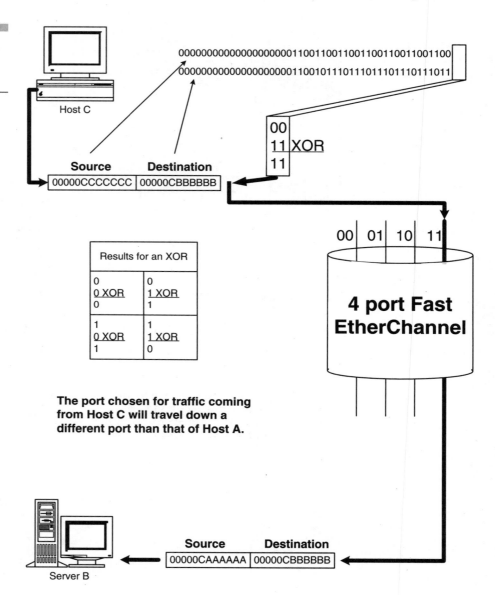

Figure 6-22
Fast EtherChannel load balancing for Host B

The port chosen for traffic coming from Host C will travel down a different port than that of Host A.

cuits (ASICs). Each ASIC works independently of other ASICs, ensuring that one process or task does not slow down the entire switch.

Cisco has introduced a proprietary method of bundling Fast Ethernet ports to create a large pipe between Fast EtherChannel-capable devices, such as a switch, router, or server with a Fast EtherChannel-capable

Figure 6-23
Fast EtherChannel
redundancy

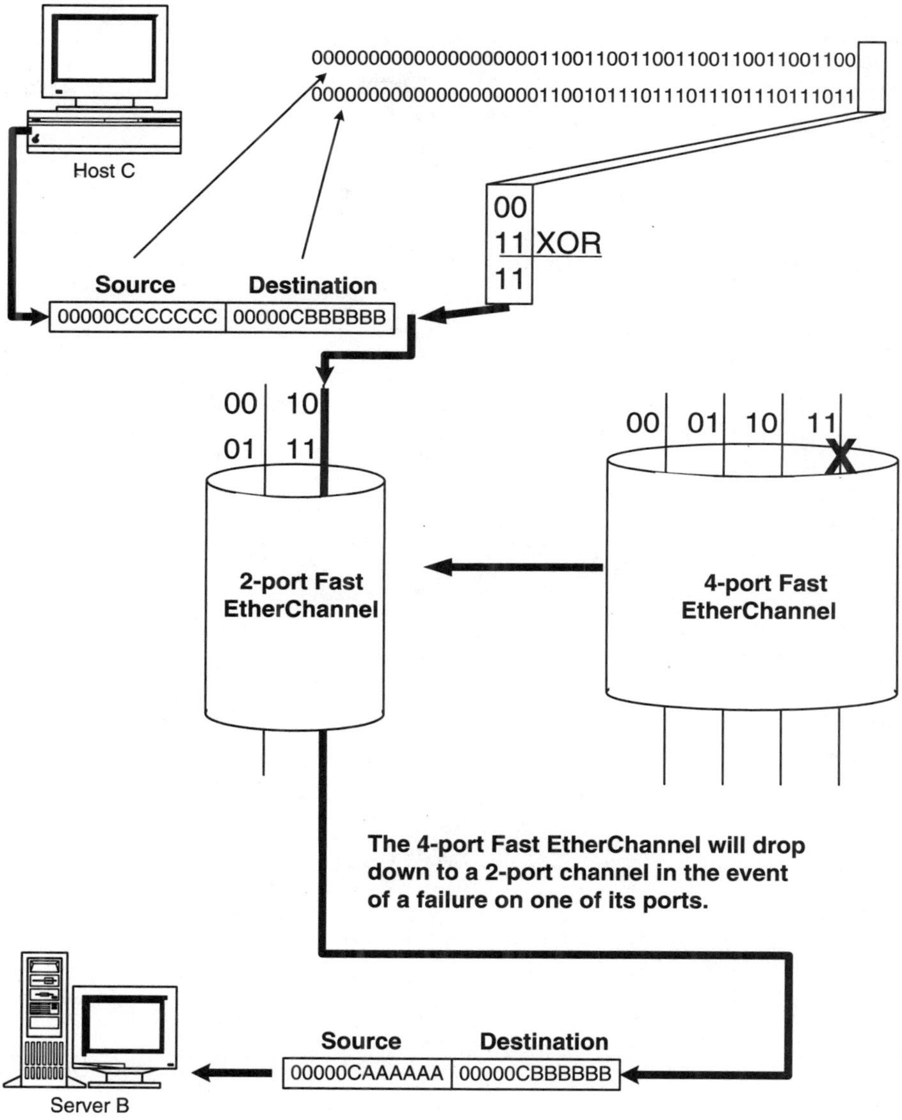

Host C

00000000000000000000011001100110011001100110011001100

000000000000000000000110010111011101110111011011

00
11 XOR
11

Source	Destination
00000CCCCCCC	00000CBBBBBB

00	10
01	11

2-port Fast EtherChannel

00	01	10	11

4-port Fast EtherChannel

The 4-port Fast EtherChannel will drop down to a 2-port channel in the event of a failure on one of its ports.

Server B

Source	Destination
00000CAAAAAA	00000CBBBBBB

NIC installed. Fast EtherChannel load sharing is performed by the Ethernet bundling controller (EBC) and is based on the source and destination MAC addresses of the frame.

Cisco's efficient use of the Catalyst backplane allows for switching performance that is measured in millions of frames per second. It is the

Figure 6-24
Fast EtherChannel
between a Sun server
and a catalyst switch

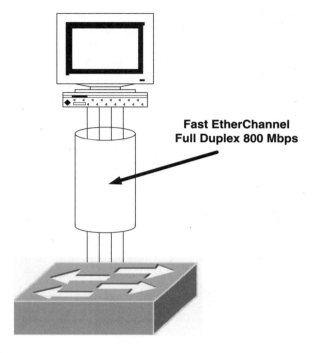

**Fast EtherChannel
Full Duplex 800 Mbps**

Figure 6-25
Fast EtherChannel
between a Cisco
router and a catalyst
switch

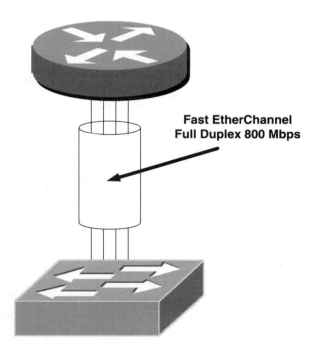

**Fast EtherChannel
Full Duplex 800 Mbps**

elimination of the shared memory area that limits the frame to traversing the backplane only once.

EXERCISES

1. Which of the supervisor engines will allow access to the 3.6-Gb/s crossbar matrix of the Catalyst 5500 series of switches? What component of supervisor engine III makes this possible?

2. In which slot of all Catalyst switches must the supervisor engine be placed? Can more than one supervisor engine be installed in a single chassis? If so, which slot must the second engine be placed in? What version of supervisor engine supports this redundant configuration?

3. List the three main areas of memory in a supervisor engine and what is stored in each of them.

4. What is the difference between single-mode fiber (SMF) and multimode fiber (MMF), and which of them is a supported port on the supervisor engine?

5. Why is latency associated with FDDI line cards, and why is the Catalyst 5000 series of switches not ideal for FDDI switching applications?

6. What are the advantages and disadvantages of using the route switch module (RSM) as opposed to an external Cisco router? What is the difference in configurations between the RSM and an external router?

7. What are the advantages and disadvantages of using the versatile interface processor (VIP) option with the RSM?

8. Why is the Catalyst 5509 considered to be one of the best options for Gigabit Ethernet?

9. What is the difference between a full 3.6-Gb/s backplane and 3.6-Gb/s crossbar matrix like the one used in the Catalyst 5500 series of switches?

10. How is it possible to use Gigabit Ethernet line cards on a Catalyst 5000 series product without oversubscribing the backplane bandwidth to the point where it is unusable?

11. Why is it recommended that the Gigabit Ethernet line card be used only with supervisor engine III?

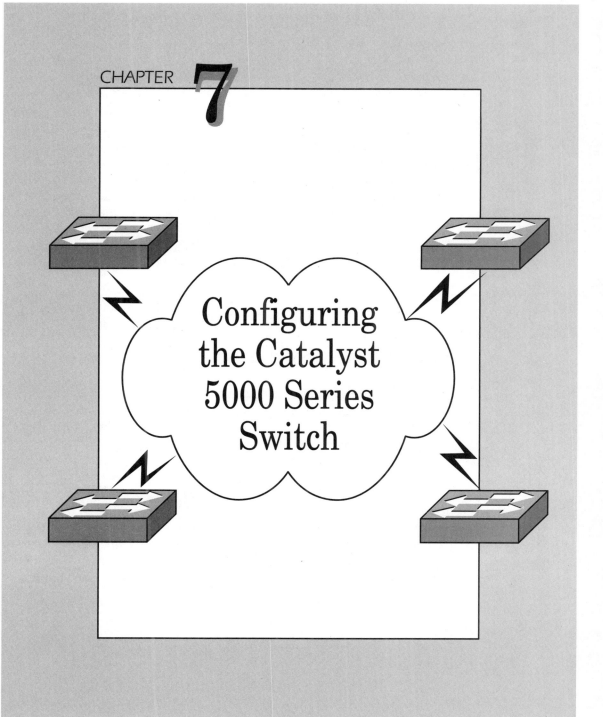

CHAPTER 7

Configuring the Catalyst 5000 Series Switch

Configuring the Catalyst 5000 series of switches can be done in two ways. You can purchase a product called *Cisco Works for Switched Internetworks* (*CWSI*), or you can configure the switch from the command line interface (CLI). After working with Cisco routers for years, many engineers find it easier to work with the CLI than to work with a graphic user interface (GUI). Here, I will discuss only the CLI. CWSI currently has no books written about it. However, Cisco training partners are currently teaching CWSI classes all over the world.

The CLI is accessed through the console port initially. Once IP has been configured on the switch, engineers can use the Telnet application to access the CLI. The console connection is a standard 9600 baud, 8 stop bits, and no error correction terminal port. Any terminal application will do. Just connect the console cable provided to a com port on your machine and the other end to the console port of the switch (shown in Chapter 6).

Introduction to the Catalyst Operating System

Catalyst switches do not use Cisco IOS. I have heard engineers call it "COS," for the "Catalyst operating system," and I have seen Cisco's documentation call it "Catalyst IOS." Personally, I use these terms interchangeably because they both refer to the same thing. COS or Catalyst IOS has been made to look as much as possible like Cisco IOS, so I will often make mention of the equivalent Cisco IOS command to make it easier for users of Cisco IOS. If you are not a user of Cisco IOS, please disregard such remarks.

When a Catalyst switch is turned on initially, it will run the normal bootstrap program with all its POST tests. The following output is taken from a Catalyst 5000 switch with a supervisor engine II. Your POST tests may be different depending on the type of supervisor engine and version of Catalyst IOS.

```
ATE0
ATS0 = 1

Catalyst 5000 Power Up Diagnostics

Init NVRAM Log
LED Test
ROM CHKSUM
DUAL PORT RAM r/w
```

```
RAM r/w
RAM address test
Byte/Word Enable test
RAM r/w 55aa
RAM r/w aa55
EARL test

BOOTROM Version 2.1, Dated Apr  6 1998 16:49:40
BOOT date: 00/00/00 BOOT time: 06:10:23
SIMM RAM address test
SIMM Ram r/w 55aa
SIMM Ram r/w aa55
Start to Uncompress Image . . .
IP address for Catalyst not configured
BOOTP will commence after the ports are online
Ports are coming online . . .
Cisco Systems Console

Enter password:
Mon Apr 14 1999  13:22:11   Module 1 is online
Mon Apr 14 1999  13:22:11   Module 2 is online
Mon Apr 14 1999  13:22:11   Module 3 is online
Mon Apr 14 1999  13:22:11   Module 4 is online
```

If this is the first time the switch has been turned on, or if the configuration file of the switch has been erased, the switch will send out a BOOTP request and a RARP to resolve its IP address. This is built into the Catalyst IOS, and messages will appear on the console letting you know:

```
Sending RARP request with address 00:40:02:24:25:ff.
Sending bootp request with address: 00:40:02:24:25:ff
Sending RARP request with address 00:40:02:24:25:ff
Sending bootp request with address: 00:40:02:24:25:ff
Sending RARP request with address 00:40:02:24:25:ff
Sending bootp request with address: 00:40:02:24:25:ff
Sending RARP request with address 00:40:02:24:25:ff
Sending bootp request with address: 00:40:02:24:25:ff
Sending RARP request with address 00:40:02:24:25:ff
Sending bootp request with address: 00:40:02:24:25:ff
Sending RARP request with address 00:40:02:24:25:ff
Sending bootp request with address: 00:40:02:24:25:ff
Sending RARP request with address 00:40:02:24:25:ff
Sending bootp request with address: 00:40:02:24:25:ff
Sending RARP request with address 00:40:02:24:25:ff
Sending bootp request with address: 00:40:02:24:25:ff
Sending RARP request with address 00:40:02:24:25:ff
Sending bootp request with address: 00:40:02:24:25:ff
Sending RARP request with address 00:40:02:24:25:ff
Sending bootp request with address: 00:40:02:24:25:ff
```

The CLI of the Catalyst IOS is made to look like the Cisco IOS CLI, so you may recognize some of the CLI features. Catalyst IOS has an online help feature. At any time you can type ? or the word help for a listing of available commands or the correct syntax for a command (see below).

```
console> (enable) ? or help <enter>
Commands:
----------------------------------------
cd              Setdefault flash device
clear           Clear, use 'clear help' for more info
configure       Configure system from network
copy            Copy files between TFTP/module/flash devices
delete          Delete a file on flash device
dir .           Show list of files on flash device
disable         Disable privileged mode
disconnect      Disconnect user session
download        Download code to a processor
enable          Enable privileged mode
format          Format a flash device
help            Show this message
history         Show contents of history substitution buffer
ping            Send echo packets to hosts
pwd             Show default flash device
quit            Exit from the Admin session
reconfirm       Reconfirm VMPS
reload          Force software reload to linecard
reset           Reset system or module
session         Tunnel to ATM or Router module
set             Set, use 'set help' for more info
—More—
```

The —More— indicates that there are more possible commands. At the —More— prompt, the <enter> key will display a line at a time, the <q> key will exit the list, and any other key will display a page at a time.

In addition commands can be truncated, provided the first characters are unique:

```
console> (enable) he <enter>
Commands:
----------------------------------------
cd              Set default flash device
clear           Clear, use 'clear help' for more info
configure       Configure system from network
copy            Copy files between TFTP/module/flash devices
delete          Delete a file on flash device
dir             Show list of files on flash device
disable         Disable privileged mode
disconnect      Disconnect user session
download        Download code to a processor
enable          Enable privileged mode
format          Format a flash device
help            Show this message
history         Show contents of history substitution buffer
ping            Send echo packets to hosts
pwd             Show default flash device
quit            Exit from the Admin session
reconfirm       Reconfirm VMPS
```

```
reload          Force software reload to linecard
reset           Reset system or module
session         Tunnel to ATM or Router module
set             Set, use 'set help' for more info
—More—
```

When a command is typed incorrectly, the CLI will respond with an unknown command message:

```
Cat5000> (enable) hlp
Unknown command "hlp". Use 'help' for more info.
Cat5000> (enable)
```

Command line editing at the CLI of Catalyst switches has several different keystrokes, as shown in Table 7-1.

Sometimes your terminal and the terminal length of the switch may not be synchronized or, in other words, when a large list is displayed, the top of the list scrolls off the top of the page. In this case, the termi-

TABLE 7-1

CLI Keystrokes for Command Line Editing (Taken from the Cisco Documentation CD)

Keystroke	Function
Ctrl-A	Jumps to the first character of the command line
Ctrl-B or left arrow key	Moves the cursor back one character
Ctrl-C	Escapes and terminates prompts and lengthy tasks
Ctrl-D	Deletes the character at the cursor
Ctrl-E	Jumps to the end of the current command line
Ctrl-F or right arrow key	Moves the cursor forward one character
Ctrl-K	Deletes from the cursor to the end of the command line
Ctrl-L; Ctrl-R	Repeats current command line on a new line
Ctrl-N or down arrow key	Enters next command line in the history buffer
Ctrl-P or up arrow key	Enters previous command line in the history buffer
Ctrl-U; Ctrl-X	Deletes from cursor to beginning of command line
Ctrl-W	Deletes last word typed
Esc B	Moves cursor backward one word
Esc D	Deletes from cursor to end of word
Esc F	Moves cursor forward one word
Delete or Backspace key	Erases mistake when entering a command; reenter command after using this key

nal length needs to be shortened. The following command will set the terminal length to 24 lines:

```
Cat5000> (enable) set length 24
Screen length for this session set to 24.
Console> (enable)
```

Catalyst Modes

If this is the first time the switch has been turned on, or if the configuration file of the switch has been erased, the switch will prompt you for a password:

```
Cisco Systems Console

Enter password:
```

Many engineers have been led to believe that there is a default password on the switch and proceed to start guessing. This is a waste of time. The default password is <return>, or "the carriage return," or <enter>. If you were to type in anything else, the switch would display the following:

```
Enter password:
Sorry. Try again.

Enter password:
Sorry. Try again.

Enter password:
Sorry. Try again.
```

Once the correct password has been entered, you will enter what is commonly referred to as user mode. The prompt will indicate that you are in user mode by displaying the name of the switch followed by the ">" character.

If this switch has no system name, the word console will be used in place of the name:

```
console>
```

While in user mode, you will only be able to view parameters. No changes can be made to the configuration while in user mode. This is very similar to the Cisco IOS. The command `enable` will change modes from the user to privileged mode. A password is required, and if the switch has no configuration file, the default password is `<return>`. In privileged mode, the prompt will have the word `(enable)` appended to the name of the switch:

```
Cat5000> enable              User mode
Enter password:
Cat5000> (enable)            Privileged mode
```

In privileged mode, you can make changes to the configuration file. This is done by using a collection of numerous `set` commands. The `set` command takes the place of the configuration modes of Cisco IOS.

The Banner

The banner that is displayed when logging into the switch by Telnet or by the terminal port on the supervisor engine is configured using the `set banner motd` command. The `motd` is short for the "message of the day." The banner should have a stern warning against unauthorized access (if you can have a stern banner?) and possibly a philosophical sonnet.

```
Cat5000> (enable) set banner motd [beginning delimiter] <enter>

                        A banner

[end delimiter]
```

The beginning and ending delimiter must be the same character.

EXAMPLE

To set the banner of a Catalyst switch:

```
Cat5000> (enable) set banner motd^C

                        CAT 5000

          Unauthorized Access is Prohibited!!

          Have you hugged an Engineer Today?

^C
Cat5000> (enable)
```

Automatic Session Logout

A sometimes-annoying feature is the automatic session logout. When a user is logged into the switch and performs no keystrokes or, in other words, is "idle" for a set number of minutes, the switch automatically logs that user out. In the event the user were to forget to log out and leave his or her terminal unattended, this feature prevents someone from coming up to the terminal and having access to the switch. The default setting of the automatic session logout feature is 5 minutes. This can be changed using the set logout command:

```
Cat5000> (enable) set logout [number of minutes]
```

EXAMPLE

To configure the automatic session logout to 20 minutes instead of the usual 5 minutes:

```
Cat5000> (enable) set logout 20
Sessions will be automatically logged out after 20 minutes of idle
time.
Cat5000> (enable)
```

Supervisor Engine's Console Baud Rate

The baud rate of the supervisor engine's console is 9600 baud by default, but this can be changed using the set system baud command:

```
Cat5000> (enable) set system baud [baudrate]
```

Possible baud rates include 600, 1200, 2400, 4800, 9600, 19,200, and 38,400.

EXAMPLE

To set the baud rate of the supervisor engine's console port to 38,400 baud:

```
Cat5000> (enable) set system baud 38400
System console port baud rate set to 38400.
Cat5000> (enable)
```

Terminal Message Logging

When you are working on the console of a Catalyst switch, terminal messages are displayed. These messages can be a nuisance. When you are typing on the CLI, a message may appear and interrupt the command you are typing. The `set logging` commands can be used to configure the format and location of these messages.

To send Terminal messages to the console (default):

```
Cat5000> (enable) set logging console enable
System logging messages will be sent to the console.
Cat5000> (enable)
```

Once again, this command is the `logging console` command from the Cisco IOS preempted with the word `set`. To send terminal messages to the current Telnet session:

```
Cat5000> (enable) set logging console enable
System logging messages will be sent to the current login session.
Cat5000> (enable)
```

To have a logging file created and maintained on a TFTP server with the IP address of 172.16.1.10:

```
Cat5000> (enable) set logging server enable
System logging messages will be sent to the configured syslog
servers.
Cat5000> (enable) set logging server 172.16.1.10
172.16.1.10 added to System logging server table.
Cat5000> (enable)
```

To view the current logging settings:

```
Cat5000> (enable) show logging
Logging console:           enabled
Logging server:            enabled
{172.16.1.10}
Current Logging Session:   enabled
```

Setting Passwords

If you want to set the initial password, the password that leads to user mode, you would type in the command `set password <return>`. You would then be prompted for the old password. After typing in the old password, you would be asked to type in the new password. After typing in the new password, you would be asked to retype the new password to verify that it is was typed correctly the first time. Of course, you could make the same typo twice, but hopefully the chances are slim.

```
Cat5000> (enable) set password
Enter old password: [old user mode password]
Enter new password: [new user mode password]
Retype new password: [new user mode password]
Password changed.
Cat5000> (enable)
```

To set the password for access to privileged mode, the command `set enablepass <return>` is used. The same procedure used for the user mode password is followed:

```
Cat5000> (enable) set enablepass
Enter old password: [old enable password]
Enter new password: [new enable password]
Retype new password: [new enable password]
Password changed.
Cat5000> (enable)
```

EXAMPLE

To set both passwords for the first time, enter the following:

```
Cat5000> (enable) set password
Enter old password: <enter>
Enter new password: cisco   (These characters would not be echoed to the termi-
nal screen.)
Retype new password: cisco
Password changed.
Cat5000> (enable)
```

Password Recovery

If you forget the password or acquire a switch from another business unit and do not know the password, password recovery is possible. During the first 60 seconds from power on, the switch will use the default password for both the user mode password and the privileged mode password. Note that this is 60 seconds from power on, not from the time the prompt is displayed. Depending on the model of supervisor engine, the actual time you would have to change the password could be as little as 15 seconds. The steps for password recovery are as follows:

Step 1:   Power cycle the switch.

Step 2: Wait for the password prompt and log in to user mode. The password will be <return>, the default.

```
ATE0
ATS0 = 1

Catalyst 5000 Power Up Diagnostics

Init NVRAM Log
LED Test
ROM CHKSUM
DUAL PORT RAM r/w
RAM r/w
RAM address test
Byte/Word Enable test
RAM r/w 55aa
RAM r/w aa55
EARL test

BOOTROM Version 2.1, Dated Apr  6 1998 16:49:40
BOOT date: 00/00/00 BOOT time: 06:10:23
SIMM RAM address test
SIMM Ram r/w 55aa
SIMM Ram r/w aa55
Start to Uncompress Image . . .
IP address for Catalyst not configured
BOOTP will commence after the ports are online
Ports are coming online . . .

Cisco Systems Console
Enter password:
Mon Apr 14 1999  13:22:11    Module 1 is online
Mon Apr 14 1999  13:22:11    Module 2 is online
Mon Apr 14 1999  13:22:11    Module 3 is online
Mon Apr 14 1999  13:22:11    Module 4 is online

Enter password:<return>
Cat5000>
```

Step 3: Type the command enable <return>, and enter the default password to enter privileged mode:

```
Console> enable
Enter Password:
Cat5000> (enable)
```

Step 4: Change the user mode password by using the set password <return> command or the truncated command set pass <return>. You will be prompted for the old password, and the old password is the default password, <return>. You will then be prompted for the new password. Enter the password you would like to use for the user mode password. You will then be prompted to retype the password for verification.

```
Cat5000> (enable) set password
Enter old password: <return>
```

```
Enter new password: [new user mode password]
Retype new password: [new user mode password]
Password changed.
Cat5000> (enable)
```

Step 5: Change the privileged mode password using the set enablepass <return> command. It is a good idea to truncate the command to set en <return>. You will be prompted for the old password, and the old password is the default password, <return>. You will then be prompted for the new password. Enter the password you would like to use for the privileged mode password. You will then be prompted to retype the password for verification.

```
Cat5000> (enable) set enablepass
Enter old password: <return>
Enter new password: [new enable password]
Retype new password: [new enable password]
Password changed.
Cat5000> (enable)
```

Once the Privileged Mode password has been set, password recovery is complete.

Sometimes there will not be enough time to change both passwords. When the 60 seconds expires, the old passwords return, and you will not be able to change them. I usually end up changing the user mode password, and by the time I get to changing the privileged mode password, the 60 seconds are up. In such a case, I have to perform the steps again, skipping step 4.

If you are in a situation where the 60 seconds does not allow you enough time to change both passwords, I recommend another faster method. Perform steps 1 to 5, except instead of typing in the new passwords, hit the <return> key.

```
Cat5000> (enable) set password
Enter old password:<return>
Enter new password: <return>
Retype new password: [new password]
Password changed.
console> (enable) set enablepass
Enter old password: <return>
Enter new password: <return>
Retype new password:[new enable password]
Password changed.
Cat5000> (enable)
```

This will expedite the process now because you do not need to type out new passwords. Once the passwords have been set to <return>, you can take your time and change the passwords to whatever you would like.

Configuring SNMP Parameters

Whether or not you are planning on running an SNMP management station, I recommend configuring the SNMP parameters on all Catalyst switches. To set the system name, use the `set system name` command:

```
console> (enable) set system name [the system name] <enter>
System name set.
The system name> (enable)
```

NOTE: *In Catalyst IOS version 4.1(2), the prompt was changed to the SNMP system name with an ">" appended. However, in prior releases, the* `set prompt` *command was necessary to change the prompt:*

```
console> (enable) set prompt Cat5000>
Cat5000> (enable)
```

The SNMP community strings must be set the same on the SNMP management station and the Catalyst switch. Three strings are used by Catalyst switches, read-only, read-write, and read-write-all. By default, Catalyst switches have their community string values set to public, private, and secret, respectively. This can be a serious security issue. An SNMP management server can make configuration changes to a switch provided that the strings are set the same. If a switch is left with the default strings, anyone with a SNMP management server and who knows the default community string values of a Catalyst switch can make configuration changes. For this reason, I recommend setting the SNMP values regardless of whether SNMP is in use or not.

To set the community strings, the commands are as follows:

Read-only:

```
console> (enable) set snmp community read-only [read-only string]
```

Read-write:

```
console> (enable) set snmp community read-write [read-write string]
```

Read-write-all:

```
console> (enable) set snmp community read-write-all [read-write-all
string]
```

Following is an example of a switch that has its strings changed:

```
console> (enable) set snmp community read-only Star
```

```
SNMP read-only community string set to 'Star'.
console> (enable) set snmp community read-write Wars
SNMP read-write community string set to 'Wars'.
console> (enable) set snmp community read-write-all Epsisode1
SNMP read-write-all community string set to 'Episode1'.
```

SNMP is an IP-based protocol and therefore requires IP to be configured on the switch. With a Cisco router, an IP address is on all the router's interfaces. However, with a Catalyst switch, there are no interfaces, only bridge ports. These ports do not require a Layer 3 address. It is for this reason that Catalyst switches have a virtual interface called the *interface sc0*. This interface has all the IP settings found on a regular IP node: IP address, subnet mask, and default gateway. This interface also needs to be assigned to a virtual local-area network (VLAN). The switch will have multiple VLANs and must have its interface sc0 assigned to one. It is important to remember that the VLAN will have an IP subnet assigned to it, and the IP address, subnet mask, and default gateway of the interface sc0 must match the IP subnet. This will be explored further in the next chapter.

The Interface sc0

The `set interface sc0` command sets the VLAN, IP address, subnet mask, and broadcast address of the interface sc0:

```
console> (enable) set interface sc0 [VLAN] [ip_address [subnet-
mask] [broadcast]]
```

Following is an example of a switch having its interface sc0 assigned an IP address of 172.16.100.5 with a subnet mask of 255.255.255.0. With no VLAN specified, the interface sc0 will remain in its current VLAN.

```
console> (enable) set interface sc0 172.16.100.5 255.255.255.0
```

TECH TIP: *The subnet mask is optional, and if it is not specified, the subnet mask will be set to the default mask of the IP address. For example, had the preceding command been entered:*

```
console> (enable) set interface sc0 172.16.100.5
```

the default mask would be set to 255.255.0.0, the default mask of a class B address.

The default VLAN of the interface sc0 is VLAN 1, and the default IP address, subnet mask, and broadcast address is 0.0.0.0. When the IP address of the interface sc0 is set to 0.0.0.0, the switch will automatically perform a BOOTP and RARP to obtain an IP address. To set the switch to perform a BOOTP and RARP, you need only set the IP address and subnet mask of the interface sc0 to 0.0.0.0 and power cycle the switch. To determine the MAC address of the interface sc0, the `show module` command can be used:

```
Cat5000> (enable) show module
Mod Module-Name        Ports Module-Type        Model      Serial-Num Status
--- ------------------ ----- ------------------ ---------- ---------- --------
1                      2     1000BaseSX Supervisor WS-X5530 010847706 ok
2                      24    10/100BaseTX Ethernet WS-X5224 010904347 ok
3                      24    10/100BaseTX Ethernet WS-X5224 010907441 ok
5                      12    100BaseFX MM Ethernet WS-X5201R 009976930 ok

Mod MAC-Address(es)                        Hw     Fw       Sw
--- -------------------------------------- ------ -------- -------------------
1   00-90-21-0d-9c-00 to 00-90-21-0d-9f-ff 2.0    3.1.2    4.3(1a)
2   00-10-7b-e9-83-e8 to 00-10-7b-e9-83-ff 1.4    3.1(1)   4.3(1a)
3   00-50-a2-30-84-c0 to 00-50-a2-30-84-d7 1.4    3.1(1)   4.3(1a)
5   00-60-70-99-f0-1c to 00-60-70-99-f0-27 1.1    4.1(1)   4.3(1a)

Mod Sub-Type Sub-Model Sub-Serial Sub-Hw
--- -------- --------- ---------- ------
1   EARL 1 + WS-F5520  0010851091 1.1
1   uplink   WS-U5534  0009999149 1.0
```

The last MAC address in the range of MAC addresses for the supervisor engine (slot 1) will be the MAC address used in the BOOTP and ARP request of the interface sc0.

The broadcast address sets the IP address to be used when a broadcast is sent. By default, the broadcast address will be the IP address with all ones in the host field. For example, if the IP address of the interface sc0 is 172.16.100.5 with a subnet mask of 255.255.255.0, the host bits will be replaced with all ones and will yield a broadcast address of 172.16.100.255. The only instance when the broadcast address should be changed from the default is when the switch is operating in a UNIX environment that uses all zeros in the host field as its broadcast address.

The `set ip route` command allows you to configure individual routes for the interface sc0:

```
Cat5000> (enable) set ip route [destination-network] [gateway-
    address]
```

For example, to create a route to the 172.16.2.0 network using the gateway 172.16.1.1 (see Figure 7-1):

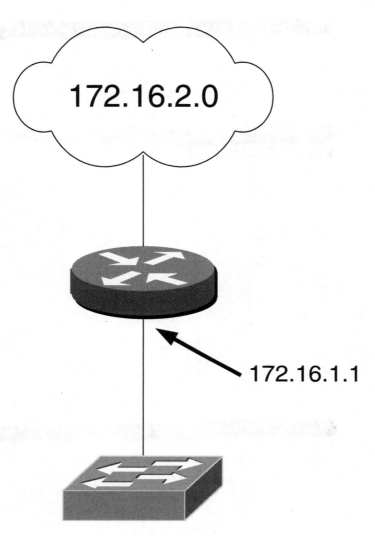

Figure 7-1
Creating a Route to
the 172.16.2.0
Network Using
Gateway 172.16.1.1

```
Console> (enable) set ip route 172.16.2.0 172.16.1.1
Route added.
```

This will create a route only to 172.16.2.0, not to the remainder of networks on both the intranet and the Internet. It is a waste of time to manually configure routes for each network, and most of the time the default gateway of the interface sc0 will be set using the set ip route default command:

```
Cat5000> (enable) set ip route default [default-gateway-address]
[primary]
```

The "primary" option will indicate that this is the primary gateway to use in the event that there is more than one default gateway. If more than one gateway is configured without the "primary" option, the first gateway entered will be the default gateway. In the event that the first gateway fails, the switch will look to the second gateway configured, and so on. If multiple gateways are configured with the "primary" option, the last gateway entered will be the primary. A maximum of three default gateways can be configured, except on the Catalyst 4000 and 2926G, on which only one can be configured. In the following example, a Catalyst switch has two gateways that can be used. The 172.16.1.1 gateway will be set as the primary, and the 172.16.1.2 will be the backup (see Figure 7-2).

Figure 7-2
Gateway 172.16.1.1
Is the Primary and
Gateway 172.16.1.2
is the Backup

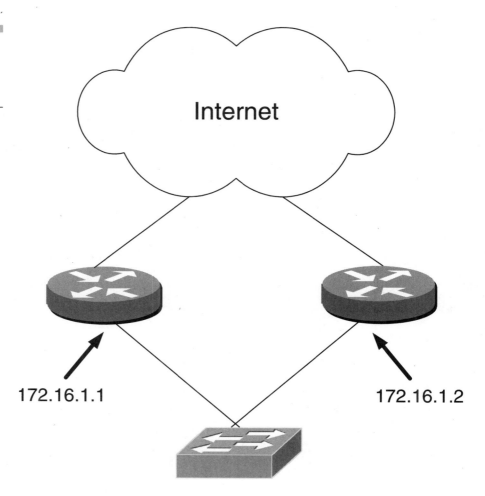

```
Cat5000> (enable) set ip route default 172.16.1.1 primary
Route added.
Cat5000> (enable) set ip route default 172.16.1.2
Route added.
```

To verify that all routes that have been configured, the show ip
route command can be used:

```
Cat5000> (enable) show ip route
Fragmentation    Redirect    Unreachable
-------------    --------    -----------
enabled          enabled     enabled
The primary gateway: 172.16.1.1
Destination                     Gateway        Flags  Use   Interface
---------------  ------------   ------------   ------ ----- ---------
default                         172.16.1.1     G      0     sc0
default                         172.16.1.2     G      0     sc0
172.16.1.0                      172.16.1.5     U      0     sc0
default                         default        UH     0     sl0
Cat5000> (enable)
```

Some of you may recognize the ip route command from the Cisco IOS.
It is used in the same manner on the switch, except that you have to
remember to put set before the command.

If you want to remove a route or default gateway from the routing
table of the interface sc0, the following command may be used:

```
Cat5000> (enable) clear ip route default 172.16.1.2
Route deleted.
Cat5000> (enable) show ip route
Fragmentation    Redirect    Unreachable
-------------    --------    -----------
enabled          enabled     enabled
The primary gateway: 172.16.1.1
Destination      Gateway        Flags     Use    Interface
---------------  ------------   --------   -----  ---------
default          172.16.1.1     G         0      sc0
172.16.1.0       172.16.1.5     U         0      sc0
default          default        UH        0      sl0
Cat5000>   (enable)
```

TECH TIP: *In older versions of the Catalyst IOS it was necessary to
clear the old default route before adding a new one. The error displayed
when this was attempted did not clearly reflect this.*

IP Permit Lists

The only purpose of the interface sc0 is for Telnet and SNMP access. Access to the interface sc0 can be restricted to a list of user-configurable IP addresses for security. This list is called the IP permit list. The set ip permit command is used to configure the list:

```
Cat5000> (enable) set ip permit [enable | disable]
```

This will enable or disable IP security. By default, IP security is disabled.

```
Cat5000> (enable) set ip permit [ip_address subnet-mask]
```

And to verify the IP permit list, the show ip permit command can be used:

```
Cat5000> (enable) show ip permit
```

EXAMPLE

To permit all stations on the 172.16.2.0 network and the IP node 172.16.3.10 access to the interface sc0 of a Catalyst switch, the following commands are used (Figure 7-3):

```
Cat5000> (enable) set ip permit enable
IP permit list enabled.
WARNING!! IP permit list has no entries.
Cat5000> (enable)
```

This enables the IP permit list.

BONEHEAD ALERT: *Do not Telnet into the switch and perform this command without first creating a permit list that grants you access. You will disconnect yourself!*

```
Cat5000> (enable) set ip permit 172.16.3.10
172.16.3.10 added to IP permit list.
Cat5000> (enable)
```

This allows 172.16.3.10 access.

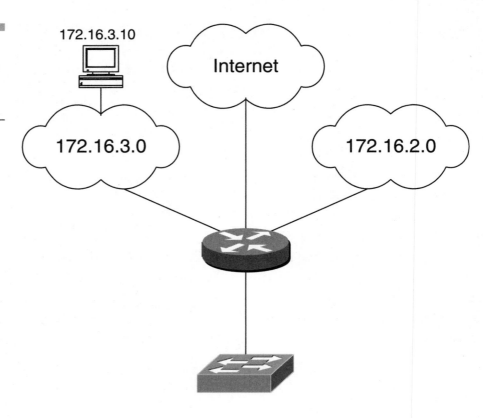

Figure 7-3
All Stations on
Network 172.16.2.0
and IP Node
172.16.3.10 Can
Access Interface sc0

```
Cat5000> (enable) set ip permit 172.16.2.0 255.255.255.0
172.16.2.0 with mask 255.255.255.0 added to IP permit list.
Cat5000> (enable)
```

This permits all the 172.16.2.0 subnet.

Moreover, to verify the IP permit list:

```
Cat5000> show ip permit
IP permit list feature enabled.
Permit List          Mask
----------------     --------------
172.16.3.10
172.16.2.0           255.255.255.0

Denied IP Address    Last Accessed Time    Type
-----------------    -------------------   ------
172.16.3.1           03/20/99,12:45:20     Telnet
Cat5000>
```

To clear any or all the entries in the IP permit list, the following command is used:

```
Cat5000> (enable) clear ip permit [ip_address or all] [subnet-
mask(if necessary)]
```

For example, the following command clears all the entries in the IP permit list (please see the preceding "Bonehead Alert"):

```
Cat5000> (enable) clear ip permit all
IP permit list cleared.
WARNING!! IP permit list is still enabled.
Cat5000> (enable)
```

DNS and an IP Host Table

Catalyst switches can use either a DNS or have their own internal host table. To configure a switch to use a DNS, the set ip dns command is used:

```
Cat5000> (enable) set ip dns enable
DNS is enabled.
Cat5000> (enable)
```

This will enable DNS. By default, DNS is disabled.

```
Cat5000> (enable) set ip dns server 172.16.1.6
198.92.30.32 added to DNS server table as primary server.

Cat5000> (enable) set ip dns server 172.16.1.7 primary
171.69.2.132 added to DNS server table as primary server.

Cat5000> (enable) set ip dns server 172.16.1.8 primary
171.69.2.143 added to DNS server table as primary server.
```

This will set the IP address of the DNS server. There can be a maximum of three entries in the DNS server table. The "primary" option indicates that this entry should be the primary.

```
Cat5000> show ip dns
DNS is currently enabled.
The default DNS domain name is: ar-inc.com

DNS name server          status
--------------------     -------
172.16.1.6
172.16.1.7               primary
172.16.1.8
console>
```

This will show the current DNS settings.

Instead of using a DNS, a host or alias table may be created manually using the `set ip alias` command:

```
Cat5000> (enable) set ip alias [name] [ip_address mapped to name]
```

This will add an entry to the host table.

```
Cat5000> (enable) show ip alias [name]
```

EXAMPLE

The following commands configure a switch with appropriate name to IP address mappings:

```
Cat5000> (enable) set ip alias Cat-1 172.16.1.1.
IP alias added.
Cat5000> (enable) set ip alias Cat-2 172.16.1.2
IP alias added.
Cat5000> (enable) set ip alias Cat-3 172.16.1.3
IP alias added.
Cat5000> (enable) set ip alias Cat-4 172.16.1.4
IP alias added.
Cat5000> (enable)
```

To verify the host table:

```
Cat5000> (enable) sh ip alias
default          0.0.0.0
cat-1            172.16.1.1
cat-2            172.16.1.2
cat-3            172.16.1.3
cat-4            172.16.1.4
Cat5000> (enable)
```

The default network listed is the address that is commonly given to represent the destination network of the default route. I prefer to use IP addresses rather than names. This allows me to become familiar with the IP addressing scheme of the environment.

The Interface sl0

To enable remote access to a Catalyst switch through a dial-up plain old telephone system (POTS) line, the interface sl0 allows a Serial Line Internet Protocol (SLIP) connection to be established on the console port. The command `set interface sl0` configures the console port to accept a SLIP connection.

The format of the interface sl0 command is

```
Cat5000> (enable) set interface sl0 [slip_address]
[destination_address]
```

To enable the console port to accept SLIP calls, the `slip attach` command is used. To set the slip address to 172.16.1.1 and the destination address to 172.16.1.2 and then enable SLIP on the console port, the following is entered:

```
Cat5000> (enable) set interface sl0 172.16.1.1 172.16.1.2
Interface sl0 slip and destination address set.
Cat5000> (enable) slip attach
Console Port now running SLIP.
```

The `show interface` command gives a summary of both the interface sc0 and interface sl0 settings:

```
Cat5000> (enable) show interface
sl0: flags = 51<UP,POINTOPOINT,RUNNING>
        slip 172.16.1.1 dest 172.16.1.2
sc0: flags = 63<UP,BROADCAST,RUNNING>
        vlan 1 inet 172.16.100.1 netmask 255.255.255.0 broadcast
172.16.100.255
Cat5000> (enable)
```

The Reset Command

To reset the switch, the command `reset system` may be used, or you could simply power cycle the switch. The command also can be shortened to `reset`:

```
Cat5000> (enable) reset
```

A module can be reset individually, which comes in handy when you need to rest a module without rebooting the entire switch.

EXAMPLE

To reboot the line card in slot 3:

```
Cat5000> (enable) reset 3
This command will reset module 3 and may disconnect your telnet
session.
```

```
Do you want to continue (y/n) [n]? y
Resetting module 3 . . .
Cat5000> (enable) 04/06/1999,18:53:35:SYS-5:Module 3 reset from
  telnet/172.16.1.5/
Cat5000> (enable) 04/06/1999,18:53:57:SYS-5:Module 3 is online
```

The Configuration File

Chapter 6 discusses the location of the configuration file. The configuration file is the file that contains all the set commands that have been entered on the CLI of the switch. The configuration file resides in both NVRAM and RAM. The file in NVRAM is used only when the switch boots; it is then copied into RAM. It is the file in RAM that is used while the switch is running. This concept is the same as for Cisco IOS-based routers. However, with a Cisco router, you must copy the configuration file in RAM to NVRAM after changes have been made. Catalyst switches synchronize the two files automatically. There is no "running config" or "startup config" for Catalyst switches. There is only *the configuration*. The upside of this is the fact that you do not have to worry about saving the configuration file to NVRAM like you do with a router. The downside is the fact that you can no longer just reboot the device when you totally "hose" (a technical term) up its configuration file.

As with Cisco routers, the configuration file is a text file, but unlike Cisco routers, the file contains all the configuration commands including the defaults. It can be viewed using the show config command.

Sample Catalyst Switch Config

(Commands that are going to be or have been discussed in this chapter are italicized.)

```
Cat5000> (enable) show config
. . .
. . . . . . . . .
. . . . . . . . .
. . . . . . . . .

. . . . . . . . .
. .

begin
set password $1$CBqb$g1WZqrZFaNmPu/UcRRqfF1
set enablepass $1$FMFQ$HfZR5DUszVHIRhrz4h6V70
set prompt Cat5000>
```

```
set length 24 default
set logout 20
set banner motd ^C
  CAT 5000

                        Unauthorized Access is Prohibited!!
^C
!
#system
set system baud  9600
set system modem disable
set system name Cat5000
set system location
set system contact
!
#snmp
set snmp community read-only      public
set snmp community read-write     private
set snmp community read-write-all secret
set snmp rmon disable
set snmp trap disable module
set snmp trap disable chassis
set snmp trap disable bridge
set snmp trap disable repeater
set snmp trap disable vtp
set snmp trap disable auth
set snmp trap disable ippermit
set snmp trap disable vmps
set snmp trap disable entity
set snmp trap disable config
set snmp trap disable stpx
set snmp extendedrmon vlanmode disable
set snmp extendedrmon vlanagent disable
set snmp extendedrmon enable
!
#ip
set interface sc0 1 172.16.1.1 255.255.255.0 172.16.1.255

set interface sc0 up
set interface sl0 0.0.0.0 0.0.0.0
set interface sl0 up
set arp agingtime 1200
set ip redirect    enable
set ip unreachable    enable
set ip fragmentation enable
set ip route 0.0.0.0            172.16.1.1      1
set ip route 172.16.2.0        172.16.1.1      1
set ip alias default           0.0.0.0
set ip alias cat-1             172.16.1.1
set ip alias cat-2             172.16.1.2
set ip alias cat-3             172.16.1.3
set ip alias cat-4             172.16.1.4
!
#Command alias
!
#vmps
set vmps server retry 3
set vmps server reconfirminterval 60
set vmps tftpserver 0.0.0.0 vmps-config-database.1
```

```
set vmps state disable

!
#dns
set ip dns disable
!
#tacacs+
set tacacs attempts 3
set tacacs directedrequest disable
set tacacs timeout 5
set authentication login tacacs disable
set authentication login local enable
set authentication enable tacacs disable
set authentication enable local enable
!
#bridge
set bridge ipx snaptoether     8023raw
set bridge ipx 8022toether     8023
set bridge ipx 8023rawtofddi snap
!
#vtp
set vtp mode server
set vtp v2 disable
set vtp pruning disable
set vtp pruneeligible 2-1000
clear vtp pruneeligible 1001-1005
!
#spantree
#uplinkfast groups
set spantree uplinkfast disable
#backbonefast
set spantree backbonefast disable
#vlan 1
set spantree enable         1
set spantree fwddelay  15     1
set spantree hello     2      1
set spantree maxage    20     1
set spantree priority  32768 1
#vlan 1003
set spantree enable         1003
set spantree fwddelay  15     1003
set spantree hello     2      1003
set spantree maxage    20     1003
set spantree priority  32768 1003
set spantree portstate 1003   block 0
set spantree portcost  1003   62
set spantree portpri   1003   4
set spantree portfast  1003   disable
#vlan 1005
set spantree disable          1005
set spantree fwddelay         15    1005
set spantree hello            2     1005
set spantree maxage           20    1005
set spantree priority         32768 1005
set spantree multicast-addres 1005  ieee
!
#cgmp
set cgmp disable
set cgmp leave disable
```

```
!
#syslog
set logging console enable
set logging server disable
set logging level cdp 2 default
set logging level mcast 2 default
set logging level dtp 5 default
set logging level dvlan 2 default
set logging level earl 2 default
set logging level fddi 2 default
set logging level ip 2 default
set logging level pruning 2 default
set logging level snmp 2 default
set logging level spantree 2 default
set logging level sys 5 default
set logging level tac 2 default
set logging level tcp 2 default
set logging level telnet 2 default
set logging level tftp 2 default
set logging level vtp 2 default
set logging level vmps 2 default
set logging level kernel 2 default
set logging level filesys 2 default
set logging level drip 2 default
set logging level pagp 5 default
set logging level mgmt 5 default
set logging level mls 5 default
set logging level protfilt 2 default
set logging level security 2 default
!
#ntp
set ntp broadcastclient disable
set ntp broadcastdelay 3000
set ntp client disable
clear timezone
set summertime disable
!
#set boot command
set boot config-register 0x2
set boot system flash bootflash:cat5000-sup3.4-3-1.bin
!
#permit list
set ip permit disable
set ip permit 172.16.3.10 255.255.255.255
set ip permit 172.16.2.0 255.255.255.0
!
#drip
set tokenring reduction enable
set tokenring distrib-crf disable
!
#igmp
set igmp disable
!
#standby ports
set standbyports disable
!
#module 1 : 2-port 1000BaseSX Supervisor
set module name    1
set vlan 1    1/1-2
```

```
set port enable        1/1-2
set port level         1/1-2  normal
set port duplex        1/1-2 full
set port trap               1/1-2  disable
set port name               1/1-2
set port security           1/1-2  disable
set port broadcast          1/1-2  100%
set port membership         1/1-2  static
set port negotiation        1/1-2 enable
set port flowcontrol send             1/1-2 desired
set port flowcontrol receive          1/1-2 off
set cdp enable        1/1-2
set cdp interval       1/1-2 60
set trunk 1/1  auto negotiate 1-1005
set trunk 1/2  auto negotiate 1-1005
set spantree portfast       1/1-2 disable
set spantree portcost       1/1-2  4
set spantree portpri        1/1-2  32
set spantree portvlanpri  1/1  0
set spantree portvlanpri  1/2  0
set spantree portvlancost 1/1  cost 3
set spantree portvlancost 1/2  cost 3
!
#module 2 : 24-port 10/100BaseTX Ethernet
set module name      2
set module enable    2
set vlan 1      2/1-24
set port enable       2/1-24
set port level        2/1-24  normal
set port speed        2/1-24  auto
set port trap               2/1-24  disable
set port name         2/1-24
set port security           2/1-24  disable
set port broadcast          2/1-24  0
set port membership         2/1-24  static
set cdp enable        2/1-24
set cdp interval            2/1-24 60
set spantree portfast 2/1-24 disable
set spantree portcost 2/1-24  100
set spantree portpri  2/1-24  32
!
#module 3 : 24-port 10/100BaseTX Ethernet
set module name      3
set module enable    3
set vlan 1      3/1-24
set port enable       3/1-24
set port level        3/1-24  normal
set port speed        3/1-24  auto
set port trap               3/1-24  disable
set port name         3/1-24
set port security           3/1-24  disable
set port broadcast          3/1-24  0
set port membership         3/1-24  static
set cdp enable        3/1-24
set cdp interval            3/1-24 60
set spantree portfast 3/1-24 disable
set spantree portcost 3/1-24  100
set spantree portpri  3/1-24  32
!
```

```
#module 4 empty
!
#module 5 : 12-port 100BaseFX MM Ethernet
set module name      5
set module enable    5
set vlan 1           5/1-12
set port channel     5/1-4 off
set port channel     5/5-8 off
set port channel     5/9-12 off
set port channel     5/1-4 auto
set port channel     5/5-8 auto
set port channel     5/9-12 auto
set port enable  5/1-12
set port level   5/1-12  normal
set port duplex  5/1  full
set port duplex  5/2-12  half
set port trap        5/1-12  disable
set port name        5/1-12
set port security    5/1-12  disable
set port broadcast   5/1-12  100%
set port membership  5/1-12  static
set port negotiation 5/1-12 enable
set port flowcontrol send    5/1-12 off
set port flowcontrol receive 5/1-12 on
set cdp enable       5/1-12
set cdp interval     5/1-12 60
set trunk 5/1  off isl 1-1005
set trunk 5/2  auto negotiate 1-1005
set trunk 5/3  auto negotiate 1-1005
set trunk 5/4  auto negotiate 1-1005
set trunk 5/5  auto negotiate 1-1005
set trunk 5/6  auto negotiate 1-1005
set trunk 5/7  auto negotiate 1-1005
set trunk 5/8  auto negotiate 1-1005
set trunk 5/9  auto negotiate 1-1005
set trunk 5/10 auto negotiate 1-1005
set trunk 5/11 auto negotiate 1-1005
set trunk 5/12 auto negotiate 1-1005
set spantree portfast      5/1-12 disable
set spantree portcost      5/1-12  19
set spantree portpri       5/1-12  32
set spantree portvlanpri   5/1  0
set spantree portvlanpri   5/2  0
set spantree portvlanpri   5/3  0
set spantree portvlanpri   5/4  0
set spantree portvlanpri   5/5  0
set spantree portvlanpri   5/6  0
set spantree portvlanpri   5/7  0
set spantree portvlanpri   5/8  0
set spantree portvlanpri   5/9  0
set spantree portvlanpri   5/10 0
set spantree portvlanpri   5/11 0
set spantree portvlanpri   5/12 0
set spantree portvlancost 5/1  cost 18
set spantree portvlancost 5/2  cost 18
set spantree portvlancost 5/3  cost 18
set spantree portvlancost 5/4  cost 18
set spantree portvlancost 5/5  cost 18
set spantree portvlancost 5/6  cost 18
```

```
set spantree portvlancost 5/7  cost 18
set spantree portvlancost 5/8  cost 18
set spantree portvlancost 5/9  cost 18
set spantree portvlancost 5/10 cost 18
set spantree portvlancost 5/11 cost 18
set spantree portvlancost 5/12 cost 18
!
#switch port analyzer
!set span 1 1/1 both inpkts disable
set span disable
!
#cam
set cam agingtime 1,1003,1005 300
end
```

Sample Router Config

On a router, the defaults are left out of the configuration file, making it easy to read and hard to determine the default settings. On a switch, however, the defaults are listed in the configuration file, making it hard to read and easy to determine the default settings

Backing Up and Restoring a Configuration File

In the event a switch were to fail and then have to be replaced with an entirely new switch, it is a good idea to have a backup of the configuration file on a TFTP server. Thus, rather than having to configure the new switch from scratch, the file can be copied easily from the TFTP server. Once the configuration file has been completed with all the settings desired, the file can be backed up using the following commands.

For a supervisor engine I or II, the `write network` command is used. For example, to back up a configuration file with the name `switch.txt` to a TFTP server with address 172.16.1.10, the following would be entered:

```
Cat5000> (enable) write network
IP address or name of remote host? 172.16.1.10
Name of configuration file? switch.txt
Upload configuration to config-file-name on address (y/n) [n]? y
. . . . .
. . . . . . . . .
. . . . . . . . .
. .
/
Finished network upload. (124356 bytes)
Console> (enable)
```

For a supervisor engine III or a Catalyst 4000, the command `copy config tftp` is used in place of the `write network` command:

```
Cat5000> (enable) copy config tftp
IP address or name of remote host? 172.16.1.10
Name of configuration file? switch.txt
Upload configuration to config-file-name on address (y/n) [n]? y
. . . . .
. . . . . . . . . .
. . . . . . . . . .
. .
/
Finished network upload. (124356 bytes)
Cat5000> (enable)
```

These commands will back up the configuration file to the TFTP server. In the event that the configuration file is lost or the original switch fails, the file can be retrieved easily from the TFTP server. Use the `config network` command on a supervisor engine I or II or the `copy tftp config` command on a supervisor engine III or Catalyst 4000.

To restore a configuration file that was backed up previously, for a supervisor engine I or II, use

```
Cat5000> (enable) configure network
IP address or name of remote host []? 172.16.1.10
Name of file to copy from []? switch.txt

Configure using tftp:switch.txt (y/n) [n]? y
/
Finished network download. (124356 bytes)
```

For a supervisor engine III, use

```
Cat5000> (enable) copy tftp config
IP address or name of remote host []? 172.16.1.10
Name of file to copy from []? switch.txt

Configure using tftp:switch.txt (y/n) [n]? y
/
Finished network download. (124356 bytes)
```

BONEHEAD ALERT: *The new switch must have its interface sc0 configured with an IP address for connectivity to the TFTP server.*

It is important to note that the configuration files for the supervisor engines are *not* the configuration files used for the route switch module

(RSM) or ATM LANE card. These modules run Cisco IOS and have their own CLI and configuration files.

Managing the Catalyst IOS Files

The Catalyst IOS, as mentioned earlier, resides in both RAM and flash memory when the switch is powered on. To upgrade the version of Catalyst IOS on a switch, I recommend the following procedure:

Step 1: Decide on which version you would like to upgrade to and download it from Cisco.

Step 2: Set up the TFTP server, and place the Catalyst IOS image in the directory that is set up as the TFTP server.

Step 3: Back up the current version of Catalyst IOS in case there is a problem with the new version. Use the `show version` command to view the current version of Catalyst IOS:

```
Cat5000> (enable) sh ver
WS-C5000 Software, Version McpSW: 4.3(1a) NmpSW: 4.3(1a)
Copyright (c) 1995-1998 by Cisco Systems
NMP S/W compiled on Nov 23 1998, 15:22:34
MCP S/W compiled on Nov 23 1998, 15:19:30

System Bootstrap Version: 3.1.2

Hardware Version: 2.0  Model: WS-C5000  Serial #: 010847706

Mod     Port   Model       Serial #      Versions
-------  ------ ----------  -----------   ---------------------------------
1       2      WS-X5530    010847706     Hw : 2.0
                                         Fw : 3.1.2
                                         Fw1: 4.2(1)
                                         Sw : 4.3(1a)
2       24     WS-X5224    010904347     Hw : 1.4
                                         Fw : 3.1(1)
                                         Sw: 4.3(1a)
3       24     WS-X5224    010907441     Hw : 1.4
                                         Fw : 3.1(1)
                                         Sw : 4.3(1a)
5       12     WS-X5201R   009976930     Hw : 1.1
                                         Fw : 4.1(1)
                                         Sw : 4.3(1a)
        DRAM                    FLASH              NVRAM
Module  Total   Used    Free    Total   Used   Free   Total Used  Free
-------  ------- ------  ------  ------  -----  -----  ----- ----- ----
1       32640K  13309K  19331K  8192K   3979K  4213K  512K  113K  399K
Uptime is 0 day, 7 hours, 14 minutes
Cat5000> (enable)
```

To back up the image, use the `upload` command on a supervisor engine I or II or the `copy flash tftp` command on a supervisor engine III:

```
Cat5000> (enable) upload 172.16.10.1 sup-412a.img
Upload Module 1 image to sup-412.img on 172.16.10.1 (y/n) [n]?
 y -
Finished network upload. (2718432 bytes)
Cat5000> (enable)
```

The naming convention of the images from Cisco is too long for my taste, and I often change the names to a short but descriptive word. For instance, sup-412.img is Catalyst IOS version 4.1(2a) for a Supervisor Engine I or II.

Step 4: Download the new image into the switch. The command to copy an image into flash memory is either the `download` command on a supervisor engine I or II or the `copy tftp flash` command on a supervisor engine III. Depending on the model of supervisor engine, there can be several different areas of flash memory. Supervisor engines I and II have only one area of flash memory, thus making it easy to work with. To upgrade the Catalyst IOS of a supervisor engine I or II, use the `download` or `copy tftp flash` command:

```
Cat5000> (enable) copy tftp flash
Upload Module 1 image to sup-412.img on 172.16.10.1 (y/n) [n]?
 y -
Finished network upload. (2718432 bytes)
Cat5000> (enable)
```

Step 6: At this point the image has been loaded into flash memory, but the version of Catalyst IOS running is the version in RAM. To load the version of Catalyst IOS from flash memory to RAM, reset the switch using the `reset` command. The upgrade is now complete.

If there are any problems with the new version, repeat steps 5 and 6 with the old version of Catalyst IOS.

On a supervisor engine III, there are three areas of flash memory, as shown in Figure 7-4. When working with the image files on a supervisor engine III, the `copy` command is used:

```
Cat5000> (enable) copy [source-memory-area]:[file-name]
  [destination-memory-area]
```

To change the file name during the copy process, you can specify the destination file name:

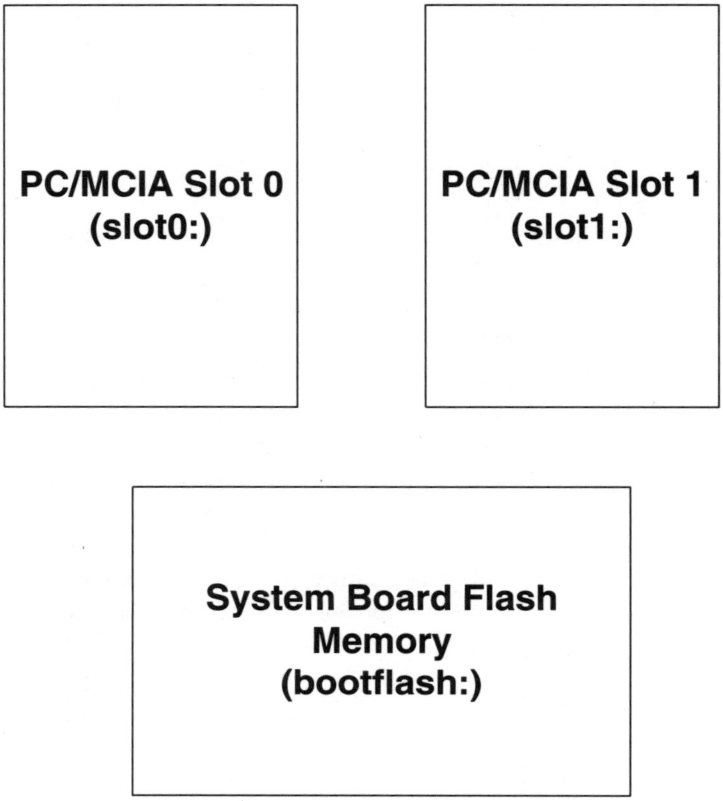

Figure 7-4
Flash Memory Areas
of a Supervisor
Engine III

```
┌─────────────────┐        ┌─────────────────┐
│                 │        │                 │
│ PC/MCIA Slot 0  │        │ PC/MCIA Slot 1  │
│    (slot0:)     │        │    (slot1:)     │
│                 │        │                 │
└─────────────────┘        └─────────────────┘

         ┌─────────────────────────┐
         │                         │
         │   System Board Flash    │
         │        Memory           │
         │     (bootflash:)        │
         │                         │
         └─────────────────────────┘
```

```
Cat5000> (enable) copy [source-memory-area]:[file-name]
    [destination-memory-area]:[new-file-name]
```

EXAMPLE

To move the image that resides in system flash memory to the PC/MCIA card in the second slot, the following command is used (Figure 7-5):

```
Cat5000> (enable) copy bootflash:sup-412a.img slot0:
```

An interesting feature of supervisor engine III's flash memory is its ability to store configuration files as well as Catalyst IOS images. The word `config` can be used to store configuration files in any of the memory areas. For example, to back up the configuration of a switch to the bootflash: device:

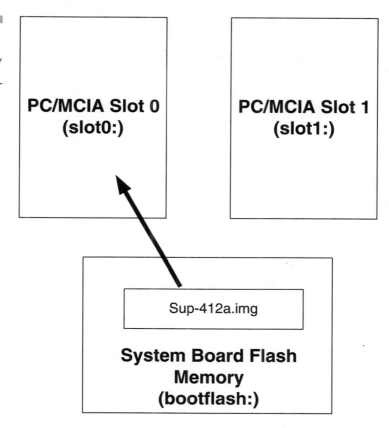

Figure 7-5
Moving the Image in
System Flash Memory
to the PC/MCIA Card

```
Cat5000> (enable) copy config flash
Flash device [bootflash]? bootflash:
Name of file to copy to [test_image]? Switch.txt
Upload configuration to bootflash:switch.txt
678324 bytes available on device slot1, proceed (y/n) [n]? y
. . . . . . . .
. . . . . . . . .
. . . . . . . . .
. . . . . . .
.
/
Configuration has been copied successfully. (175664 bytes).
Cat5000> (enable)
```

The copy command will prompt for the necessary parameters if they are
not specified.

The Boot System Command

When using a supervisor engine III with its various memory areas, it is possible to have multiple images in multiple areas. The `set boot system` command specifies the file to load as the operating system when the switch boots. The `set boot system` command also may be used to load the operating system from a TFTP server. The proper syntax of the command is

```
Cat5000> (enable) set boot system flash [memory area]:[filename]
```

EXAMPLE

The following command specifies to load the operating system from the file sup3-441.img that resides on the PCMCIA card in slot 0 when it boots the next time:

```
Cat5000> (enable) set boot system flash slot0:sup3-441.img
```

Multiple files may be listed to specify the order in which the switch will attempt to load the operating system in the event of a failure. If the first file is not present or corrupt, the second file will be attempted, and so on.

Configuring the Ethernet, Fast Ethernet, and Gigabit Ethernet Ports

Catalyst switches have line cards that support all Ethernet, Fast Ethernet, and Gigabit Ethernet applications, as discussed in Chapter 6. Any port other than an ATM port can have a name assigned to it. This can be very helpful when troubleshooting. Documenting the physical connectivity on the switch will save many hours of troubleshooting when something goes wrong. By default, there is no port name.

To set a port name, the command `set port name` is used:

```
Cat5000> (enable) set port name [module_number/port_number]
  [name_string]
```

EXAMPLE

To set a port name to "Connection to Backbone Catalyst 5500," the following is entered:

```
Cat5000> (enable) set port name 1/1 Connection to Backbone Catalyst
    5500
Port 1/1 name set.
```

A port's access to the backplane is determined by the *port priority* or *port level,* and there are three port priorities or port levels—normal, high, and critical. As mentioned in Chapter 5, the critical level is not configurable. However, to configure a port to either normal or high priority, the `set port level` command is used. The default port level is normal.

```
Cat5000> (enable) set port level [module_number/port_number]
    [Normal or High]
```

EXAMPLE

To configure the left-most port in slot 1 to high priority level, the following command is used:

```
Cat5000> (enable) set port level 1/1 high
Port 1/1 level set to high.
Cat5000> (enable)
```

Some of Catalyst line cards have ports that support either 10- or 100-Mb/s Ethernet. The command `set port speed` is used to configure the port's speed. There is also an automatic mode, in which the speed is negotiated with the hub or the directly connected neighbor. I have had numerous reports from students that this option will not work with certain NICs. The solution is to simply set the speed. By default, the port speed will be set to 100 Mb/s. If you are having connectivity problems, it might be a good idea to set the speed:

```
Cat5000> (enable) set port speed module_number/port_number
    [10/100/auto]
```

EXAMPLE

To set the port speed of the left-most port in slot 1 to 100 Mb/s, the following command is used:

```
Cat5000> (enable) set port speed 1/1 100
Port 1/1 speed set to 100 Mbps.
Cat5000> (enable)
```

Depending on which Catalyst line card is in use, the Ethernet and Fast Ethernet port may be configured for full-duplex operation. Gigabit Ethernet line cards do not support half-duplex. The set port duplex command can be used to set the duplex method of a port. By default, a 10-Mb/s-*only* port and a 100-Mb/s-*only* port will have the duplex method set to half-duplex.

```
Cat5000> (enable) set port duplex module_number/port_number [full |
  half]
```

EXAMPLE

To set the port duplex method of the left-most port in slot 1 to full-duplex, the following command is used:

```
Cat5000> (enable) set port duplex 1/1 full
Port 1/1 set to full-duplex.
Cat5000> (enable)
```

The 10/100-Mb/s Ethernet ports, by default, have their duplex method set to auto. These ports have their duplex method tied to the port's speed. If the port speed is set to auto, the port duplex will be AUTO. If the port's speed is set to either 10 or 100 Mb/s, the port duplex will default to half-duplex but can be changed to full-duplex. The port cannot be configure to automatically detect the duplex method when the port speed is set to auto.

BONEHEAD ALERT: *If one tries to improperly configure the port duplex method, an error will not be displayed. Instead, the switch simply will reply with the correct setting. This is confusing and frustrating to a lot of engineers. Following is an example of what is displayed when one tries to set the port duplex to full when the port speed is set to auto.*

```
Cat5000> (enable) set port duplex 1/1 full
Port 1/1 set to auto.
Cat5000> (enable)
```

To verify the settings, the command show port may be used:

```
Cat5000> (enable) show port <Enter>
Port Name              Status      Vlan   Level     Duplex   Speed Type
---- -------------- ---------- ----- -------- -------- ----- -------------
1/1  BB-Connection  connected 1       high      half      100 10/100BaseTX
1/2                 connected 1       normal    half      100 10/100BaseTX
2/1                 connected 1       normal    a-full  a-100 10/100BaseTX
2/2                 connected 1       normal    a-half   a-10 10/100BaseTX
2/3                 connected 1       normal    a-full  a-100 10/100BaseTX
2/4                 connected 1       normal    a-full  a-100 10/100BaseTX
2/5                 connected 1       normal    a-full  a-100 10/100BaseTX
2/6                 connected 1       normal    a-full  a-100 10/100BaseTX
2/7                 connected 1       normal    a-full  a-100 10/100BaseTX
2/8                 connected 1       normal    a-full  a-100 10/100BaseTX
2/9                 connected 1       normal    a-full  a-100 10/100BaseTX
2/10                connected 1       normal    a-full  a-100 10/100BaseTX
2/11                connected 1       normal    a-full  a-100 10/100BaseTX
2/12                connected 1       normal    a-full  a-100 10/100BaseTX
3/1                 connected 1       normal    half      100 FDDI
3/2                 connected 1       normal    half      100 FDDI
4/1                 connected trunk   normal    full      155 OC3 MMF ATM
4/2                 connected trunk   normal    full      155 OC3 MMF ATM
...
Cat5000> (enable)
```

Working with the Spanning Tree Protocol

A switch is a bridge and must run the Spanning Tree Protocol (STP). Catalyst switches run a version of STP for every VLAN. I realize that we have not yet discussed creating VLANs, But this is not necessary yet. Chapter 4 talked about the STP and all its related parameters. This section explains how to configure those parameters.

The root bridge is the bridge with the lowest priority. To change the bridge priority from the default of 32768, use the set spantree priority command:

```
Cat5000> (enable) set spantree priority [bridge_priority] [vlan]
```

If no VLAN is specified, this sets the bridge priority for VLAN 1.

BONEHEAD ALERT: *It is a common mistake to forget to specify the VLAN after the bridge priority. This can cause problems when you intend to configure another VLAN's bridge priority.*

EXAMPLE

To set a switch as the root for VLAN 10:

```
Cat5000> (enable) set spantree priority 1 10
```

This will set the bridge priority low enough that it will become the root bridge. If there is another bridge with its priority set to 1 for VLAN 10, the tiebreaker will be the MAC address.

The ports that will be placed in the forwarding state will be determined by several parameters, as mentioned earlier. Two of them are *port priority* and *port cost*. To set the port cost two commands may be used. If the port cost is going to be changed on a port for all VLANs, the command `set port cost` is used. However, if the port cost of a single VLAN is to be changed, then `set portvlan cost` is used. The default cost of a port is based on its bandwidth and typically is 1000/bandwidth, except for Fast Ethernet, which uses a default cost of 19 instead of 10.

To set the port cost for all VLANs:

```
Cat5000> (enable) set spantree portcost [module_number/port_number]
   [cost]
```

To set the port cost for a specific VLAN:

```
Cat5000> (enable) set spantree portvlancost [module_number/
   port_number] cost [cost] [VLAN]
```

EXAMPLE

To set the port cost of port 1/1 to 10 from the default value of 19 for all VLANs:

```
Cat5000> (enable) set spantree portcost 1/1 10
Spantree port 1/2 path cost set to 10.
```

To set the port cost of port 1/1 to 10 for only VLAN 1, leaving the port cost at 19 for all other VLANs:

```
Cat5000> (enable) set spantree portvlancost 1/2 cost 10 1
Port 1/1 VLANs 2-1005 have path cost 19.
Port 1/1 VLANs 1 have path cost 10.
Cat5000> (enable)
```

The port that is placed in the forwarding mode also can rely on the port priority. By default, all ports are set to a priority of 32 (1-63). The lower the priority, the better are the port's chances of being placed in the forwarding mode. The priority, like the port cost, can be configured for all VLANs or for a single VLAN with the set spantree portvlan priority and set spantree priority commands.

To set the priority of a port for all VLANs:

```
Cat5000> (enable) set spantree portpri mod_num/port_num priority
    [vlans]
```

To set the priority of a port for one VLAN:

```
Cat5000> (enable) set spantree portvlanpri mod_num/port_num priority
    [vlans]
```

EXAMPLE

To configure the 2/1 port with a priority of 1 for all VLANs:

```
Cat5000> (enable) set spantree portpri 2/1 1
Bridge port 2/1 port priority set to 1.
Cat5000> (enable)
```

To configure the 2/1 port with a priority of 1 for only VLAN 1:

```
Cat5000> (enable) set spantree portvlanpri 2/1 1 10
Port 2/1 vlans 1-9,11-1005 using portpri 32.
Port 2/1 vlans 10 using portpri 1
Cat5000> (enable)
```

A problem with switched Ethernet to the desktop, as mentioned in Chapter 2, and the listening and learning states that a port must traverse before being placed in the forwarding state can be remedied easily with the set spantree portfast command. This command causes the port to forward while it is listening and learning. Workstations connected to the port therefore will have connectivity to the appropriate servers while the BPDUs are being transmitted and the STP is making its calculations. This does not shut off the STP! If a loop is present, the switch will identify it and block on the culprit port. There may be a small loss of connectivity, but I have observed these times to be fewer than 10 seconds.

To enable a port to forward while in the listening and learning states:

```
Cat5000> (enable) set spantree portfast [module_number/port_number]
  [enable or disable]
```

EXAMPLE

If port 2/1 is connected directly to a workstation or server, it is not necessary to block during the listening and learning modes:

```
Cat5000> (enable) set spantree portfast 2/1 enable
Warning: Spantree port fast start should only be enabled on ports
connected to a single host. Connecting hubs, concentrators, switch-
es, bridges, etc. to a fast start port can cause temporary spanning
tree loops. Use with caution.
Spantree port 2/1 fast start enabled.
```

These parameters can all be viewed with the show spantree command:

```
Cat5000> (enable) show spantree [module/number] [vlan_number]
```

EXAMPLE

To view the STP settings for the 2/1 port:

```
Cat5000> (enable) show spantree 2/1
Port     Vlan    Port-State      Cost  Priority  Fast-Start Group-method
-------- ------- --------------- ----  --------  ---------- -----------
2/1      1       forwarding      10    32        enabled
2/1      10      forwarding      19    1         enabled
2/1      20      forwarding      19    1         enabled
2/1      30      forwarding      19    1         enabled
2/1      40      forwarding      19    1         enabled
2/1      1003    not-connected   19    1         enabled
2/1      1005    not-connected   19    1         enabled
Console> (enable)
```

To view the spanning tree statistics for all the ports of VLAN 1:

```
Cat5000> show spantree 1
VLAN 1
Spanning tree enabled

Designated Root                 00-40-0b-73-64-c2
Designated Root Priority        1
Designated Root Cost            0
Designated Root Port            1/0
Root Max Age   6  sec    Hello Time 2  sec    Forward Delay 4  sec
```

```
Bridge ID MAC ADDR          00-40-0b-73-64-c2
Bridge ID Priority          1
Bridge Max Age 6  sec     Hello Time 2  sec    Forward Delay 4  sec

Port     Vlan    Port-State      Cost Priority Fast-Start Group-method
------   ------  ------------   ------ --------- ----------- -----------
1/1       1      forwarding       10      1       enabled
1/2       1      forwarding       10      32      enabled
2/1       1      forwarding       10      32      enabled
2/2       1      forwarding       10      32      enabled
2/3       1      forwarding       10      32      enabled
2/4       1      forwarding       10      32      enabled
2/5       1      forwarding       10      32      enabled
2/6       1      forwarding       10      32      enabled
2/7       1      forwarding       10      32      enabled
2/8       1      forwarding       10      32      enabled
2/9       1      forwarding       10      32      enabled
2/10      1      forwarding       10      32      enabled
2/11      1      forwarding       10      32      enabled
2/12      1      forwarding       10      32      enabled
3/1-2     1      forwarding       10      32      enabled
```

This show screen can be very helpful when troubleshooting an STP problem. The designated root port is the port that is the closest to the root bridge. In this case it is the 1/0 port. There is no 1/0 port! This indicates that this switch is the root bridge for VLAN 1. However, this switch may not be the root bridge for VLAN 10. This show screen also gives the MAC address and priority of the root bridge. This information will be helpful when determining what priority at which to place a switch if that switch is to be made the root.

Uplink Fast

Uplink Fast is a Cisco proprietary feature to increase the convergence time for the STP when a failure is detected and to provide load balancing over the redundant paths. It is only useful when redundant connections are used and therefore should never be configured on a port that is connected directly to a switch or a server (if there are multiple links, Fast EtherChannel should be used).

Figure 7-6 shows a redundant configuration. The four switches are connected together via four uplink ports. If all ports were configured for Uplink Fast and U1 were to fail, the blocking path, U2, would be placed in the forwarding state without passing through the listening and learning states, thus increasing the recovery time. According to the Cisco documentation, this usually occurs within 5 seconds (Figure 7-7).

The proper syntax for configuring Uplink Fast is

Figure 7-6
Uplink Fast
Connection

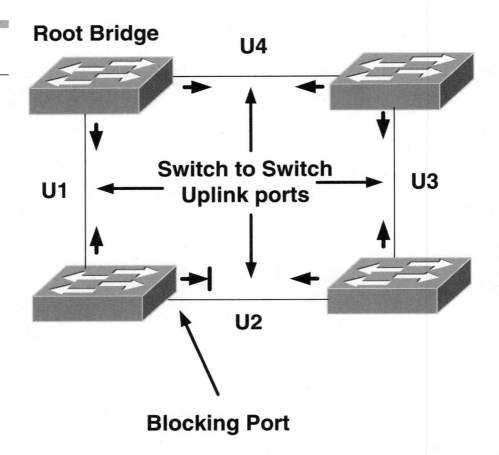

Root Bridge

U4

**Switch to Switch
Uplink ports**

U1

U3

U2

Blocking Port

```
Cat5000> (enable) set spantree uplinkfast enable
VLANs 1-1005 bridge priority set to 49152.
The port cost and portvlancost of all ports set to above 3000.
Station update rate set to 15 packets/100ms.
uplinkfast all-protocols field set to off.
uplinkfast enabled for bridge.
Cat5000> (enable)
```

There is no way to configure Uplink Fast on only a single port. Uplink Fast sets the bridge priority and port costs to extremely large values to reduce the chances that they will be selected as the root bridge. This configuration is only recommended in the wiring closet by Cisco Systems.

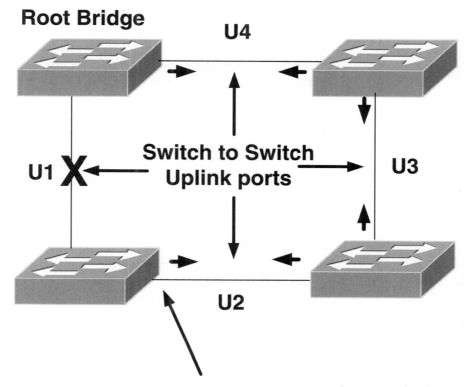

Figure 7-7
A Failure Occurs
in U1

Root Bridge

U4

**Switch to Switch
Uplink ports**

U1 **X**

U3

U2

**Blocking Port bypasses the listening
and learning modes and proceeds
directly to the Forwarding State**

SUMMARY

The Cisco Catalyst command line interface (CLI) was designed to look and feel like the true Cisco IOS, but it has many differences. This chapter explored working with the CLI. The one interesting difference between the Cisco IOS and the Catalyst IOS is the Catalyst IOS's use of the set command rather than the configuration modes of Cisco IOS. The configuration file also is very large compared with that of a router.

The architecture of a Catalyst switch also resembles that of a Cisco Router. Flash memory, NVRAM, and RAM serve basically the same purpose on Catalyst switches that they do on a Cisco router. This chapter examined the commands to work with these areas of memory.

Management of a switch can be achieved through use of an SNMP management server or the CLI. The CLI can be accessed via the console port or through the IP application Telnet. The interface sc0 is a virtual interface configured on the switch to allow IP connectivity for SNMP or Telnet access to the switch. Remote access via a POTS line can be achieved through use of interface sl0.

Security of a switch is controlled by two passwords. The user mode password is necessary to log in to user mode, whereas the privileged mode or enable password is necessary to log in to privileged mode or enable mode (that was simple!). Additional security can be created by using an IP permit list (not an access list).

The Spanning Tree Protocol (STP) can be difficult to manage when there are many VLANs configured on a switch. With one STP per VLAN, it is recommended to keep the STP customization to a minimum to prevent unwanted administrative overhead. The Portfast and Uplink Fast features of the switch can reduce the length of time it takes a port to go into the forwarding mode.

EXERCISES

1. Describe the requirements for a Catalyst switch to perform a RARP or BOOTP to resolve its IP address during the boot procedure.

2. What password(s) is(are) required to log into a switch and view parameters? What mode is this called?

3. What password(s) is(are) required to log into a switch and change the configuration file? What mode is this called? What is(are) the command(s) to configure these password(s)?

4. Why must one type quickly to perform password recovery? What shortcuts can you think of to speed password recovery?

5. Why is it suggested that the SNMP parameters be changed from the default values?

6. Why is it suggested that only the default gateway be configured as opposed to individual routes? What is the command to configure the default gateway of a switch to 172.16.1.64 255.255.255.192?

7. Given the following output, what is the MAC address that will be used by this switch when performing a RARP or BOOTP?

```
Cat5000> (enable) sh module
Mod Module-Name          Ports Module-Type            Model      Serial-Num Status
--- -------------------- ----- -------------- --------- ---------- ---------- -------
1                        2     1000BaseSX Supervisor WS-X5530   010847706 ok
2                        24    10/100BaseTX Ethernet WS-X5224   010904347 ok
3                        24    10/100BaseTX Ethernet WS-X5224   010907441 ok
5                        12    100BaseFX MM Ethernet WS-X5201R 009976930 ok

Mod MAC-Address(es)                            Hw    Fw      Sw
--- ---------------------------------------- ----- ------- ----------------
1   00-30-56-76-7c-00 to 00-30-56-76-7f-ff  2.0   3.1.2   4.3(1a)
2   00-10-7b-e9-83-e8 to 00-10-7b-e9-83-ff  1.4   3.1(1)  4.3(1a)
3   00-50-a2-30-84-c0 to 00-50-a2-30-84-d7  1.4   3.1(1)  4.3(1a)
5   00-60-70-99-f0-1c to 00-60-70-99-f0-27  1.1   4.1(1)  4.3(1a)

Mod Sub-Type Sub-Model Sub-Serial Sub-Hw
--- -------- --------- ---------- -------
1   EARL 1 + WS-F5520  0010851091 1.1
1   uplink   WS-U5534  0009999149 1.0
Cat5000> (enable)
```

8. What is the alternative to using a DNS server to resolve addresses on a Catalyst switch?

9. In what area of memory is the configuration file of a Catalyst switch stored? What is the command to copy the configuration file from RAM to NVRAM?

10. Why are the ATM ports not configured on the CLI of a Catalyst switch?

11. Describe the differences between the flash memory areas of a supervisor engine I or II compared with a supervisor engine III? What are the different memory areas called, and where do they reside physically?

12. Why is it important to configure a port name on a Catalyst switch? What is the command to name a port?

13. What are the default costs of Ethernet, Fast Ethernet, Gigabit Ethernet, FDDI, and 16-Mb/s Token Ring ports (your answer should be based on the typical method)?

14. Given the following configuration commands:

```
Cat5000> (enable) set port speed 1/1 100
Cat5000> (enable) set port duplex 3/1 auto
```

what duplex method will be used by the 3/1 port? What speed will be used by the 3/1 port?

15. What is the difference between the `set spantree portcost` command and the `set spantree portvlancost` command? What is the difference between the `set spantree priority` command and the `set spantree portvlan priority` command?

16. What is the default STP priority of a port? What does it mean?

17. Why is the `set spantree portfast` command used only with connections to servers, workstations, and routers, not hubs or switches?

18. What are the advantages and disadvantages to using Uplink Fast?

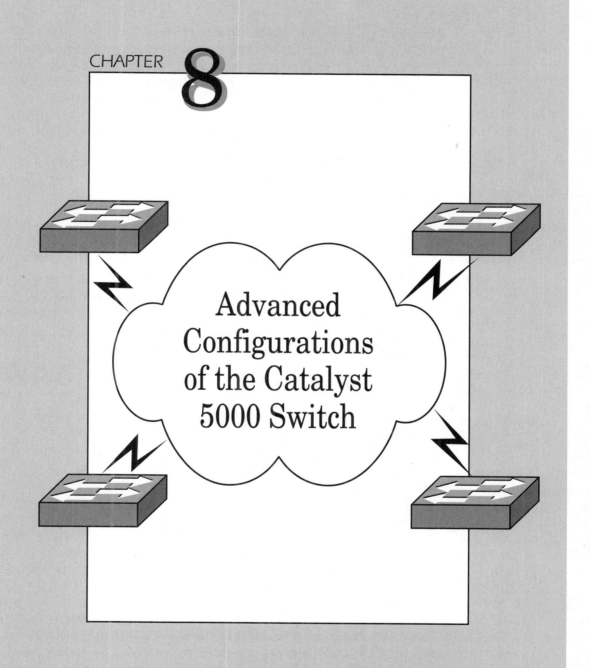

Advanced
Configurations
of the Catalyst
5000 Switch

Chapter 7 gave the commands for configuring a Catalyst switch to operate in a single virtual local-area network (VLAN) environment. This chapter explores configuration commands for a multi-VLAN environment as well as some sample "real world" configurations. Proprietary features such as Dynamic VLANs and Fast EtherChannel also will be discussed.

VLAN Trunking Protocol (VTP)

Two steps are required to create and implement VLANs:

1. Create the VLAN (the `set vlan` command, discussed later).
2. Assign the appropriate ports to the VLAN (also the `set vlan` command).

A switch will have a list of VLANs that it knows exist and will have its ports assigned to some or all of the VLANs in the list. VLANs that have ports assigned to them are said to be *active VLANs* on the switch to which the ports are assigned. It is possible for a switch to have one or more VLANs in its VLAN list and *not* have ports assigned to them. These VLANs are often referred to as *transit VLANs*. A transit VLAN is known to the switch but has no ports assigned to it so that VLAN traffic can pass through the switch's trunk ports. In Figure 8-1, switch B has no ports assigned to VLAN 20, but VLAN 20 appears in the VLAN list. Switch B must know about VLAN 20 to properly recognize traffic coming from switches A and C that are tagged VLAN 20. Switch B only forwards these frames out its trunk ports because it has no ports assigned to VLAN 20. VLAN 20 is said to be a *transit VLAN* on switch B.

When VLANs are configured on a Catalyst switch, several parameters may be defined. The VLAN number is the parameter that uniquely identifies the broadcast domain. The VLAN name is an optional parameter for documentation purposes. All ports that are to be in the same broadcast domain are assigned to the same VLAN number; the switch does not assign ports based on VLAN name. When VLANs span multiple switches, it is helpful to have these parameters consistent. The *VLAN Trunking Protocol (VTP)* is a protocol to exchange information about VLANs between switches to keep VLANs consistent. For example, if two switches are configured to trunk, switch A has two

Figure 8-1
Active and Transit
VLANs

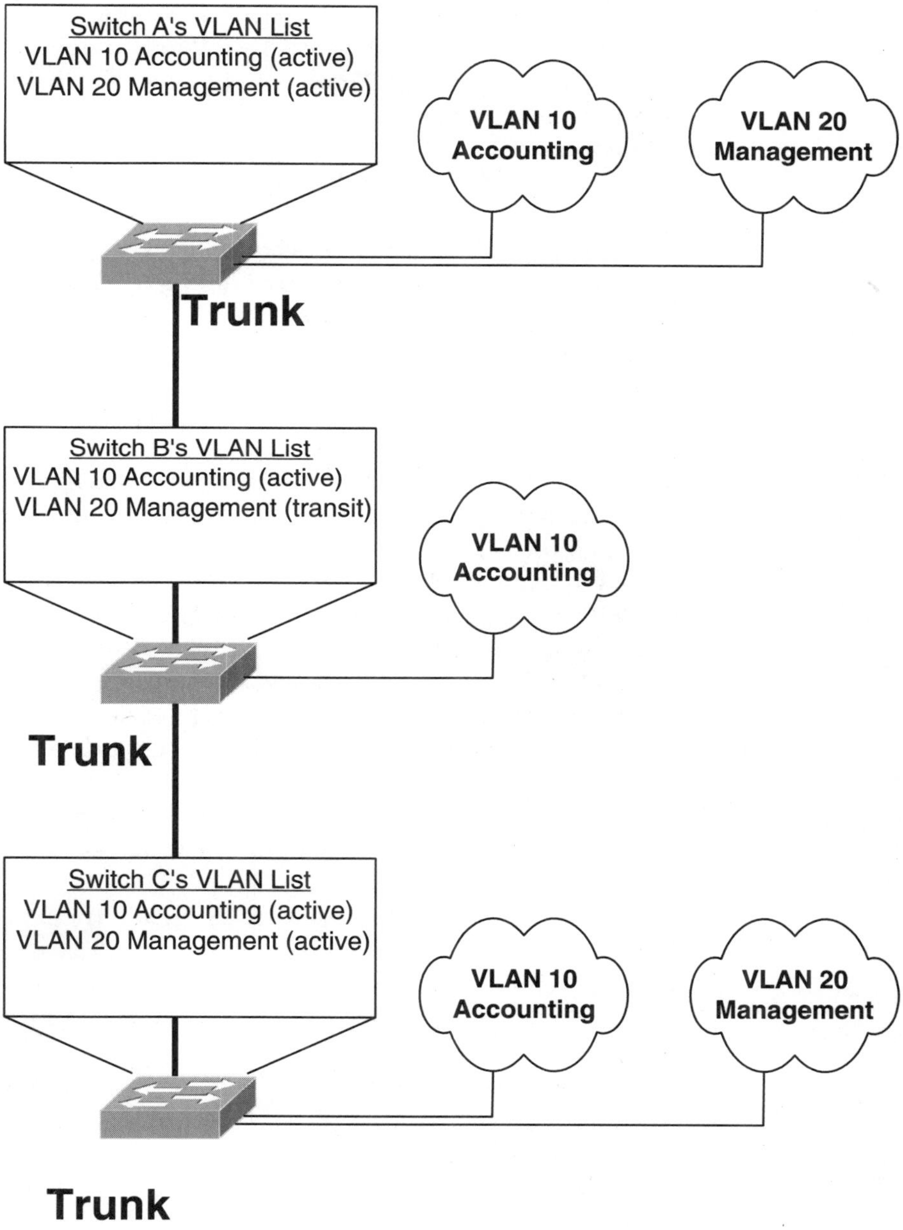

Switch A's VLAN List
VLAN 10 Accounting (active)
VLAN 20 Management (active)

VLAN 10
Accounting

VLAN 20
Management

Trunk

Switch B's VLAN List
VLAN 10 Accounting (active)
VLAN 20 Management (transit)

VLAN 10
Accounting

Trunk

Switch C's VLAN List
VLAN 10 Accounting (active)
VLAN 20 Management (active)

VLAN 10
Accounting

VLAN 20
Management

Trunk

VLANs, VLAN 10, named Accounting, and VLAN 20, named Management. Switch B has the same two VLAN numbers but different names. VLAN 10 is named Management, and VLAN 20 is named Accounting—perhaps because of a configuration error on someone's part (see Figure 8-2).

I realize that this is not a large issue, but it could lead to further configuration errors and lengthy troubleshooting in the future. Remember that documentation is very important for troubleshooting and future configurations. By naming a VLAN, you are creating documentation.

VTP is a protocol that runs *only* over trunk lines to exchange information about VLANs between switches to ensure that VLANs are consistent. The problem is automatically corrected by a VTP update, as shown in Figures 8-3 and 8-4.

When the VTP update is sent by switch 1 to switch 2, switch 2 changes its VLAN configuration to match that of switch 1. This ensures that VLANs are kept consistent (Figure 8-4).

Without VTP, an engineer would have to physically go to each switch's CLI and configure a new VLAN. With VTP, new VLAN data are automatically propagated out all trunk lines, making it unnecessary to create VLANs on multiple switches. In Figure 8-5, an engineer configures VLAN 30 with the name of Engineering on switch 1.

A VTP update is sent from switch 1 immediately. VTP uses *flash updates,* meaning that updates are sent immediately after a VLAN configuration change. When switch 2 receives the VTP update from switch 1, it updates its VLAN configuration and sends a VTP update to switch 3 (Figure 8-6).

When switch 3 receives the VTP update from switch 2 (Figure 8-7), it updates its VLAN configuration, and all three switches have a consistent configuration for VLAN 30. By configuring VLAN 30 on a single switch and using VTP updates, a consistent configuration for VLAN 30 has been created. With only three switches, you may not be impressed. However, when there are 40 switches, you will be singing a different tune!

There are currently two versions of VTP—version 1 and version 2 (very imaginative). By default, a switch will run VTP version 1, but it may be configured to run version 2. There are several differences between version 1 and version 2, but the main difference is version 2's support of Token Ring VLANs.

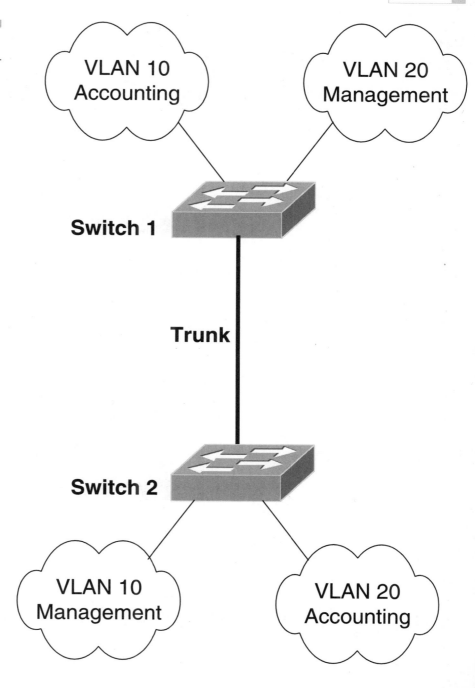

Figure 8-2
Misconfigured VLANs

Figure 8-3
AVTP Update Is Sent

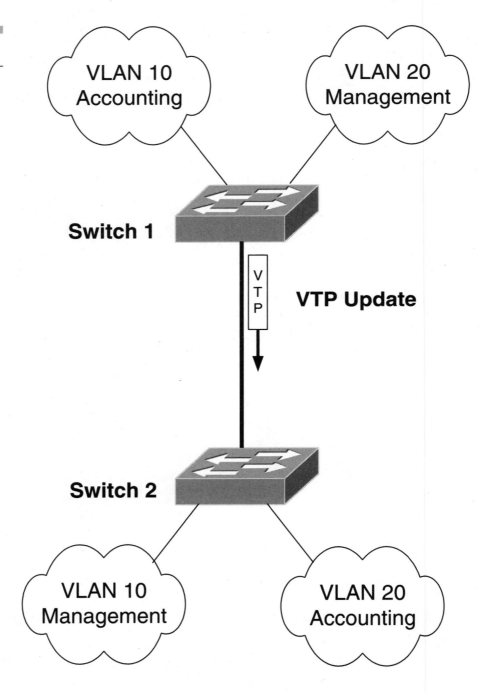

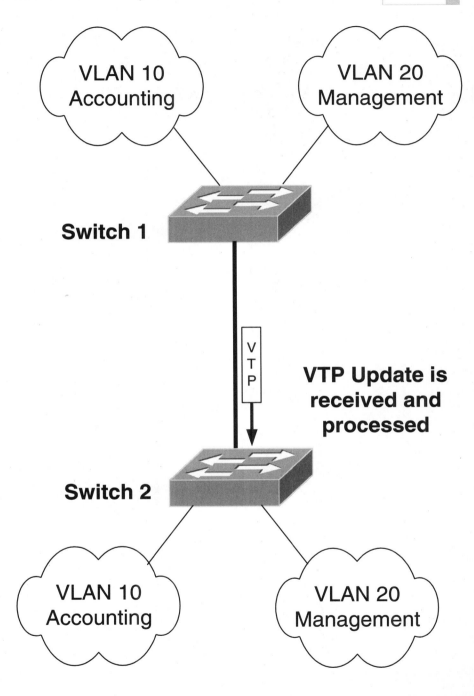

Figure 8-4
The VTP Update
Is Received and the
VLAN Names
Are Synchronized

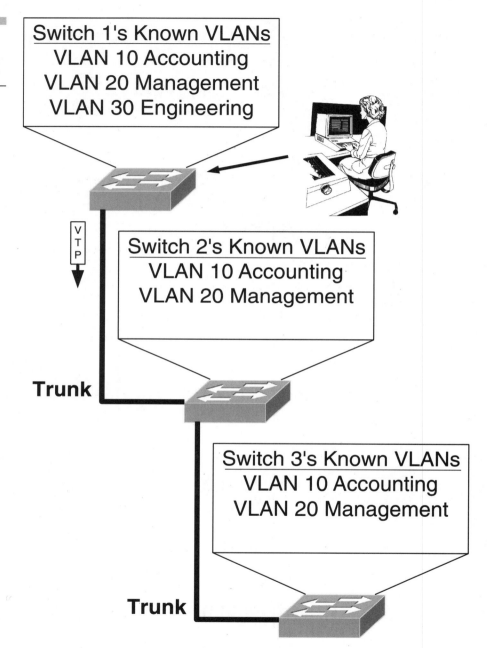

Switch 1's Known VLANs
VLAN 10 Accounting
VLAN 20 Management
VLAN 30 Engineering

V
T
P

Switch 2's Known VLANs
VLAN 10 Accounting
VLAN 20 Management

Trunk

Switch 3's Known VLANs
VLAN 10 Accounting
VLAN 20 Management

Trunk

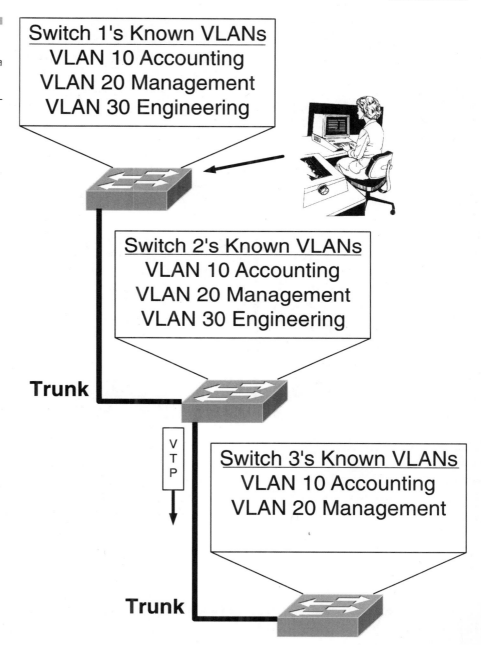

Figure 8-6
The VLAN Configuration Is Updated and a VTP Updates Is Sent to Switch 3

Switch 1's Known VLANs
VLAN 10 Accounting
VLAN 20 Management
VLAN 30 Engineering

Switch 2's Known VLANs
VLAN 10 Accounting
VLAN 20 Management
VLAN 30 Engineering

Trunk

V
T
P

Switch 3's Known VLANs
VLAN 10 Accounting
VLAN 20 Management

Trunk

Figure 8-7
Switch 3 Receives the VTP Update and Updates Its VLAN Configuration

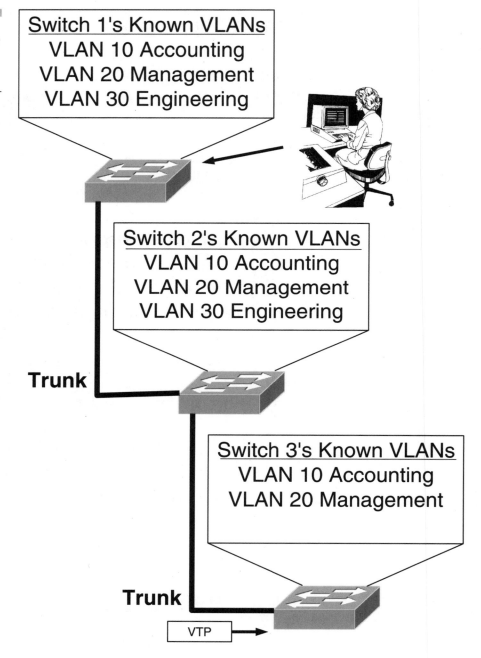

Switch 1's Known VLANs
VLAN 10 Accounting
VLAN 20 Management
VLAN 30 Engineering

Switch 2's Known VLANs
VLAN 10 Accounting
VLAN 20 Management
VLAN 30 Engineering

Trunk

Switch 3's Known VLANs
VLAN 10 Accounting
VLAN 20 Management

Trunk

VTP

VTP Modes

A switch can be in one of three VTP modes.

A switch in the *VTP server mode,* which is the default, sends updates out all its trunk ports, reads and learns from the updates it receives on its trunk ports, and can have VLANs configured on its CLI.

Figure 8-8
Broadcast from VLAN 20 Is Received by Switch A

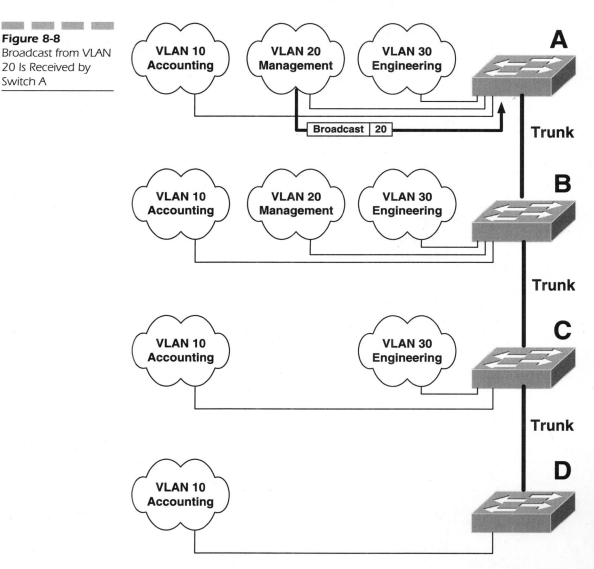

A switch in the *VTP client mode* sends updates out all its trunk ports, reads and learns from the updates it receives on its trunk ports, and *cannot* have VLANs configured on its CLI. This mode is ideal for a switch that may be in a remote wiring closet where major configuration changes, such as adding or deleting VLANs, are unwise because of the inability to judge the impact of such changes.

A switch in the VTP transparent mode does not listen to VTP updates received on its trunk ports but forwards any updates it receives from another switch in its management domain. I have been unable to ascertain the purpose of this mode, nor have the 600 or so students I have had while teaching the Authorized Catalyst LAN Switching Class (CLSC). The only reason that I mention it is that it may be asked on the CLSC written exam for CCNP.

VTP Pruning

VTP pruning is a feature of VTP that reduces unwanted traffic on trunk lines. In Figure 8-8, switch A receives a broadcast from a VLAN 20 port.

Switch A forwards the broadcast out VLAN 20 ports and all trunk ports, in this case the trunk port to switch B (see Fig. 8-9), which will do the same, i.e., forward the broadcast out all VLAN 20 ports and all trunk ports (except the trunk port on which it was received).

Switch C repeats the same process, except that it has no ports in VLAN 20, so it only forwards frames to all trunk ports (see Figure 8-10).

When switch D receives the broadcast for VLAN 20, it discards it because it has no ports in VLAN 20 or trunk ports other than the one on which the broadcast was received (see Figure 8-11). The broadcast traffic coming from switch B to switch C and then from switch C to switch D is unnecessary. VTP pruning enables the switch to not forward the unnecessary traffic. By exchanging information about active VLANs, switches can determine whether traffic is necessary. In this example, with VTP pruning enabled the unnecessary traffic would not be forwarded.

Management Domains

Cisco's implementation of VLANs in a multiswitch environment uses the concept of a *management domain*. The management domain is to switches what an autonomous system is to routers. It is a group of

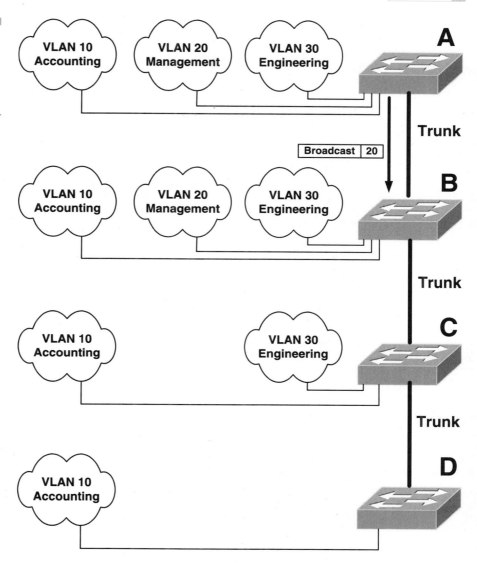

Figure 8-9
The Broadcast from
VLAN 20 Is
Forwarded by Switch
A to All VLAN 20 and
Trunk Ports

switches under a common administration. Only instead of sending routing updates to one another, they send VTP updates via trunk lines. In
the preceding section I talked about the VLAN Trunking Protocol (VTP).
It is this protocol that runs over the trunk lines to exchange information
about VLANs between switches.

When running IGRP or EIGRP on a Cisco router, all routers must be
configured with the same autonomous system number. All Catalyst

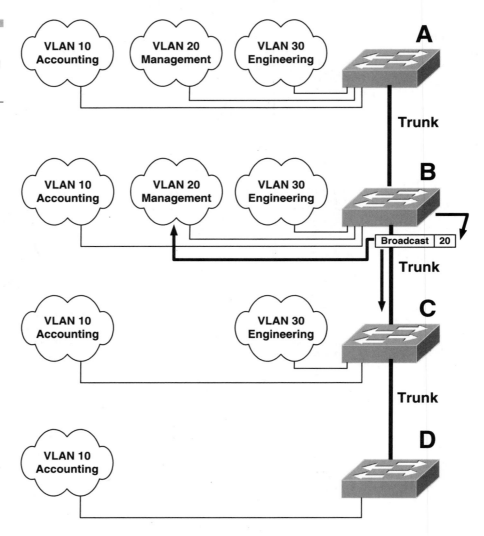

Figure 8-10
Switch B Forwards
the Broadcast Out All
VLAN 20 and Trunk
Ports

switches that exchange VTP updates must be configured with the same management domain name and must be connected together via trunks. In Figure 8-12, there are three management domains.

Switch E has no trunk lines and therefore will not send any VTP updates. In contrast, switches A, B, C, and D are connected together via trunk lines, so these switches will have to be configured with the same management domain name so that they can all learn about each other's VLAN lists. Switches F, G, H, and I are also connected together via

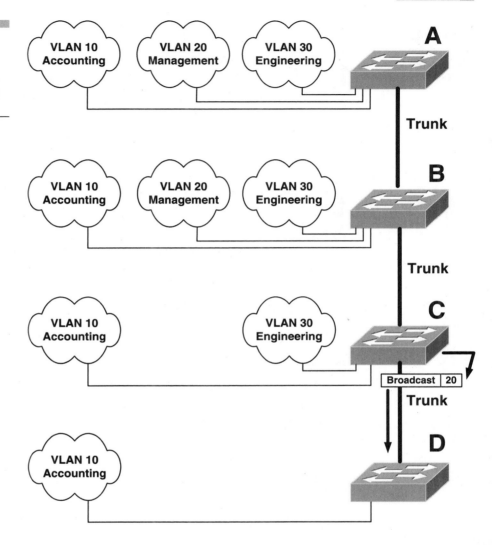

Figure 8-11
Switch C Does Not
Have Any VLAN 20
Ports, but Does For-
ward the Broadcast
to Switch D

trunk lines and thus are also in the same management domain. The
third management domain is switch E itself. Although this switch does
not send updates, it still most likely will have VLANs other than VLAN
1, the default. For a switch to have any VLANs other than VLAN 1, it
must be configured as part of a management domain, even if it is the
only switch in the management domain. If you were to attempt to configure a VLAN using the `set vlan` command (discussed later), the following error would be displayed:

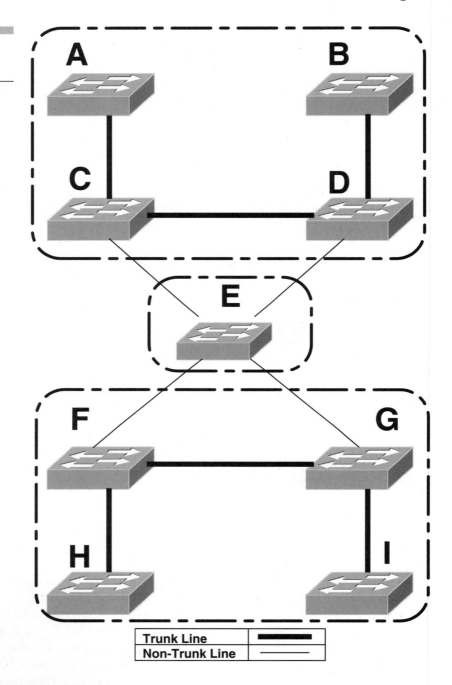

Figure 8-12
Management
Domains

```
Switch_A> (enable) set vlan 10
Cannot add/modify VLANs on a VTP server without a domain name.
Switch_A> (enable)
```

Switches connected to an existing management domain automatically join the management domain if it is an unsecured management domain. The thought process behind this "feature" was the ability of new switches to learn all new VLANs without having to configure each new switch with even so much as a management domain name.

TECH TIP: *At the time of this writing, this "feature" is extremely dangerous and can result in all VLANs, except VLAN 1, being erased from the existing management domain. When VLANs are erased from the VLAN list of a switch, all ports assigned to those VLANs are placed in the "inactive" state; i.e., they do not work anymore. This brings down all VLANs except VLAN 1, a situation that is undesirable, to say the least. When a new switch is added to an existing management domain, I recommend manually configuring that switch with all VLANs. Do not depend on VTP!*

Routers may be connected to switches via trunk lines, but they do not listen to or forward VTP updates. Therefore, they will create management domain segmentation. In Figure 8-13, router E is configured to trunk on all ports.

Router E does not pass the VTP updates and will segment the network into four separate management domains.

Configuring Management Domains

A switch need only be configured with a management domain name to have multiple VLANs configured and pass VTP updates. The management domain name is *case sensitive*. Do *not* learn this the hard way. The set vtp domain command is used to configure several VTP parameters, including the management domain name:

```
console> (enable) set vtp domain [name]
```

For example, to configure switches A and B in Figure 8-14 to be in management domain ACC (note the case), the following command is used:

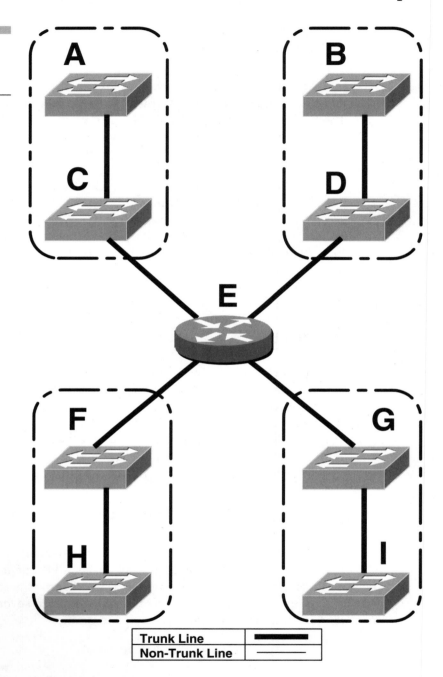

Figure 8-13
Routers and
Management
Domains

Trunk Line	▬▬▬▬
Non-Trunk Line	────

Figure 8-14
Configuring Switches
A and B to Be in
Management
Domain ACC

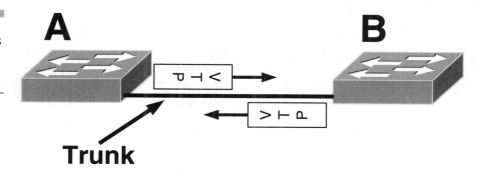

Trunk

```
Switch_A> (enable) set vtp domain ACC
VTP domain ACC modified
Switch_A> (enable)
```

It is not necessary to configure the VTP domain name on switch B because switch B automatically joins the management domain via trunk-line switch A.

To set the VTP mode of a switch, the `set vtp mode` command is used. The default mode is server.

```
Switch_A> (enable) set vtp mode [mode]
```

For example, to change the VTP mode to client for switch A:

```
Switch_A> (enable) set vtp mode client
VTP domain ACC modified
Switch_A> (enable) set vlan 30
Cannot add/modify VLANs on a VTP client.
Switch_A> (enable)
```

Once the mode has been set, the switch no longer allows modifications to the VLAN configuration. To restore the ability to modify the VLAN configuration, simply change the mode back to server.

Configuring Secure Management Domains

In the event that you do not want new switches to automatically join a management domain, a password may be configured. When the password is set, a new switch will be unable to join the existing management domain until it has been configured with the correct password. This ensures that someone has taken the time to configure the new switch.

To secure a management domain, the domain name and password must be configured on each switch in the domain.

To configure the ACC management domain to be a secure domain, the following must be completed:

On switch A:

```
Switch_A> (enable) set vtp domain ACC passwd TobaccoRoad
Generating MD5 secret for the password ....
VTP domain ACC modified
Switch_A> (enable)
```

On switch B:

```
Switch_B> (enable) set vtp domain ACC passwd TobaccoRoad
Generating MD5 secret for the password ....
VTP domain ACC modified
Switch_B> (enable)
```

TECH TIP: *Note the syntax of the command carefully. When specifying the password, the command is* passwd, *not password!*

Configuring VTP Version 2

Catalyst switches that are capable of VTP version 2, by default, do not have these capabilities enabled. When enabling the VTP version 2 capabilities on one switch, VTP advertisements will be sent, and all switches will enable VTP version 2. If there is a switch in the management domain that does not support VTP version 2, that switch will not be able to communicate with the rest of the switches. Do not enable VTP version 2 unless all switches are capable of VTP version 2.

To enable the VTP version 2 capabilities of a Catalyst switch:

```
Switch_A> (enable) set vtp v2 enable
This command will enable the version 2 function in the entire man-
agement domain.
All devices in the management domain should be version2-capable
before enabling.
Do you want to continue (y/n) [n]? y
VTP domain ACC modified
Switch_A> (enable)
```

Configuring VTP Pruning

VTP pruning is disabled by default and must be set manually on one switch in each management domain. VTP pruning cannot be configured on one or two switches in a management domain. If one switch is configured with VTP pruning, all switches in that management domain will be configured with VTP pruning. The proper syntax of the command is

```
console> (enable) set vtp pruning enable <enter>
```

For example, to configure VTP pruning on the ACC management domain, enter

```
Switch_A> (enable) set vtp pruning enable
This command will enable the pruning function in the entire
  management domain.
All devices in the management domain should be pruning-capable
  before enabling.
Do you want to continue (y/n) [n]? y
VTP domain ACC modified
Switch_A> (enable)
```

The warning message informs the user that VTP pruning will be activated in the entire management domain and all switches must be capable of VTP pruning. If one switch is running VTP version 1, it would not be capable of using VTP pruning, and this may create problems.

Verifying the VTP Settings

To verify the VTP settings on a switch, the show vtp domain and show vtp statistics commands can be used:

```
Switch_A> (enable) sh vtp domain
Domain Name                 Domain Index VTP Version  Local Mode Password
---------------------       ------------ -----------  ---------- ---------
ACC                         1            2            server     configured

Vlan-count   Max-vlan-storage   Config Revision   Notifications
------------ ------------------ ----------------- -------------
7            1023               4                 disabled

Last Updater    V2 Mode    Pruning    PruneEligible on Vlans
--------------- ---------- ---------  ------------------------
172.16.0.10     enabled    enabled    2-1000
Switch_A> (enable)
```

TABLE 8-1

Output of the
`show vtp`
`domain`
Command

Title	Description
Domain Name	The name of the management domain to which this switch belongs
Domain Index	An index number to identify the domain VTP Version. The switch is either capable or incapable of handling version 2
Local Mode	The VTP mode of this switch
Password	The management domain is secure or not
VLAN-count	The number of VLANs defined in the management domain
Max-VLAN-storage	The maximum number of VLANs that can be configured in this management domain
Config Revision	A revision number so as to sequence VTP updates
Notifications	SNMP notifications are enabled or not enabled
Last Updater	The last switch to send this switch a VTP update
V2 Mode	V2 mode is enabled or not enabled
Pruning	VTP pruning is enabled or not enabled
PruneEligible on VLANs	VLANs eligible to be pruned on this switch's trunk ports

Table 8-1 defines `show vtp domain` output.

Configuring VLANs

Once the management domain has been created, VLANs may be created. There are five properties of a VLAN that can be defined when creating the VLAN (Table 8-2).

In order to set the VLAN number and name, the following syntax is used:

```
Switch_A> (enable) set vlan [vlan_number] name [VLAN_name]
```

For example, to create a VLAN numbered 10 and named FSU and a VLAN numbered 20 and named Duke:

Table 8-2

VLAN Parameters

Parameter	Description
Number	The VLAN number is a unique number on the management domain to identify the broadcast domain.
Type	The VLAN type defines the type of VLAN. When using Ethernet or FDDI, the VLAN type will be "Ethernet." When trunking over FDDI, the VLAN type will be FDDI. When using Token Ring, the VLAN type will be either TR-CRF or TR-BRF.
Name	The VLAN name is for documentation purposes and has no functional effect on the switch.
MTU	The maximum transmission unit (MTU) of frames for the VLAN.
SAID	Security association and identifier (used for FDDI only).

```
Switch_A> (enable) set vlan 10 name FSU
Vlan 10 configuration successful
Switch_A> (enable) set vlan 20 name Duke
Vlan 20 configuration successful
```

The show vlan command can be used to verify the VLAN settings:

```
Switch_A> (enable) sh vlan
VLAN    Name                     Status   IfIndex  Mod/Ports, Vlans
-----   ----------------------   -------  -------  ----------------
1       default                  active   5        1/1-2
                                                   3/1-24
                                                   5/1-12

10      FSU                      active   46
20      Duke                     active   47
1002    fddi-default             active   6
1003    token-ring-default       active   9
1004    fddinet-default          active   7
1005    trnet-default            active   8
```

Once the VLAN has been created on one switch, it will be advertised via VTP to all switches in the management domain.

To assign ports to a VLAN, the set vlan command is used again with a different syntax:

```
Switch_A> (enable) set vlan [vlan_num] [module/ports]
```

Multiple ports may be listed with a hyphen, if they are in numerical order, or a comma.

For example, to assign the first 12 ports on module 3 to VLAN 10 and the last 12 ports on module 3 to VLAN 20:

```
Switch_A> (enable) set vlan 10 3/1-12
VLAN 10 modified.
VLAN 1 modified.
VLAN  Mod/Ports
----  ----------------------
10    3/1-12

Switch_A> (enable) set vlan 20 3/13-23,24
VLAN 20 modified.
VLAN 1 modified.
VLAN  Mod/Ports
----  ----------------------
20    3/13-24

Switch_A> (enable)
```

The results will indicate that both the VLAN to which the ports were assigned previously and the VLAN that is being assigned are being modified.

To verify that the ports have been properly assigned:

```
Switch_A> (enable) sh vlan
VLAN   Name                    Status     IfIndex   Mod/Ports, Vlans
------ ----------------------- ---------- --------- -------------------
1      default                 active     5         1/1-2
                                                    5/1-12
10     FSU                     active     46        3/1-12
20     Duke                    active     47        3/13-24
1002   fddi-default            active     6
1003   token-ring-default      active     9
1004   fddinet-default         active     7
1005   trnet-default           active     8
```

To change the MTU, SAID, or type of a VLAN, the set vlan command is used:

```
Switch_A> (enable) set vlan 10 type FDDI said 10 mtu 2000
Switch_A> (enable) sh vlan
VLAN   Name                    Status     IfIndex   Mod/Ports, Vlans
------ ----------------------- ---------- --------- -------------------
1      default                 active     5         1/1-2
                                                    5/1-12
10     FSU                     active     46        3/1-12
20     Duke                    active     47        3/13-24
1002   fddi-default            active     6
1003   token-ring-default      active     9
1004   fddinet-default         active     7
1005   trnet-default           active     8

VLAN Type  SAID   MTU  Parent RingNo BrdgNo Stp BrdgMode Trans1 Trans2
---- ----- ------ ---- ------ ------ ------ --- -------- ------ ------
1    enet  100001 1500 -      -      -      -   -        0      0
10   fddi  10     2000 -      -      -      -   -        0      0
20   enet  100020 1500 -      -      -      -   -        0      0
1002 fddi  101002 1500 -      -      -      -   -        0      0
```

```
1003 trcrf 101003 1500 0    0x0    -      -    -      0      0
1004 fdnet 101004 1500 -    -      0x0    ieee -      0      0
1005 trbrf 101005 1500 -    -      0x0    ibm  -      0      0

VLAN   AREHops   STEHops   Backup CRF
------ --------- --------- ----------
1003   7         7         off
Switch_A>  (enable)
```

This will set the VLAN type to FDDI, which on this switch is not necessary because there are no FDDI ports. The SAID value will be discussed in Chapter 9.

Configuring Dynamic VLANs

Ports that are configured in dynamic VLANs will dynamically assign themselves to a VLAN based on the source MAC address of the first frame it receives. This is done using a VLAN membership policy server (VMPS). The VMPS is a Catalyst switch that has downloaded a text file from a TFTP server. This text file will have VLAN-to-MAC address mappings. As dynamic VLAN ports become active, the switch will check with the VMPS server (which may be itself) and compare the source MAC address of the first frame with the database. If there is an entry in the database, the port will assign itself to the designated VLAN. If there is no entry in the database, the port will do one of the following:

1. It will return an "access-denied" message if the VMPS database is not in secure mode and no fallback VLAN is specified.
2. It will shut down if the VMPS database is in secure mode.
3. It will be assigned to the specified fallback VLAN.

All these options are user-configurable.

The first step in configuring dynamic VLANs is to gather the MAC address-to-VLAN mappings. This can be an arduous process, but it is necessary. This information is collected and placed in a text file that is placed on a TFTP server. The VMPS database is done in text. A sample VMPS database (text file) follows:

```
!VMPS Database for ACC
!
!
vmps domain ACC              Indicates the management domain name
vmps mode open               Specifies the VMPS mode (open or secure)
```

```
vmps fallback —NONE—                          Specifies the VLAN to place ports
                                              with MAC addresses that are not
!                                             in the MAC address-to-VLAN table
!
!MAC Addresses
!
vmps-mac-addrs
!
!address <addr> vlan-name <vlan_name>
!
address 0001.1111.1111 vlan-name hardware     The MAC address-to-VLAN
address 0001.2222.2222 vlan-name hardware     mappings
address 0001.3333.3333 vlan-name Green
```

When the database is complete, it is stored on a TFTP server. A Catalyst switch will be chosen as the primary VMPS. To configure a Catalyst switch as the primary VMPS, use the following commands.

```
Switch_A> (enable) set vmps tftpserver [ip_address]
[filename_VMPS_Database]
```

This command tells the VMPS where to find the database. The VMPS loads this file after the boot sequence and stores it in RAM. Each time the switch boots, it reloads the file from the TFTP server, so it is very important that the TFTP server be accessible at all times when using dynamic VLANs. The file name of the VMPS database can be anything. If no file name is specified, the default file name is *vmps-config-database.1* (a little too long for me).

After the TFTP server and file name has been defined, activate VMPS on the Catalyst switch with the following command:

```
Switch_A> (enable) set vmps state enable
```

Configure the ports to use dynamic VLANs using the following command:

```
Switch_A> (enable) set port membership [mod_num/port_num] dynamic
```

This tells the ports to get their VLAN information from the VMPS server, which in this case is the same switch. When the dynamic VLAN ports become active, they will assign themselves to the VLANs specified in the VMPS database.

To configure other switches as VMPS clients, use the following command:

```
Switch_A> (enable) set vmps server [ip_address_of_VMPS] [primary]
```

This informs the client where to find the VMPS.

EXAMPLE

Figure 8-15 shows three switches. Switch A is the VMPS server, and switches B and C are configured as VMPS clients. The VMPS database has already been created and resides on the TFTP server as shown. The following will configure VMPS as described above:

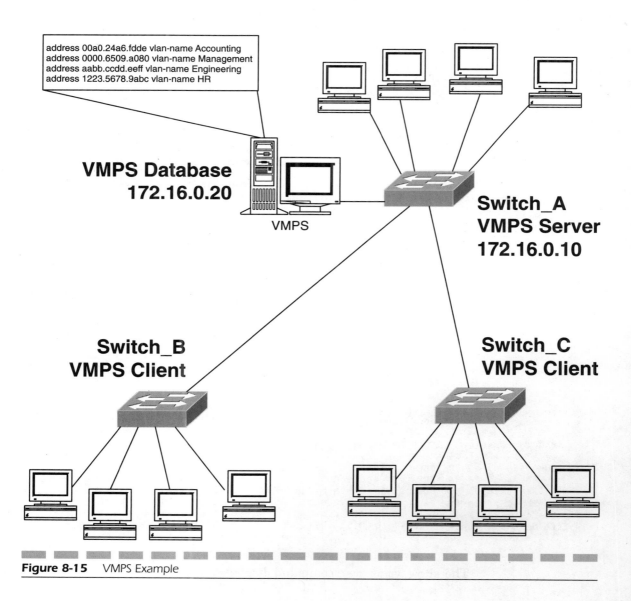

Figure 8-15 VMPS Example

On switch A:

```
Switch_A> (enable) set vmps tftpserver 172.16.0.20 vmps.txt
IP address of the TFTP server set to 172.16.0.20
VMPS configuration filename set to vmps.txt
Switch_A> (enable) set vmps state enable
Switch_A> (enable) 1999 Apr 13 01:31:43 %VMPS-2-PARSEMSG:PARSER:
26 lines parsed, Errors 0
Switch_A> (enable) set port membership 3/1-12 dynamic
Ports 3/1-12 vlan assignment set to dynamic.
Switch_A> (enable)
```

On switch B:

```
Switch_B> (enable) set vmps server 172.16.0.10 primary
172.16.0.10 added to VMPS table as primary domain server.
Switch_B> (enable) set port membership 3/1-12 dynamic
Ports 3/1-12 vlan assignment set to dynamic.
Switch_B> (enable)
```

On switch C:

```
Switch_C> (enable) set vmps server 172.16.0.10 primary
172.16.0.10 added to VMPS table as primary domain server.
Switch_C> (enable) set port membership 3/1-12 dynamic
Ports 3/1-12 vlan assignment set to dynamic.
Switch_C> (enable)
```

TECH TIP: *Not all ports need to be configured for dynamic VLANs.*

To verify the VMPS settings on all switches, use the following commands:

On switch A:

```
Switch_A> (enable) show vmps mac

MAC Address        VLAN Name  Last Requestor Port ID Last Accessed Last Response
------------------ ---------- -------------- ------- ------------- -------------
00-00-65-09-a0-80  FSU        0.0.0.0                0,00:00:00    Success
00-a0-24-a6-fd-de  FSU        0.0.0.0                0,00:00:00    Success
12-23-56-78-9a-bc  DUKE       0.0.0.0                0,00:00:00    Success
aa-bb-cc-dd-ee-ff  FSU        0.0.0.0                0,00:00:00    Success
fe-dc-ba-23-12-45  DUKE       0.0.0.0                0,00:00:00    Success
fe-dc-ba-98-76-54  -NONE-     0.0.0.0                0,00:00:00    Success
```

The show vmps mac **command displays the entire VMPS database:**

```
Switch_A> (enable) show vmps
VMPS Server Status:
-------------------
Management Domain:      ACC
State:                  enabled
Operational Status:     active
TFTP Server:            209.86.82.33
TFTP File:              vmps.txt
Fallback VLAN:          default
Secure Mode:            open
VMPS No Domain Req:     allow
```

The show vmps command displays the current status of VMPS, whether the switch is the server or a client.

On switch B:

```
Switch_B> (enable) show vmps server

VMPS Client Status:
-------------------
VMPS VQP Version:     1
Reconfirm Interval:   60 min
Server Retry Count:   3
VMPS domain server:   172.16.0.10 (primary)
```

On switch C:

```
Switch_C> (enable) show vmps server

VMPS Client Status:
-------------------
VMPS VQP Version:     1
Reconfirm Interval:   60 min
Server Retry Count:   3
VMPS domain server:   172.16.0.10 (primary)
```

VMPS has been configured successfully.

Configuring Trunking

To allow multiple VLANs across a single port, trunking must be configured on that port. Chapter 4 discussed two methods of trunking across Fast Ethernet and Gigabit Ethernet. Now I will discuss the commands to enable trunking.

All ports are not capable of trunking. To examine a port's capabilities, the show port capabilities command will display whether or not a port is capable of trunking and what encapsulation methods are supported. For example, on switch A, a supervisor engine III with a Gigabit Ethernet module is installed.

```
Switch_A> (enable) show module
Mod Module-Name Ports Module-Type          Model      Serial-Num Status
--- ----------- ----- --------------------- ---------- ---------- --------
1               2     1000BaseSX Supervisor WS-X5530   010847706  ok
3               24    10/100BaseTX Ethernet WS-X5224   010904347  ok
5               12    100BaseFX MM Ethernet WS-X5201R  009976930  ok

Mod   MAC-Address(es)                          Hw    Fw      Sw
----  ---------------------------------------- ----- ------- ------
1     00-90-21-0d-9c-00 to 00-90-21-0d-9f-ff   2.0   3.1.2   4.5(1)
3     00-10-7b-e9-83-e8 to 00-10-7b-e9-83-ff   1.4   3.1(1)  4.5(1)
5     00-60-70-99-f0-1c to 00-60-70-99-f0-27   1.1   4.1(1)  4.5(1)

Mod   Sub-Type   Sub-Model   Sub-Serial    Sub-Hw
----  ---------  ----------  ------------  --------------------
1     EARL 1+    WS-F5520    0010851091    1.1
1     uplink     WS-U5534    0009999149    1.0
Switch_A> (enable)
```

To verify whether or not the two ports on the supervisor engine III are capable of trunking and, if so, what encapsulation methods they support:

```
Switch_A> (enable) show port capabilities 1/1
Model                   WS-X5530
Port                    1/1
Type                    1000BaseSX
Speed                   1000
Duplex                  full
Trunk encap type        802.1Q,ISL
Trunk mode              on,off,desirable,auto,nonegotiate
Channel                 no
Broadcast suppression   percentage(0-100)
Flow control            receive-(off,on,desired),send-(off,on,desired)
Security                no
Membership              static
Fast start              yes
Rewrite                 no
Switch_A> (enable) show port capabilities 1/2
Model                   WS-X5530
Port                    1/2
Type                    1000BaseSX
Speed                   1000
Duplex                  full
Trunk encap type        802.1Q,ISL
Trunk mode              on,off,desirable,auto,nonegotiate
Channel                 no
Broadcast suppression   percentage(0-100)
Flow control            receive-(off,on,desired),send-(off,on,desired)
Security                no
Membership              static
Fast start              yes
Rewrite                 no
Switch_A> (enable)
```

These ports are capable of trunking and will support either Cisco's ISL or the IEEE's 802.1Q encapsulation method.

There are five different trunk modes in which a trunk port may be placed (see Table 8-3).

The modes listed in the table may seem a little unusual, especially when compared with the states of a 10/100Mb/s port. With a 10/100-Mb/s port, if the speed is set to auto, the ports will configure themselves to run at 100 Mb/s if both ports are capable because 100 Mb/s is obviously better than 10 Mb/s. With trunking, this is not as cut and dry. If two ports are connected together and they are set to auto trunk on both sides, is it better to trunk or not trunk? Trunking may not be the desired type of connection. This explains the numerous states in which a trunk port can be placed.

Table 8-4 gives the possible port states of two ports connected together and the resulting connection.

Table 8-3

Trunk States Defined

Trunk Mode	Description
On	This port encapsulates frames in ISL or 802.1Q frames.
Off	This port will not trunk and therefore not encapsulate frames.
Desirable	This port wants to trunk, yearns to be a trunk, but will not trunk unless the port to which it is connected is capable of trunking.
Auto (Default)	This port does not care whether or not it trunks and will do whatever the port to which it is connected wants.
Nonnegotiate	The port will be a trunk but will not negotiate with the other port, i.e., the other side must have trunking turned on.

Table 8-4

To Trunk or Not to Trunk, That Is the Question

Trunk Mode	On	Off	Desirable	Auto (Default)	Nonnegotiate
On	Trunk	Misconfigured	Trunk	Trunk	Trunk
Off	Misconfigured	Not trunk	Not trunk	Not trunk	Misconfigured
Desirable	Trunk	Not trunk	Trunk	Trunk	Trunk
Auto (Default)	Trunk	Not Trunk	Trunk	Not trunk (default)	Misconfigured
Nonnegotiate	Trunk	Misconfigured	Trunk	Misconfigured	Trunk

Table 8-5

Cisco's ISL or IEEE's
802.1Q

Trunk Mode	ISL	802.1Q	Autonegotiate (Default)
ISL	ISL	Not trunk	ISL
802.1Q	Not trunk	802.1Q	802.1Q
Auto-negotiate (default)	ISL	802.1Q	ISL

The nonnegotiate state should be used when trunking to a Cisco router. It is not necessary to negotiate whether or not to form a trunk because the router must be manually configured to trunk in order for it to trunk.

With Fast Ethernet and Gigabit Ethernet ports that are capable of both Cisco's ISL encapsulation and the IEEE's 802.1Q encapsulation, the method of encapsulation can be specified. By default, the encapsulation method is set to auto. Table 8-5 gives the possible settings of the trunk encapsulations and the results of those settings.

TECH TIP: *If a port's trunk encapsulation method is set to auto, its trunk state also must be set to auto. If you were to try to set the state while the trunk encapsulation method was set to auto, the following error would be displayed:*

```
Switch_A> (enable) set trunk 1/1 on
Failed to set port 1/1 to trunk mode on.
Trunk mode `on' not allowed with trunk encapsulation type `negotiate'.
Switch_A> (enable)
```

To configure a port that is capable of trunking, the set trunk command is used:

```
Switch_A> (enable) set trunk [module_number/port_number]
[on|off|desirable|auto|nonegotiate] [trunk_encapsulation_method]
```

For example, switch A's 1/1 port is connected to switch B's 2/49 port (see Figure 8-16). To configure switch A to trunk with switch B, one could use the following:

```
Switch_A> (enable) set trunk 1/1 on isl
Port(s) 1/1 trunk mode set to on.
Port(s) 1/1 trunk type set to isl.
```

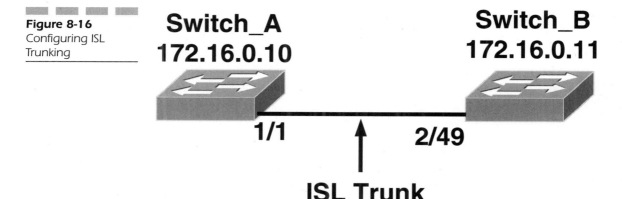

Figure 8-16
Configuring ISL
Trunking

```
Switch_A> (enable)
1999 Apr 12 20:31:18 %DTP-5-TRUNKPORTON:Port 1/1 has become isl
trunk
Switch_A> (enable)
```

Once the port on switch A has trunking turned on, the port to which it is connected on switch B will autonegotiate ISL trunking. A message will appear on the console screen indicating that the port has become trunked.

Trunking can be verified with the show trunk command:

```
Switch_A> (enable) show trunk
Port      Mode          Encapsulation   Status         Native vlan
--------  ------------  --------------  -------------  --------------
 1/1      on            isl             trunking       1

Port      Vlans allowed on trunk
--------  ------------------------------------------------------------
 1/1      1-1005

Port      Vlans allowed and active in management domain
--------  ------------------------------------------------------------
 1/1      1,10,20,1003,1005

Port      Vlans in spanning tree forwarding state and not pruned
--------  ------------------------------------------------------------
 1/1      1,10,20,1003,1005
Switch_A> (enable)
```

Port 1/1 is trunking. It was not necessary to perform any modifications on switch B. However, it should be noted that this is the most dangerous part of configuring trunking. When trunking was turned on between switch A and switch B, one of the switch's VLAN lists was going to overwrite the others. Before turning trunking on, one should verify that the

VLAN list on both switches is consistent because if the VLAN list is inconsistent, some ports may be placed in the inactive state and users will lose connectivity.

To change the encapsulation method to 802.1Q:

```
Switch_A> (enable) set trunk 1/1 dot1q
Port(s) 1/1 trunk type set to dot1q.
Switch_A> (enable) show trunk
1999 Apr 12 20:47:42 %DTP-5-TRUNKPORTCHG:Port 1/1 has changed from
isl trunk to dot1q trunk
Port      Mode         Encapsulation  Status        Native vlan
--------  -----------  -------------  ------------  --------------
 1/1      on           dot1q          trunking      1

Port      Vlans allowed on trunk
--------  ----------------------------------------------------------
 1/1      1-1005

Port      Vlans allowed and active in management domain
--------  ----------------------------------------------------------
 1/1      1,10,20,1003,1005

Port      Vlans in spanning tree forwarding state and not pruned
--------  ----------------------------------------------------------
 1/1      1,10,20,1003,1005
Switch_A> (enable)
```

With Switch B's 2/49 port in the autonegotiate trunk state, it is easy to make changes because they only have to be made on one end of the trunk.

```
Switch_B> (enable) show trunk
Port      Mode         Encapsulation    Status    Native vlan
--------  -----------  ---------------  --------  ----------------
 2/49     auto         dot1q            trunking  1

Port      Vlans allowed on trunk
--------  ----------------------------------------------------------
 2/49     1-1005

Port      Vlans allowed and active in management domain
--------  ----------------------------------------------------------
 2/49     1,10,20

Port      Vlans in spanning tree forwarding state and not pruned
--------  ----------------------------------------------------------
 2/49     1
Switch_B> (enable)
```

However, if switch B's 2/49 port were not configured to autonegotiate, changes would have to be made on both ends.

At this point I like to verify that the two VLAN lists have been synchronized. This can be done using the show vlan command that was discussed earlier:

```
Switch_B> (enable) sh vlan
VLAN Name             Status    IfIndex   Mod/Ports, Vlans
----- ---------------  --------- --------- -------------------------
1     default          active    4         2/1-48,2/50
10    FSU              active    59
20    Duke             active    60
1002  fddi-default     active    5
1003  trcrf-default    active    8
1004  fddinet-default  active    6
1005  trbrf-default    active    7                   1003

VLAN Type  SAID   MTU  Parent RingNo BrdgNo Stp BrdgMode Trans1 Trans2
----  ----  ------ ---- ------ ------ ------ --- ------- ------ -----
1     enet  100001 1500 -      -      -      -   -        0      0
10    enet  100010 1500 -      -      -      -   -        0      0
20    enet  100020 1500 -      -      -      -   -        0      0
1002  fddi  101002 1500 -      -      -      -   -        0      0
1003  trcrf 101003 4472 1005   0xccc  -      -   srb      0      0
1004  fdnet 101004 1500 -      -      0x0    ieee -       0      0
1005  trbrf 101005 4472 -      -      0xf    ibm  -       0      0

VLAN AREHops STEHops Backup CRF
---- ------- ------- ------ ---
1003 7       7       off
Switch_A> (enable) sh vlan
VLAN  Name                 Status    IfIndex  Mod/Ports, Vlans
------ -------------------- --------- -------- -----------------
1     default              active    5        1/2
                                              3/1
                                              5/1-12
10    FSU                  active    46       3/2-12
20    Duke                 active    47       3/13-24
1002  fddi-default         active    6
1003  trcrf-default        active    9
1004  fddinet-default      active    7
1005  trbrf-default        active    8                1003

VLAN Type  SAID   MTU  Parent RingNo BrdgNo Stp  BrdgMode Trans1 Trans2
----  ----  ------ ---- ------ ------ ----- ---- -------- ----- ------
1     enet  100001 1500 -      -      -      -    -        0      0
10    enet  100010 1500 -      -      -      -    -        0      0
20    enet  100020 1500 -      -      -      -    -        0      0
1002  fddi  101002 1500 -      -      -      -    -        0      0
1003  trcrf 101003 4472 1005   0xccc  -      -    srb      0      0
1004  fdnet 101004 1500 -      -      0x0    ieee -        0      0
1005  trbrf 101005 4472 -      -      0xf    ibm  -        0      0

VLAN AREHops STEHops Backup CRF
---- ------- ------- ----------
1003 7       7       off
Switch_A> (enable)
```

TECH TIP: *Both switch A and switch B have identical VLAN lists in this case, but I have discovered that sometimes the VTP updates are going across the trunk, but the VLANs do not become synchronized. This can be remedied easily by creating a VLAN on one of the switches. This will trigger a flash VTP update and will synchronize the VLANs.*

BONEHEAD ALERT: *When trunking, be sure that you have the VTP settings correct on both switches if you are using secure management domains. In other words, verify your password in the* set vtp *command. They are case-sensitive!*

To verify that the switches are exchanging VTP updates over the new trunk, the show vtp domain command may be used:

On switch A:

```
Switch_A> (enable) sh vtp domain
Domain Name           Domain Index VTP Version Local Mode  Password
-------------------- ------ ----- --- ------- ----- ----- --------
ACC                     1            2           server    configured

Vlan-count  Max-vlan-storage  Config Revision  Notifications
----------- ----------------- ---------------- -------------
7           1023              4                disabled

Last Updater    V2 Mode   Pruning   PruneEligible on Vlans
--------------- --------- --------- ---------------------------
172.16.0.10     enabled   enabled   2-1000
Switch_A> (enable)
```

On switch B:

```
Switch_B> (enable) sh vtp domain
Domain Name           Domain Index VTP Version Local Mode Password
-------------------- ------ ----- --- ------- ----- ----- --------
ACC                     1            2           server   configured

Vlan-count  Max-vlan-storage  Config Revision  Notifications
----------- ----------------- ---------------- -------------
7           1023              4                disabled

Last Updater    V2 Mode   Pruning   PruneEligible on Vlans
--------------- --------- --------- ---------------------------
172.16.0.10     enabled   enabled   2-1000
Switch_B> (enable)
```

The VLAN counts are the same, which is a good indication that the VLAN lists are consistent. The VTP domain names are the same.

Configuring Fast EtherChannel and Gigabit EtherChannel

In Figure 8-16, switch A and switch B had one Gigabit Ethernet connection between them. If that connection were Fast Ethernet, it might be necessary to bond together multiple ports to increase bandwidth between the switches.

Ports that are going to become part of the same channel, on both switches, must be configured with the exact same parameters. They must be in the same VLAN and must have the same STP parameters (i.e., port priority and port cost).

To configure Fast EtherChannel, the set port channel command is employed. The proper syntax of the command is as follows:

```
Switch_B> (enable) set port channel [ports_to_be_channeled]
[on|off|desirable|auto]
```

For example, to configure ports 1/1 and 1/2 on switch A to perform Fast EtherChannel to ports 2/49 and 2/50 on switch B:

On switch A:

```
Switch_A> (enable) set port channel 1/1-2 <Enter>
Port(s) 1/1-2 channel mode set to on.
```

On switch B:

```
Switch_A> (enable) set port channel 2/49-50 <Enter>
Port(s) 2/49-50 channel mode set to on.
```

The show port channel command can be used to verify that the channel is up and operational:

```
Switch_A> (enable) show port channel <Enter>
Port  Status     Channel   Channel   Neighbor              Neighbor
                 mode      status    device                port
----- ---------- --------- --------- -------------------- -------
 1/1  connected  on        channel   WS-C5000  006047419   2/49
 1/2  connected  on        channel   WS-C5000  006047419   2/50
----- ---------- --------- --------- -------------------- -------
Switch_A> (enable)
```

TECH TIP: *When trunking on a Fast EtherChannel, it is helpful if you disable a port before turning trunking on and then reenable the port after trunking has been turned on.*

Configuring Port Protocol Filtering

There are several different options to choose from for securing ports on a Catalyst switch. Traffic may be filtered based on protocol or by MAC address. Protocol filters restrict traffic to a particular port based on protocol. This feature can be extremely useful in an environment where both IP and IPX are running. Workstations that are configured for IP-*only* will receive IPX broadcasts unnecessarily. This will reduce the amount of bandwidth for valid traffic and increase CPU utilization. Protocol filters can stop IPX traffic from being transmitted to the IP-only workstations.

When using protocol filtering, packets are grouped into four categories:

1. IP packets
2. IPX packets
3. Appletalk, DECnet, and Banyan Vines packets
4. All others

NOTE: *On the Catalyst 4000 and 2948G series switches, Banyan Vines packets are classified as "all others."*

Ports that support protocol filtering can have each of the groups set to one of three modes (see Table 8-6).

Table 8-6

Protocol Filter Group Modes

Mode	Description
On	Traffic from this group will be transmitted out the port.
Off	Traffic from this group will not be transmitted out the port.
Auto	Traffic will be not be forwarded out this port unless traffic from this group is received. A port that has the IPX group set to the auto mode will not forward IPX traffic until IPX traffic is received on that port.

Before protocol filtering can be enabled on any one port, it must first be enabled on the switch using the `set protocolfilter` command:

```
Switch_B> (enable) set protocolfilter enable
Protocol filtering enabled on this switch.
Switch_B> (enable)
```

TECH TIP: *Protocol filtering is a relatively new feature and is not supported on all Catalyst switches:*

```
Switch_A> (enable) set protocolfilter enable
Protocol filtering not supported by this hardware.
Switch_A> (enable)
```

After protocol filtering has been enabled on a switch, the ports may have their groups assigned to one of the three modes:

```
Switch_B> (enable) set port protocol [mod_num/port_num]
[ip|ipx|group] [on|off|auto]
```

For example, to allow only IP traffic on ports 2/1-12 of switch B:

```
Switch_B> (enable) set port protocol 2/1-12 ip on
IP protocol set to on mode on ports 2/1-12.
Switch_B> (enable) set port protocol 2/1-12 ipx off
IPX protocol disabled on ports 2/1-12.
Switch_B> (enable) set port protocol 2/1-12 group off
Group protocol disabled on ports 2/2-12.
Switch_B> (enable)
```

BONEHEAD ALERT: *Do not set the protocol filter of the IP group to auto for the port to which you are telneted. You will loose connectivity for an indefinite period of time.*

To verify that port filtering has been correctly configured:

```
Switch_B> (enable) show port protocol
Port   Vlan  IP  IP Hosts   IPX      IPX Hosts   Group    Group Hosts
------ ----- --- ---------- -------- ----------- -------- -----------
 2/1   1     on  0          off      0           off      0
 2/2   1     on  0          off      0           off      0
```

```
2/3    1    on  0           off       0           off       0
2/4    1    on  0           off       0           off       0
2/5    1    on  0           off       0           off       0
2/6    1    on  0           off       0           off       0
2/7    1    on  0           off       0           off       0
2/8    1    on  0           off       0           off       0
2/9    1    on  0           off       0           off       0
2/10   1    on  0           off       0           off       0
2/11   1    on  0           off       0           off       0
2/12   1    on  0           off       0           off       0
2/13   1    on  0           auto-off  0           auto-off  0
2/14   1    on  0           auto-off  0           auto-off  0
2/15   1    on  0           auto-off  0           auto-off  0
2/16   1    on  0           auto-off  0           auto-off  0
2/17   1    on  0           auto-off  0           auto-off  0
2/18   1    on  0           auto-off  0           auto-off  0
2/19   1    on  0           auto-off  0           auto-off  0
2/20   1    on  0           auto-off  0           auto-off  0
2/21   1    on  0           auto-off  0           auto-off  0
2/22   1    on  0           auto-off  0           auto-off  0
2/23   1    on  0           auto-off  0           auto-off  0
2/24   1    on  0           auto-off  0           auto-off  0
```

Configuring Port Security

Another filtering technique that can be employed with Catalyst switches is *secure port filtering*. Secure port filtering will allow only frames from a certain MAC address to be received on a secure port. This MAC address may be specified or can be determined dynamically. If a frame with an invalid source MAC address is detected on the secure port, the port will be shut down.

Secure port filtering allows the network administrators to have strict control over which stations connect into the switch. This feature is practical in organizations that are slightly paranoid as to who might connect to a switch port. In my experience, this has been a rare case, usually only seen in the military. The administrative headaches created by this feature are numerous.

TECH TIP: *Secure port filtering allows only a single MAC address to be secured on a port. Therefore, if a hub is connected to a secure port on a switch, only a single workstation will have access through the switch.*

The MAC address that is locked into the port can be specified manually or determined automatically. If the port is set to automatically determine the locked-in MAC address, it will learn (for lack of a better word) the first source MAC address it sees on that port. This address will be stored in NVRAM, locking this MAC address on that port even after the switch is rebooted.

To configure secure port filtering:

```
Switch_B> (enable) set port security [mod_num/port_num]
[enable|disable] [mac_addr]
```

If no MAC address is specified, the port will automatically lock in the source MAC address received on that port.

For example, to configure the 2/2 port on switch B to automatically lock in the source MAC address of the first frame it receives, the following command would be typed:

```
Switch_B> (enable) set port security 2/2 enable
Port 2/2 port security enabled with the learned mac address.
Trunking disabled for Port 2/2 due to Security Mode
Switch_B> (enable)
```

The MAC address that was learned can be examined using the show port security command:

```
Switch_B> (enable) show port security 2/2
Port  Security Secure-Src-Addr   Last-Src-Addr Shutdown Trap IfIndex
----- -------- ----------------- ------------- -------- ---- ------
 2/2  enabled  22-22-22-22-22-22               No       disabled 10
Switch_B> (enable)
```

Working with Sniffers

When troubleshooting networks with switches, it can be difficult to use common protocol analyzers and packet analyzers because a switch does not forward all traffic out all ports like a hub. If a packet analyzer were plugged directly into a switch, it would see only broadcast and multicast traffic. Often this does not help with the problem at hand.

Port mirroring or spanning is the ability of a Catalyst switch to mirror all traffic seen on its ports to one port. This port is referred to as the *span port*. However, this port has nothing to do with the Spanning Tree Protocol (STP). It is used only when it is necessary to capture frames for troubleshooting or network management.

Catalyst switches allow traffic to be mirrored from one port, multiple ports, or all ports in a VLAN. The span port will have a packet analyzer connected to it and will capture these frames.

The set span command is used to mirror frames to a span port:

```
Switch_B> (enable)  set span [source] [span port] [rx | tx | both]
```

The source may be a single port, multiple ports, or a VLAN number. If a VLAN number is specified, then all VLAN traffic will be forwarded to the span port. The [rx | tx | both] is optional; if no direction is specified, it defaults to both.

For example, to mirror frames from the 2/3 port to the 2/2 port:

```
Switch_B> (enable) set span 2/3 2/2
Enabled monitoring of Port 2/3 transmit/receive traffic by Port 2/2
Switch_B> (enable)
```

To mirror frames from the 2/3-12 ports to the 2/2 port:

```
Switch_B> (enable) set span 2/3-12 2/2
Enabled monitoring of Port 2/3-12 transmit/receive traffic by Port
2/2
Switch_B> (enable)
```

To mirror frames from VLAN 10 to the 2/2 port:

```
Switch_B> (enable) set span 10 2/2
Enabled monitoring of VLAN 10 transmit/receive traffic by Port 2/2
Switch_B> (enable)
```

To examine the current span settings:

```
Switch_B> (enable) show span
Status          : enabled
Admin Source    : VLAN 10
Oper Source     : Port 2/49
Destination     : Port 2/2
Direction       : transmit/receive
Incoming Packets: disabled
Switch_B> (enable)
```

Controlling Broadcasts

A Catalyst switch can be configured to limit the amount of broadcast traffic that is received on a port. This will help prevent the backplane fabric from being overloaded with broadcast traffic. Broadcast traffic can be limited in either the percentage of overall traffic in a 1-second window or the number of broadcast packets received in 1 second. Once the threshold is reached, no broadcast packets will be received on that port for the remainder of that 1-second interval.

TECH TIP: *Broadcast control can vary from module to module. Some line modules do not allow individual ports to be configured with broadcast control. Instead, all ports on the line module must be configured with broadcast control. Some line modules do not support broadcast suppression by the number of broadcast packets per second. You will have to toy around a bit to determine which type of broadcast control is supported on your switch.*

To limit the number of broadcasts as a percentage of overall traffic, the following may be used:

```
Switch_A> (enable) set port broadcast [mod_num/port_num] [thresh-
hold%]
```

For example, to limit the number of broadcasts below 50 percent of overall traffic on port 2/1-12:

```
Switch_A> (enable) set port broadcast 3/1-12 50%
Port 3/1-24 broadcast traffic limited to 50%.
Switch_A> (enable) show module
Mod Module-Name Ports Module-Type          Model    Serial-Num Status
--- ----------- ----- -------------------- -------- ---------- ------
1               2     1000BaseSX Supervisor WS-X5530 010847706  ok
3               24    10/100BaseTX Ethernet WS-X5224 010904347  ok
5               12    100BaseFX MM Ethernet WS-X5201R 009976930 ok

Mod   MAC-Address(es)                        Hw     Fw         Sw
----  ------------------------------- ------ ---------- ----------------
100-90-21-0d-9c-00 to 00-90-21-0d-9f-ff  2.0   3.1.2      4.5(1)
300-10-7b-e9-83-e8 to 00-10-7b-e9-83-ff  1.4   3.1(1)     4.5(1)
500-60-70-99-f0-1c to 00-60-70-99-f0-27  1.1   4.1(1)     4.5(1)

Mod   Sub-Type   Sub-Model   Sub-Serial    Sub-Hw
----  --------   ----------  ------------- ------
1     EARL 1+    WS-F5520    0010851091    1.1
1     uplink     WS-U5534    0009999149    1.0
```

On this particular line module I was unable to limit only ports 3/1-12; all ports on the line card were configured to limit broadcast traffic (please see earlier Tech Tip).

To limit broadcast traffic to 500 broadcast packets per second on ports 3/1-12:

```
Switch_A> (enable) set port broadcast 3/1-12 500
Ports 3/13-24 broadcast traffic unlimited.
Ports 3/1-12 broadcast traffic limited to 500 packets/second.
Switch_A> (enable)
```

When the broadcast traffic is limited by the number of broadcasts per second, the line module will accept different values per port. Notice that ports 3/1-12 have their broadcasts limited but 3/13-24 do not.

To verify the broadcast restrictions:

```
Switch_A> (enable) show port broadcast
Port       Broadcast-Limit   Broadcast-Drop
--------   ----------------  ----------------
  1/1             -                  0
  1/              -                  0
  3/1           500 p/s              0
  3/2           500 p/s              0
  3/3           500 p/s              0
  3/4           500 p/s              0
  3/5           500 p/s              0
  3/6           500 p/s              0
  3/7           500 p/s              0
  3/8           500 p/s              0
  3/9           500 p/s              0
  3/10          500 p/s              0
  3/11          500 p/s              0
  3/12          500 p/s              0
  3/13            -                  0
  3/14            -                  0
  3/15            -                  0
  3/16            -                  0
  3/17            -                  0
  3/18            -                  0
  3/19            -                  0
  3/20            -                  0
  3/21            -                  0
  3/22            -                  0
  3/23            -                  0
  3/24            -                  0
  5/1             -                  0
  5/2             -                  0
  5/3             -                  0
  5/4             -                  0
  5/5             -                  0
  5/6             -                  0
  5/7             -                  0
  5/8             -                  0
  5/9             -                  0
  5/10            -                  0
  5/11            -                  0
  5/12            -                  0
Switch_A> (enable)
```

Working with the CAM Table

Sometimes it can be helpful to read the bridge table of a Catalyst switch. This table is referred to as the *content addressable memory (CAM) table.* There are several commands on Catalyst switches with which one can manipulate this table or view it.

The `set cam` command adds entries to the CAM table of the switch. These entries can be unicast or multicast entries. This can be extremely useful when Layer 2 multicasts are commonplace. By default, a switch forwards multicasts out all ports, treating them like broadcasts. With the `set cam` command these multicasts can be mapped statically to only those ports which need the multicast.

The syntax of the `set cam` command is as follows:

```
Switch_A> (enable) set cam [dynamic|static|permanent] [MAC_address]
[mod/port] [VLAN]
```

TECH TIP: *All ports specified must be in the same VLAN.*

Entries that are placed in the CAM table can be placed there temporarily or, in other words, may be subject to the normal aging process. By default, entries that are learned dynamically will remain in the table for 5 minutes. After 5 minutes of idle use, the entry is dropped. To add an entry temporarily to the CAM table, use the "dynamic" option. To add an entry to the CAM table until the switch is rebooted, use the "static" option. To add an entry to the CAM table permanently, use the "permanent" option. The MAC address will be the destination MAC address. If a frame is destined for the specified MAC address, it will be forwarded to the port(s) specified.

To add an entry to the CAM table, just until the next reboot, for the unicast address 01-00-12-11-11-11 with the destination ports of 3/3, 3/5, 3/7, and 3/12, the following command will be used:

```
Switch_A> (enable) set cam static 01-00-12-11-11-11 3/3,3/5,3/7,3/12
Static multicast entry added to CAM table.
Switch_A> (enable)
```

To permanently map the destination MAC address AA-AA-03-22-33-44 to the port 3/11:

```
Switch_A> (enable) set cam permanent AA-AA-03-22-33-44 3/11
Permanent unicast entry added to CAM table.
Switch_A> (enable)
```

To view the cam table, use the show cam command:

```
Switch_A> (enable) show cam [dynamic|static|permanent|system]
```

The system option will show addresses that are entered into the CAM table by the switch itself:

```
Switch_A> (enable) show cam system
* = Static Entry. + = Permanent Entry. # = System Entry. R = Router
Entry. X = Port Security Entry
VLAN  Dest MAC/Route Des    Destination Ports or VCs / [Protocol Type]
-----  -------------------   ------------------------------------------
1      00-90-21-0d-9f-ff#    1/9
1      01-00-0c-cc-cc-cc#    1/9
1      01-00-0c-cc-cc-cd#    1/9
1      01-00-0c-ee-ee-ee#    1/9
1      01-80-c2-00-00-00#    1/9
1      01-80-c2-00-00-01#    1/9
10     01-00-0c-cc-cc-cc#    1/9
10     01-00-0c-cc-cc-cd#    1/9
10     01-80-c2-00-00-00#    1/9
10     01-80-c2-00-00-01#    1/9
20     01-00-0c-cc-cc-cc#    1/9
20     01-00-0c-cc-cc-cd#    1/9
20     01-80-c2-00-00-00#    1/9
20     01-80-c2-00-00-01#    1/9
1003   01-80-c2-00-00-00#    1/9
1003   80-01-43-00-00-00#    1/9
1003   c0-00-08-00-00-00#    1/9
1005   80-01-43-00-00-00#    1/9
1005   c0-00-08-00-00-00#    1/9
Total Matching CAM Entries Displayed = 19
Switch_A> (enable)
```

To view the permanent entries:

```
Switch_A> (enable) show cam permanent
* = Static Entry. + = Permanent Entry. # = System Entry. R = Router
Entry. X = Port Security Entry

VLAN  Dest MAC/Route Des    Destination Ports or VCs / [Protocol Type]
-----  -------------------   ------------------------------------------
10     aa-aa-03-22-33-44+    3/11
Total Matching CAM Entries Displayed = 1
Switch_A> (enable)
```

To view the static entries:

```
Switch_A> (enable) show cam static
* = Static Entry. + = Permanent Entry. # = System Entry. R = Router
```

```
Entry. X = Port Security Entry
VLAN  Dest MAC/Route Des   Destination Ports or VCs / [Protocol Type]
----- -------------------- ------------------------------------------
10    01-00-12-11-11-11*   3/3,3/5,3/7,3/12
Total Matching CAM Entries Displayed = 1
Switch_A (enable)
```

To view the dynamic entries in the CAM:

```
Switch_A> (enable) show cam dynamic
* = Static Entry. + = Permanent Entry. # = System Entry. R = Router
Entry. X = Port Security Entry
VLAN  Dest MAC/Route Des   Destination Ports or VCs / [Protocol Type]
----- -------------------- ------------------------------------------
1     00-60-5c-f4-b6-6c    3/1 [ALL]
1     00-a0-24-51-2b-d1    3/1 [ALL]
1     02-00-22-22-09-80    3/1 [ALL]
1     00-90-21-69-23-9e    3/1 [ALL]
1     00-90-21-69-23-cf    1/2 [ALL]
1     00-00-81-39-e8-ce    3/1 [ALL]
Total Matching CAM Entries Displayed = 6
Switch_A> (enable)
```

TECH TIP: *The dynamic CAM table is the learned MAC addresses. When troubleshooting, it is a good idea to verify that this table is correct.*

Entries that are in the dynamic portion of the CAM table will timeout in 5 minutes by default, as mentioned earlier. This value can be changed using the set cam agingtime command.

To extend the timeout aging time of the dynamic CAM table to 10 minutes, use the following command:

```
Switch_A> (enable) set cam agingtime 1-1005 600
Vlans 1-1005 CAM aging time set to 600 seconds.
Switch_A> (enable)
```

A VLAN must be specified. In this case I specified all VLANs, but this is not required. VLANs can be configured with different aging times.

Routing VLANs with an External Router (One-Armed Routing)

To configure an external router to route for multiple VLANs, subinterfaces are configured. One subinterface must be configured for each

VLAN that needs to be routed. The router must have Cisco IOS version 11.1(2).

Figure 8-17 shows a Cisco 4500 router connected directly to a Catalyst 5000 switch with two VLANs.

To configure the router to route for VLANs 10 and 20, two subinterfaces are created on the 4500 as follows:

```
interface FastEthernet0.10
 description VLAN 10 FSU
 encapsulation isl 10
```

Figure 8-17
External Routing of
VLANs

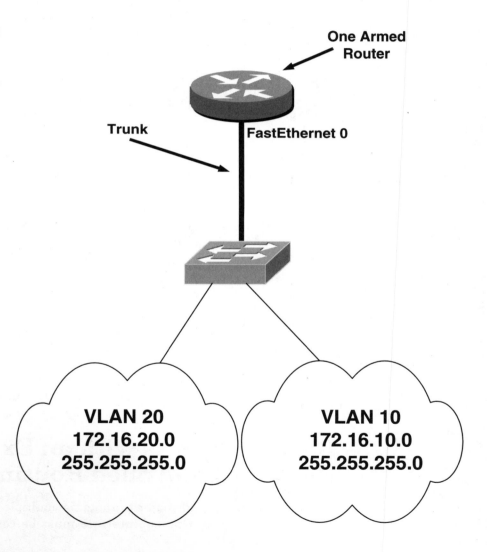

One Armed
Router

Trunk

FastEthernet 0

VLAN 20
172.16.20.0
255.255.255.0

VLAN 10
172.16.10.0
255.255.255.0

```
 ip address 172.16.10.1 255.255.255.0
!
interface FastEthernet0.20
 description VLAN 20 Duke
 encapsulation isl 20
 ip address 172.16.20.1 255.255.255.0
```

The subinterface numbers can be any value between 1 and 65535. However, only 255 subinterfaces can be configured on a single interface. The `encapsulation isl` command specifies the VLAN that has been assigned to the subinterface and the trunking method used. If IEEE 802.1Q had been the trunk encapsulation method, the command `encapsulation dot1q 20` would be used.

Configuring the Route Switch Module (RSM)

The Catalyst route switch module (RSM) is a modified route switch processor (RSP). It runs its own version of an operating system. The operating system is true Cisco IOS. The RSM is configured with the same commands that are used to configure a Cisco router. The only difference is that instead of having physical interfaces, the RSM has virtual interfaces called *VLAN interfaces*. These VLAN interfaces are configured the same as interfaces on a normal external router.

Figure 8-18 shows a Catalyst switch with an RSM installed in its chassis. The configuration is the same as in Figure 8-17 but now uses the RSM to route between VLANs.

For the RSM to route between VLAN 10 and VLAN 20, it would have the following configuration on its interfaces:

```
interface Vlan10
 description VLAN 10 FSU
 ip address 172.16.10.1 255.255.255.0
!
interface Vlan20
 description VLAN 20 Duke
 ip address 172.16.20.1 255.255.255.0
!
```

The RSM should be treated no differently than if it were an external router. It simply has a high-speed connection to the backplane and instead of subinterfaces uses VLAN interfaces.

Figure 8-18
RSM

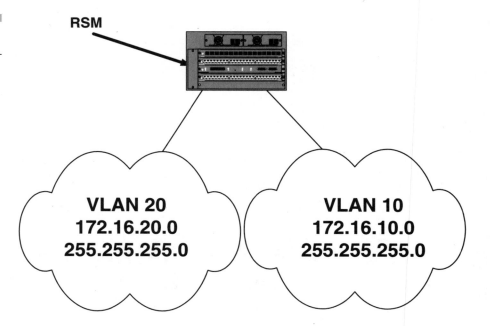

Multilayer Switching (MLS) Defined

Multilayer switching or *Layer 3 switching* is the ability of a switch to mimic the actions of a router. I use the word *mimic* because an MLS or Layer 3 switch does not actually look up a route in a routing table like a router.

Figure 8-19 shows a switch connected to a router. The switch has two VLANs, and the router is behaving as a "one-armed router."

When station A transmits to station B, the frame travels from station A to the switch. The frame has the destination MAC address of the router and the source MAC address of station A. The encapsulated packet will have a source IP address of 172.16.1.11 and a destination IP address of 172.16.2.23 (Figure 8-20).

The frame with the encapsulated packet will be transmitted to the switch, and the switch will forward the frame to the router after it is tagged identifying the frame as belonging to VLAN 10 (Figure 8-21).

When the router receives the frame, it reads the tag that identifies the frame as belonging to VLAN 10, unencapsulates the packet, and

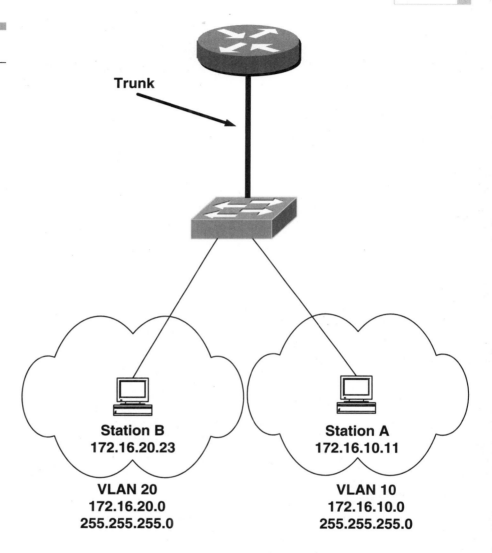

Figure 8-19
One-Armed Routing

Trunk

Station B
172.16.20.23

Station A
172.16.10.11

VLAN 20
172.16.20.0
255.255.255.0

VLAN 10
172.16.10.0
255.255.255.0

makes a routing decision based on the destination IP address. Station B is on the IP subnet 172.16.1.0, so the packet needs to be sent back to the switch. The router then reencapsulates the frame, only this time the source MAC address is that of the router and the destination MAC address is that of station B. Moreover, before transmitting the frame back to the switch, the router tags the frame with VLAN 20, indicating that the frame now belongs to VLAN 20. The router has changed only

Figure 8-20
The Frame Is
Transmitted First to
the Switch

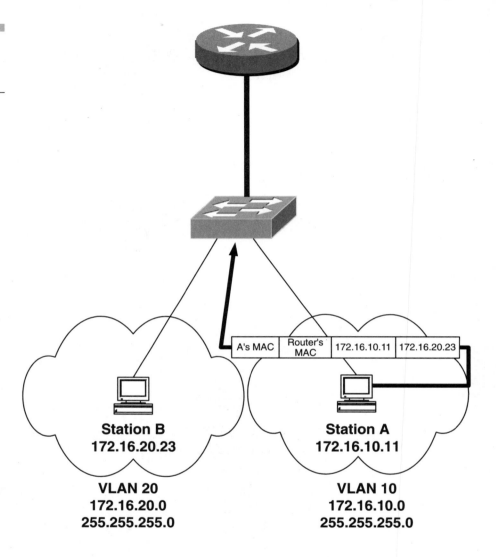

| A's MAC | Router's MAC | 172.16.10.11 | 172.16.20.23 |

Station B
172.16.20.23

Station A
172.16.10.11

VLAN 20
172.16.20.0
255.255.255.0

VLAN 10
172.16.10.0
255.255.255.0

the three fields just mentioned (with the exception of decrementing the TTL field by 1 and recalculating the check sum in the IP packet header) (Figure 8-22.)

The switch then receives the frame, reads the tag and the destination MAC address, and finally forwards the frame to station B (Figure 8-23).

The frame has to travel over the trunk line between the router and the switch twice. The router must make a routing decision based on its routing tables. Remember in Chapter 1 when a router was described as

Figure 8-21
The Frame Is Then
Transmitted to the
Router

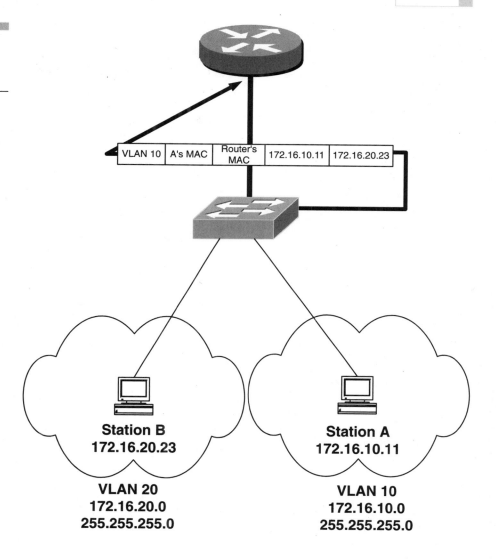

| VLAN 10 | A's MAC | Router's MAC | 172.16.10.11 | 172.16.20.23 |

Station B
172.16.20.23

Station A
172.16.10.11

VLAN 20
172.16.20.0
255.255.255.0

VLAN 10
172.16.10.0
255.255.255.0

being slow or having high latency. MLS or Layer 3 switching gives the switch the ability to change the frame in the same way the router did, without having to look up the destination in a routing table or having to send the frame across the trunk twice.

The switch will take a before and after "picture" of the first frame in a flow. A *flow* is defined as traffic coming from one particular host and going to another particular host for a particular application. Cisco defines *flow* as "a unidirectional sequence of packets between a particu-

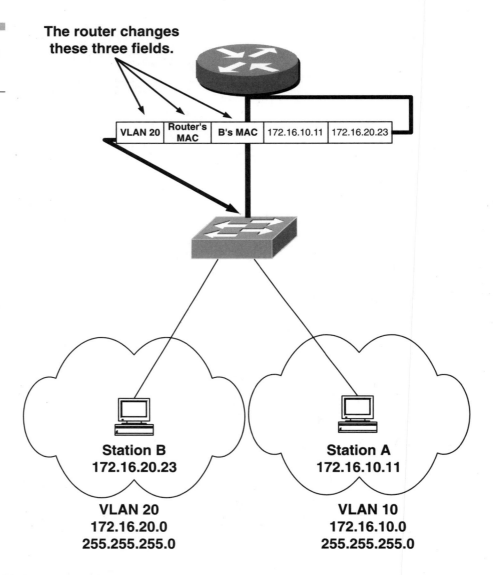

Figure 8-22
The Router Changes
the Frame and the
Tag

The router changes these three fields.

| VLAN 20 | Router's MAC | B's MAC | 172.16.10.11 | 172.16.20.23 |

Station B
172.16.20.23

Station A
172.16.10.11

VLAN 20
172.16.20.0
255.255.255.0

VLAN 10
172.16.10.0
255.255.255.0

lar source and destination that share the same protocol and transport-layer information. Communications from a client to a server and from a server to a client are separate flows. For example, Telnet traffic transferred from a particular source to a particular destination comprises a separate flow from File Transfer Protocol (FTP) packets between the same source and destination....[Moreover] the previous figures illustrated a flow from station A to station B. Had MLS been configured, the first

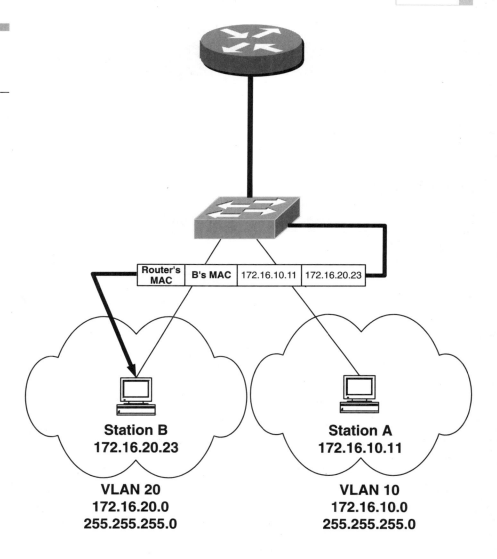

Figure 8-23
The Frame Is For-
warded to Its Final
Destination

| Router's MAC | B's MAC | 172.16.10.11 | 172.16.20.23 |

Station B
172.16.20.23

Station A
172.16.10.11

VLAN 20
172.16.20.0
255.255.255.0

VLAN 10
172.16.10.0
255.255.255.0

frame between station A and station B would take the path illustrated
[in Figures 8-18 through 8-22]. However, every subsequent frame would
be Layer 3 switched by the Catalyst switch" (quoted from the Cisco Connection Online *http://www.cisco.com/univercd/cc/td/doc/product/
lan/cat5000/rel_4_5/config/mls.htm*).

Figure 8-24 shows the same configuration except that the router and
switch are configured to perform MLS. The first frame in the flow has

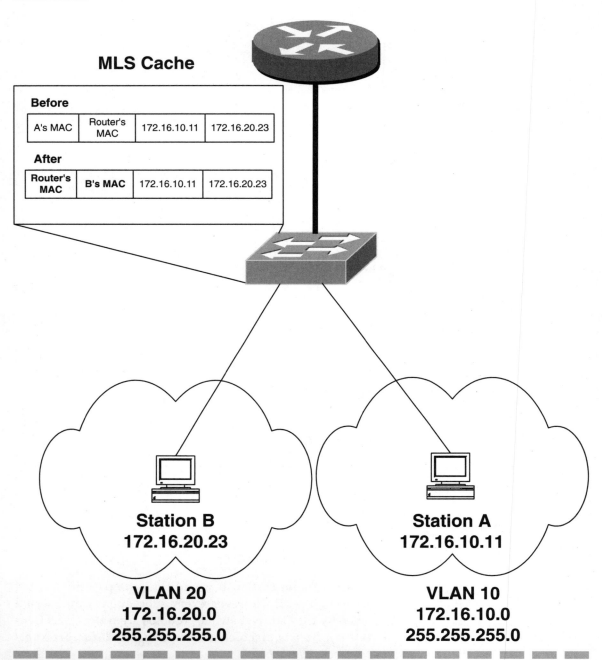

Figure 8-24   Multilayer Switching Enabled

already followed the path illustrated in Figures 8-18 through 8-22, and the Catalyst switch has taken the before and after pictures.

When station A transmits the second frame in the flow, the switch recognizes the destination MAC address as that of the router and checks the MLS cache (Figure 8-25).

When the header is matched in the MLS, instead of sending the frame to the router, the switch changes the header to the "after" picture in the MLS Cache. Cisco refers to this procedure as a *packet rewrite*. All fields that were changed in Figures 8-18 through 8-22, including the TTL and IP check sum, will be changed during the packet rewrite (Figure 8-26).

The frame reaches the destination without having to go through the router. This will improve performance immensely.

There are three modes of MLS operation on a switch—destination-IP mode, source-destination-IP mode, and IP-flow mode. These modes will determine which fields are checked after a flow has been established. If an MLS is configured in the destination-IP mode, only the destination IP address will be checked to determine if there is a match in the MLS cache. The source-destination-IP mode checks both the source and destination IP addresses. And the IP-flow mode checks not only the source and destination IP addresses, but also the source and destination port numbers in the segment header. The mode of operation depends on the whether or not an access list is configured on the router and what type of access list is in use (see Table 8-7).

In most cases, supervisor engine III does the actual changing of the frame or packet rewrite, but if either the Catalyst WS-X5225R or WS-X5201R is used, the frames can be changed on the local line module, increasing performance further.

A common misconception about MLS and Layer 3 switching is that it replaces the need for a router. This is completely false. The router must route the first frame of all flows; the MLS can only Layer 3 switch the subsequent frames in the flow.

Another common misconception is that MLS or Layer 3 switching will prevent access lists from working. This is also not entirely true. Since the first frame of a flow must go through the router, had an access list been configured, there would be no "after" picture. But what if an access list is added after a flow has been established? MLS uses a special protocol between the switch and the router—the Multi-Layer Switching Protocol (MLSP). It is through this protocol that the router can update the switch about a particular flow. When an access list is added or modified on a router interface that is configured with MLSP, a message is sent to

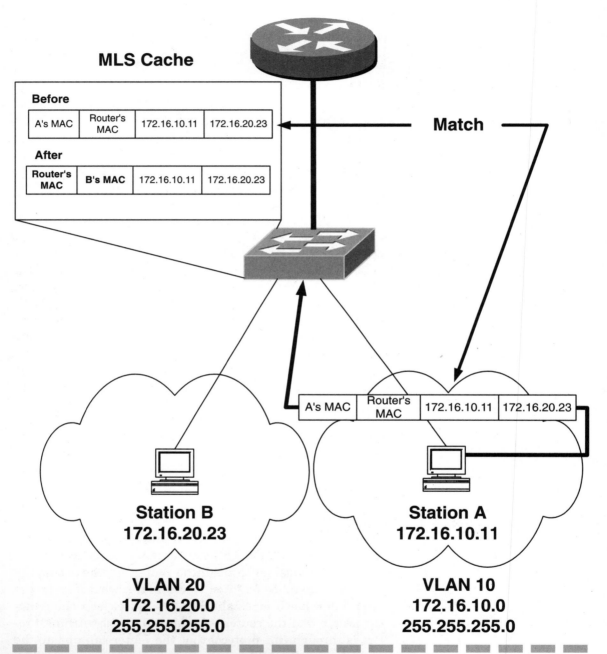

Figure 8-25 The Switch Recognizes the Flow

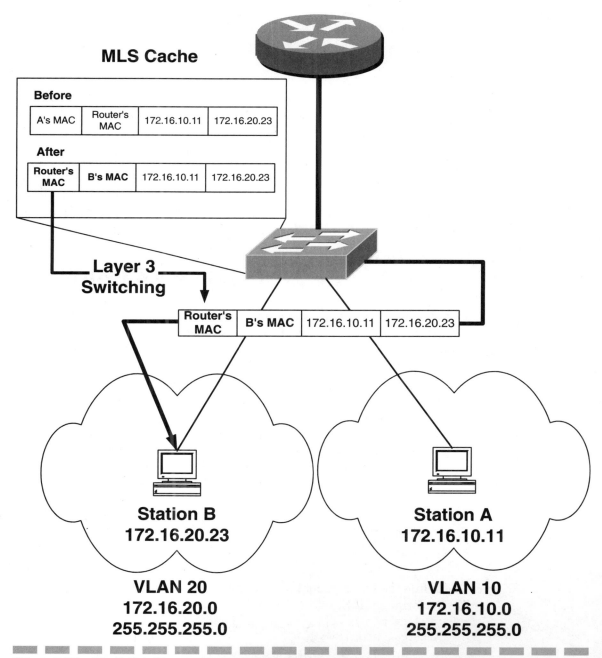

Figure 8-26   The Switch Changes the Frame Header

Table 8-7

Modes of MLS
Operation

Type of Access List	MLS Mode	Performance
No access list configured	destination-IP mode	Best
Standard IP access list	source-destination-IP mode	Better
Extended IP access list	IP-flow mode	Worst

the Layer 3 switch to flush all MLS cache entries, thus ensuring that the first frame of all flows will go through the access list. An input access list cannot be placed on an interface configured with MLS, but an output access list can. NAT (network address translation) interfaces also may not participate in MLS.

Configuring Multilayer Switching

When configuring MLS, a router must be used. The router may be an external router or the Cisco Catalyst route switch module (RSM). In either case, the release of software required on the router is 11.3(3)Wa4(4) or later. The router is referred to as the *MLS-RP*.

The actual Layer 3 switch will be a Catalyst switch with a supervisor engine III with the NetFlow Feature Card (NFFC). The switch must be running Catalyst IOS version 4.1(1) to support MLS. The Layer 3 switch is referred to as the *MLS-SE*.

Figure 8-27 shows the Cisco 4500 router from Figure 8-17 and the Catalyst 5000 switch from Figure 8-18 connected together.

To configure MLS on the router, the following steps must be taken:

1. Enable MLS on the router. The command `mls ip rp` enables MLS on a Cisco router:

```
C4500(config)#mls rp ip
C4500(config)#
```

2. Define the management domain name on the interface that will be performing MLS:

```
C4500(config-if)#mls rp vtp-dom ACC
C4500(config-if)#
```

3. One of the interfaces that is connected to the Catalyst switch must be configured as the management interface. It is through this

Figure 8-27
One-Armed Router

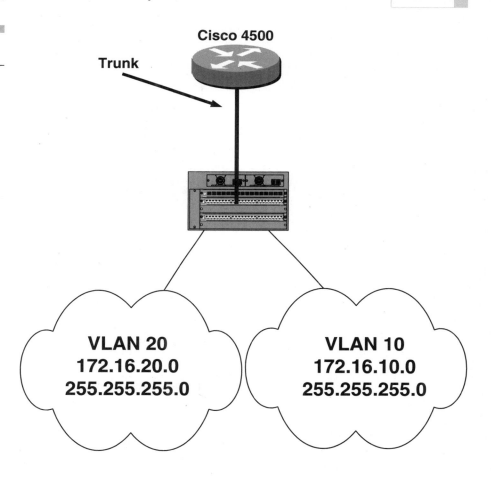

interface that MLSP packets will be exchanged. In this example I
have chosen to use the interface FastEthernet 0.10, but it could be
any of the subinterfaces:

```
C4500(config)#int fa0.10
C4500(config-subif)#mls rp management-interface
C4500(config-subif)#
```

4. Enable MLS on all interfaces that will participate in MLS:

```
C4500(config-subif)#int fa0.10
C4500(config-subif)#mls rp ip
C4500(config-subif)#int fa0.20
C4500(config-subif)#mls rp ip
C4500(config-subif)#
```

5. Verify that MLS has been configured properly:

```
C4500#sh mls rp
multilayer switching is globally enabled
mls id is 0010.7b9b.3eb1
mls ip address 209.118.4.184
mls flow mask is destination-ip
number of domains configured for mls 1

vlan domain name: ACC
 current flow mask: destination-ip
 current sequence number: 3513170556
 current/maximum retry count: 0/10
 current domain state: no-change
 current/next global purge: false/false
 current/next purge count: 0/0
 domain uptime: 00:12:15
 keepalive timer expires in 0 seconds
 retry timer not running
 change timer not running
 fcp subblock count = 3

 1 management interface(s) currently defined:
    vlan 10 on FastEthernet0.10

 2 mac-vlan(s) configured for multi-layer switching:

 mac 0010.7b9b.3eb1
    vlan id(s)
    10   20

 router currently aware of following 0 switch(es):
    no switch id's currently exists in domain
```

TECH TIP: *Configuring the RSM to be the MLS-RP is done in exactly the same way.*

When configuring MLS on a Catalyst switch, the default settings often can be enough. By default, a Catalyst switch capable of MLS will have MLS enabled. If the router that is the MLS-RP is an internal RSM, the switch will automatically begin conversing via MLSP (provided that MLS has been configured on the RSM). If an external router is being used, which is the case in Figure 8-27, the following steps must be taken to configure MLS on the switch:

1. Enable MLS on the Catalyst switch (if it was disabled):

```
Switch_A> (enable) set mls enable
Multilayer switching is enabled.
Switch_A> (enable)
```

2. Specify the address of the MLS-RP:

```
Switch_A> (enable) set mls include 172.16.10.1
Multilayer switching enabled for router 172.16.10.1.
Switch_A> (enable)
```

3. Optionally specify an MLS aging time. By default, an entry will timeout of the MLS cache after that entry has not been used for 256 seconds. This can be configured for 64-second increments between 64 and 1920 seconds. If you cannot count in multiples of 64 seconds, the switch automatically rounds to closest value:

```
Switch_A> (enable) set mls agingtime 340
Multilayer switching agingtime set to 344
Switch_A> (enable)
```

4. Optionally specify an MLS fast aging time. The MLS fast aging time is a method of clearing MLS entries that are used soon after they have been created. For example, if a workstation were to send a DNS request, a flow would be created, and an entry in the MLS cache would be allocated. However, the workstation may never send another packet to the DNS. MLS fast aging clears entries from the table if a second packet is not seen for a certain period of time. In the case of the DNS, the entry only stays in the MLS cache for the fast aging time and not the full aging time. This frees up memory for the most widely used flows. Table 8-8 shows the two parameters of the MLS fast aging time. To configure a switch to clear all entries in the MLS cache that have had packets match three times or fewer after 64 seconds from the entry's creation:

```
Switch_A> (enable) set mls agingtime fast 64 3
Multilayer switching fast agingtime set to 64 seconds for entry
with no more than 3 packets switched
Switch_A> (enable)
```

6. Verify that MLS has been enabled properly and that the proper address has been specified for the MLS-RP:

```
Switch_A> (enable) sh mls include
Included MLS-RP
```

Table 8-8

MLS Fast Aging
Time Parameters

Parameter	Description
Time	The fast aging time in seconds
Packet threshold	The maximum number of packets an entry in the MLS cache can match before the regular MLS aging time is used

```
----------------------
172.16.10.1
Switch_A> (enable)
```

And verify the aging times:

```
Switch_A> (enable) show mls
Multilayer switching enabled
Multilayer switching aging time = 344 seconds
Multilayer switching fast aging time = 64 seconds, packet threshold = 3
Current flow mask is Destination flow
Configured flow mask is Destination flow
Total packets switched = 0
Active shortcuts = 0
Netflow Data Export disabled
Netflow Data Export port/host is not configured.
Total packets exported = 0


MLS-RP IP          MLS-RP ID     XTAG MLS-RP MAC-Vlans
---------------- ------------ ---- ------ ------------------------
Switch_A> (enable)
```

MLS has been configured on both the MLS-RP and the MLS-SE.

MLS is a derivative of a Cisco proprietary switching service called *NetFlow switching*. Most of the features that were supported with NetFlow switching are supported with MLS. One of the major advantages of NetFlow switching was its ability to audit traffic flows. Using a variety of commands, many detailed statistics about traffic flow can be viewed.

For example, the `show mls entry` command can be used to view all the current flows that have been established:

```
console> (enable) show mls entry
Destination IP Source IP      Port DstPrt SrcPrt Destination Mac     Vlan  Port
-------------- -------------- ---- ------ ------ ------------------- ----- -----
MLS-RP 172.16.10.1:
172.16.10.21   172.16.20.11   UDP  7203   69     00-21-4a-00-23-34 10    4/1
172.16.10.32   172.16.20.203  TCP  23     10342  00-21-4a-12-45-87 10    4/7
172.16.10.45   172.16.20.153  TCP  23     10362  00-21-4a-23-23-51 10    4/3
172.16.10.24   172.16.20.167  UDP  69     3458   00-21-4a-17-38-56 10    4/12
172.16.10.12   172.16.20.135  TCP  21     2598   00-21-4a-12-23-03 10    4/21
172.16.10.145  172.16.20.34   UDP  80     1764   00-21-4a-38-23-97 10    4/23
172.16.10.134  172.16.20.18   UDP  12567  23     00-21-4a-02-30-64 10    4/2
console> (enable)
```

For more information on NetFlow switching and the data that can be obtained, visit the Cisco Connection Online (CCO) Web site.

SUMMARY

At this point you should be able to configure just about anything on the Catalyst 2900 series, 4000 series, or 5000 series switches having to do with Ethernet, Fast Ethernet, or Gigabit Ethernet. This chapter looked at the more advanced concepts involved when working with Catalyst switches.

VLANs are configured within a management domain and advertised throughout the domain via the VLAN Trunking Protocol (VTP). VTP keeps a consistent VLAN configuration throughout the management domain. VTP pruning can be configured to reduce unnecessary traffic on trunk lines, and VTP version 2 is required for Token Ring VLANs.

Ports may be assigned to VLANs either by having them assigned statically or by having them learned dynamically through the use of a VLAN membership policy server (VMPS). Static VLANs are much easier to configure but make VLAN management difficult. Dynamic VLANs are difficult to implement but will make VLAN administration much easier.

Security on a switch can be configured by restricting a specific protocol or a specific MAC address. Spanning must be configured to work with a packet analyzer and a Catalyst switch. Broadcasts can be limited by a percentage of overall traffic or by a packet per second threshold.

Multilayer switching (MLS) allows Catalyst switches to switch frames between VLANs using an interesting before and after picture method. MLS can greatly improve the performance of a network.

EXERCISES

1. Define the concept of a management domain. Why is it analogous to an autonomous system?

2. Define an active VLAN. Define a transit VLAN.

3. What are the advantages of naming VLANs in a management domain?

4. What is the purpose of the VLAN Trunking Protocol (VTP)? Does VTP have a comparable entity with respect to routing? If so, what is it and why?

5. What are the three VTP modes into which a switch may be placed? What does each mode allow and disallow?

6. How does VTP pruning know when to block traffic on a trunk port?

7. What is the default management domain name? What is the default VTP mode? What is the command to configure the management domain name and the VTP mode?

8. Why are unsecured management domains especially dangerous? What can be done to overcome this limitation?

9. How many management domains are there in Figure 8-28? Identify which switches are in which management domains.

10. What is the syntax of the command to create VLANs on a Catalyst switch? What command would be typed on the CLI of a Catalyst switch to create an Ethernet VLAN, numbered 100, named management, with an MTU of 1500?

11. When creating VLANs in a management domain, why is it not necessary to create the VLAN on all switches?

12. What command would assign ports 1/1 and 1/2 to VLAN 10 and ports 3/1-11 and 4/1 to VLAN 20? What two commands could you use to verify that the ports were assigned properly?

13. What are the advantages and disadvantages of static VLANs? What are the advantages and disadvantages of dynamic VLANs? (Do not regurgitate from the Summary!)

14. What device is the VLAN membership policy server? Where does it get the VMPS database? What file format is the VMPS database created in?

15. What will happen when a station with a MAC address that is not in the VMPS database connects to a dynamic VLAN port if no "fallback" VLAN is defined in the VMPS database?

16. What is the command to display the entire VMPS database? What command will display the current VMPS TFTP settings such as IP address and file name?

17. How could you find out which trunking methods are supported on a particular port? Describe the relationship between the trunk mode and the trunk encapsulation method. What is this relationship similar to? (*Hint:* It was covered in the last chapter.)

Figure 8-28
Figure for Exercise 9

| Trunk Line | ▬▬▬▬ |
| Non-Trunk Line | ———— |

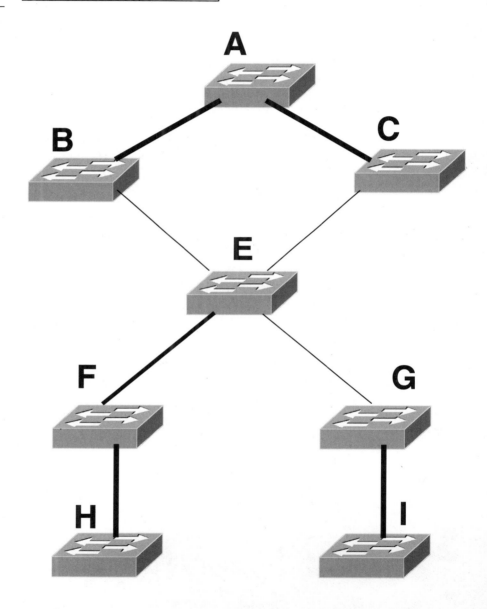

18. What is the difference between the nonnegotiate trunk state and the off trunk state? What is the purpose of the desirable state? List all the circumstances where two ports would form a trunk.

19. What is the syntax of the command to configure trunking on a port? When does this syntax change?

20. Describe the advantages and disadvantages of using a secure management domain.

21. Write the command to configure Fast EtherChannel on ports 4/1-4 of a Catalyst switch. What is the command to verify that Fast EtherChannel is working?

22. What is the difference between port protocol filtering and port security? Describe both.

23. Why must the `set span` command be used if a packet analyzer is to be employed? What port or ports can be mirrored to the span port?

24. What will the `show span` command display?

25. Describe the two methods in which broadcasts can be controlled on a Catalyst port.

26. What is the CAM table? List the three types of entries that can be placed in the CAM table, and describe the differences between each.

27. What is the difference between using an external router and Cisco's route switch module (RSM) to route between VLANs?

28. Describe the advantages to using multilayer switching (MLS).

29. Which of the MLS modes will produce the best performance, and how are the switch and router configured to operate in this mode?

30. What do the terms *MLS-RP* and *MLS-SE* describe?

31. List the instances when MLS cannot be applied to an interface.

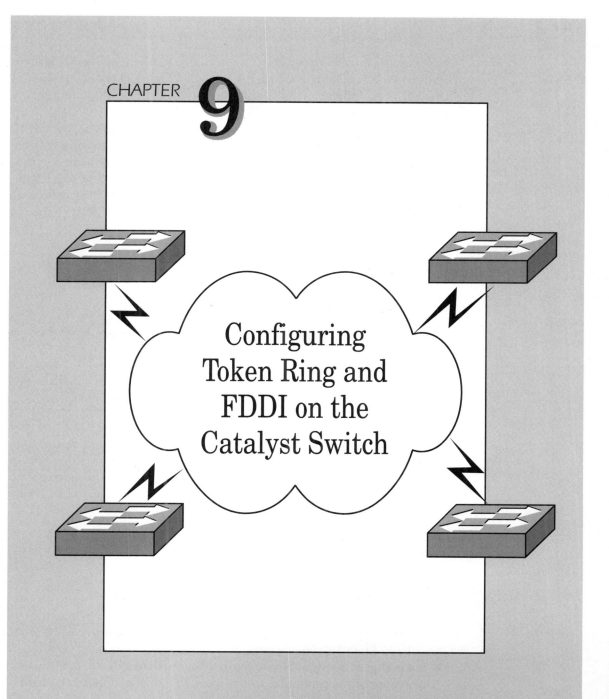

CHAPTER 9

Configuring
Token Ring and
FDDI on the
Catalyst Switch

Chapters 7 and 8 discussed commands that could be used to configure a Catalyst switch to operate in an Ethernet, Fast Ethernet, or Gigabit Ethernet environment. This chapter looks at commands to configure a switch with Token Ring and FDDI ports.

Although Token Ring and FDDI are slowly falling out of favor with many large organizations, there are still large implementations of these legacy media. I do not recommend installation of these media as new installations, but I also do not recommend ripping out these older technologies without good reason. "If it ain't broke, don't fix it!" It is for this reason that Cisco still supports the Token Ring and FDDI media on most of its switches.

Token Ring Features

As mentioned in Chapter 3, Token Ring features that are supported on Catalyst switches are

- Ring speeds of 4 and 16 Mb/s
- High-density switching modules (16 RJ-45 ports)
- Dedicated Token Ring support (DTR)
- Early Token Release
- ARE reduction
- Source-route bridging
- Source-route switching
- Source-route transparent bridging

Configuring the Port Speed

The Token Ring ports on a Catalyst line card can support 4 or 16 Mb/s. Like 10/100-Mb/s Ethernet ports, Token Ring ports have an autodetection mode that automatically configures the ports to the detected speed.

The syntax of the command to configure the Token Ring port speed is

```
Switch_A> (enable) set port speed [module_number/port_number]
[4|16|auto]
```

For example, to configure the 3/1 port to operate at 16 Mb/s:

```
Switch_A> (enable) set port speed 3/1 16
Port 3/1 speed set to 16Mbps.
Switch_A> (enable)
```

The default setting is auto.

NOTE: *When changing the port speed, the port will open and then close. If you improperly set the speed of a port that connects to a multiaccess unit (MAU), all stations connected to that MAU may experience an interruption in service.*

Configuring the Duplex Method

Token Ring ports support full duplex, but they also support full duplex to the MAU. This differs from Ethernet ports. Ethernet ports only operate at full duplex if stations are connected directly. There are four duplex methods by which a Token Ring port may operate (Table 9-1). The default duplex method is auto.

To configure the Token Ring port duplex method, use the following syntax:

```
Switch_A> (enable) set tokenring portmode [mod_num/port_num]
[duplex_method_from Table 9-1]
```

TABLE 9-1

Token Duplex Methods Supported on Catalyst Switches

Notation	Mode	Description
Hdxstation	Half duplex connected directly	The Token Ring port is connected directly to a station transmitting at half duplex
Fdxstation	Full duplex connected directly	The Token Ring port is connected directly to a station transmitting at full duplex
Hdxcport	Half duplex connected to a MAU	The Token Ring port is connected into a MAU transmitting at half duplex
Fdxcport	Full duplex connected to a MAU	The Token Ring port is connected into a MAU transmitting at full duplex
Auto	Autodetection	The port will automatically detect the transmission method

For example, to configure the 3/1 port, which is connected to a MAU, to operate in the full-duplex mode:

```
Switch_A> (enable) set tokenring portmode 3/1 fdxcport
Port 3/1 mode set to fdxcport
Switch_A> (enable)
```

Configuring Early Token Release

Catalyst Token Ring line cards support Early Token Release. To enable a Token Ring port to use Early Token Release, use the following syntax:

```
Switch_A> (enable) set tokenring etr [module_number/port_number]
[enable|disable]
```

For example, to enable Early Token Release on the 3/1 port:

```
Switch_A> (enable) set tokenring etr 3/1 enable
Port 3/1 Early Token Release enabled.
Switch_A> (enable)
```

By default, Early Token Ring Release is enabled on all ports.

Reducing the Number of All Routes Explorer (ARE) Packets

ARE reduction works in accordance with the IEEE 802.1d source route transparent bridging standard that ensures that only one ARE is received on each ring in a Token Ring virtual local-area network (VLAN).

To turn on or off ARE reduction, use the following command:

```
Switch_A> (enable) set tokenring reduction [enable | disable]
```

By default, all ports have ARE reduction enabled.

Viewing Token Ring Port Settings

To view the settings of a particular port, the following command is used:

```
Console> (enable) show tokenring 3/1
Ports  Crf/Brf    Ring#  Port-Mode     Early-Token   AC-bits
-----  -------    -----  -----------   -----------   --------
3/1    1003/1005  105    fdx-cport     enabled       enabled

Ports  Prior-Thresh   Min-Xmit   MAC-Address
-----  ------------   --------   ----------------
3/1    4              5          20:32:0b:45:2c:d5

Ports Cfg-Loss-Thresh Cfg-Loss-Intvl Cfg-Loss-Count Cfg-Loss-Reason
----- --------------- -------------- -------------- ---------------
3/1   50              20             0              none
```

Token Ring VLANs

A Token Ring network with multiple rings is usually connected together via a source-route bridge (SRB) or a source-route transparent (SRT) bridge. Catalyst switches support both methods of bridging as well as source-route switching.

From Chapter 3 we know that each port on the Token Ring card is a physical ring. Typically, in Token Ring environments, each physical ring receives a ring number, and an SRB or SRT will be used for connectivity between these rings, forming a single logical ring (Figure 9-1).

On a Catalyst switch, the ports may be grouped together into "virtual rings," with all ports in the virtual ring having the same ring number. This is *source-route switching (SRS)*. I use the term *virtual ring* as a matter of convention. I have found no documentation that uses this terminology.

The rings in Figure 9-2 have been grouped to form three virtual rings. All ports on the switch could have been configured with the same ring number. This can make administration somewhat easier. Ports that are grouped together into a single virtual ring will be assigned to a *Token Ring concentrator relay function (TrCRF)* VLAN.

To bridge between TrCRFs, *Token Ring bridge relay function (TrBRF)* VLANs are created. The TrBRFs perform either SRB or SRT bridging between the TrCRFs (Figure 9-3). And logically, Figure 9-3 looks like Figure 9-4.

Figure 9-1
Typical Token Ring
Environment

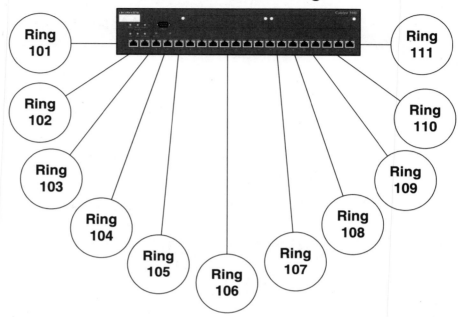

Source Route Bridge

Ring 101, Ring 102, Ring 103, Ring 104, Ring 105, Ring 106, Ring 107, Ring 108, Ring 109, Ring 110, Ring 111

TrBRF VLANs are SRB or SRT bridges. They are given ring numbers and are assigned as parents to TrCRFs. TrCRFs typically are created on only one switch. However, it is possible to distribute the default TrCRFs across multiple switches using Cisco's ISL trunking encapsulation (Figure 9-5).

This will help reduce the number of ring numbers and avoid problems with the maximum SRB hop count.

NOTE: *By default, a TrBRF VLAN and a TrCRF VLAN are created, and a parent-child relationship is defined. Therefore, Token Ring switching can be plug and play.*

Configuring Token Ring VLANs

To configure Token Ring VLANs on a Catalyst switch, one must decide whether or not to use the default settings. By default, there is a TrCRF

Figure 9-2
Virtual Ring
Configuration

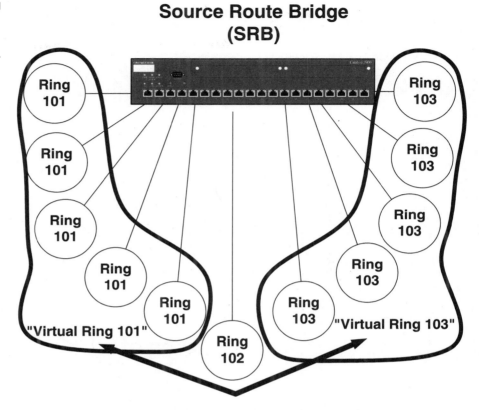

VLAN and a TrBRF VLAN. All Token Ring ports are assigned to the TrCRF, and the TrBRF is the parent of the TrCRF.

```
Switch_A> (enable) show vlan <Enter>
VLAN  Name                         Status     Mod/Ports
----  ---------------------------  ---------  -----------------
1     default                      active     1/1-2
                                              2/1-12
                                              3/1-2
1002  fddi-default                 active
1003  trcrf-default                active
1004  fddinet-default              active
1005  trbrf-default                active
```

VLAN 1003 is the default TrCRF, and VLAN 1005 is the default TrBRF.

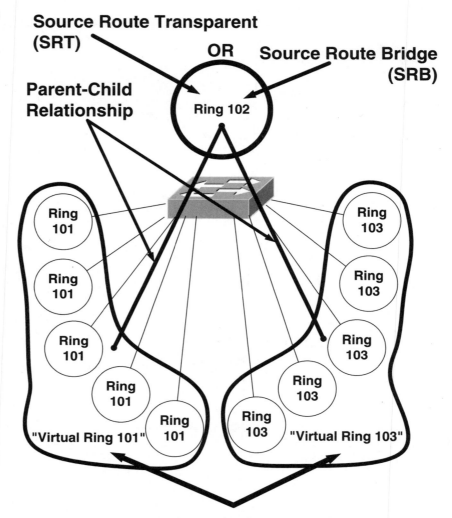

Figure 9-3
TrBRFs and TrCRFs

Source Route Transparent (SRT)

OR

Source Route Bridge (SRB)

Parent-Child Relationship

Ring 102

Ring 101

Ring 101

Ring 101

Ring 101

Ring 101

"Virtual Ring 101"

Ring 103

Ring 103

Ring 103

Ring 103

Ring 103

"Virtual Ring 103"

Source Route Switching (SRS)

To create more TrCRFs, a parent TrBRF must be created. You cannot use the default TrBRF; one must be created manually before any TrCRFs can be created.

NOTE: *VTP version 2 must be enabled to create Token Ring VLANs.*

Figure 9-4
Logical Representation
of Figure 9-3

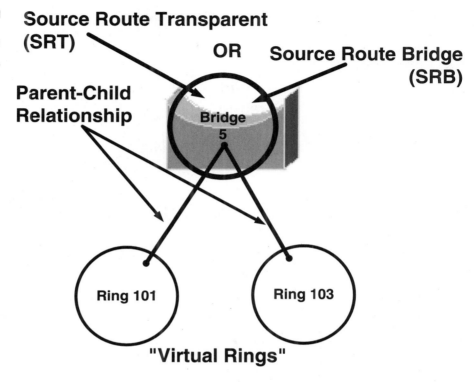

Figure 9-5
Distributed TrCRFs

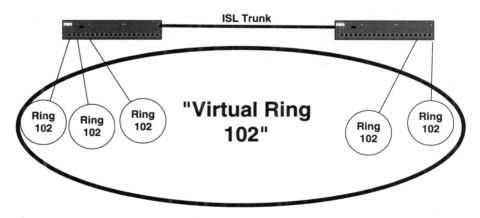

When creating a TrBRF, a bridge number must be given and an STP protocol chosen. The Catalyst Token Ring modules currently support the IBM and IEEE versions of STP for Token Ring *only*. The IEEE version is the only STP supported on Ethernet ports. The maximum transmission unit (MTU) can be set to 1500 or 4472. By default, it is 4472. The command to create a TrBRF is as follows:

```
Switch_A> (enable) set vlan [vlan_num] name [name] type trbrf mtu
                   [mtu] bridge
                   bridge_number stp [ieee | ibm]
```

NOTE: *The default STP is IBM.*

To configure a TrCRF, the following syntax must be followed:

```
Switch_A> (enable) set vlan vlan_num name [name] type trcrf mtu [mtu]
                   ring [hex_ring_number or decring
                   decimal_ring_number] parent [vlan_num]
```

The ring number may be specified in either hex or decimal. To specify the ring number in decimal, the word `decring` must be inserted before the ring number is entered.

NOTE: *The parent VLAN must exist or the TrCRF will not be created.*

EXAMPLE

To configure a Catalyst switch with the configuration shown in Figure 9-6, the following commands must be entered:

```
Switch_A> (enable) set vlan 900 name Bridge_1 type trbrf bridge 1
Vlan 900 configuration successful
Switch_A > (enable) set vlan 901 name Ring_101 type trcrf ring 101
parent 900
Vlan 901 configuration successful
Switch_A > (enable) set vlan 902 name Ring_102 type trcrf ring 102
parent 900
Vlan 902 configuration successful
Switch_A> (enable) set vlan 901 3/1-8
VLAN 1003 modified.
VLAN 901 modified.
VLAN  Mod/Ports
----  ---------------------
900    3/1-8
```

Figure 9-6
Configuring a
Catalyst Switch

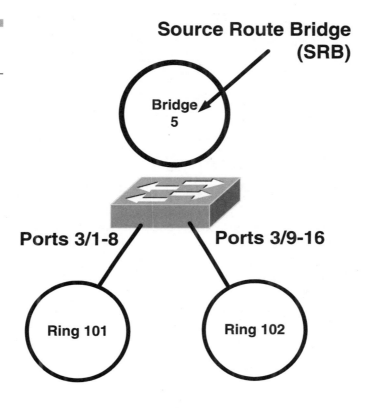

```
Switch_A> (enable) set vlan 901 3/9-16
VLAN 1003 modified.
VLAN 902 modified.
VLAN  Mod/Ports
----  ---------------------
902    3/9-16
```

Configuration complete.

FDDI and Catalyst Switches

Currently, Cisco has a single-port FDDI module to support connectivity to legacy backbones like those discussed in Chapter 1. Most of the time FDDI makes up a campus backbone or a server backbone. The Catalyst FDDI module allows connectivity by translationally bridging to and from FDDI to Ethernet, and vice versa.

FDDI supports larger maximum transmission units (MTUs) than Ethernet, and therefore, the Catalyst FDDI modules support IP fragmentation. The FDDI module discovers the MTU in use on the FDDI ring.

FDDI Automated Packet Recognition and Translation (APaRT)

APaRT is a feature best used in a Novell environment. It was common to have FDDI server backbones when using Novell's netware NOS. Clients would be attached to Ethernet ports on a switch, and the switch would have an FDDI connection to the server ring, as shown in Figure 9-7.

When a server on the FDDI ring transmits a frame to one of the workstations on the Ethernet segments, how will it know what Ethernet frame type into which to translate the frame? Chapter 1 discussed the four different frame types commonly found in a Novell environment. Figure 9-7 shows several clients, all with different Ethernet frame types.

APaRT occurs when the switch creates a table to associate source MAC addresses with frame types. The FDDI module will learn (in the same manner as a transparent bridge) what frame type a MAC address is using. Once an Ethernet frame type has been learned, the switch will know what Ethernet frame type to use when forwarding frames to that MAC address.

In Figure 9-8, frames with destination MAC addresses in the APaRT table will be translated to the listed Ethernet frame type. If a MAC address is not in the APaRT table, default translations will be used based on the FDDI frame type.

NOTE: *APaRT is enabled by default. The process of looking up entries in the APaRT table reduces the packets per second (pps) of the FDDI module by approximately 15,000. APaRT is only useful with protocols other than IP. IP always uses the ARPA Ethernet frame type. In an IP-only environment, APaRT should be disabled.*

Figure 9-7
FDDI-to-Ethernet
Translational Bridging

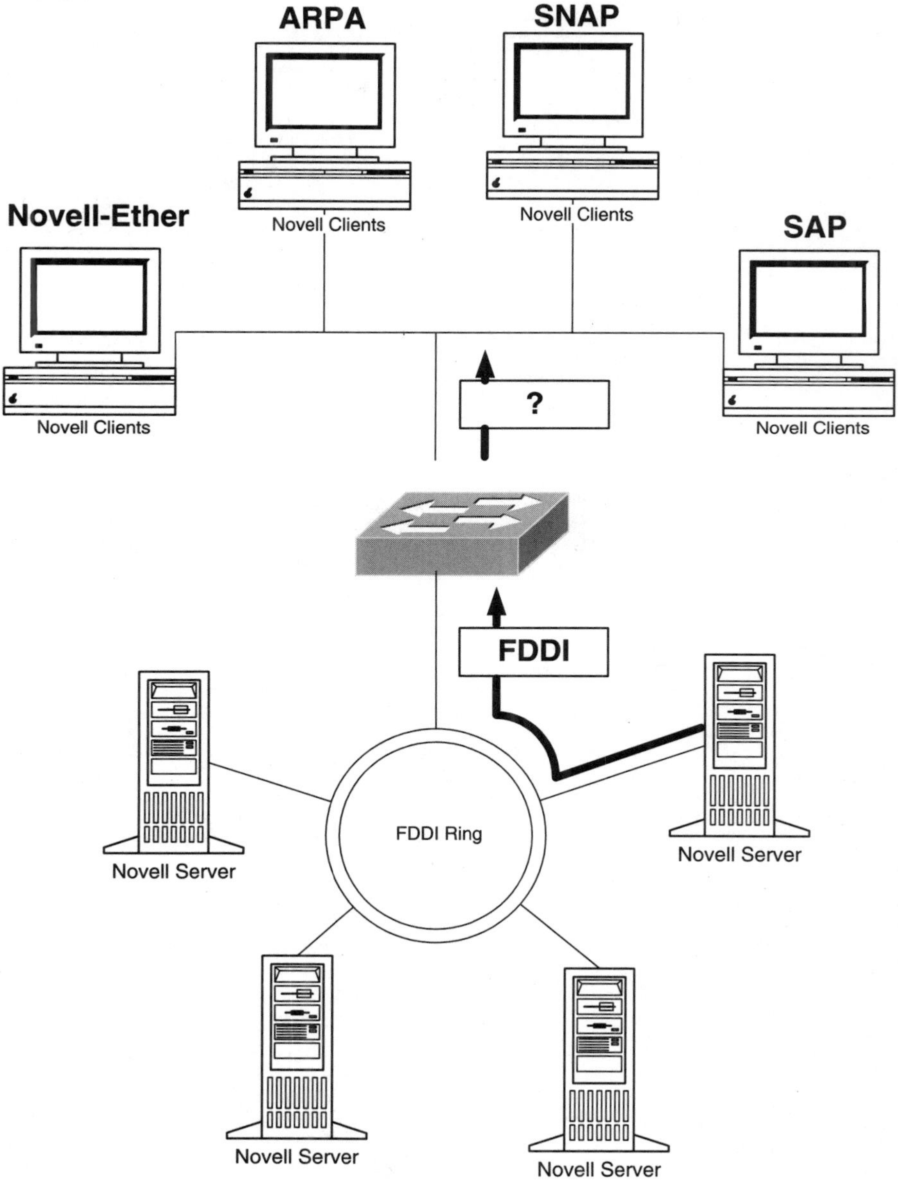

Figure 9-8
APaRT

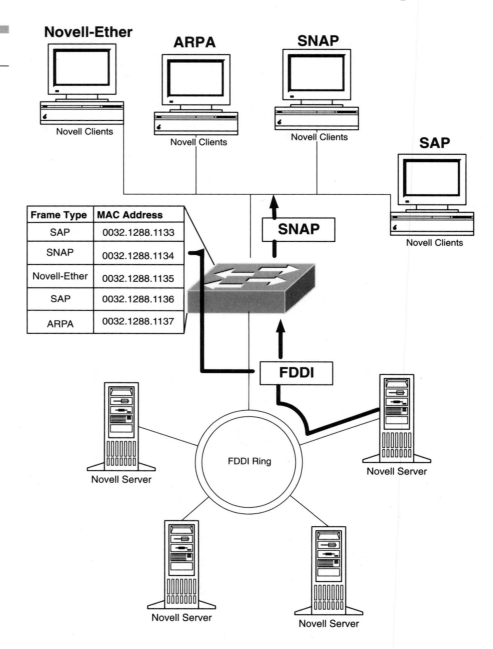

Frame Type	MAC Address
SAP	0032.1288.1133
SNAP	0032.1288.1134
Novell-Ether	0032.1288.1135
SAP	0032.1288.1136
ARPA	0032.1288.1137

To disable APaRT, use the following command:

```
Switch_A> (enable) set bridge apart disable
APaRT disabled
Switch_A> (enable)
```

FDDI and Catalyst Switches

I have observed three different methods of implementing Catalyst switches.

1. Translational bridging between a server farm to workstations, as in Figure 9-7.
2. Trunking across FDDI to provide a connectivity backbone in a large LAN or MAN (Figure 9-9).
3. Both translational bridging to those servers on the ring and trunking to those switches on the FDDI ring (Figure 9-10).

Each method requires a different configuration.

Configuring Translational Bridging

To provide connectivity to workstations on an FDDI ring, the FDDI port can be assigned to an Ethernet VLAN. The switch will automatically translate frames destined for workstations on the FDDI ring into FDDI, and vice versa.

To configure a switch to translationally bridge between Ethernet ports and an FDDI ring (Figure 9-11), assign the FDDI port to the Ethernet VLAN that is assigned to the Ethernet ports. This sounds funny, but an FDDI port must be assigned to an Ethernet VLAN. The FDDI ring will now be in the same broadcast domain. As far as the workstations in Figure 9-11 are concerned, the servers are on the same IP subnet, IPX network, and Appletalk cable-range (Figure 9-12).

The FDDI ring is easily incorporated into the Ethernet VLAN, making administration at Layer 3 very easy. A disadvantage to be considered is the latency associated with switching between the Ethernet and FDDI ports. Remember that in an IP environment, disabling APaRT will reduce this latency.

Figure 9-9
Trunking with FDDI

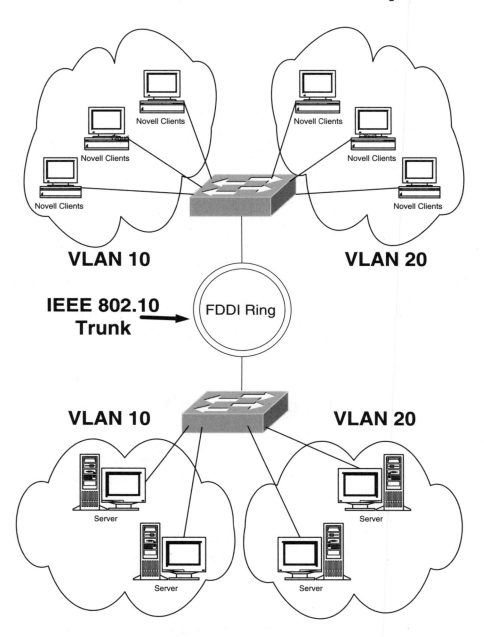

VLAN 10

VLAN 20

IEEE 802.10
Trunk

FDDI Ring

VLAN 10

VLAN 20

Novell Clients

Novell Clients

Novell Clients

Novell Clients

Novell Clients

Novell Clients

Server

Server

Server

Server

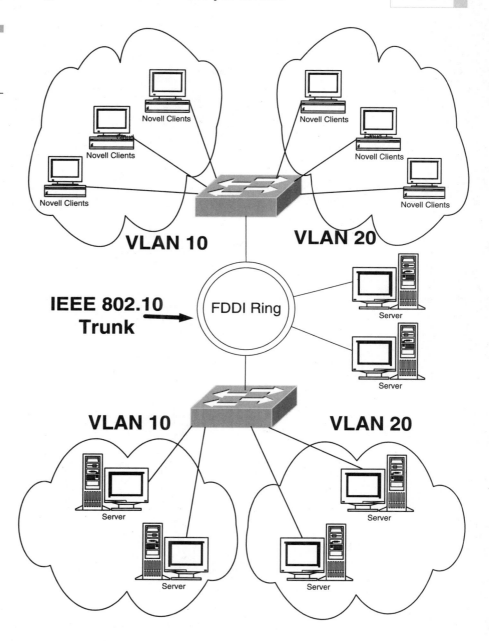

Figure 9-10
Trunking and
Translationally
Bridging

Figure 9-11
FDDI Translational
Bridge

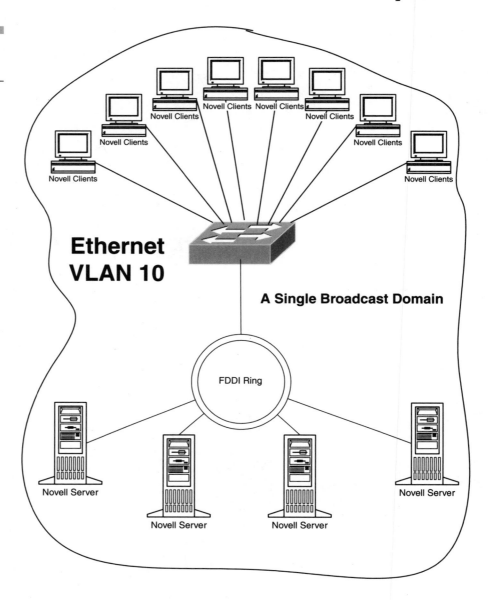

To assign an FDDI port to an Ethernet VLAN, use the command from Chapter 8:

```
Switch_A> (enable) set vlan [Ethernet VLAN number]  [FDDI ports]
```

For example, to assign the FDDI ports 3/1-2 to VLAN 10 as in Figure 9-12,

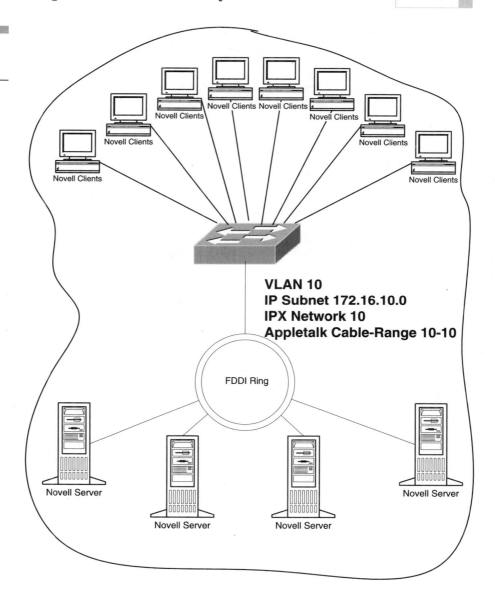

Figure 9-12
A Single Broadcast Domain

VLAN 10
IP Subnet 172.16.10.0
IPX Network 10
Appletalk Cable-Range 10-10

use the following command (this example sets VLAN 10 for a Catalyst 5000 series switch in building A):

```
Switch_A> (enable) set vlan 10 2/1-2
VLAN 10 modified.
VLAN 1 modified.
```

```
VLAN   Mod/Ports
----   ---------------------
10     2/1-2
```

By default, the FDDI ports are in the default VLAN, Ethernet VLAN 1.

Multiple switches can be connected to the FDDI ring, so VLAN 10 can be extended as in Figure 9-13.

All the switches in the figure are connected to Ethernet VLAN 10, which allows Ethernet VLAN 10 to span multiple switches. This is *not* trunking. Frames are not being tagged with a VLAN number, and there are no VTP updates passing across the ring. The result is four separate management domains. This type of configuration would be used in a single VLAN environment. The configuration *only* allows VLAN 10 traffic to cross the FDDI ring. The servers that have been placed on the FDDI ring are also in VLAN 10. When configuring the two switches in Figure 9-13, both must have their FDDI ports assigned to VLAN 10.

Figure 9-13
Extending an
Ethernet VLAN Across
an FDDI Ring

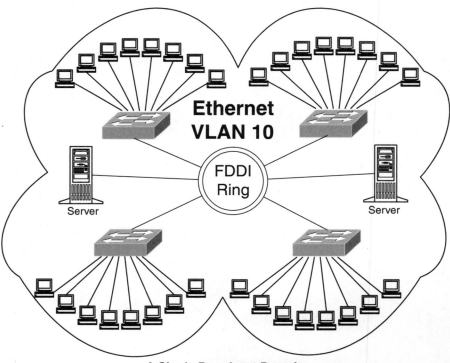

Configuring FDDI Trunking

If trunking is necessary, FDDI VLANs must be created. Figure 9-14 shows an environment similar to Figure 9-13 but with the need to have multiple VLAN traffic traverse the FDDI ring.

VLAN 10 and VLAN 20 are spread across the four switches, so trunking must be configured on the FDDI ring. The IEEE 802.10 header will identify the VLAN to which the encapsulated frame belongs.

When configuring trunking on an FDDI ring, there are three steps:

1. Turn on trunking on the FDDI port connected to the FDDI ring on which trunking is to be configured.

2. Create an FDDI VLAN for every Ethernet VLAN to be trunked across the FDDI ring.

3. Map the FDDI VLANs to the corresponding Ethernet VLAN.

To configure trunking for the scenario in Figure 9-15, complete the following steps:

Figure 9-14
FDDI Trunking Is required

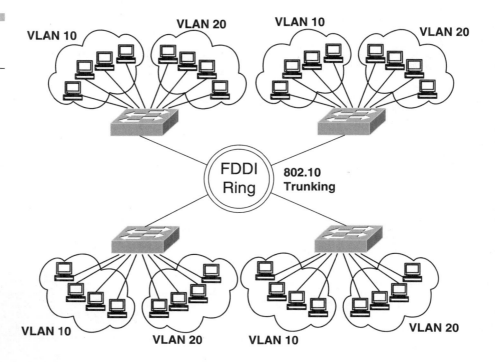

Figure 9-15
FDDI Trunking
Example

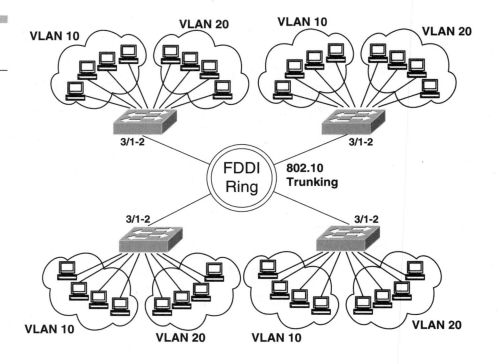

1. Turn on trunking on the FDDI port connected to the FDDI ring on which trunking is to be configured.

    The switches in Figure 9-15 are using the 3/1-2 ports to connect to the FDDI ring. To turn on trunking on those ports, use the following commands:

    On switch A:

```
Switch_A> (enable) set trunk 3/1 on
Port(s) 3/1-2 trunk mode set to on.
Switch_A> (enable)
1999 Apr 12 20:31:18 %DTP-5-TRUNKPORTON:Port 1/1 has become dot10
trunk
Switch_A> (enable)
```

    On switch B:

```
Switch_B> (enable) set trunk 3/1 on
Port(s) 3/1-2 trunk mode set to on.
Switch_B> (enable)
1999 Apr 12 20:32:48 %DTP-5-TRUNKPORTON:Port 3/1-2 has become dot10
trunk
Switch_B> (enable)
```

On switch C:

```
Switch_C> (enable) set trunk 3/1 on
Port(s) 3/1-2 trunk mode set to on.
Switch_C> (enable)
1999 Apr 12 20:36:21 %DTP-5-TRUNKPORTON:Port 3/1-2 has become dot10
trunk
Switch_C> (enable)
```

On switch D:

```
Switch_D> (enable) set trunk 3/1 on
Port(s) 3/1-2 trunk mode set to on.
Switch_D> (enable)
1999 Apr 12 20:33:12 %DTP-5-TRUNKPORTON:Port 3/1-2 has become dot10
trunk
Switch_D> (enable)
```

Notice that the command typed only specified the 3/1 port. The 3/2 port was set automatically to trunk. This occurs because the FDDI ports, although two ports physically, act as a single logical port.

2. Create an FDDI VLAN for every Ethernet VLAN to be trunked across the FDDI ring.

Two Ethernet VLANs need to be trunked across the FDDI ring. Thus I create two FDDI VLANs, one for each of the Ethernet VLANs. They can be numbered in any way, but I find it helpful to come up with a logical VLAN numbering scheme. For example, in this scenario I use the Ethernet VLAN number + 800. The FDDI VLAN created for Ethernet VLAN 10 will be numbered 810, and the FDDI VLAN created for Ethernet VLAN 20 will be numbered 820.

When creating FDDI VLANs, a security association identifier (SAID) can be specified. It is this number that is used in the IEEE 802.10 header to identify the VLAN of the encapsulated frame. By default, the SAID value will be 100000 plus the VLAN number. I do not recommend changing the SAID value from the default.

When creating an FDDI VLAN, it is necessary to specify the "type" as FDDI.

To create the FDDI VLANs necessary for trunking, use the following commands:

```
Switch_A> (enable) set vlan 810 name FDDI_810-Ethernet_10 type fddi
VTP: vlan addition successful
Switch_A> (enable) set vlan 820 name FDDI_820-Ethernet_10 type fddi
VTP: vlan addition successful
```

It is only necessary to create these VLANs on a single switch. The VTP will advertise the newly created VLANs to the other switches.

NOTE: *Depending on the version of Catalyst IOS you are using, you may receive a message indicating that the VLAN you are creating is "of an unsupported VLAN type." This message is to remind you that an FDDI VLAN is never to be assigned to a port.*

BONEHEAD ALERT: *Do not forget to specify the "type" as FDDI. If you do, the VLAN will be created as an Ethernet VLAN, and you will not be able to perform step 3. To rectify this mistake, the VLAN must be removed from the switch and recreated. Do not simply retype the command specifying FDDI as the "type."*

3. Map the FDDI VLANs to the corresponding Ethernet VLAN.

The final step is to inform the switches of the Ethernet-to-FDDI VLAN mappings. Figure 9-16 shows the FDDI-to-Ethernet mappings.

Figure 9-16
FDDI-to-Ethernet
VLAN Mappings

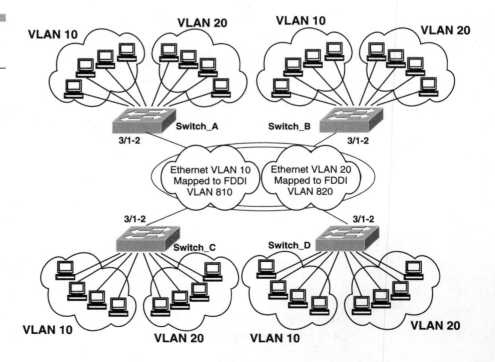

To specify the mappings, use the following commands:

```
Switch_A> (enable) set vlan 10 translation 810
VTP: vlan modification successful
Switch_A> (enable) set vlan 20 translation 820
VTP: vlan modification successful
```

These translations need only be specified on one switch. VTP will advertise the translations to all switches via the trunk ports.

NOTE: *The order in which the VLANs are specified is not significant. The commands could have been typed*

```
Switch_A> (enable) set vlan 810 translation 10
VTP: vlan modification successful
Switch_A> (enable) set vlan 820 translation 20
VTP: vlan modification successful
```

To verify the translations, use the show vlan command:

```
Switch_A> (enable) show vlan
```

VLAN	Name	Type	Status	Mod/Ports
1	default	enet	active	1/1-2,2/1-12
10	FSU	enet	active	3/1-2
20	Duke	enet	active	2/13-24
810	FDDI_810-Ethernet_10	fddi	active	
820	FDDI_820-Ethernet_20	fddi	active	
1002	fddi-default	fddi	active	
1003	token-ring-default	tring	active	
1004	fddinet-default	fdnet	active	
1005	trnet-default	trnet	active	

VLAN	SAID	MTU	RingNo	BridgeNo	StpNo	Parent	Trans1	Trans2
1	1	1500	0	0	0	0	0	0
10	100010	1500	0	0	0	0	810	0
20	100020	1500	0	0	0	0	820	0
810	100810	1500	0	0	0	0	10	0
820	100820	1500	0	0	0	0	20	0
1002	1002	1500	0	0	0	0	0	0
1003	1003	1500	0	0	0	0	0	0
1004	1004	1500	0	0	0	0	0	0
1005	1005	1500	0	0	0	0	0	0

```
Switch_A> (enable)
```

The Trans1 field indicates what VLANs are being translated. At this point VLAN 10 and 20 traffic may be transmitted across the FDDI ring.

Configuring an FDDI Port to Trunk and Translationally Bridging at the Same Time

In the event that an FDDI ring is doubling as both a server backbone and a switch backbone, as in Figure 9-17, a Catalyst switch can have its FDDI ports configured as both a trunk and be assigned to an Ethernet VLAN. The servers on the FDDI ring will belong to the Ethernet VLAN to which the FDDI ports are assigned, whereas 802.10 frames will carry VLAN traffic between the switches (trunking).

The servers on the right-hand side are part of the FDDI ring. With the FDDI ports assigned to Ethernet VLAN 10 and trunking turned on, there is connectivity to the servers as well as trunking capabilities.

To configure the environment shown in Figure 9-17, simply configure translational bridging and trunking on the same port. To verify that

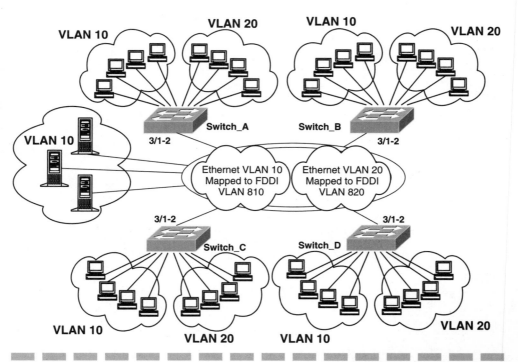

Figure 9-17   Trunking and Translationally Bridging on the Same FDDI Ring

both trunking and translational bridging are configured properly, use the show port command:

```
Switch_A> (enable) show port <Enter>
Port Name  Status     Vlan      Level    Duplex   Speed   Type
---------  ---------  --------  -------  -------  -----   ----------
1/1        connected 1         high      half      100   10/100BaseTX
1/2        connected 1         normal    half      100   10/100BaseTX
2/1        connected 1         normal    a-full   a-100   10/100BaseTX
2/2        connected 1         normal    a-half    a-10   10/100BaseTX
2/3        connected 1         normal    a-full   a-100   10/100BaseTX
2/4        connected 1         normal    a-full   a-100   10/100BaseTX
2/5        connected 1         normal    a-full   a-100   10/100BaseTX
2/6        connected 1         normal    a-full   a-100   10/100BaseTX
2/7        connected 1         normal    a-full   a-100   10/100BaseTX
2/8        connected 1         normal    a-full   a-100   10/100BaseTX
2/9        connected 1         normal    a-full   a-100   10/100BaseTX
2/10       connected 1         normal    a-full   a-100   10/100BaseTX
2/11       connected 1         normal    a-full   a-100   10/100BaseTX
2/12       connected 1         normal    a-full   a-100   10/100BaseTX
3/1        connected 10/trunk  normal    half      100   FDDI
3/2        connected 10/trunk  normal    half      100   FDDI
4/1        connected trunk     normal    full      155   OC3 MMF ATM
4/2        connected trunk     normal    full      155   OC3 MMF ATM
.. .
Switch_A> (enable)
```

The ports are listed as being configured as trunk and as members of VLAN 10.

SUMMARY

Token Ring and FDDI media types are supported by Catalyst switches. Although diminishing, there is still a large installed base of these media. It is for this reason that Cisco continues to produce line modules to support these legacy media.

The Catalyst 3900 series of switches is entirely a Token Ring, whereas the Catalyst WS-X5030 is a 16-port line module for the Catalyst 5000 series of switches. Catalyst switches can support source-route bridging (SRB), source-route switching (SRS), and source-route translational bridging (SRT). Bridging methods are configured using Token Ring concentrator relay function (TrCRF) VLANs and Token Ring bridge relay function (TrBRF) VLANs. TrBRFs are VLANs that behave as an SRB or SRT bridge. A TrBRF will be a parent of a TrCRF and will see each TrCRF as a bridge port. Individual ports are then assigned to a TrCRF.

A Catalyst switch can be configured as an FDDI-to-Ethernet translational bridge as well as have its FDDI ports configured for trunking to other Catalyst switches. FDDI VLANs are only used when configuring trunking. An FDDI port will always be assigned to an Ethernet VLAN. By default, this is VLAN 1.

EXERCISES

1. Describe the dedicated Token Ring (DTR) feature of a Catalyst line module? What are the advantages and requirements of using DTR?

2. When would you use the hdxstation duplex method as opposed to the hdxcport duplex method?

3. What does the term *virtual ring* refer to? What are the advantages to using source-route switching (SRS)?

4. Describe the difference between a TrBRF and a TrCRF. When would you use one as opposed to the other?

5. What first must be done before creating a TrCRF?

6. What are the two formats in which the ring number of a TrCRF may be specified? How is each specified in the `set vlan` command.

7. What is the APaRT feature? What is the default setting? When should it be used?

8. When is an FDDI port assigned to an FDDI VLAN? Why?

9. What is the effect of assigning a Ethernet VLAN to an FDDI port?

10. What are the three steps to configuring FDDI trunking? What is the purpose of the FDDI VLAN? What is the difference between configuring trunking on Ethernet ports as compared with trunking on FDDI ports?

11. What is the SAID? When should you alter the default value?

12. Why do FDDI-to-Ethernet VLAN translations need to be configured only on one switch and not every switch in the management domain?

13. How can you verify that your translations have been configured correctly?

14. In Figure 9-17, who will have connectivity to the servers on the FDDI ring? Who will not? Why?

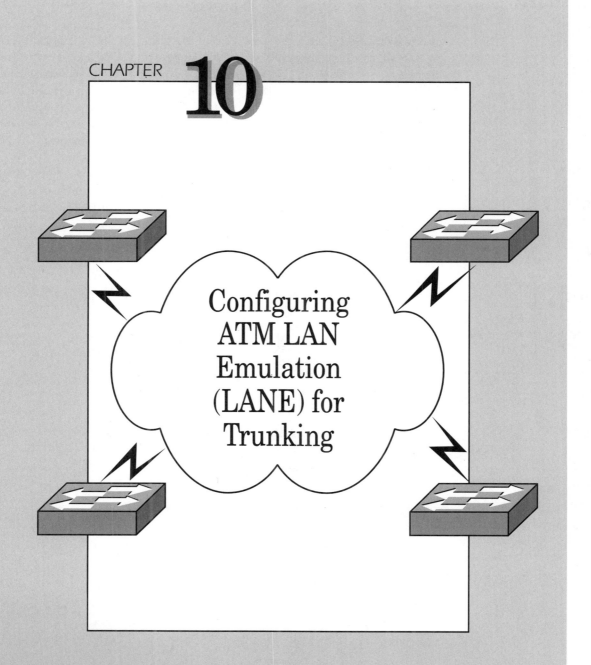

CHAPTER 10

Configuring
ATM LAN
Emulation
(LANE) for
Trunking

A Catalyst switch, with the exception of the Catalyst 5500, is not an ATM switch. It can be configured as an end node of an ATM cloud but is not part of the cloud. An ATM cloud is constructed using ATM switches, much in the same way a Frame Relay cloud is constructed with Frame Relay switches. Local-area network emulation (LANE) is a standard developed by the ATM Forum (a consortium of ATM vendors) to make an ATM cloud appear as a LAN, either Ethernet or Token Ring. It is through LANE that LAN workstations may commnicate across an ATM cloud.

In Figure 10-1, the Catalyst switches connect into a port on one of the ATM switches that make up the ATM cloud. The ATM switches may be a Cisco light stream or the bottom five slots of a Catalyst 5500 if it has the appropriate modules installed.

Cisco currently has several line modules that support ATM LANE. There is currently an ATM LANE module that supports OC-3 and a module that supports OC-12. These have speeds of 155 and 622 Mb/s, respectively. ATM is an excellent high-speed backbone. Besides the

Figure 10-1
An ATM Cloud

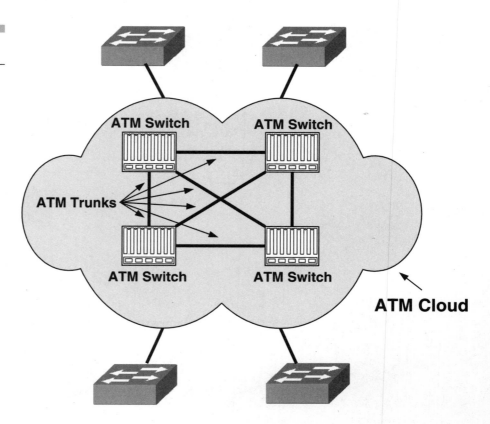

speed advantages over other high-speed bandwidth options, ATM also supports quality of service (QoS) for applications that may require it. It uses permanent and switched virtual circuits (PVCs and SVCs), with bandwidth on demand. Here, I will only discuss SVCs.

ATM and Gigabit Ethernet

I am often asked if ATM or Gigabit Ethernet should be used. Each medium has its advantages and disadvantages. Table 10-1 provides a summary.

ATM supports high-speed bandwidths of 155 and 622 Mb/s, as mentioned before. Gigabit Ethernet supports a bandwidth of 1 Gb/s, a little faster than ATM. However, the ATM Forum is currently working on an OC-48, a 2.4-Gb/s standard. There is also little latency associated with ATM switching owing to the fixed-length cells. Gigabit Ethernet uses variable-length frames, which increase latency when performing Gigabit Ethernet switching. ATM uses a cloud technology, which allows the use of virtual circuits (VCs) and permits customization of traffic and traffic shaping (the ability to control the amount of bandwidth used by a particular type of traffic). The cloud technology also reduces the number of ports required in the same way that fewer serial interfaces are required when using Frame Relay (point-to-multipoint) as opposed to dedicated lease lines (point-to-point). As the number of connections required increases, so does the cost savings over Gigabit Ethernet.

TABLE 10-1

Advantages and Disadvantages to ATM and Gigabit Ethernet

ATM Advantages	ATM Disadvantages	GE Advantages	GE Disadvantages
155 or 622 Mb/s bandwidth	Difficult to understand	1 Gb/s bandwidth	Point-to-point technology
QoS	Difficult to configure	Known and proven Ethernet technology	Somewhat expensive
Cloud technology	Somewhat expensive	Well-defined standards	Loosely defined QoS
Support of switched virtual circuits	Not well standardized	Easy to implement	
Bandwidth on demand			
Fixed-length data unit to reduce latency			

Which to use? It depends. Do you need the advantages of ATM, or are you looking for a high-speed medium to connect together several locations in a small geographic area? If this is the case, Gigabit Ethernet is the way to go. If you would like a little more control over how traffic goes across your backbone, ATM provides excellent bandwidth with QoS. ATM is also ideal when it is used as a large backbone.

ATM and LAN Emulation

ATM LAN emulation is used on the switch for trunking across an ATM cloud. Trunking is configured across ATM in much the same way we configured trunking across FDDI. With FDDI, we created an FDDI VLAN for every Ethernet VLAN that we wanted to trunk across the FDDI ring. With ATM, we create an ATM VLAN for every Ethernet VLAN that we want to trunk across the ATM cloud. Only we do not call an ATM VLAN an ATM VLAN; we call it an emulated LAN (ELAN). An ELAN is created for every Ethernet VLAN that will be trunked across an ATM cloud. Figure 10-2 shows the same environment we used in Chapter 9; only now the switches are connected together using an ATM cloud.

The three steps for trunking VLANs over an FDDI ring are translated to ATM trunking (LANE) as follows:

1. Turn trunking on. With an ATM port, trunking is always enabled. See the following output:

```
Switch_A> (enable) show port <Enter>
Port Name    Status    Vlan     Level   Duplex Speed Type
---- -----   --------- -------- ------- ------ ----- --------------
1/1          connected 1        high    half   100   10/100BaseTX
1/2          connected 1        normal  half   100   10/100BaseTX
2/1          connected 1        normal  a-full a-100 10/100BaseTX
2/2          connected 1        normal  a-half a-10  10/100BaseTX
2/3          connected 1        normal  a-full a-100 10/100BaseTX
2/4          connected 1        normal  a-full a-100 10/100BaseTX
2/5          connected 1        normal  a-full a-100 10/100BaseTX
2/6          connected 1        normal  a-full a-100 10/100BaseTX
2/7          connected 1        normal  a-full a-100 10/100BaseTX
2/8          connected 1        normal  a-full a-100 10/100BaseTX
2/9          connected 1        normal  a-full a-100 10/100BaseTX
2/10         connected 1        normal  a-full a-100 10/100BaseTX
2/11         connected 1        normal  a-full a-100 10/100BaseTX
2/12         connected 1        normal  a-full a-100 10/100BaseTX
3/1          connected 10/trunk normal  half   100   FDDI
3/2          connected 10/trunk normal  half   100   FDDI
4/1          connected trunk    normal  full   155   OC3 MMF ATM
4/2          connected trunk    normal  full   155   OC3 MMF ATM
. . .
Switch_A> (enable)
```

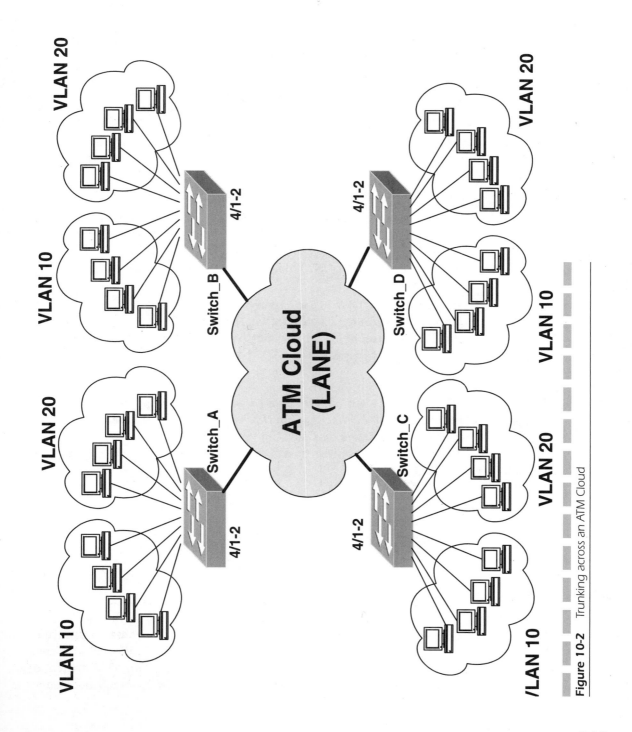

Figure 10-2 Trunking across an ATM Cloud

The 4/1-2 ports are ATM OC-3 ports connected into the ATM cloud. Both ports will always be listed as trunks, whether they are connected or not. With trunking always enabled, it is not necessary to turn trunking on.

NOTE: *The two ports are both connected to the same ATM cloud. Multiple connections are only for redundancy; there is no load balancing. This feature is called dual PHY, for the "dual physical connections."*

2. Create an FDDI VLAN for every Ethernet VLAN that needs to be trunked across the FDDI ring. With ATM, an ELAN needs to be created for every Ethernet VLAN that needs to be trunked across the ATM cloud. Creating an ELAN is not nearly as simple as configuring an FDDI VLAN. This procedure will be discussed in the next section.

3. Map the FDDI VLAN to the Ethernet VLAN. With ATM, the mapping must be created on each switch that is trunking over the ATM cloud. This is unlike FDDI trunking, where the translations were automatically advertised via VTP updates. ATM translations are not.

NOTE: *The translations can be created automatically using VTP. This procedure will not be discussed in this book. However, the step-by-step procedure can be found on Cisco Connection Online (CCO) at http://www.cisco.com/univercd/cc/td/doc/product/lan/cat5000/rel_4_5/config/atm.htm#42173.*

It is important to recognize the similarities between FDDI trunking and ATM trunking. Logically, you are doing the same procedure. However, the configurations are completely different.

Creating an ATM LANE Cloud

To create ELANs, a set of software components must be configured. These software components can run on a number of different devices, including, but not limited to, an ATM attached router, an ATM switch, a Catalyst switch, or other ATM devices. The four components necessary to create an ATM LANE cloud are

1. LAN emulation client (LEC)

2. Broadcast and unknown server (BUS)

3. LAN emulation server (LES)

4. LAN emulation configuration server (LECS)

Each component has a hand in the process of trunking VLAN traffic across the ATM LANE cloud. The organization of these components can be compared with that of a medium-sized business.

Every business has one individual who is ultimately responsible for all decisions. This individual runs the organization and answers to no one. This is, of course, the chief executive officer (CEO) or president. In an ATM cloud, the LAN emulation configuration server (LECS) is in charge of running the cloud. As in a business, there can be only *one* LECS.

NOTE: *In LANE version 2 and with Cisco's Simple Server Redundancy Protocol (SSRP), a second LECS, LES, and BUS can be configured for redundancy.*

A medium-sized business is split into departments. An ATM LANE cloud is split into emulated LANs (ELANs). Each department has a single individual who runs the department. In a business this is usually a vice president or a department head. In an ATM cloud, the LAN emulation server (LES) runs the ELAN. There will be only one LES per ELAN.

A typical department head or vice president often has an assistant to help with the day-to-day operation of the department, typically referred to as an *administrative assistant.* In an ATM cloud, each LES has a broadcast and unknown server (BUS) as its administrative assistant. There will be only one BUS per LES.

Finally, all companies have employees that actually perform the work dictated by management. The LAN emulation clients (LECs) are the employees or "worker bees" of the ATM LANE cloud. The translation between VLAN and ELAN is defined by the LEC, and all user traffic passes through a LEC. Typically, there will be one LEC per ELAN per switch (Figure 10-3).

To create the ELANs necessary, all the components described above must be created. Please do not lose sight of why the ELANs are being

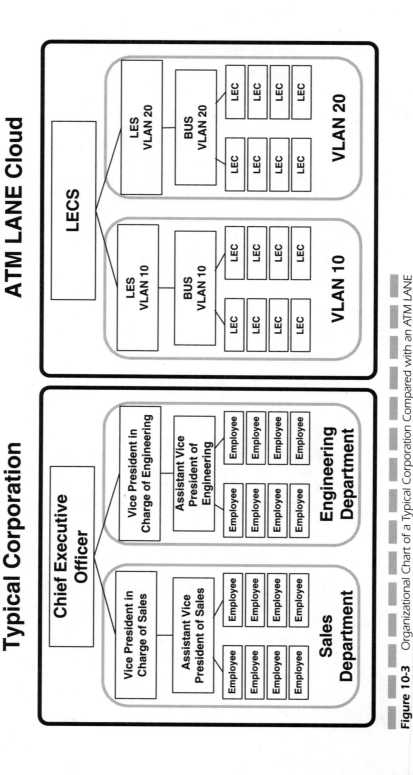

Figure 10-3   Organizational Chart of a Typical Corporation Compared with an ATM LANE

created. For every VLAN to be trunked, there must be a corresponding ELAN. For example, the ATM LANE components may be designed as in Figure 10-4 for the environment shown in Figure 10-2. In this case, two ELANs, ELAN 10 and ELAN 20, have been created for VLAN 10 and VLAN 20, respectively. The LANE components are drawn as external devices but are actually software running on the switch.

Please note that if a VLAN does not need to be trunked to a switch, it is not necessary to create a LEC for the corresponding ELAN on the switch. For example, if switch D had no ports assigned to VLAN 20, there would be no reason to configure a LEC for ELAN 20 (Figure 10-5).

Configuring these components will be discussed later in this chapter.

LANE Component Virtual Circuits

The LANE components communicate using virtual circuits, more specifically switched virtual circuits (SVCs). It is over SVCs that the LANE components pass data traffic. All user traffic passes through the LECs (as in multiple LECs, not LECS). It is for this reason that the SVCs I will discuss are centered around the LEC.

When the LEC is activated (i.e., the software is loaded), it will go through the following steps:

1. It will contact the LECS and establish a bidirectional SVC between the LEC and the LECS. This SVC is called the *configure direct VC*. Its primary purpose is to allow the LEC to communicate with the LECS and to determine the location of the LES for the ELAN of which the LEC is a member (Figure 10-6).

2. After the LECS directs the LEC to the LES of the ELAN of which it is member, a bidirectional SVC will be created between the LEC and the LES. This SVC is called the *control direct VC*. This SVC is used by the LEC and LES to communicate control information (Figure 10-7).

3. The LES will communicate with the LECS to determine if the LEC can join the ELAN. This communication occurs over an SVC called the *configure direct server VC*. Once the LES establishes that the LEC is a valid member of the ELAN, a unidirectional SVC is created between the LES and the LEC. This SVC is called the *control distribute VC* (Figure 10-8).

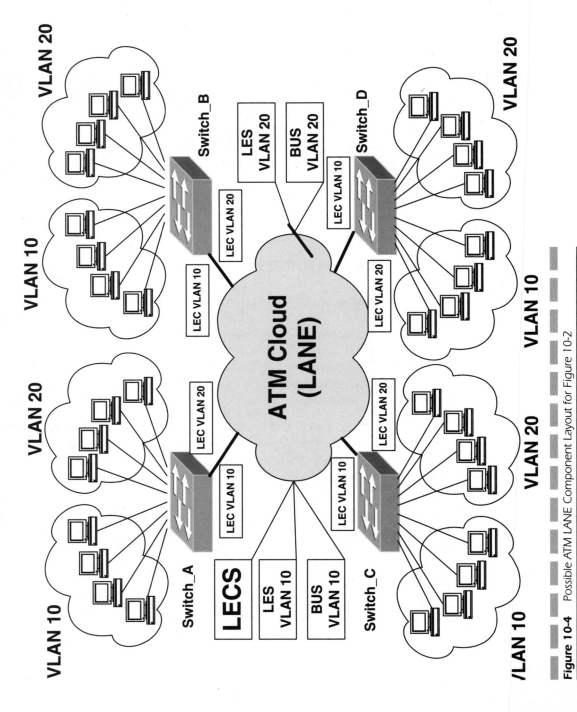

Figure 10-4 Possible ATM LANE Component Layout for Figure 10-2

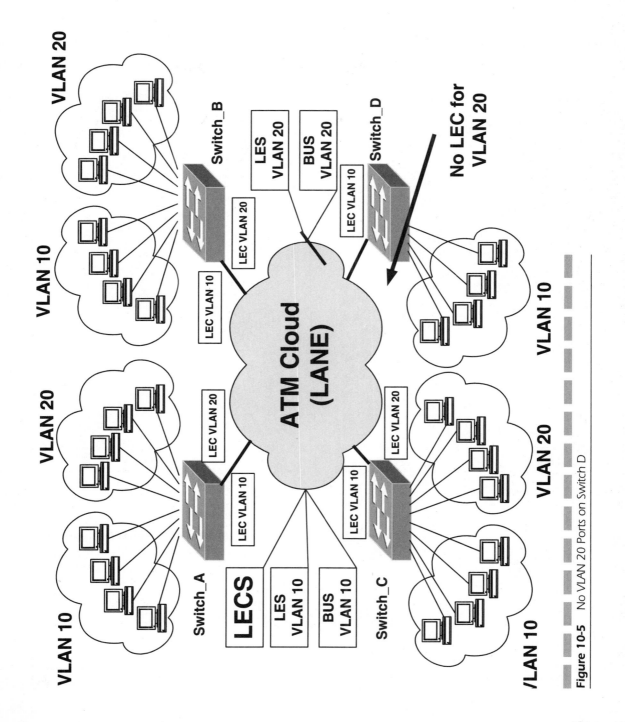

VLAN 20

VLAN 10

Switch_B

LES VLAN 20

BUS VLAN 20

Switch_D

No LEC for VLAN 20

VLAN 10

LEC VLAN 20

LEC VLAN 10

LEC VLAN 10

ATM Cloud (LANE)

VLAN 20

VLAN 10

LEC VLAN 20

LEC VLAN 10

LEC VLAN 20

Switch_A

LECS

LES VLAN 10

BUS VLAN 10

LEC VLAN 10

Switch_C

VLAN 20

/LAN 10

Figure 10-5   No VLAN 20 Ports on Switch D

309

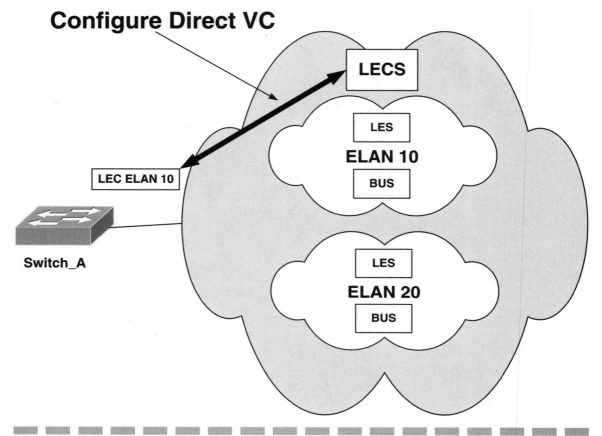

Figure 10-6   The Configure Direct VC

4. After the control distribute VC has been built, the LEC establishes a bidirectional SVC with the BUS. This SVC is called the *multicast send VC*. The name is somewhat misleading in that it is not limited to multicast traffic (Figure 10-9).

5. The BUS also establishes a unidirectional SVC called the *multicast forward VC* between itself and the LEC. Broadcasts, multicasts, and unicasts to unknown nodes received on the multicast send VC are forwarded out the multicast forward VC (Figure 10-10).

These SVCs are created automatically when the LEC is configured. At this point, no data have been transferred.

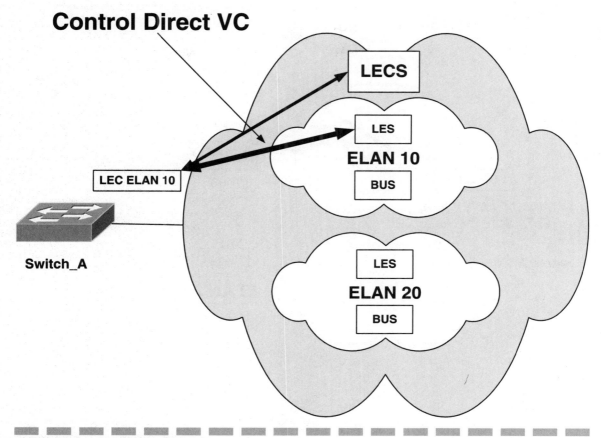

Figure 10-7 The Control Direct VC

ATM Addressing

On an ATM cloud, a different addressing scheme is used than on Ethernet or Token Ring (MAC addresses). An ATM address is 160 bits long! It is usually displayed in hex, creating a 40-hex-digit address. Each of the ATM LANE components receives a unique ATM address. When configuring ATM LANE, it is important to understand how the last 56 bits are derived. The first 104 bits are defined by the ATM provider or the ATM switches that are in use (Figure 10-11).

The Catalyst switch where the component resides determines the end

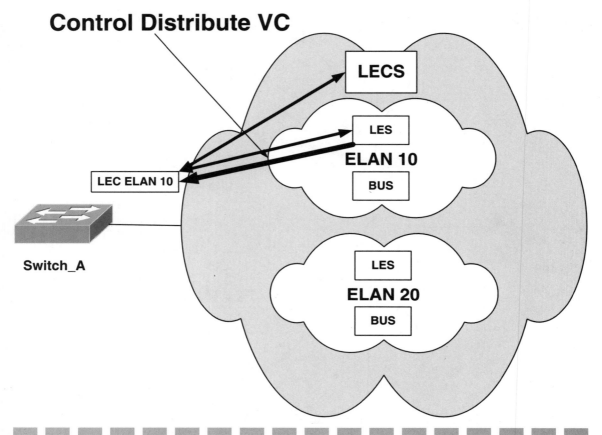

Figure 10-8   The Control Distribute VC

system identifier (ESI) of that component. A Catalyst Switch will have a pool of 16 MAC addresses assigned to an ATM port. One ESI will be assigned to each of the LANE components configured on that switch. All like components on the same switch will have the same ESI. The ESI is assigned from the pool shown in Table 10-2.

For example, if the pool of addresses assigned to an ATM port consists of 0000.0C20.1000 through 0000.0C20.100F, the ESIs would be assigned as shown in Table 10-3.

The selector byte makes up the last 8 bits of the ATM address. It will be the subinterface number of the subinterface where the component resides (subinterfaces will be discussed under "Configuring LANE" later in this chapter).

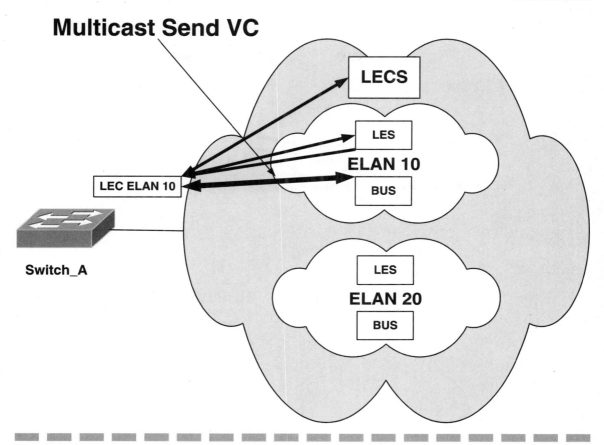

Figure 10-9   The Multicast Send VC

LANE Operation

In the preceding section the SVCs that are created automatically were described. How will user data be forwarded across the ATM LANE cloud? Figure 10-12 shows two ELANs, ELAN 10 and ELAN 20, that are being used to carry traffic for VLANs 10 and 20. The SVCs that are created automatically when the LECs are created are shown.

When host A goes to transmit data to host B using an IP-based application, the following will occur:

1. Host A will ARP for the address of host B. This is a broadcast that is sent to the switch. The switch will forward the broadcast out all

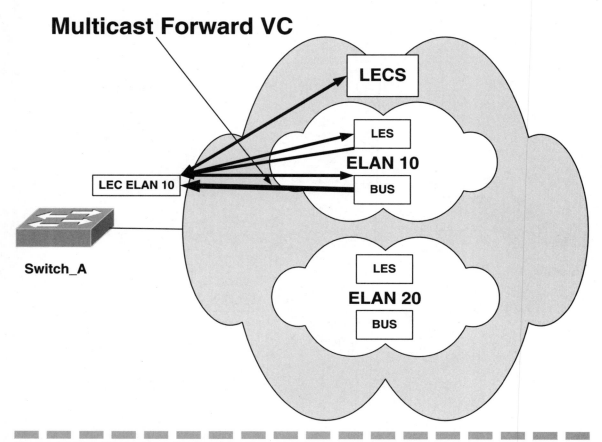

Figure 10-10   The Multicast Forward VC

ports in VLAN 10 and all trunk ports. Since the ATM port is always a trunk, it will receive the broadcast (Figure 10-13).

2. When the ATM port receives a broadcast from VLAN 10, based on the translation that is created when configuring the LEC for ELAN 10, it will translate the VLAN 10 broadcast into an ELAN 10 broadcast, and the ARP will be forwarded to the BUS (Figure 10-14).

3. The BUS will forward the ARP broadcast that it receives on the multicast send VC to the multicast distribute VC. The multicast send VC is a unidirectional point-to-multipoint SVC that connects the BUS to every LEC in its ELAN. In this case, the BUS in ELAN 10 receives the ARP broadcast and forwards it out the mul-

ATM Address

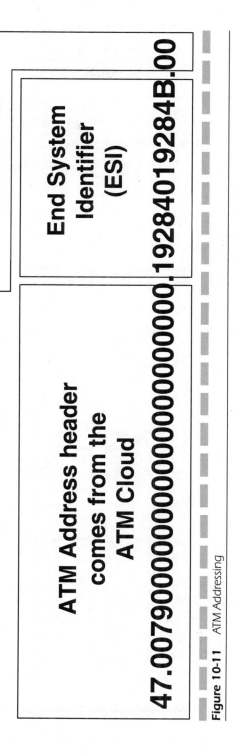

Selector Byte

End System Identifier (ESI)

ATM Address header comes from the ATM Cloud

47.007900000000000000000000.192840192848.00

Figure 10-11 ATM Addressing

TABLE 10-2

ESI MAC Address
Assignments

MAC Address	Component
First MAC address in the pool	All LECs
Second MAC address in the pool	All LESs
Third MAC address in the pool	All BUSs
Fourth MAC address in the pool	All LECSs
Fifth through sixteenth address in the pool	Reserved

TABLE 10-3

Example ESI Assign-
ments

MAC Address	Component
0000.0C20.1000	All LECs
0000.0C20.1001	All LESs
0000.0C20.1002	All BUSs
0000.0C20.1003	All LECSs
0000.0C20.1004-0000.0C20.100F	Reserved

ticast forward VC. The multicast forward VC includes switch A
(Figure 10-15).

4. On switch A, the LEC for ELAN 10 will discard the ARP request,
realizing that it originated the ARP. On switch B, the LEC for
ELAN 10 will translate the ARP into VLAN 10. Switch B will forward the ARP out all VLAN 10 ports, which would include the
port to which host B is connected (Figure 10-16).

5. When host B replies to the ARP request, the destination MAC
address will be unknown to the LEC for ELAN 10 and therefore
will be forwarded to the BUS (broadcast and unkown server)
(Figure 10-17).

6. The BUS then forwards the ARP reply out the multicast forward
VC, which will include the LEC where the ARP reply originated
(Figure 10-18).

7. When switch A receives the ARP reply, the LEC for ELAN 10
translates it to VLAN 10, and the switch forwards the ARP reply
out all VLAN 10 ports. This will include host A (Figure 10-19).

8. At this point, host A has resolved the MAC address of host B and
will begin to send application data to host B (Figure 10-20).

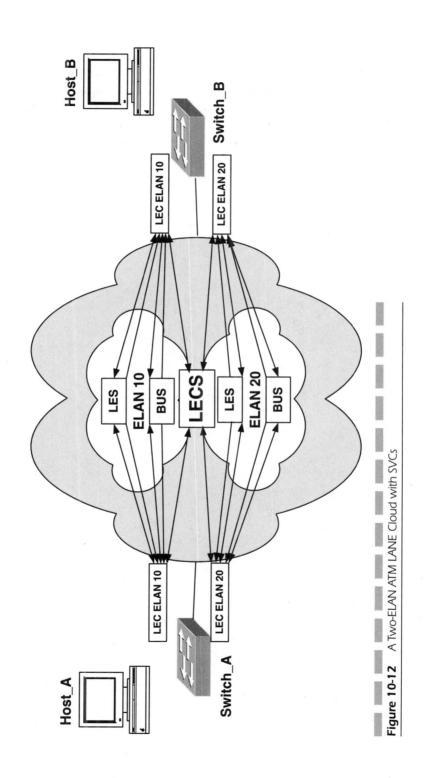

Figure 10-12　A Two-ELAN ATM LANE Cloud with SVCs

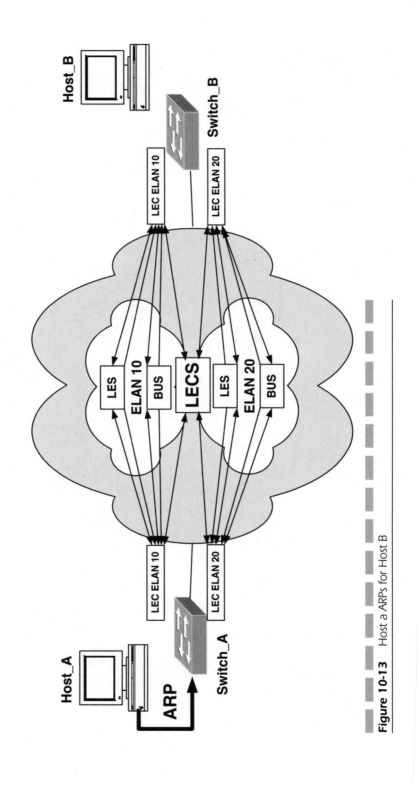

Figure 10-13 Host a ARPs for Host B

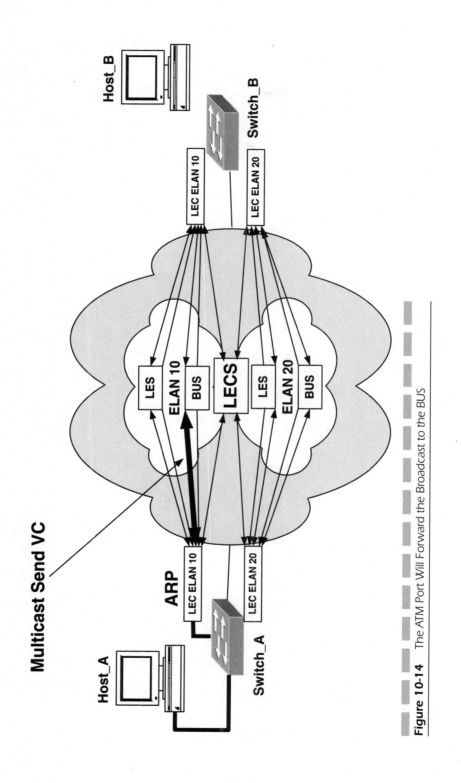

Figure 10-14 The ATM Port Will Forward the Broadcast to the BUS

319

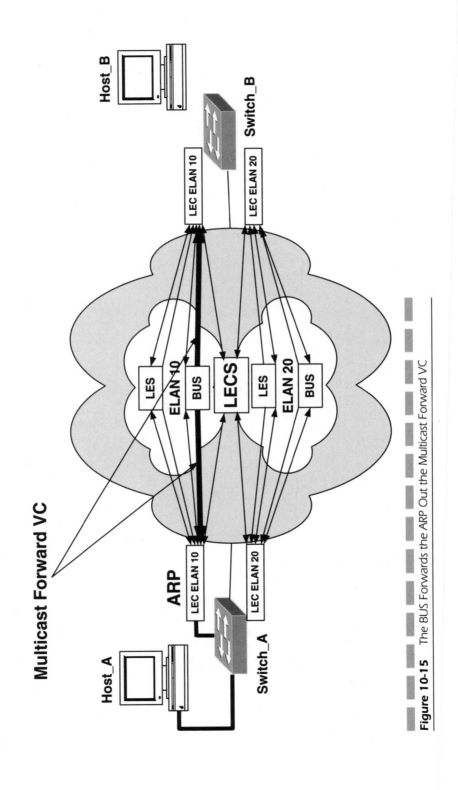

Multicast Forward VC

Figure 10-15 The BUS Forwards the ARP Out the Multicast Forward VC

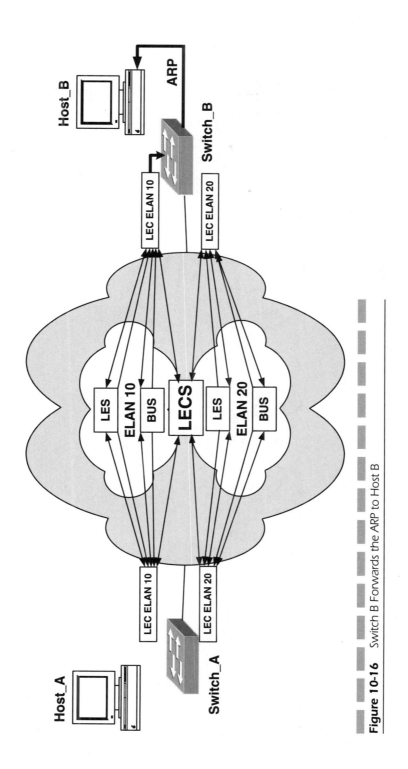

Figure 10-16 Switch B Forwards the ARP to Host B

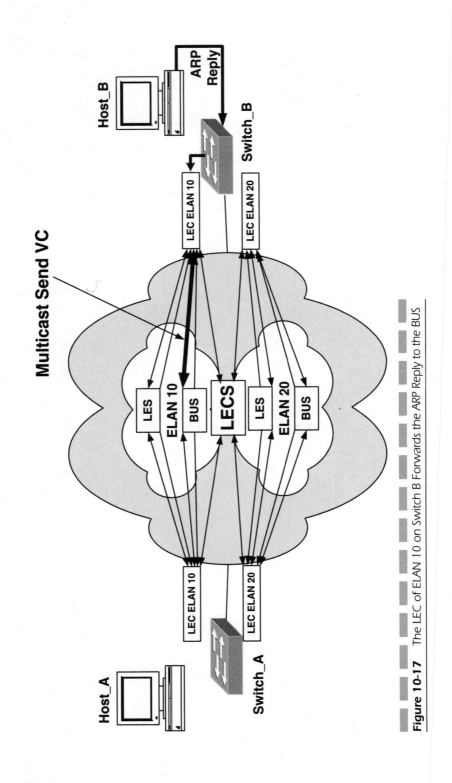

Figure 10-17 The LEC of ELAN 10 on Switch B Forwards the ARP Reply to the BUS

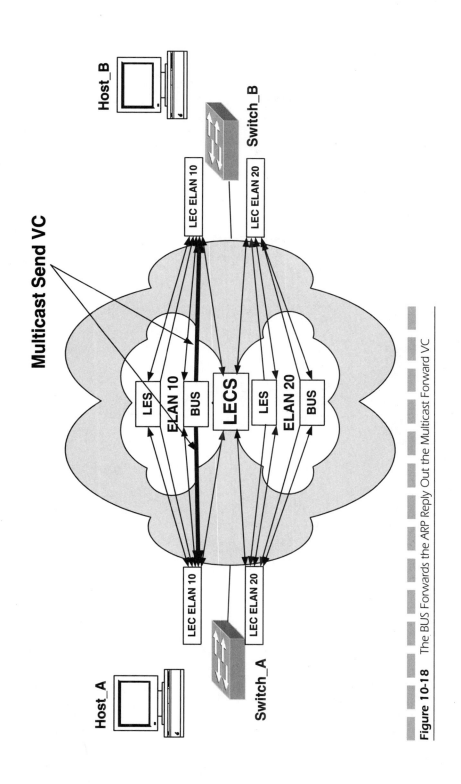

Figure 10-18   The BUS Forwards the ARP Reply Out the Multicast Forward VC

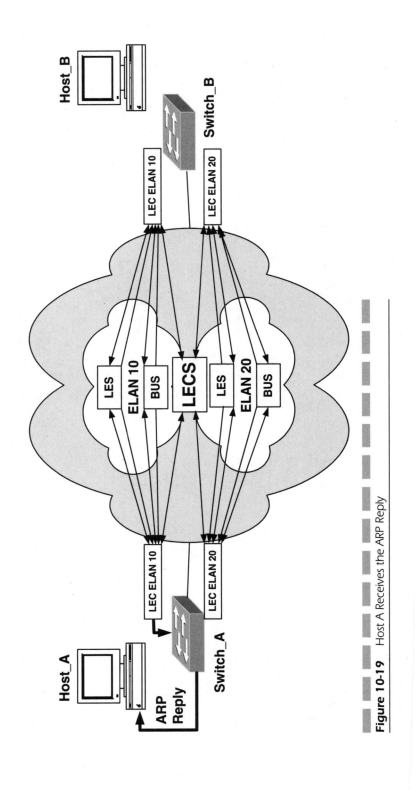

Figure 10-19 Host A Receives the ARP Reply

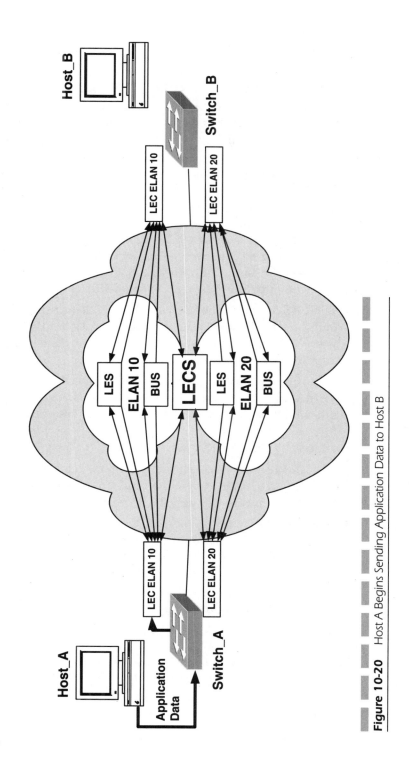

Figure 10-20   Host A Begins Sending Application Data to Host B

9. When switch A receives the stream of application data for host B's MAC address, which it has learned from the ARP reply, it forwards the data to the LEC for ELAN 10. The LEC for ELAN 10 does not know what the destination ATM address is and therefore begins forwarding the data to the BUS. However, using the BUS is extremely inefficient because the BUS forwards this data traffic to all ELAN 10 LECs. The LEC for ELAN 10 on switch A will try to resolve the ATM address of the LEC for ELAN 10 on switch B and then create a data direct VC. A data direct VC bypasses the BUS and creates a more efficient path between the two switches. Using a procedure called *inverse ARP* allows switch A to resolve the ATM address of switch B's LEC for ELAN 10. At this point, switch A begins the inverse ARP process by sending an inverse ARP request to the LES for ELAN 10. At the same time, the application data are being transmitted to the BUS (Figure 10-21).

10. The LES forwards the inverse ARP out the control distribute VC, and the BUS forwards the application data out the multicast forward VC. These processes are now occurring independently of one another (Figure 10-22).

11. When the application data are received by switch B, they are forwarded directly to host B because the destination MAC address is known by the switch. On switch A, the inverse ARP is discarded. Switch B responds to the inverse ARP request with its ATM address to the LES (Figure 10-23).

12. The LES receives the ARP reply from switch B and forwards the reply to switch A. At the same time, application data are still being transmitted through the BUS (Figure 10-24).

13. When the ARP reply is received by switch A from the LES, the LEC for ELAN 10 builds a data direct VC between itself and switch B. However, before the application data can begin over it, a *flush cell* is sent through the BUS to the LEC for ELAN 10 on switch B to indicate that the application data will now begin to flow over the data direct VC (Figure 10-25).

NOTE: *The LECS has been removed from Figure 10-26 for illustrative purposes. It is still present after the data direct VC has been created.*

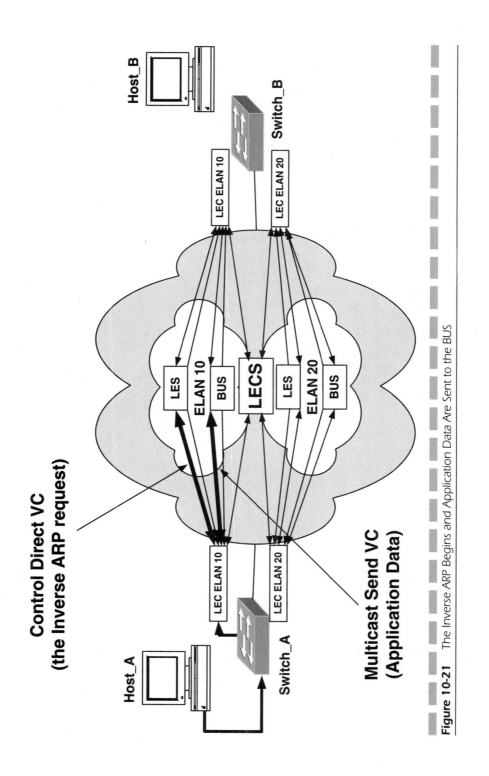

Figure 10-21 The Inverse ARP Begins and Application Data Are Sent to the BUS

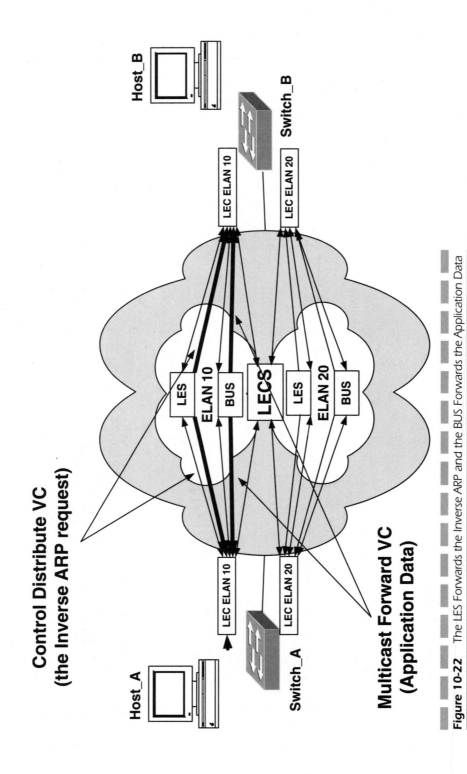

Figure 10-22 The LES Forwards the Inverse ARP and the BUS Forwards the Application Data

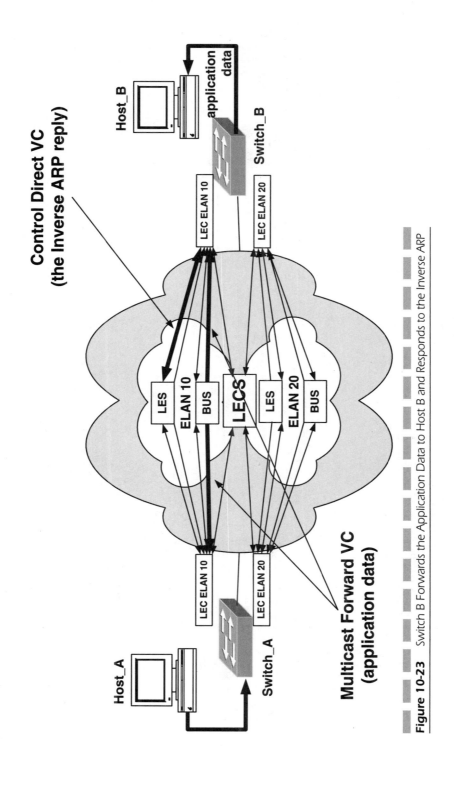

**Control Direct VC
(the Inverse ARP reply)**

**Multicast Forward VC
(application data)**

Host_B

Switch_B

application
data

LEC ELAN 10

LEC ELAN 20

LES

ELAN 10

BUS

LECS

LES

ELAN 20

BUS

LEC ELAN 10

LEC ELAN 20

Host_A

Switch_A

Figure 10-23   Switch B Forwards the Application Data to Host B and Responds to the Inverse ARP

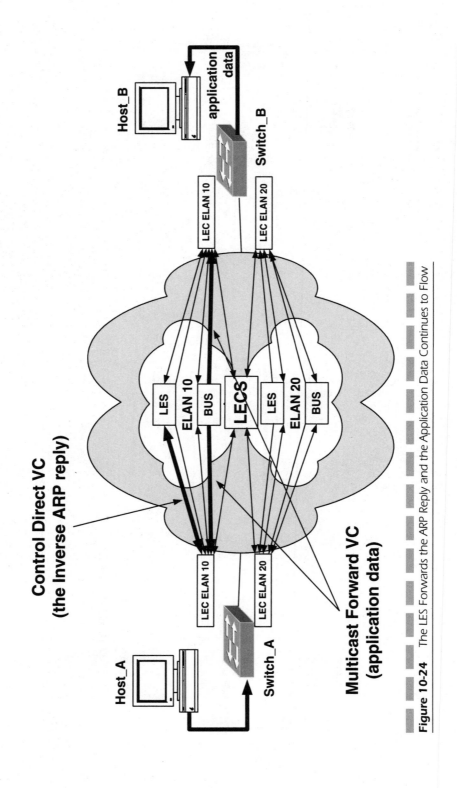

**Control Direct VC
(the Inverse ARP reply)**

**Multicast Forward VC
(application data)**

Figure 10-24 The LES Forwards the ARP Reply and the Application Data Continues to Flow

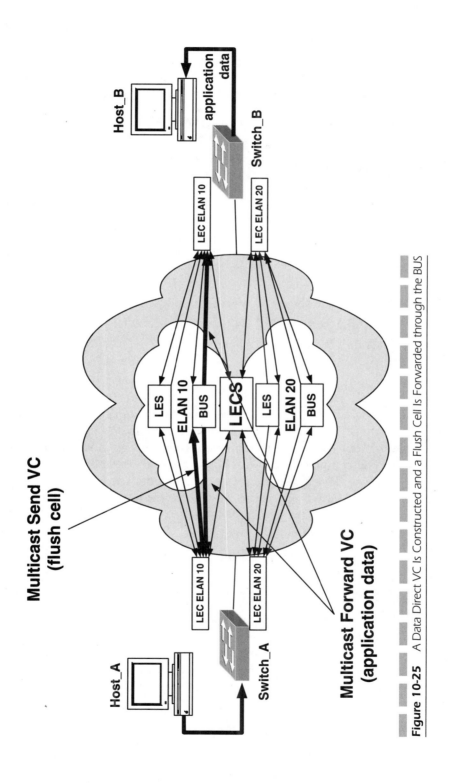

Figure 10-25   A Data Direct VC Is Constructed and a Flush Cell Is Forwarded through the BUS

331

14. When the flush cell has been received, the LEC for ELAN 10 on switch A will begin forwarding application data across the data direct VC (Figure 10-26).

This process occurs for all data flows.

Configuring LANE

Configuring all the LANE components can become somewhat overwhelming. However, if the process is broken into pieces and then performed step by step, it can be much easier. The following is a list of the procedures to configure LANE:

1. Create a LANE component layout.

2. Determine the ATM addressing method.

3. Configure the LESs, BUSs, and LECs.

4. Create the LECS database.

5. Enable the LECS.

6. Tell the ATM LANE cloud where the LECS is.

1. *Create a LANE component layout.* One of the hardest parts of configuring LANE is figuring out where all the little components go. By laying them out beforehand, implementation will go much more smoothly. The LANE component layout should have all the LANE components listed and the device on which they will reside. In the next section I give an example LANE component layout. Rules to remember when creating the LANE component layout:

■ There will be only one LECS.

■ There will be one LES per ELAN.

■ There will be one BUS per LES or one BUS per ELAN.

■ There will be one LEC per ELAN per switch.

2. *Determine the ATM addressing method.* All LANE components must have an ATM address. These can be set manually, or they can be determined automatically by the components themselves. Remember that ATM is a 160-bit address represented in hex, not exactly easy to work with. For this reason I recommend using the auto addressing method.

3. *Configure the LESs, BUSs, and LECs.* To configure the any of these components on a Catalyst switch, you must first go to the

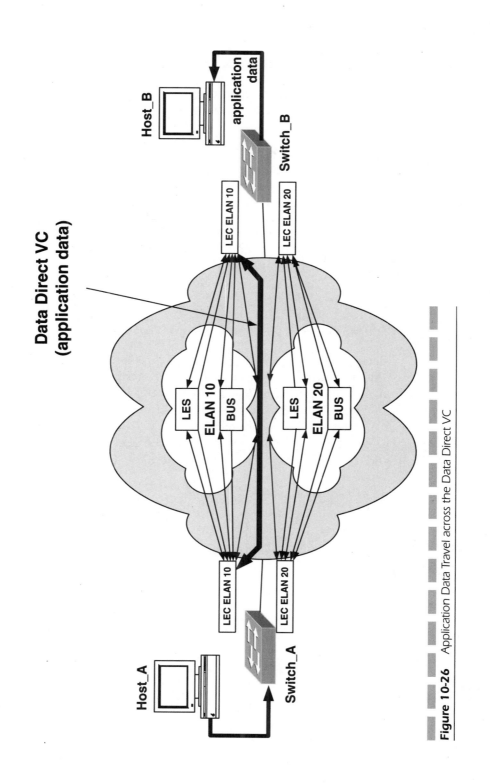

Figure 10-26 Application Data Travel across the Data Direct VC

CLI of the ATM LANE module. This can be done using the `session` command:

```
console> (enable) session 5 <Enter>
Trying ATM-5...
Connected to ATM-5.

Escape character is '^]'.

ATM>
```

Thus "5" is the slot number where the ATM LANE module is installed.

The ATM LANE module uses Cisco IOS. Therefore, all configuration changes will need to be made in privileged mode. The `enable` command changes the mode to privileged mode:

```
ATM> enable <Enter>
ATM#
```

The "#" indicates that you are in privileged mode.

Each LANE component will be configured on a subinterface. For every ELAN, the switch will have at least one subinterface. The LANE components are configured on the subinterfaces. Only components of the same ELAN may be placed on the same subinterface. The subinterface number may be any value between 1 and 254. To create a subinterface, enter the global configuration mode using the `configure terminal` command (the command may be shortened to `conf t`):

```
ATM# configure terminal <Enter>
ATM(config)#
```

NOTE: *The prompt will indicate that the CLI is in global configuration mode with* `ATM(config)#`*.*

The `interface` command will be used to create the subinterface:

```
ATM(config)# interface atm 0.[subinterface number (1-254)] <enter>
ATM(config-subif)#
```

NOTE: *The prompt will indicate that the CLI is in subinterface configuration mode with* `ATM(config-subif)#`*.*

To configure the LES and the BUS, only one command is necessary:

```
ATM(config-subif)# lane server-bus [ethernet | token-ring] [the
elan name] <enter>
```

The ELAN may emulate either an Ethernet or a Token Ring LAN. ELANs are identified by name, not by number.

TECH TIP: *It is a good idea to choose ELAN names that represent the VLAN for which they are being created for translation. For example, VLAN 10 and VLAN 20 in the preceding figures were translated into ELAN10 and ELAN20. It is easy to deduce that ELAN10 is being translated into VLAN 10 and ELAN20 is being translated into VLAN 20.*

The LEC may be created on the same subinterface as the LES and BUS (as long as they are in the same ELAN). However, Cisco recommends that they be placed on separate subinterfaces for performance reasons. To create the LEC, the following command is used:

```
ATM(config-subif)# lane client ethernet [vlan_number] [elan-name]
<enter>
```

NOTE: *This command is very important. It is here that the ELAN and VLAN are mapped together.*

Configure all switches with the appropriate LANE components, as shown in the LANE component layout from step 1.

TECH TIP: *When configuring the LECS, the ATM address of every LES is necessary. This can sometimes be difficult and often leads to configuration errors. I would suggest creating a text file and recording the ATM addresses as they are being created. To view the ATM address of the LES, use the command* show lane server:

```
ATM#show lane server <enter>
LE Server ATM0.1  ELAN name: default  Admin: up  State: operational
type: ethernet        Max Frame Size: 1516
ATM address: 47.009181000000009245AE74329.AA00D2946591.01
LECS used: 47.007900000000000000000000.192840192843.00 NOT yet connected
```

The ATM address of the LES is in boldface. Do not be alarmed by the message "Not yet connected." The LECS has not yet been configured, and this is the expected result.

4. *Create the LECS Database.* The LECS of an ATM cloud must have the ATM address of every LES in the cloud so that it may direct the LEC to the appropriate LES when the LEC joins the cloud. The LECS database is a listing of all LES, the ELAN to which they are assigned, and their ATM address. To create the LECS database, use the following command from global configuration mode:

```
ATM(config)#lane database [LANE database name]
ATM(lane-config-database)#
```

NOTE: *When in the LECS database configuration mode, the prompt will be* ATM(lane-config-database)#.

The LANE database name may be any alphanumeric value. The name should be small because to change the database, the command must be reentered to enter the LECS database configuration mode. The name is only significant to the device where it is being created.

Once in the LECS database configuration mode, enter the LES ATM addresses using the following command:

```
ATM(lane-config-database)# name [elan-name] server-atm-address
[atm-address of LES] <enter>
ATM(lane-config-database)#
```

Enter all the necessary entries into the database. Once all LESs have been entered, the LECS database is complete.

NOTE: *If an ELAN was defined as being restricted, all LEC ATM addresses would have to be entered as well.*

5. *Enable the LECS.* The LECS must be enabled on the major interface (i.e., *not* a subinterface) of a Cisco IOS device (this includes the Catalyst LANE module). Before enabling the LECS, the ATM address of the LECS must be specified. If the LECS is going to use the automatically generated ATM address, use the following command:

```
ATM(config)#interface atm 0
ATM(config-if)#lane config auto-config-atm-address <enter>
```

If the LECS address is to specified manually, use this command:

```
ATM(config)#interface atm 0
ATM(config-if)#lane config config-atm-address lecs_atm_address <enter>
```

I would recommend using the automatically generated address. This makes configuration easier on the ATM switches that make up the ATM cloud. The ATM switches will need to be configured with the ATM address of the LECS. Contact the administrator of the ATM cloud and inform him or her of the correct address.

NOTE: *On a LightStream 1010 ATM switch, the ATM address of the LECS may be configured using the following command:*

```
ATM(config)#atm lecs-address [atm address of LECS] <enter>
```

To enable the LECS:

```
ATM(config-if)#lane config database [LANE database name] <enter>
```

The database name is the name that was created in step 4.

BONEHEAD ALERT: *The LANE database name is case-sensitive!*

ATM LANE configuration is complete.

Example LANE Configuration

Using the preceding section's steps, configure the environment shown in Figure 10-27 to trunk all VLANs across the ATM cloud. Make sure that all switches have connectivity to all VLANs.

1. *Create a LANE component layout.* There are two VLANs in Figure 10-27 that must be trunked across the ATM LANE cloud. Two ELANs will need to be created, each with a LES and a BUS. For VLAN 10, ELAN10 will be created, and for VLAN 20, ELAN20 will be created. In addition, one LECS also will be needed for the ATM LANE cloud. All components

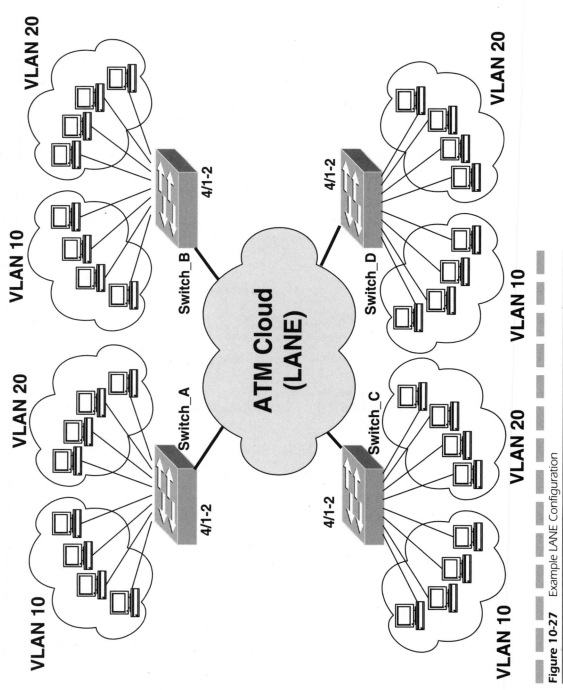

Figure 10-27   Example LANE Configuration

must be placed on one of the four switches. In this example the LECS will be placed on switch A, and the LES and BUS for ELAN10 and the LES and BUS for ELAN20 will be placed on switch B (Figure 10-28).

LEC placement will be determined by the VLAN connectivity for each switch. Since each switch must have connectivity to both VLANs, each switch will need to have a LEC for each ELAN (Figure 10-29).

2. *Determine the ATM addressing method.* In this example, the autoaddressing method will be used.

3. *Configure the LESs, BUSs, and LECs.* Each switch will be configured with the components outlined in the LANE component layout (see Figure 10-29). And using the Tech Tip, all LES addresses will be recorded.

On switch A:

Enter the CLI of the ATM LANE module:

```
Switch_A> (enable) session 4 <enter>
Trying ATM-4...
Connected to ATM-4.
Escape character is '^]'.

ATM> enable <enter>
ATM# configure terminal <enter>
```

Figure 10-28
LECS, LES, and BUS
Placement

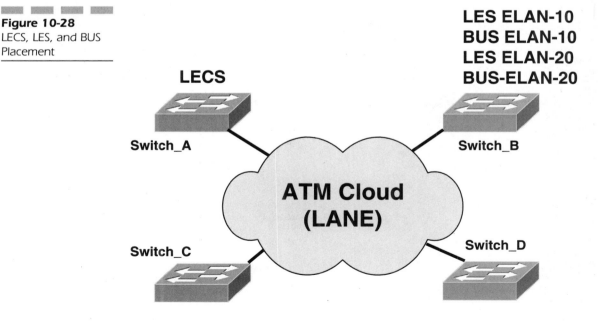

LES ELAN-10
BUS ELAN-10
LES ELAN-20
BUS-ELAN-20

LECS

Switch_A

Switch_B

ATM Cloud
(LANE)

Switch_C

Switch_D

Figure 10-29
LEC Placement

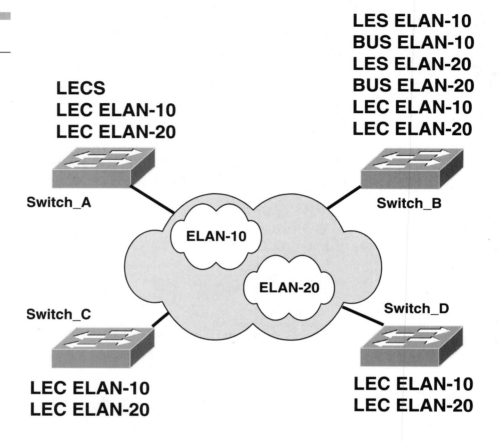

LECS
LEC ELAN-10
LEC ELAN-20

LES ELAN-10
BUS ELAN-10
LES ELAN-20
BUS ELAN-20
LEC ELAN-10
LEC ELAN-20

Switch_A

Switch_B

ELAN-10

ELAN-20

Switch_C

Switch_D

LEC ELAN-10
LEC ELAN-20

LEC ELAN-10
LEC ELAN-20

Configure the LEC for ELAN10:

```
ATM(config-subif)# interface atm 0.11 <enter>
ATM(config-subif)# lane client ethernet 10 ELAN-10 <enter>
```

Configure the LEC for ELAN20:

```
ATM(config-subif)# interface atm 0.21 <enter>
ATM(config-subif)# lane client ethernet 10 ELAN-20 <enter>
```

On switch B:

Enter the CLI of the ATM LANE Module:

```
Switch_A> (enable) session 4 <enter>
```

```
Trying ATM-4...
Connected to ATM-4.
Escape character is '^]'.

ATM> enable <enter>
ATM# configure terminal <enter>
```

Configure the LES and BUS for ELAN10:

```
ATM(config)# interface atm 0.10 <enter>
ATM(config-subif)# lane server-bus ethernet ELAN-10 <enter>
```

Configure the LEC for ELAN10:

```
ATM(config-subif)# interface atm 0.11 <enter>
ATM(config-subif)# lane client ethernet 10 ELAN-10 <enter>
```

Configure the LES and BUS for ELAN20:

```
ATM(config-subif)# interface atm 0.20 <enter>
ATM(config-subif)# lane server-bus ethernet ELAN-20 <enter>
```

Configure the LEC for ELAN20:

```
ATM(config-subif)# interface atm 0.21 <enter>
ATM(config-subif)# lane client ethernet 10 ELAN-20 <enter>
```

To record the ATM address of the LES:

```
ATM#show lane server <enter>
LE Server ATM0.10  ELAN name: ELAN-10  Admin: up  State: operational
type: ethernet         Max Frame Size: 1516
ATM address: 47.009181000000009245AE74329.AA00D2946591.0A
LECS used: 47.007900000000000000000000.192840192843.00 NOT yet connected
LE Server ATM0.20  ELAN name: ELAN-20  Admin: up  State: operational
type: ethernet         Max Frame Size: 1516
ATM address: 47.009181000000009245AE74329.AA00D2946591.14
LECS used: 47.007900000000000000000000.192840192843.00 NOT yet connected
```

On switch C:

Enter the CLI of the ATM LANE module:

```
Switch_C> (enable) session 4 <enter>
Trying ATM-4...
Connected to ATM-4.
Escape character is '^]'.

ATM> enable <enter>
ATM# configure terminal <enter>
```

Configure the LEC for ELAN10:

```
ATM(config-subif)# interface atm 0.11 <enter>
ATM(config-subif)# lane client ethernet 10 ELAN-10 <enter>
```

Configure the LEC for ELAN20:

```
ATM(config-subif)# interface atm 0.21 <enter>
ATM(config-subif)# lane client ethernet 10 ELAN-20 <enter>
```

On switch D:

Enter the CLI of the ATM LANE module:

```
Switch_D> (enable) session 4 <enter>
Trying ATM-4...
Connected to ATM-4.
Escape character is '^]'.

ATM> enable <enter>
ATM# configure terminal <enter>
```

Configure the LEC for ELAN10:

```
ATM(config-subif)# interface atm 0.11 <enter>
ATM(config-subif)# lane client ethernet 10 ELAN-10 <enter>
```

Configure the LEC for ELAN20:

```
ATM(config-subif)# interface atm 0.21 <enter>
ATM(config-subif)# lane client ethernet 10 ELAN-20 <enter>
```

4. *Create the LECS database.* The LECS database needs to be conifgured on switch A. With only two ELANs, only two entries are needed:

```
ATM(config)#lane database Example-1 <enter>
ATM(lane-config-database)# name ELAN-10 server-atm-address
   47.009181000000009245AE74329.AA00D2946591.0A <enter>
ATM(lane-config-database)# name ELAN-20 server-atm-address
   47.009181000000009245AE74329.AA00D2946591.14 <enter>
ATM(lane-config-database)# <ctrl-C>
ATM#
```

5. *Enable the LECS.* To enable the LECS on switch A:

```
ATM(config)#interface atm 0
ATM(config-if)#lane config auto-config-atm-address <enter>
ATM(config-if)#lane config database Example-1
```

6. Tell the ATM LANE cloud where the LECS is.

The final step is to tell the ATM LANE Cloud what the ATM Address of the LECS is. This can be accomplished using the "atm-lecs-address-default" command. It is placed in the global configuration mode of the Lightstream switch. If Cisco Lightstream ATM switches are not in use, you will have to refer to the documentation of the switches that are in use.

```
ATM(config-if)#atm-lecs-address-default
47.007900000000000000000000.192840192843.00      <enter>
```

This will complete the configuration. I have noticed that it may be a minute or two before traffic will start to flow so be patient. I would recommend using the show lane config command on the switch that is the LECS to verify that the LESs are active:

```
ATM#show lane config
LE Config Server ATM0 config table: ATM_Cloud
Admin: up   State: operational
LECS Mastership State: active master
list of global LECS addresses (38 seconds to update):
47.007900000000000000000000.192840192843.00   <----- me
ATM Address of this LECS: 47.007900000000000000000000.192840192843.00
  (auto)
 vcd  rxCnt  txCnt  callingParty
2732    5      5    47.009181000000009245AE74329.AA00D2946591.0A
  LES ELAN-10 0 active
2744    4      4    47.009181000000009245AE74329.AA00D2946591.14
  LES ELAN-20 0 active
cumulative total number of unrecognized packets received so far: 0
cumulative total number of config requests received so far: 23940
cumulative total number of config failures so far: 14413
    cause of last failure: no configuration
    culprit for the last failure:
47.009181000000000905FF4A001.00905FAC3E41.15
```

The "active" at the end of each line in bold indicates that there is connectivity to the LES from the LECS.
Configuration complete.

In this example there are two VLANs; trunking over the ATM cloud has been established with the preceding configuration, but it should be noted that without a router there will be no connectivity between VLANs 10 and 20.

SUMMARY

A Cisco Catalyst switch can be configured to use ATM LANE. By configuring trunking over an ATM LANE cloud, a high-speed backplane can be created to provide connectivity to other switches, servers, and routers. ATM LANE has many advantages over Gigabit Ethernet when used in environments where quality of service (QoS) and traffic control are concerned

Configuring ATM LANE on a Catalyst switch is logically similar to trunking with FDDI. However, the configurations are totally different. ATM LANE uses ELANs as opposed to the VLANs used with FDDI. ATM LANE is performed by four software components:

1. LAN emulation client (LEC)
2. Broadcast and unknown server (BUS)
3. LAN emulation server (LES)
4. LAN emulation configuration server (LECS)

All user traffic passes through a LEC, which is the interface to the ATM LANE cloud. Five VCs are created automatically. However, none of these VCs actually handles user traffic on a regular basis. User traffic passes over data direct VCs. An LE-ARP is used to resolve an ATM address from a destination MAC address. When the ATM address is determined, the data direct VC can be configured.

An ATM address is 160 bits in length and is represented in hex. The ESI portion of the ATM address is an automatically assigned MAC address from a pool of MAC addresses that are assigned to the ATM port. The selector byte, which is the last 8 bits of the address, is the subinterface number represented in hex.

EXERCISES

1. Describe how LAN emulation (LANE) is used on a Catalyst switch.
2. Compare and contrast an ELAN and a VLAN.
3. In what circumstances is ATM more advantageous than Gigabit Ethernet?

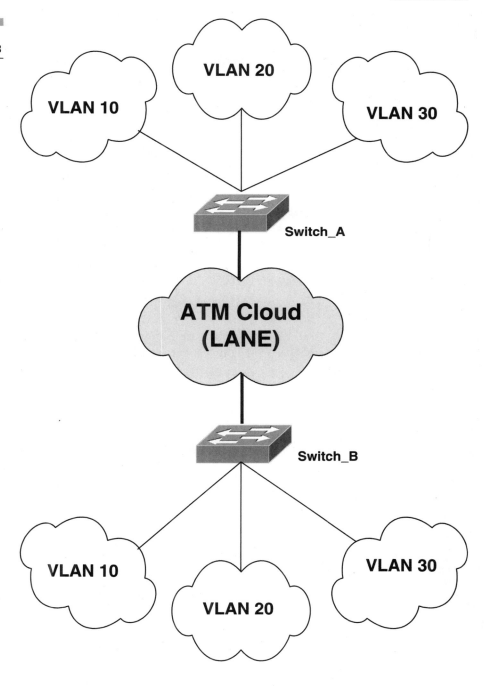

Figure 10-30
Figure for Exercise 13

4. Compare and contrast the three steps involved in configuring trunking on FDDI with configuring trunking with ATM.

5. When is trunking not configured on an ATM port?

6. Describe the four components of LANE, and give a brief overview of each component's job function.

7. How many LECSs must be configured on an ATM LANE cloud assuming LANE version 1 and that SSRP is not in use? How many LESs? How many BUSs?

8. What is the relationship between the number of VLANs in a management domain and the number of ELANs on an ATM LANE cloud?

9. Give an example of when it is not necessary to configure a LEC on an ATM port.

10. List the five automatically created SVCs on a LEC. Include the direction and the LANE component to which they connect.

11. Given a MAC address range for a LANE module of 0000.0CAA.9370 to 0000.0CAA.937F and a subinterface number of 127 for the the LES, determine the ESI and selector byte fields of the ATM address of that LES.

12. Describe what occurs during the LE-ARP process.

13. Given the environment in Figure 10-30, create a LANE component layout (assume that connectivity to every VLAN is required of all switches). Include ELAN names and *all* LANE components.

14. When is the mapping between an ELAN and a VLAN defined?

15. What is the purpose of the "dual phy" option?

GLOSSARY

4B/5B Encoding methods for packing four bits of data into every five bits transmitted over the data network. Encoding and decoding is performed by a standardized look-up table, which precludes certain recurring signal transitions. Fast Ethernet must achieve 125 MHz in signaling speed to provide a 100-MHz data rate.

10Base-2 A 10-Mbit/s baseband network using thin Ethernet coaxial cable.

10Base-5 A 10-Mbit/s baseband network using thick Ethernet coaxial cable.

10Base-F The IEEE specification for baseband Ethernet over fiberoptic cabling. *See also* **10Base-FB**; **10Base-FL**; **10Base-FP**.

10Base-FB Part of the IEEE 10Base-F specification providing a synchronous signaling backbone that allows additional segments and repeaters to be connected to the network.

10Base-FL Part of the IEEE 10Base-F specification that is designed to replace the Fiber-Optic Inter-Repeater Link (FOIRL) standard providing Ethernet over fiberoptic cabling; interoperability is provided between the old and new standards.

10Base-FP Part of the IEEE 10Base-F specification that allows the organization of a number of end nodes into a star topology without the use of repeaters.

10Base-T IEEE standard enabling telephone UTP cable to be used for Ethernet LANs.

10Base-TX The IEEE 802.3u physical layer device (PHY) sublayer using a two-pair wiring standard with UTP Category 5 or STP.

100Base-F Standard for fiberoptic cabling used with Fast Ethernet, often used to mean Fast Ethernet with fiberoptic cabling.

100Base-FX The IEEE 802.3u physical layer device (PHY) sublayer using a two-strand fiber-optic standard for Ethernet signal transmission.

100Base-T Standard for copper cabling used with Fast Ethernet, often used to mean Fast Ethernet with copper cabling.

Some definitions in this Glossary are reproduced with permission from Datapro Information Services Group, February 1999. *Glossary*.

100Base-VG   LAN standard of the IEE 802 committee for transmission of 100 Mbits/s over UTP (unshielded twisted-pair) cable promoted originally by Hewlett-Packard and AT&T, among others. With 100VG-AnyLAN, an alternative to 100Base-T with Fast Ethernet.

100VG-AnyLAN   Method of LAN transmission based on 100Base-VG that builds on aspects of both token ring and Ethernet to run at 100 Mbits/s with resilience and high realization of potential. Generally considered better technically than Fast Ethernet, the alternative, but less successful in the marketplace.

802.1d   IEEE standard for spanning tree.

802.1p   The IEEE standard which adds important filtering controls to 802.1d with VLANs in mind.

802.1Q   The IEEE encapsulation standard, which calls for adding 4 bytes to a packet to tag it for virtual LAN purposes.

802.3   IEEE broadband bus networking system that uses CSMA/CD protocol. Ethernet has become the generic name, although it is one trademarked version of 802.3.

802.4   IEEE standard that governs broadband bus and broadband token bus. Usually used in industrial applications.

802.5   IEEE standard that governs token-ring networking systems.

802.6   IEEE standard that governs metropolitan area networks (MANs).

802.9   Integrated voice and data LAN IEEE standard.

802.10   Standard from the IEEE for packet tagging for security within LANs; also used by some companies to tag packets for virtual LANs.

802.11   Unfinished IEEE standard for wireless LANs which use Ethernet bridges with roaming to join them to the network.

802.12   IEEE standard that specifies the physical layer and the MAC sublayer of the data-link layer of the seven-layer OSI reference model.

AAL5   ATM adaptation layer type 5, part of ATM.

AARP   *See* **AppleTalk Address Resolution Protocol**.

abnormal preamble   A packet error that occurs when the preamble doesn't match the legal eight-byte Ethernet synchronization pattern.

ABR   *See* **available bit rate**.

ac   Alternating current (electricity).

active hub   A multiported device that amplifies LAN transmission signals.

adaptive   A type of bridge or switch which can use adaptive or store-and-forward techniques as needed.

address   Station or user identifier. *See also* **IP address**; **network address**.

address error   A packet improperly labeled with either source or destination information.

Address Resolution Protocol   Internet protocol used to map an IP address to a MAC address. Abbreviated ARP.

alignment error   1. In IEEE 802.3 networks, an error that occurs when a received frame's total number of bits is not divisible by eight. Alignment errors usually are caused by frame damage due to collisions. 2. A frame that has not been synchronized correctly.

American National Standards Institute   The coordinating body for voluntary standards groups within the United States, this group is also a member of the International Organization for Standards. This is a governmental agency that maintains standards for science and commerce, including a list of acceptable standards for computer languages, character sets, connection compatibility, and many other aspects of the computer and data communications industries. Better known by the ANSI acronym.

AppleTalk   Apple protocol consisting of a seven-layer stack similar to the OSI stack.

AppleTalk Address Resolution Protocol   Protocol that maps a MAC address to a network address. Abbreviated AARP.

architecture   The way hardware or software is structured, usually based on a specific design philosophy. Architecture affects both a computer's abilities and its limitations.

ARP   *See* **Address Resolution Protocol**.

ASIC   Application-specific integrated circuit.

Asynchronous Transfer Mode   1. A cell relay packet network providing from 25 Mbps to Gbits/s from central offices to central offices. 2. A form of packet switching; a subset of Cell Relay that uses 53-byte cells (five bytes of overhead, and another four bytes for LAN sequencing adaptation) as the basic transport unit. In concept, circuits of different signaling speeds can move data from desktop to desktop and across long-distance services without major changes in data format. Abbreviated ATM.

ATM   *See* **Asynchronous Transfer Mode**.

ATM Forum   The main standards-developing body for ATM.

ATM LANE   LAN Emulation for ATM; allows logically separated LANs within an ATM network.

ATM route server   In a native ATM LAN, the route server addresses the layer 3 requirements, allowing network layer traffic to be routed from one layer 3 domain to another when two ATM LANs are interconnected.

attachment unit interface   An IEEE 802.3 cable connecting the MAU (Media Access Unit) to the networked device. The term AUI also can be used to refer to the host back-panel connector to which an AUI cable might attach. Abbreviated AUT. Also called transceiver cable or drop cable.

attenuation   Loss of communication signal energy.

AUI   *See* **attachment unit interface**.

AUI cable   The attachment unit interface cable that connects a workstation to a transceiver or fan-out box. Often called a drop cable.

auto-negotiation   The algorithm that allows two or more nodes on a transmission link to negotiate transmission services. This usually relates to discovering the highest possible transmission speed, as in 10/100Base-T.

available bit rate   Quality-of-service class (one of five) defined by the ATM Forum for ATM networks where a timing relationship is not required between sending and receiving stations. Abbreviated ABR.

backbone   1. See bus. 2. A collapsed (that is, minimized) wiring concentrator.

bandwidth   1. The range (band) of frequencies that are transmitted on a channel. The difference between the highest and lowest frequencies is expressed in Hertz (Hz) or millions of Hertz (MHz). 2. The wire speed of the transmission channel.

baseband   A transmission channel that carries a single communications channel, on which only one signal can transmit at a given time.

baseline   The normalized traffic or performance level. An interesting although perhaps flawed metric for network and computer performance management.

baselining   The process of generating a baseline or making comparisons to a baseline.

beatdown   The condition a switch suffers when it becomes congested and cells or cell streams representing layer 3 VLAN packets are missed or dropped, leading to the VLAN becoming unstable. Also known as "VC starvation" on an ATM network and "transit VLAN starvation" on a non-ATM network.

B-ISDN   Broadband ISDN; the foundation for ATM.

bit   An abbreviation for binary digit, A unit used in the binary numbering system; it can be 0 or 1.

bit error rate   The percentage of erroneous transmitted bits received by a network node or server.

bits per second   Basic unit of measurement for serial data transmission capacity; abbreviated as kbit/s, for thousands of bits per second; Mbits/s for millions of bits per second; Gbits/s for billions of bits per second; Tbits/s, for trillions of bits per second. The numbers are not exact—kbits/s is really 1024 bits per second, and so on. This is because capacity expands exponentially, not sequentially.

BootP   See **Bootstrap Protocol**.

Bootstrap Protocol   Allows a computer on the network to act as an address server, automatically giving IP addresses on request.

B PDU   See **Bridge protocol data units**.

break   A physical break (electrical or optical) in the network media that prohibits passage of the transmission signal.

bridge   A relatively simple device that passes data without examining it. Bridges interconnect networks, or network segments, running the same protocols. Operating at the MAC layer, they are protocol-independent—the decision as to whether to forward a signal depends only on the address. There are various types of bridges: encapsulating, translating, and source routing are the main categories.

bridge protocol data units   Formatted frames in spanning-tree networks. Abbreviated BPDUs.

bridge/router   Strictly provides bridging at level 2 and routing at level 3, but this very precise meaning has been largely superseded by a looser categorization that includes any device that combines the functions of bridge and router. *See also* **bridge**; **router**.

broadcast   1. Delivery of a transmission to two or more stations at the same time, such as over a bus-type local network or by satellite.

2. Protocol mechanism in which group and universal addressing is supported.

broadcast storm   An enterprise network event in which many broadcasts are sent at once, overloading intermediate nodes and creating a time-out or network panic. This is an undesirable network event in which many broadcasts are sent all at once, using substantial network bandwidth and typically causing network saturation at intermediate nodes. See also **network cascade**.

Carrier Sense Multiple Access with Collision Detection   1. A communications protocol in which nodes contend for a shared communications channel and all nodes have equal access to the network. Simultaneous transmissions from two or more nodes result in random restarts of those transmissions. 2. A channel access mechanism wherein devices wishing to transmit first check the channel for a carrier. If no carrier is sensed for some period of time, devices can transmit. If two devices transmit at once, a collision occurs and is detected by all colliding devices, which subsequently delays their retransmissions for some random length of time. This access scheme is used by Ethernet and IEEE 802.3. 3. The Ethernet protocol. Abbreviated CSMA/CD.

cascading hubs   Hierarchy of hubs allowing many LAN segments to be connected to a backbone efficiently but without great expense.

Category 1   The TIA/EIA recommendation for two-pair twisted (TP) to support data transmission rates to 1 Mbps. This is voice-grade wire suitable for analog telephone, facsimile, and modem connections. It is not typically used for digital lines. It is not in any way similar to IBM Type 1 cable.

Category 2   The TIA/EIA recommendation for two-pair twisted-pair (TP) to support data transmission rates to 4 Mbps. This grade of wire is suitable for ARCNET and 4-Mbps Token-Ring.

Category 3   The TIA/EIA recommendation for two-pair twisted-pair (TP) to support data transmission rates to 10 Mbps. This is suitable for Ethernet and 4-Mbps Token-Ring.

Category 4   The TIA/EIA recommendation for two-pair twisted-pair (TP) to support data transmission rates to 16 Mbps. This is suitable for Ethernet and 16-Mbps Token-Ring, but not necessarily suitable for switched or full-duplex data transmission because of the near-end crosstalk and impedance problems. IBM Type 1 cable does correspond to these performance recommendations.

Category 5 The TIA/EIA recommendation for two-pair twisted-pair (TP) to support data transmission rates to 155 Mbps. This is suitable for TCNS, ARCNET PLUS, Fast Ethernet, FDDI, and ATM. IBM Type 1 (coaxial) cable may correspond to these performance recommendations.

CCITT *See* **Consultative Committee for International Telephone and Telegraph**.

cell In data transmission, a fixed number of bytes of data sent together, as opposed to a frame, which is of variable length.

cell delay variation One of three negotiated QoS parameters defined by the ATM Forum. Abbreviated CDV.

cell delay variation tolerance Parameter defined by the ATM Forum for ATM traffic management. Abbreviated CDVT.

cell loss ratio One of three negotiated QoS parameters defined by the ATM Forum. Abbreviated CLR.

cell relay Transmission technique used in circuit-switching services with fixed-length cells. The main example of cell relay is ATM.

cell transfer delay One of three negotiated QoS parameters defined by the ATM Forum. Abbreviated CTD.

Challenge Handshake Authentication Protocol Security protocol with encryption that allows access between data communications systems prior to and during data transmission. CHAP uses challenges to verify that a user has access to a system. *See also* **Password Authentication Protocol**.

CHAP *See* **Challenge Handshake Authentication Protocol**.

chatter The condition resulting when NIC electronics fail to shut down after a transmission and the NIC floods the network with random signals.

circuit Means of two-way communication between two or more points.

classical IP over ATM Specification for running IP over ATM as defined in RFC1577. An end station registers its own address with an address server in the ATM network. It then uses the server to learn the ATM addresses of other similar stations. This differs from traditional IP, whose ARP (Address Resolution Protocol) uses broadcasts to learn remote addresses.

client 1. A network user or process, often a device or workstation. 2. A secondary processor that relies upon a primary processor or server.

client/server architecture The division of an application into separate processes capable of operating on separate CPUs connected over a network.

client/sever model In most cases, the "client" is a desktop computing device or program "served" by another networked computing device. Computers are integrated over the network by an application which provides a single system image. The server can be a minicomputer, workstation, or microcomputer with attached storage devices. A client can be served by multiple servers.

collision 1. The event occurring when two or more nodes contend for the network at the same time. This is usually caused by the time delay that the signal requires to travel the length of the network. 2. The Ethernet protocol mechanism by which simultaneous or overlapping network access requests are handled. This network event is not an error in and of itself; it is an indication that two or more nodes attempted to transmit within the same slot. Unless the number of collisions is excessive, this is a normal condition.

collision detection A node's ability to detect when two or more nodes are transmitting simultaneously on a shared network.

collision enforcement The transmission of extra jam bits, after a collision is detected, to insure that all other transmitting nodes detect the collision.

congestion A slowdown in a network due to a bottleneck. Excessive network traffic. *See also* **traffic congestion**.

congestion error 1. An indication that a station does not have sufficient buffer space to copy a cell, frame, or packet addressed to it. 2. A packet sent to the file server, which then cannot buffer the frame, indicates that the server NIC may be considered congested. The board may require reconfiguration to allocate an additional incoming packet buffer.

connection The establishment of a communication path for the transfer of information according to agreed-on conventions.

connection-oriented service A service where a connection (real or virtual) is set up and maintained for the duration of the call.

connectionless service In a connectionless service, no fixed path is set up between sender and recipient. Every unit of data that is exchanged is self-contained in that it contains all the necessary control and address information to ensure correct delivery, such as packet switching.

constant bit rate   One of five service categories defined by the ATM Forum for ATM. Where the number of bits sent or received per time unit is constant, or very nearly so.

Consultative Committee for International Telephone and Telegraph   An international organization that makes recommendations for networking standards like X.25, X.400, and facsimile data compression standards. Abbreviated CCITT. Now called the International Telecommunications Union Telecommunication Standardization Sector, and abbreviated ITU or ITU-TSS.

contention   An access method in which network devices compete for the right to access the physical medium.

controller   The device in a network node that physically connects that device to the network media.

CRC   Acronym for Cyclic Redundancy Check.

CRC error   Acronym for Cyclic Redundancy Check Error.

CRC errors/s   1. An indication of a corrupted packet, either due to a faulty network interface board or a faulty cabling system. 2. A high number of CRC errors per second attributed to a single station indicates a faulty network interface board. If CRC errors are attributed to numerous stations on the network, this indicates a cabling problem.

crosstalk   A technical term indicating that stray signals from other wavelengths, channels, communication pathways, or twisted-pair wiring have polluted the signal. It is particularly prevalent in twisted-pair networks or when telephone and network communications share copper-based wiring bundles. A symptom of interference that is caused by two cell sites causing competing signals to be received by the mobile subscriber. This can also be generated by two mobiles causing competing signals that are received by the cellular base station. Crosstalk sounds like two conversations, and often a distortion of one or the other or both.

CSMA/CD   *See* **Carrier Sense Multiple Access with Collision Detection**.

CSMA/CD   Carrier sense multiple access with collision detection; the method by which Ethernet keeps traffic separated on a network.

cut-through   A type of switching in which the frame is forwarded after the initial header is processed. *See also* **adaptive**; **store-and-forward switching**.

cut-through switch mode   A switching technology that has the least latency because the MAC address is stripped from the header on-the-fly and the packet is redirected to the destination at wire speed. It provides no store-and-forward buffering. At high traffic loading or high error rates, the switch forwards bad packets, and drops all those it cannot immediately forward. *See also* **modified cut-through switch mode, store-and-forward switch mode**.

cyclic redundancy check   A checksum—an error-checking algorithm that the transmitting station includes within a frame. The receiving station generates its own CRC to check against the transmitted CRC. If the results are different, the receiver usually requests a retransmission of the frame. This encoded value is appended to each frame by the data link layer to allow the receiving NIC to detect transmission errors in the physical channel. *See also* **frame check sequence**.

daisychaining   The connection of multiple devices in a serial fashion. An advantage of daisychaining is savings in transmission facilities. A disadvantage is that if a device malfunctions, all the devices daisychained behind it are disabled.

data   When used in the context of communications, data refers to transmitted information, particularly information that is not interpreted by a particular protocol entity but merely delivered to a higher-level entity, possibly after some processing.

data link   Any serial data communications transmission path, generally between two adjacent nodes or devices and without any intermediate switching nodes.

data-link control   1. Procedures to ensure that both the sending and receiving devices agree on synchronization, error detection and recovery methods, and initialization and operation methods for point-to-point or multipoint configurations. 2. The second layer in the ISO reference model for Open Systems Interconnection.

data-link control layer   Layer 2 of the SNA architectural model, responsible for the transmission of data over a particular physical link. Corresponds approximately to the data-link layer of the OSI model.

data-link layer   The logical entity in the OSI model concerned with transmission of data between adjacent network nodes; it is the second layer processing in the OSI model, between the physical and the network layers.

data rate The effective speed at which data is transferred over a transmission link. The data rate is the actual transmission rate after errors, synchronization, and overhead are factored out.

de facto According to actual practice; protocols and architectures such as Sun Microsystems' Network File System (NFS) and IBM's Systems Network Architecture (SNA) are called de facto standards because they are so widely used, although they have not been sanctioned by any official standards bodies.

de jure Standards specified by an accredited standards organization. IEEE 802.3 is an example of a de jure standard.

delay The time between the initiation of a transaction by a sender and the first response received by the sender. Also, the time required to move a packet from source to destination over a given path.

destination address The receiving station's address. *See* **address**.

Differential Manchester Encoding Digital coding scheme where a mid-bit-time transition is used for clocking, and a transition at the beginning of each bit time denotes a zero. The coding scheme used by 100BaseVG-AnyLAN.

DHCP *See* **Dynamic Host Configuration Protocol**.

discrete-event simulation Modeling technique in which the traffic is represented as sequences of messages, packets, or frames.

DNS *See* **Domain Naming System**.

domain A group of nodes on a network forming an administrative entity.

Domain Naming System Used in the Internet for translation of names of network nodes into IP addresses. Abbreviated DNS.

duplexed Ethernet A method to provide paired, full-duplexed Ethernet transmission circuits.

Dynamic Host Configuration Protocol Dynamically allocates IP addresses to end stations for fixed periods of time.

email Electronic mail; a computer network and software by which messages can be sent to others on the network.

EIA Electronic Industries Association. *See* **Electronics Industry Association/Telecommunication Industry Association**.

EIA/TIA *See* **Electronics Industry Association/Telecommunication Industry Association**.

EIA/TIA 568/569 Premise wiring recommendations for telecommunications and data communications in commercial and high-rise buildings and campus facilities. These are not standards or specifications, but represent rather a concept. Conformance testing to wiring category definitions is based on an industry-based general adaptation and consensus to these wiring concepts.

EIAN   *See* **Emulated LAN**.

Electronics Industry Association/Telecommunication Industry Association   Two industry groups merging telephonics and communications experience that have created a series of joint standards for consolidating premise wiring and measuring quality and performance. EIA was established in 1924 by common-carrier radio interests and the electronic industry community to respond to governmental regulatory matters. Abbreviated EIA/TIA.

EMI   Electromagnetic Interference.

Emulated LAN   Defined by the LANE specification for LANs within an ATM network, there can be multiple emulated LANs comprising many Ethernets or token rings. Abbreviated ELAN.

encapsulation   The wrapping of data in a particular protocol header. For example, Ethernet data is wrapped in a specific Ethernet header before network transmission. Also, a method of bridging dissimilar networks where the entire frame from one network is simply enclosed in the header used by the link-layer protocol of the other network.

end-system designator   Part of GSE for IPv6. Abbreviated ESD.

ER   *See* **explicit rate**.

enterprise network   A campus or wide area network that services all (or most) organizational sites supporting multiple point-to-point routes and/or integrating voice, facsimile, data, and video into the same channel. A (usually large and diverse) network connecting most major points in a company. An enterprise network differs from a WAN in that it is typically private and contained within a single organization.

error rate   Ratio of the number of bits, elements, characters, or blocks incorrectly received to the total number of bits, elements, characters, or blocks transmitted.

ESD   *See* **end-system designator**.

Ether   The lumeniferous ether was the omnipresent passive medium theorized in 1765 by Christiaan Huygens. It was proposed as the medium that carried light (electromagnetic) waves from the Sun to the Earth.

Ethernet   A popular baseband local area network from which the IEEE 802.3 standard was derived. Ethernet applies the IEEE 802.2 MAC protocols and uses the persistent CSMA/CD protocol. It is built on a bus topology based on original specifications invented by Xerox Corporation and developed jointly by Xerox, Intel, and Digital Equipment Corporation. Sometimes abbreviated Enet.

Ethernet address   A coded value indicating the manufacturer, machine type, and a unique identifying number. There are source and destination addresses in every valid Ethernet packet.

Ethernet controller   An interface device that provides protocol access for computer equipment to a network. Each node on the network must have an Ethernet controller.

ETSI   *See* **European Telecommunications Standards Institute**.

European Telecommunications Standards Institute   An organization made up of national representatives from CEPT countries, the composition of which can include public and private telecommunications providers and equipment manufacturers and users, subject to national determination. Abbreviated ETSI.

explicit rate   In an ATM network, one of two feedback mechanisms used by the ABR service category to inform the source of the network resources available to it. Abbreviated ER.

explicit tagging   A frame is classified as belonging to a particular VLAN on the basis of a VLAN tag value that is included in the frame.

facilities management   Entering into an agreement with a service supplier to manage internal company facilities such as telecommunications services. Facilities management does not involve the transfer of ownership of facilities to the service provider.

Fast Ethernet   IEEE standard based on IEEE 802.3 but running at 100 instead of 10 Mbits/s and using 100Base-T or 100Base-F families of cabling standards.

FCS   *See* **frame check sequence**.

FDDI   *See* **fiber distributed data interface**.

fiber distributed data interface   A LAN standard specifying a LAN-to-LAN backbone for transmitting data at 100 Mbits/s over fiberoptic (or copper with TP-PMD) media. Features wrapping rings and includes SMT (surface mounting technology) management. Abbreviated FDDI.

Fiber Optical Inter-Repeater Link   The interconnection protocol required for point-to-point repeater links based on optical fiber in LANs. Abbreviated FOIRL.

fiber optics   Thin glass or plastic cables that transmit data in the form of pulse-modulated light beams.

fiber-optic cable   A thin, flexible medium capable of conducting modulated light transmission. Compared with other transmission media, fiber-optic cable is more expensive, impervious to electromagnetic interference, and capable of higher data rates.

FIFO   *See* **first in, first out**.

firewall   Router or access server, often with specialist software, designated as a buffer to ward off intrusion into a private network, particularly important in Internet-to-intranet communications.

first in, first out   A method of transmitting data through a switch to minimize delay. Also has a more general use. Abbreviated FIFO.

FOIRL   **Fiber Optic Inter-Repeater Link**.

forced collision   A collision that occurs when a packet is transmitted even if traffic (carrier sense) is detected on the network; that is, if the packet will collide with other packets already on the network. When a packet is transmitted and collides, it is received at the destination node with either a CRC error or an alignment error, if it is received at all.

fragment   1. A partial cell, frame, or packet. 2. A normal Ethernet event due to a collision. 3. A sudden increase in Ethernet fragments can indicate a problem with a network component. A good rule of thumb is to examine fragments in conjunction with utilization. If both Ethernet utilization and fragments increase, this indicates an increase in usage of the cabling system. If fragments increase and utilization remains steady, however, this indicates a faulty network component.

fragmentation   The process of breaking a packet into smaller units when transmitting over a network medium that cannot support the original size of the packet.

frame   1. A self-contained group of bits representing data and control information. The control information usually includes source and destination addressing, sequencing, flow control, preamble, delay, and error control information at different protocol levels. 2. A frame may be a packet with framing bits for preamble and delay. 3. Data transmission units for FDDI. The terms packet, datagram, segment, and message are also used to describe logical information groupings at various layers of the OSI reference model and in various technology circles.

frame check sequence   1. The encoded value appended to each frame by the data link layer to allow receiving Ethernet controllers to detect transmission errors in the physical channel. Also called a Cyclic Redundancy Check. 2. An HDLC term adopted by subsequent link-layer protocols and referring to extra characters added to a frame for error-control purposes. Abbreviated FCS.

framing   The process of assigning data bits into the network time slot.

gateway   1. A device that routes information from one network to another. It often provides an interface between dissimilar networks and provides protocol translation between the networks, such as SNA and TCP/IP or IPX/SPX. A gateway is also a software connection between different networks; this meaning is not implied in this book. The gateway provides service at levels 1 through 7 of the OSI reference model. 2. In the IP community, an older term referring to a routing device. Today, the term router is used to describe nodes that perform this function, and gateway refers to a special-purpose device that performs a Layer 7 conversion of information from one protocol stack to another. 3. System requesting service from another system. *See also* **router**.

Gbps   Abbreviation for gigabits (1,000,000,000 bits) per second. The adverse performance condition that occurs when traffic from overlapping or intersection channels prevents the free flow of traffic on the other channel(s).

GID   GARP Information Declaration.

gigabit   Usually taken to mean 1 billion bits (abbreviated Gbit); more precisely, 1,024,000 bits.

Gigabit Ethernet   Standard approaching IEEE approval for transmission of standard Ethernet traffic at speeds of 1 Gbit/s.

GIP   GARP Information Propagation.

global, site, and end system   Alternate addressing architecture for IPv6.

GMRP   GARP Multicast Registration Protocol. Provides a mechanism that allows GMRP participants to dynamically register and deregister information with the MAC bridges attached to the same LAN segment.

graphical user interface   A graphics-based front end. Common examples are Microsoft Windows and HP OpenView. Abbreviated GUI.

groupware   Networked applications capable of being shared by users.

GSE   *See* **global, site, and end system**.

GUI   *See* **graphical user interface**.

header   The initial portion of a message, which contains any information and control codes that are not part of the text (e.g., routine, priority, message type, destination addressee, and time of origination).

heterogeneous (computer) network   A system of different host computers, such as those of different manufacturers.

hop   1. The routing of a cell, frame, or packet through a network device and/or transmission channel based on destination address information. 2. The passage of a packet through one bridge, router, switch, or gateway.

hub   1. A network interface that provides star connectivity. 2. A wiring concentrator. 3. Generally, a term used to describe a device that serves as the center of a star-topology network. In Ethernet/IEEE 802.3 terminology, a hub is an Ethernet multiport repeater, which is sometimes referred to as a concentrator. The term is also used to refer to a hardware/software device that contains multiple independent but connected modules of network and internetwork equipment. Hubs can be active (where they repeat signals sent through them) or passive (where they do not repeat, but merely split, signals sent through them). *See also* **Media Access Unit**.

I/O   Abbreviation for input and output from a computer. Refers to all memory movement on the bus, data moved to and from disks, screen and speaker output, and data frames transmitted to and from the network channel.

IEEE   *See* **Institute for Electrical and Electronic Engineers**.

IEEE 802   An Institute for Electrical Engineering standard for interconnection of local area networking computer equipment. The IEEE 802 standard describes the physical and data link layers of the OSI reference model.

IEEE 802.1   A specification for media-layer physical linkages and bridging.

IEEE 802.1d   The standard that detects and manages logical loops in a network. When multiple paths exist, the bridge or router selects the most efficient one. When a path fails, it automatically reconfigures the network with a new active path. Also known as the Spanning Tree Algorithm.

IEEE 802.2   A specification for media-layer communication typified by Ethernet, FDDI, and Token-Ring.

IEEE 802.3   An Ethernet specification derived from the original Xerox

Ethernet specifications. It describes the CSMA/CD protocol on a bus topology using baseband transmissions.

IEEE 802.3u   The Fast Ethernet specification for 100-Mbps transmission on two pairs, four pairs, or fiber.

IEEE 802.5   A token ring specification derived from the original IBM Token-Ring LAN specifications. It describes the token protocol on a star/ring topology using baseband transmissions.

IEEE 802.9a   A recommendation for isochronous Ethernet with a standard 10-Mbps Ethernet channel and a second 6-Mbps isochronous channel for simultaneous videoconferencing using the BRI ISDN interface. This recommendation also provides for connectivity to WAN channels using ISDN, Switched 56, or T-1 services with a CSU/DSU interface.

IEEE 802.11   A physical- and MAC-layer specification for wireless network transmission at transmission speeds from 1 to 4 Mbps. This specification includes the basic rate set for fixed bandwidths supported by all wireless stations (for compatibility) and an extended rate set for optional speeds. Another addendum includes a dynamic data rate set.

IEEE 802.12   A 100-Mbps Ethernet specification based on four wire pairs and quartet signaling.

impedance   The mathematical combination of resistance and capacitance that is used as a measurement to describe the electrical properties of the coaxial cable and network hardware.

implicit tagging   A frame is classified as belonging to a particular VLAN on the basis of the data content of the frame and/or the receiving port.

inductance   The property of electrical fields to induce a voltage to flow on the coaxial cable and network hardware. It is usually a disruptive signal that interferes with normal network transmissions.

infrastructure   1. The premise wiring plant supporting data communications; the risers, jumpers, patch panels, and wiring closets; the hubs, PBXs, and switches; the computer operations providing services to network devices; the network division; the test equipment; and the design and support staff maintaining operations. 2. The physical and logical components of a network. Typically, this includes wiring, wiring connections, attachment devices, network nodes and stations, interconnectivity devices (such as hubs, routers, gateways, and switches), operating environment software, and software applications.

Institute for Electrical and Electronic Engineers A membership-based organization based in New York City that creates and publishes technical specifications and scientific publications. Abbreviated IEEE.

interconnection A junction (telecommunication) connecting two communication carriers (such as between cellular and land-line networks) allowing mutual access by customers to each carrier's network.

interconnectivity The process where different network protocols, hardware, and host mainframe systems can attach to each other for transferring data to each other.

interface A device that connects equipment of different types for mutual access. Generally, this refers to computer software and hardware that enable disks and other storage devices to communicate with a computer. In networking, an interface translates different protocols so that different types of computers can communicate together. In the OSI model, the interface is the method of passing data between layers on one device.

interframe spacing The 96-bit waiting time between transmissions to allow receiving Ethernet controllers to recover. This corresponds to 96 ms at 10 Mbps and 9.6 ms at 100 Mbps. PACE and priority demand systems support the interface spacing only for interoperability with standard Ethernet.

International Organization for Standardization Standards body, based in Switzerland, responsible for, among other things, the seven-layer OSI reference model.

International Telecommunications Union Previously named the CCITT (Comité Consultatif International Télégraphique et Téléphonique). This is a leading group to develop telecommunications standards. Abbreviated ITU or ITU-TTS.

International Telecommunications Union/Telecommunications Standards Sector Formerly, the Consultative Committee for International Telephone and Telegraph (CCITT), this international organization makes recommendations for networking standards like X.25, X.400, and facsimile data compression standards. Abbreviated ITU-TSS.

Internet A worldwide network of networks all connected using the TCP/IP suite of protocols and functioning as a single virtual network. It provides universal connectivity and three levels of network services: connectionless packet delivery, full-duplex stream delivery, and application-level services (mainly electronic mail).

Internet Activities Board Technical policy- and standards-setting body for the Internet, TCP/IP, and connected protocols with two task forces: Internet Engineering Task Force (IETF) and Internet Research Task Force (IRTF). Abbreviated IAB.

internet address 1. An address in the following format: username@system.type. 2. An address applied at the TCP/IP protocol layer to differentiate network stations from each other. This is in addition to the station hardware or protocol address. 3. Also called an "IP address," at least a 32-bit address (could be 128-bit) assigned to hosts using TCP/IP. The address is written as four octets separated with periods (dotted decimal format) that are made up of a network section, an optional subnet section, and a host section.

Internet Control Message Protocol Part of the Internet Protocol, handling error and control messages. Abbreviated ICMP. *See also* **Internet Protocol.**

Internet Control Message Protocol Replaces ARP in IPv6. Abbreviated ICMP.

Internet Engineering Steering Group Organization appointed by the IAB to manage the operation of the IETF. Abbreviated IESG.

Internet Engineering Task Force Committee which is a subgroup of the Internet Society and is concerned with short- and medium-term problems with TCP/IP and the Internet. It is divided into six subcommittees (with further divisions into working parties). The chairperson sits on the IAB. Abbreviated IETF.

Internet Packet Exchange A very widely used routing protocol, based on Xerox's XNS, developed by Novell. Implemented in Novell's NetWare. Abbreviated IPX.

Internet Protocol The network layer protocol of the TCP/IP suite including the ICMP control and error message protocol as an integral part. Has 32-bit addressing. Now at version 4. Abbreviated IP. *See also* **IP next generation** and **Transmission Control Protocol/Internet Protocol.**

Internet service provider A company providing public access to the Internet, usually by leased line, ISDN, and/or modem. Abbreviated ISP.

internet(work) Two or more networks linked together. A local internet is confined within a single building; a campus internet includes two or more nearby buildings.

internetworking A general term used to refer to the industry that has arisen around the problem of connecting networks with each other. The term can refer to products, procedures, and technologies.

interoperability   The process where different network protocols, network hardware, and host mainframe systems can process data together.

interpacket delay   The time between arrivals of packets on the network.

intranet   A network using Web technologies to communicate within its organization.

IP address   Internetwork Protocol address or Internet address. A unique number assigned by an Internet authority that identifies a computer on the Internet. The address consists of four groups of numbers separated by three periods (dots), each between 0 and 255. For example, 195.112.56.75 is an IP address. (See also **IP subnet.**)

IP multicast   Routing technique that allows propagation of IP traffic from one source to many destinations.

IP next generation (IPng)   Colloquial name for IPv6.

IP Security Option (IPSO)   U.S. government specification defining an optional field in the IP packet header for hierarchical packet security levels on a per interface basis.

IP subnet   A division of a network made by allocating different parts of the IP address spectrum to separate the network into IP domains. An IP subnet or subnet mask is a way to subdivide a network into smaller networks to allow a large number of computers on a network with a single *IP address.*

IPv4   The current version of IP now informally redesignated to distinguish it from IPv6.

IPv6   New standard intended to replace IP now being decided by the IETF under RFC1752; offers 128-bit addressing to overcome limitations of numbers of IP addresses. Also has facilities for mobile logins and includes authentication. Also known as *IP next generation* (IPng).

IPX   Internet Packet Exchange.

ISDN   Integrated Services Digital Network; a fully digital communications facility designed to provide transparent, end-to-end transmission of voice, data, video, and still images across the PSTN. Standards for this service are set by the ITU-T.

ISO   *See* **Internation Organization for Standardization**.

ITU   *See* **International Telecommunications Union**.

ITU-T   Part of the International Telecommunications Union.

ITU-TSS   *See* **International Telecommunications Union/ Telecommunications Standards Sector**.

ITU-TTS   *See* **International Telecommunications Union**.

jabber   1. To talk without making sense. 2. The condition that results when a transceiver's carrier-sense electronics malfunction and the transceiver broadcasts in excess of the specified time limit, thus creating an oversized frame.

jabber frame   A frame that exceeds 1518 bytes in the data field and violates the IEEE 802.3 specifications.

jam   A short encoded sequence emitted by the transmitting node to ensure that all other nodes have detected a collision, and used for collision enforcement.

jitter   A network failure that occurs when network segment preamble and the frame signal are out of phase. The jitter shows up as transmission signal distortion, decay, frequency errors, and timing errors on all dc-based hubs or switches. Analog signal distortion is caused by variation of the signal from the timing positions. Jitter can cause data loss, particularly at high speeds.

KB   Abbreviation for kilobytes (1024 bytes) of memory. Also K.

Kbps   Abbreviation for kilobits (1000 bits) per second.

Kerberos   Security method for authenticating network users and protecting network traffic based on DES encryption. An Internet Engineering Task Force (IETF) standard, Kerberos works by having a central server grant a "ticket" honored by all networked nodes running Kerberos.

kHz   *See* **kilohertz**.

kilohertz   A measure of audio and radio frequency (a thousand cycles per second). Abbreviated as kHz. The human ear can hear frequencies up to about 20 kHz. There are 1000 kHz in 1 MHz.

kilobit   Loosely, 1000 bits (actually 1024). Abbreviated kbit.

kilobyte   Loosely, 1000 bytes (actually 1024). Abbreviated KB, K, or kbyte.

kilometer   A unit representing 1000 m, or approximately 3200 SAE feet. It also may be represented by km.

km   *See* **kilometer**.

LAN   *See* **Local Area Network**.

LAN Emulation   Makes ATM resemble Ethernet or token ring (but not FDDI) to the local network. It allows broadcast and multicast messages. Sitting at the MAC layer, it is protocol-independent—not recognizing the network layer at all. Abbreviated LANE.

LAN Emulation Network Node Interface   The interface between two LANE servers. LNNI is part of the LANE 2.0 specification. Abbreviated LNNI.

LAN switch   The hublike intermediate-node hardware used for increasing overall network performance either through static microsegmentation and dynamic port switching. Typically, network devices are dynamically paired through the LAN switch for each packet transmission only for the duration of that single transmission. This technology is typically applied for LAN-to-ATM connectivity.

LANE   *See* **LAN Emulation**.

late collision   A collision indicated by an oversized runt frame, usually indicative of a network exceeding length or size specifications.

latency   1. The waiting time for a station desiring to transmit on the network. 2. The delay or process time that prevents completion of a task. Latency usually refers to the lag between request for delivery of data over the network until it is actually received. 3. The period of time after a request has been made for service before it is fulfilled. 4. The amount of time between when a device requests access to a network and when it is granted permission to transmit.

LDAP   *See* **Lightweight Directory Protocol**.

LEC   LAN Emulation client.

LES   LAN Emulation server.

Lightweight Directory Access Protocol   An emerging directory access standard for the Internet, also being adopted by NOS vendors. Abbreviated LDAP.

LLC   *See* **logical link control**.

LNNI   *See* **LAN Emulation Network Node Interface**.

load balancing   1. A technique to equalize the workload over peer and client network components. This includes workstations, storage disks, servers, network connectivity devices (such as bridges, routers, gateways, and switches), and network transmission channels. 2. In routing, the ability of a router to distribute traffic over all its network ports that are the same distance from the destination address. Good algorithms use both line speed and reliability information. Load balancing increases the utilization of network segments, thus increasing effective network bandwidth.

lobe   A section of cable or wire extending from an MAU, hub, or concentrator to a network station.

local area network   One of the several types of geographically limited communications networks intended primarily for such high-speed data transmission applications as data transfer, text, facsimile, and video. Abbreviated LAN.

logical link control   A protocol developed by the IEEE 802, common to all its local network standards, for data-link-level transmission control. The upper sublayer of the IEEE layer 2 (OSI) protocol that complements the MAC protocol (IEEE 802.2). Abbreviated LLC.

long frame   A frame that exceeds the specified protocol length maximum.

long packet   A packet that exceeds maximum packet size including address, length, and CRC fields.

loopback test   A test for faults over a transmission medium where received data is returned to the sending point (thus traveling a loop) and compared with the data sent.

MAC   *See* **media access control**.

MAN   High-speed communications network operating within a city or metropolitan area up to 50 km in diameter.

management information base   The set of specifications associated with a vendor's devices, used by management systems. Abbreviated MIB.

mapping   In network operations, the logical association of one set of values, such as addresses on one network, with quantities or values of another set, such as devices on a second network (e.g., name-address mapping, internetwork-route mapping).

MAU   *See* **Media Access Unit**.

maximum burst size   In ATM, the number of cells a source is allowed to send at the peak cell rate. Abbreviated MBS.

MB   Abbreviation for megabyte (1024 kilobytes) of data.

Mbps   *See* **megabits per second**.

MCR   *See* **minimum all rate**.

media   1. The physical material used to transmit the network transmission signal. For wired networks, it is some form of copper wire or optical fiber. However, wireless networks use infrared or radio-frequency signals with the air as the medium. 2. The substance used by a physical data-storage device to record data; magnetic tape, floptical disks, or CD-ROM, for example.

media access control   A sublayer of layer 2 of the OSI seven-layer reference model depending on characteristics of the underlying physical layer. Abbreviated MAC.

Media Access Unit   A device that connects directly to a lobe wire, broadcasts and receives information over that cable, and switches the signals to the next active downstream station. It is abbreviated as MAU. *See also* **hub**.

megabits per second   The number of millions of bits transferred per second. Abbreviated Mbps.

Megahertz   Signal frequency use for voice, data, TV, and other forms of electronic communications in the millions of cycles per second. Abbreviated as MHz.

message   1. Any cell, frame, or packet containing a response to a LAN-type network request, process, activity, or network management operation. 2. A PDU of any defined format and purpose. 3. An application-layer logical grouping of information. *See also* **frame**.

meter   A unit of measurement equivalent to 39.25 SAE inches, or 3.27 ft. Meter is abbreviated m.

metric   A formal measuring standard or benchmark. Network performance metrics include Mbps, throughput, error rates, and other less formal definitions.

metropolitan area network   A network that spans buildings, or city blocks, or a college or corporate campus. Optical fiber repeaters, bridges, routers, packet switches, and PBX services usually supply the network links. Abbreviated MAN.

MHz   *See* **Megahertz**.

microsecond 1×10^{-6} second. Abbreviated μs.

microsegmentation   1. The division of a large network into smaller isolated (and bridged) segments. 2. A typical method to decrease network performance saturation on LANs that have become a traffic bottleneck. 3. The process of increasing bandwidth and managing loads by segmenting LANs into smaller units, establishing a firewall between these smaller units, and routing or Switching traffic as necessary between units.

millisecond 1×10^{-3} second. Abbreviated ms.

minimum cell rate   In ATM, the minimum cell rate a source is allowed to maintain. Abbreviated MCR.

misaligned frame   A frame that trails a fragmentary byte (1-7 residual bits), and has an FCS error, or an Ethernet packet that was framed improperly by the receiving station and is therefore a synchronization error.

modified cut-through switch mode   A switching technology that has a latency equivalent to that of bridges because it reads the entire packet header. It can retry a failed transmission more than once, because it buffers that single packet. Packets that arrive for the same destination during this interval are dropped, because they are not buffered. *See also* **cut-through switch mode**; **store-and-forward switch mode**.

monitor   *See* **protocol analyzer**.

MPOA   *See* **Multiprotocol over ATM**.

multicast   1. The ability to broadcast to a select subset of nodes. 2. Single packets copied to a specific subset of network addresses. These addresses are specified in the destination-address field. In contrast, in a broadcast, packets are sent to all devices in a network.

Multiprotocol over ATM   A development for performing switched IP networking over an ATM network, used in conjunction with LANE. Other protocols may be added in the future. Abbreviated MPOA.

NetBIOS   Network Basic Input/Output System interface, created by Microsoft and IBM.

network   A series of points (nodes, end stations, etc.) connected by communications standards.

network address   A logical address at layer 3 of the seven-layer OSI model, rather than a physical address at layer 2.

network administrator   A person who helps maintain a network.

network analyzer   A device offering various network troubleshooting features, including protocol-specific packet decodes, specific preprogrammed troubleshooting tests, packet filtering, and packet transmission. *See* **protocol analyzer**.

network cascade   An enterprise network event in which many broadcasts are sent at once, overloading intermediate nodes and creating a time-out or network panic. This is an undesirable network event in which many broadcasts are sent all at once, using substantial network bandwidth and, typically, causing network saturation at intermediate nodes. *See also* **broadcast storm**.

network interface card   Board that plugs into an expansion slot on a workstation or server which is to be networked, with a connector for the network cabling. Abbreviated NIC.

network layer   In the OSI model, the logical network entity that services the transport layer. It is responsible for ensuring that data passed to it from the transport layer is routed and delivered through the network.

network monitor   *See* **protocol analyzer**.

network management center   Center used for control of a network. May provide traffic analysis, call-detail recording, configuration control, fault detection and diagnosis, and maintenance. Abbreviated NMC.

Network Management Forum   Consortium of over 100 equipment vendors and carriers that are developing implementation specifications for OSI-based network management.

network management system   A central software-based set of programs for control of disparate hardware elements; also the whole— both software and hardware used in bridging, routing, etc., together with the network management center. Abbreviated NMS.

network-network interface   In ATM environments, the interface between two network devices. Abbreviated NNI.

network operating system   Software that handles the administration of a network to allow resources and files to be shared. Various facilities can be provided, including file sharing, remote access, and a range of administrative functions to control the network. Abbreviated NOS.

network topology   Describes the physical and logical relationship of nodes in a network, the schematic arrangement of the links and nodes, or some hybrid combination thereof.

NIC   *See* **Network interface card**.

NMC   *See* **network management control**.

NMS   *See* **network management system**.

NMI   *See* **network management interface**.

node   1. A logical, nonphysical interconnection to the network that supports computer workstations or other types of physical devices on a network that participates in communication. 2. Alternatively, a node may connect to a fan-out unit providing network access for many devices. A device might be a terminal server or a shared peripheral such as a file server, printer, or plotter.

non-real-time variable bit rate   One of five service categories defined by the ATM Forum for ATM. Abbreviated nrtVBR.

NOS   *See* **network operating system**.

OEM   *See* **original equipment manufacturer**.

Open Shortest Path First   A link state routing protocol derived from the Dijkstra algorithm. The routers using this protocol update each other and learn network topology by periodically broadcasting link state data across the network. Abbreviated OSPF.

Open Systems Interconnection   ISO's reference model for a seven-layer network architecture used for the definition of network protocol standards enabling all OSI-compliant computers or devices to communicate with each other. Abbreviated OSI.

Open Systems Interconnection reference model   A specification definition from the International Standards Organization. It is a data communication architectural model for networking. Abbreviated OSI model.

original equipment manufacturer   Maker of equipment that is marketed by another vendor, usually under the name of the reseller. The OEM may manufacture only certain components, or complete computers, which are then often configured with software and/or other hardware by the reseller. Abbreviated OEM.

OS   Abbreviation for operating system.

OSI   *See* **Open Systems Interconnection**.

OSI seven-layer reference model   An architecture that enables the interoperable transmission of data through a network.

OSPF   *See* **Open Shortest Path First**.

outsourcing   A strategy in which an organization contracts the provision of its requirements for services such as telecommunications, data networking, or information technology to another, separate organization. In outsourcing, the outside organization normally provides the network, equipment, and management necessary to support these services. This contrasts with facilities management, where only the management and maintenance of existing facilities is normally involved.

overlapping VLANs A virtual LAN type where one user may belong to more than one VLAN at a time.

oversize error A frame or packet greater than the largest allowable size. Oversized packets indicate that a faulty or corrupted driver is in use on the network.

oversized frame A frame that exceeds the maximum frame size defined by a protocol.

oversized packet A packet that exceeds the maximum packet size including address, length, and CRC fields.

packet A group of binary digits, including data and call-control signals, that is switched as a composite whole. The data, call-control signals, and error-control information are arranged in a specified format.

packet buffer A structure created in computer memory to build, disassemble, or temporarily store network data frames.

packet burst An overwhelming broadcast of frames requesting network and station status information, requesting source or destination addresses, or indicating panic error messages.

packet switching A network transmission methodology that uses data to define a start and length of a transmission for digital communications. A process of sending data in discrete blocks. A network on which nodes share bandwidth with each other by intermittently sending logical information units (packets). In contrast, a circuit-switching network dedicates one circuit at a time to data transmission.

PAP *See* **Password Authentication Protocol**.

Password Authentication Protocol A security protocol without encryption that secures passwords for user authentication to allow access to a network or host. Abbreviated PAP. *See also* **Challenge Handshake Authentication Protocol.**

patch cord A flexible wire unit or element with quick-connects used to establish connections on a patch panel.

patch panel A cross-connect device designed to accommodate the use of a patch cord for the simplification of wiring additions, movements, and other changes.

PCR *See* **peak cell rate**.

PDU *See* **Protocol Data Unit**.

peak   1. A high volume of network traffic. 2. A local or absolute traffic volume maximum.

peak cell rate   In ATM, the maximum cell rate a source is allowed to maintain. Abbreviated PCR.

physical address   The unique address associated with each workstation on a network. A physical address is devised to be distinct from all other physical addresses on interconnected networks. A worldwide designation unique to each unit.

physical device   Any item of hardware on the network.

physical layer   Within the OSI model, the lowest level of network processing, below the data-link layer, that is concerned with the electrical, mechanical, and handshaking procedures over the interface that connects a device to a transmission medium (i.e., RS-232-C).

PIM   *See* **protocol-independent multicast**.

polling   An access method in which a primary network device inquires, in an orderly fashion, whether secondary nodes have data to transmit. The inquiry occurs in the form of messages to each secondary that gives the secondary the right to transmit.

port   Point of access into a communications switch, a network, or other electronic device.

preamble   The 64-bit encoded sequence that the physical layer transmits before each frame to synchronize clocks and other physical layer circuitry at other nodes on the Ethernet channel.

presentation layer   In the OSI model, the layer of processing that provides services to the application layer, allowing it to interpret the data exchanged, as well as to structure data messages to be transmitted in a specific display and control format.

priority-tagged frame   A tagged frame whose tag header carries no VLAN identification information.

protocol   A collection of rules, voluntarily agreed on by vendors and users, to ensure that the equipment transmitting and receiving data understand each other. In general, protocols represent three major areas: the method in which data is represented or coded (e.g., ASCII); the method in which the codes are received (e.g., synchronously or asynchronously); and the methods used to establish control, detect failures or errors, and initiate corrective action. Terminals performing the same functions under different protocols cannot be used on the same system without protocol converters or emulators.

protocol address   *See* **network address**.

protocol analyzer   Test equipment that transmits, receives, and captures Ethernet packets to verify proper network operation.

Protocol Data Unit   An OSI term for the data to be transmitted together with the headers and trailers attached by each layer. Abbreviated PDU.

protocol-independent multicast   Allows the addition of IP multicast routing in an IP network. In dense mode, packets are forwarded on all outgoing interfaces and it is assumed that receivers are most likely to want to receive the packets. In sparse mode, data distribution is limited; packets are sent only if explicitly requested at the rendezvous point. Abbreviated PIM.

protocol stack   A defined protocol, together with options applicable for specific functions, which can be implemented as a product. Also called a *functional standard* or *functional profile*.

protocol-transparent.   A device's capability to perform its function independent of the communications protocol.

PVC   In ATM, a permanent virtual circuit.

PVID   Port virtual LAN Identifier.

QoS   *See* **Quality of Service**.

quality of service   A concept by which an application can indicate its specific requirements to the network before transmitting data. Especially applicable to ATM for indicating whether delay is allowed. Soon to be implemented for IP. Abbreviated QoS.

queue   A waiting line with requests for service. Generally, an ordered list of elements waiting to be processed. In routing, a backlog of packets waiting to be forwarded over a router interface.

queueing delay   The amount of time that data must wait before it can be transmitted onto a statistically multiplexed physical circuit. *See also* **latency**.

RADIUS   *See* **Remote Authentication Dial-in User** Sevice.

RAEP   *See* **Reverse Address Resolution Protocol**.

real-time variable bit rate   One of five service categories defined by the ATM Forum for ATM. Abbreviated rtVBR.

Remote Authentication Dial-in User Service   Security protocol used to securely transport passwords between the access device and the authentication server. Abbreviated RADIUS.

Remote MONitoring Management Information Base   An extension of the SNMP MIB II which provides a standards-based method for tracking, storing, and analyzing remote network management information. Developed by the IETF. Abbreviated RMON MIB.

repeater   1. A device that boosts a signal from one network lobe or trunk and continues transmission to another similar network lobe or trunk. Protocols must match on both segments. The repeater provides service at level 1 of the OSI reference model. 2. A device that regenerates and propagates electrical signals between two network segments.

request for comments   Working documents of the Internet research and development community. These documents cover a range of topics related to computer communications ranging from Internet working-group reports to Internet standards specifications. Abbreviated RFC.

Resource Reservation Protocol   Will enhance classic IP for obtaining differentiated quality of service over an ATM network. Abbreviated RSVP.

Reverse Address Resolution Protocol   TCP/IP protocol for finding IP addresses based on MAC addresses. Abbreviated RARP. *See also* **Address Resolution Protocol.**

Revised IP Security Option (RIPSO)   RFC1108, which specifies an optional IP header field that contains a security classification and handling label.

ring   1. The connection and call signaling method on POTS. 2. A network topology that has stations in a circular configuration.

RFC   *See* **request for comments**.

RG   *See* **routing Goop**.

RIP   Routing Information Protocol.

RJ-11   Standard four-wire connectors for phone lines.

RJ-45   Standard eight-wire connectors for networks. Also used as phone lines in some cases.

RMON   Standard for Remote Network MONitoring. RMON2 is the latest version.

RMON2   A remote MONitoring standard that complements RMON (RMON1). RMON2 defines network layer and application layer statistics, providing an enterprise view of network traffic.

router   A sophisticated, protocol-specific device that examines data and finds the best route for it between sender and receiver. Selects the cheapest, fastest, or least busy of all available routes. Routers are preferable to bridges for large networks with relatively low-bandwidth connections.

routing   Assignment of the communications path by which a message or telephone call will reach its destination.

Routing Goop   Identifies the attachment point to the public Internet in GSE for IPv6. Abbreviated RG.

routing table   Table associated with a network node that states for each message (or packet) destination the preferred outgoing link that the message should use.

RSVP   *See* **Resource Reservation Protocol**.

runt frame   An Ethernet frame that is too short. A runt frame has fewer than the 60 bytes in the data fields required by the IEEE 802.3. If the frame length is less than 53 bytes, a runt frame indicates a normal collision. A frame less than 60 bytes, but at least 53 bytes, indicates a late collision.

SCR   *See* **sustainable cell rate**.

server   A processor that provides a specific service to the network; for example, a routing server connects nodes and networks of like architectures, and a gateway server connects nodes and networks of different architectures.

shared media   A reference to the "public" transport wiring used in a network topology on which all devices compete for access to the transmission media and vie for bandwidth and do not transmit over dedicated (or switched) circuits. Examples include Ethernet, FDDI, and Token-Ring with standard concentrator, hub, or MAU technology.

short packet   A packet that is less than the minimum legal size, including address, length, and CRC fields.

signal   A transmission broadcast. The electrical pulse that conveys information.

signal propagation speed   The speed at which the signal wave passes through the transmission channel. This is the speed of electrical pulses in copper, light in fiber, or radio signals through air and building materials.

Simple Network Management Protocol   A protocol recommended by the IETF for managing TCP/IP networks, internetworked LANs, and packet-switched networks; most commonly employed using TCP/IP protocols. SNMPv2 combines two updates to SNMP: Secure SNMP and Simple Management Protocol; defines everything from SMI to manager-to-manager MIB. Abbreviated SNMP.

site topology partition Corresponds to a site's subnet portion of an IPv4 address, part of GSE for IPv6. Abbreviated STP.

SNA *See* **Systems Network Architecture**.

SNMP *See* **Simple Network Management Protocol**.

source address The transmitting station's logical address.

spanning tree IEEE 802.1d committee standard for bridging LANs without loops. The algorithm ensures that only one path connects any pair of stations, selecting one bridge as the root bridge from which all paths are considered to radiate.

Spanning Tree Algorithm An algorithm, the original version of which was invented by Digital Equipment Corporation, used to prevent bridging loops by creating a spanning tree. The IEEE 802.1d standard that detects and manages logical loops in a network. When multiple paths exist, the bridge or router selects the most efficient one. When a path fails, the tree automatically reconfigures the network with a new active path. The algorithm is now documented in the IEEE 802.1d specification, although the Digital algorithm and the IEEE 802.1d algorithm are not the same, nor are they compatible. Abbreviated as STA.

STA *See* **Spanning Tree Algorithm**.

stackable Network devices that may be stacked vertically but where the stack is managed as one, as opposed to daisychaining, where each device is viewed separately by the network management system. Types of devices available in this format are hubs, switches, and routers.

standard A document that recommends a protocol, interface, type of wiring, or some other aspect of a network. It may even recommend something as general as a conceptual framework or model (e.g., a communications architecture). De jure standards are developed by internationally or nationally recognized standards bodies or vendors. De facto standards are widely used vendor-developed protocols or architectures, such as IBM's Systems Network Architecture (SNA).

star network A network topology in which each station is connected to a central station by a point-to-point link and communicates with all other stations through the central station.

star topology A LAN topology in which endpoints on a network are connected to a common central switch by point-to-point links.

station 1. A logical, nonphysical interconnection to the network that supports computer workstations or other types of physical devices on a network. Alternatively, a station may connect to a wiring concentrator providing network access for many devices. A device might be a terminal server, or a shared peripheral such as a file server, printer, or plotter. 2. A single addressable device on FDDI, generally implemented as a stand-alone computer or a peripheral device such as a printer or plotter. 3. A station might be a terminal server or a shared peripheral such as a file server, printer, or plotter. *See also* **node**; **workstation**.

store-and-forward A message-switching technique where messages are temporarily stored at intermediate points between the source and destination until such time as network resources (such as an unused link) are available for message forwarding.

store-and-forward switch mode The switching technology that has the most latency; its latency is equivalent to that of a router because it is a MAC-layer bridge and packet router. This entails a substantial delay, because arriving packets are fully buffered and checked for errors before they are switched, and when switched they vie for slot time on either the destination node or destination subnet. Note that packets can be switched not only between paired nodes, but also between paired subnets. *See also* **cut-through switch mode**; **modified cut-through switch mode**.

STP *See* **site topology partition**.

store-and-forward switching A type of packet switching in which the whole frame is processed before further transmission. *See also* **cut-through** and **adaptive.**

subnet For routing purposes, IP networks can be divided into logical subnets by using a subnet mask. Values below those of the mask are valid addresses on the subnet.

subnetwork A term sometimes used to refer to a network segment. In IP networks, a network sharing a particular subnet address. In OSI networks, a collection of ESs and ISs under the control of a single administrative domain and using a single network access protocol.

sustainable cell rate In ATM, the average cell rate a source is allowed to maintain. Abbreviated SCR.

SVC Switched virtual circuit.

switched ethernet A technology that provides a switched circuit between paired communicating Ethernet network nodes.

Systems Network Architecture A seven-layer network architecture developed by IBM. Although there is some commonality between the layers of OSI and SNA, a direct mapping is difficult as some layers do not correspond directly. Abbreviated SNA.

tag   In VLAN terms, an addition to the header that gives VLAN membership information.

tag control information   Part of the VLAN tag header in the IEEE 802.1Q draft standard. Abbreviated TCI.

tag protocol identifier   Part of the VLAN tag header in the IEEE 802.1Q draft standard. Abbreviated TPID.

tag-aware bridges   Bridges that support tagging using the format defined in 802.1Q.

tag-aware regions   Regions of a bridged LAN that support tagging using the format defined in 802.1Q.

tagged frame   A MAC frame that contains a tag header.

TCP/IP   *See* **Transaction Control Protocol/Internet Protocol**.

TDM   Time-division multiplexing. Traffic is slotted together along the same pipe with each stream remaining separate.

telecommunications   A term referring to communications (usually involving computer systems) over the telephone network.

telecommuter   A work-at-home computer user who connects to the corporate LAN backbone using remote access technologies.

teleconference   Bidirectional audio on either a one-to-many or a many-to-many basis.

telecottage   A well-equipped, well-connected small office that may be used by people working remotely for the same or different companies.

TFTP   *See* **Trivial File Transfer Protocol**.

throughput   1. A measurement of work accomplished. 2. The volume of traffic that passes through a pathway or intersection. Typically, this refers to data communications packets or cells and it is measured in packets/s, cells/s, or bits/s. 3. Rate of information arriving at, and possibly passing through, a particular point in a network system.

time-out   1. An event that occurs when one network device expects to hear from, but does not hear from, another network device within a specified period of time. The resulting time-out usually results in a retransmission of information or the outright dissolving of the virtual circuit between the two devices. 2. The explicit failure to receive a status message during a synchronization window, or the implicity failure to receive an acknowledgment message, both of which result in session failure. 3. A method to train a toddler as to appropriate behavior.

token   1. The protocol-based permission that is granted to a station in a predetermined sequence. The permission allows that station to transmit on the network. 2. A control information frame, possession of which grants a network device the right to transmit.

token bus   A local network access mechanism and topology in which all stations actively attached to the bus listen for a broadcast token or supervisory frame. Stations wishing to transmit must receive the token before doing so; however, the next physical station to transmit is not necessarily the next physical station on the bus. Bus access is controlled by preassigned priority algorithms.

token passing   A local area network access technique in which participating stations circulate a special bit pattern that grants access to the communications pathway to any station that holds the sequence; often used in networks with a ring topology.

token ring   A local network access mechanism and topology in which a supervisory frame or token is passed from station to station in sequential order. Stations wishing to gain access to the network must wait for the token to arrive before transmitting data. In a token ring, the next logical station receiving the token is also the next physical station on the ring. The ring may be a logical, rather than physical, ring in the case of switched token ring.

TopN   In *RMON,* conversation information that is imported from an external data collector.

topology   1. The logical or physical arrangement of stations on a network in relation to one another. 2. The physical layout of the network including devices and their connections.

TP-PMD   Twisted-pair–physical-media-dependent; an amalgamation of all the old proprietary standards for running FDDI over copper.

traffic   1. The communications carried by a system. 2. A measure of network load that refers to the frame transmission rate (frames per second or frames per hour).

traffic congestion   The situation when data arrivals exceed delivery times and create performance problems.

traffic jam   A metaphorical reference to congestion on a network.

Transaction Control Protocol/Internet Protocol   *See* **TCP/IP**.

transceiver   The coaxial cable interface based upon a mechanical and electrical connection to the Ethernet coaxial cable medium. It is typically a radio transmitter and receiver combined to form a single unit. A cellular phone uses a transceiver to send signals to, and receive them from, the cell site. Also known as a medium-dependent interface.

TPID *See* **tag protocol identifier.**

transit VLAN starvation The condition a switch suffers in a non-ATM network when it becomes congested and cells or cell streams representing layer 3 VLAN packets are missed or dropped, causing the VLAN to become unstable. Also known as "beatdown."

transmission Any electronic or optical signal used for telecommunications or data communications to send a message.

Transmission Control Protocol/Internet Protocol A group of transport and network layer protocols designed for wide area networks. A complete implementation of this networking protocol includes Transmission Control Protocol (TCP), Internet Protocol (IP), Internetwork Control Message Protocol (ICMP), User Datagram Protocol (UDP), and Address Resolution Protocol (ARP). Standard applications are File Transfer Protocol (FTP), Simple Mail Transfer Protocol (SMTP), and TELNET, which provide virtual terminal on any remote network system. Abbreviated TCP/IP. Abbreviated TCP/IP.

Trivial File Transfer Protocol A TCP/IP protocol that supports rudimentary file transfer over User Datagram Protocol (UDP). TFTP lacks security controls. Abbreviated TFTP.

tunneling Encapsulation. The process of enclosing one protocol inside another protocol packet for delivery over a router-defined link.

twisted pair Telephone wire twisted over its length to preserve signal strength and minimize electromagnetic interference. Abbreviated TP.

twisted-pair–physical-media-dependent (TP-PMD) ANSI standard for FDDI over copper, replacing SDDI (shielded DDI—runs on shielded cable) and CDDI (copper DDI—runs on unshielded cable).

UBR *See* **unspecified bit rate.**

undersized error A frame or packet that does not meet the minimum size requirement. Oversized packets indicate that a faulty or corrupted driver is in use on the network.

undersized packet A packet that contains less than 64 bytes, including address, length, and CRC fields.

UNI *See* **user network interface.**

unshielded twisted pair Pairs of 22 to 26 AWG wire usually in bundles of 2, 4, or 25 pairs installed for telephone service and occasionally for data networks. Referred to as voice-grade twisted-pair or voice-grade wiring. Abbreviated UTP.

unspecified bit rate One of five service categories defined by the ATM Forum for ATM. Abbreviated UBR.

untagged frame A MAC frame that does not contain a tag header.

user interface The program through which the end users interact with the computer.

user network interface In ATM environments, the point at which the user joins the network. Abbreviated UNI.

UTP *See* **unshielded twisted pair**.

VC *See* **Virtual Channel**.

VC starvation The condition a switch in an ATM network suffers when it becomes congested and cells or cell streams representing layer 3 VLAN packets are missed or dropped, leading to the VLAN becoming unstable. Also known as "beatdown."

VID Virtual LAN identifier.

virtual bridged local area network A bridged LAN in which one or more bridges are tag-aware.

virtual channel In ATM, a communications track between two nodes giving the bandwidth needed for a virtual connection across the network. Abbreviated VC.

virtual circuit Proposed ITU-T definition for a data transmission service in which the user presents a data message for delivery with a header of a specified format. The system delivers the message as though a circuit existed to the specified destination. One of many different routes and techniques could be used to deliver the message, but the user does not know which is employed.

virtual LAN A network segmented logically, rather than physically, using one of a variety of means at layer 2 or 3 of the OSI model. Abbreviated VLAN.

virtual path In ATM, bandwidth between two points on a network used by one or more virtual channels (VCs). Abbreviated VP.

virtual source/virtual destinations One of three types of feedback an ATM switch can provide. Abbreviated VS/VD.

VLAN *See* **virtual LAN**.

VLAN Membership Resolution Protocol   Protocol that uses GARP to provide a mechanism for dynamic maintenance of the contents of the port egress lists for each port of a bridge, and for propagating the information they contain to other bridges. Abbreviated VMRP.

VLAN-tagged frame   A tagged frame whose tag header carries VLAN identification information.

VMRP   *See* **VLAN Membership Resolution Protocol**.

VP   *See* **virtual path**.

WAN   *See* **wide area network**.

wide area network   A network that covers a larger geographic area than a single work site (LAN) or metropolitan area (MAN). Abbreviated WAN.

wiring closet   A specially designed room used for wiring data and voice networks. Wiring closets serve as central junction points for wiring and wiring equipment that is used for interconnecting devices.

wiring concentrator   A central wiring concentrator for a series of Ethernet, FDDI, and Token-Ring nodes. *See also* **wiring hub**.

wiring hub   A central wiring concentrator for a series of Ethernet, FDDI, and Token-Ring nodes.

workstation   1. Any computer device. 2. Any device on a network. 3. A single addressable site on FDDI that is generally implemented as a stand-alone computer or a peripheral device, connected to the ring with a controller. *See also* **node**; **station**.

X.500   ITU-T recommendation covering the implementation of addressing databases for devices attached to a network. The basis for Novell's and Banyan's directory services.

INDEX

U

V

X

ABOUT THE AUTHORS

Louis R. Rossi CCIE #3116, holds many certifications including Novell, CNE-3, Novell CNE-4, Certified Novell Instructor (CNI), Master CNE (MCNE), and Certified Cisco Systems Instructor (CCSI). He has conducted hundreds of router, Catalyst switch, and Novell classes throughout the country.

Louis D. Rossi began his career as a programmer on Wall Street before earning his key instructor certifications. He currently provides Novell and Cisco training to thousands of network professionals around the country.

Thomas L. Rossi has background in computational fluid dynamics, programming, and relational database design. He currently runs his own consulting company, Capernaum.

Advanced IP Routing in Cisco Networks

Terry Slattery, CCIE & Bill Burton, CCIE
0-07-058144-4 $55.00

Covering all the protocols that run on Cisco IP routers, this clear, illustrated guide provides all the expertise needed to design, configure, manage, and troubleshoot this vital technology. Features a wealth of network examples and actual router configurations.

Cisco Router OSPF Design and Implementation Guide

William Parkhurst, Ph.D., CCIE
0-07-048626-3 • $55.00

The CCIE exam demands full knowledge of Open Shortest Path First (OSPF). This guide reveals step-by-step how to configure, design, and implement a network using OSPF. Discusses the latest protocol OSPF2.

Get today's most authoritative, easy-to-follow guidance on how to configure, design, implement, and troubleshoot Cisco-routed networks! From solving difficult configuration problems to securing Cisco-routed networks, the help you need is here!

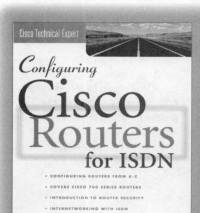

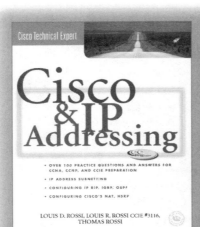